# THE OFFICIAL
# PRICE GUIDE TO
# Hŭmmel
## Figurines & Plates

**FROM THE EDITORS
OF THE HOUSE OF COLLECTIBLES**

**SIXTH EDITION
THE HOUSE OF COLLECTIBLES
NEW YORK, NEW YORK 10022**

*Important Notice.* The format of *The Official Price Guide Series*, published by *The House of Collectibles*, is based on the following proprietary features: *All facts and prices are compiled through a nationwide sampling of information* obtained from noteworthy experts, auction houses, and specialized dealers. *Detailed "indexed" format* enables quick retrieval of information for positive identification. *Encapsulated histories* precede each category to acquaint the collector with the specific traits that are peculiar to that area of collecting. *Valuable collecting information* is provided for both the novice as well as the seasoned collector: How to begin a collection; how to buy, sell, and trade; care and storage techniques; tips on restoration; grading guidelines; lists of periodicals, clubs, museums, auction houses, dealers, etc. *An average price range* takes geographic location and condition into consideration when reporting collector value. *An inventory checklist system* is provided for cataloging a collection.

All of the information, including valuations, in this book has been compiled from the most reliable sources, and every effort has been made to eliminate errors and questionable data. Nevertheless the possibility of error, in a work of such immense scope, always exists. The publisher will not be held responsible for losses which may occur in the purchase, sale, or other transaction of items because of information contained herein. Readers who feel they have discovered errors are invited to *write* and inform us, so they may be corrected in subsequent editions. Those seeking further information on the topics covered in this book are advised to refer to the complete line of Official Price Guides published by The House of Collectibles.

Published by: The House of Collectibles
201 East 50th Street
New York, New York 10022

Distributed by Ballantine Books, a division of Random House, Inc., New York and simultaneously in Canada by Random House of Canada Limited, Toronto.

Manufactured in the United States of America

Library of Congress Catalog Card Number: 84-645738

ISBN: 0-876-37243-4

10   9   8   7   6   5

# TABLE OF CONTENTS

# ACKNOWLEDGMENTS

We extend our appreciation to Ms. Millie Carpenter of Classic Boutique, Dunedin, Florida 33528, our pricing consultant, for her services.

Special thanks to Mr. and Mrs. William Perry, for letting us photograph their collection, and to McGuire Studios, Walt Disney World Village, and Mr. Ott Rabby for photographs of certain Hummel Figurines used in this book.

We would especially like to thank the Goebel Collectors' Club, and, in particular, Joan N. Ostroff, Vice President, corporate communications of Goebel Art GmbH, U.S. division, for their cooperation in supplying us with cover photographs.

# MARKET REVIEW

Every year we, as Hummel collectors, wait anxiously for the new releases from the Goebel Company. Nineteen eighty-five has been no exception. The 50th Anniversary year paved the way with a Golden Anniversary album and a glorious limited edition "Jubilee" figurine. Following the "Jubilee," our brand new M.I. Hummel figurines were released: "Baking Day," "Going Home," "Sing With Me," and "Just Fishing." Old friends released in new sizes include "Chick Girl," "Hear Ye Hear Ye," "Sensitive Hunter," "For Mother," and "Stormy Weather." These are listed below:

"Baking Day" HUM 330, 5¼": This wonderful piece was originally called "Kneading Dough." Master Sculptor Gerhard Skrobek modeled this Hummel in 1955, and later changed the name to "Baking Day."

"Going Home" HUM 383, 4¾": This Hummel was first called Fancy Free." Once again, Master Sculptor Gerhard Skrobek modeled this piece in November of 1966, and later changed the name to "Going Home."

"Sing With Me" HUM 405, 5": This figurine was also modeled by Gerhard Skrobek in 1973, and kept its original name to become one of 1985's new M.I. Hummel releases.

"Just Fishing" HUM 373, 4½": This figurine was first named "The Fisherman" and was modeled by Gerhard Skrobek in 1964. Later changed to "Just Fishing," this M.I. Hummel figurine is, by far, the collectors' choice for new releases.

"Chick Girl" HUM 57/2/0; "Hear Ye Hear Ye" HUM 15/2/0; "Sensitive Hunter" HUM 6/2/0; "For Mother" HUM 257/2/0; and "Stormy Weather" HUM 71/2/0 have all been released in a new size, ranging from 3" to 5". The new sizes add more dimension to your M.I. Hummel collecting.

The year of 1986 will be even more exciting for M.I. Hummel releases. With great tradition, the Annual M.I. Hummel Plate and the Annual M.I. Hummel Bell will open the door for more Collectors' surprises. Along with the Annual Plate and Bell, you will see the third edition of the *Little Music Makers Series*—the miniplate and minifigurine, "The Soloist." The most exciting news is the release of the very first M.I. Hummel clock, called "Chapel Time." These are listed below:

*1986 Annual M.I. Hummel Plate*: "Playmates" will be pictured on this plate. A perfect figurine match in "Playmates" HUM 58.

*1986 Annual M.I. Hummel Bell*: This is entitled "Sing Along."

*1986 Miniplate*: This is the third edition of the *Little Music Makers Series* "Soloist."

*1986 Minifigurine*: "The Soloist," 4". This matches the 1986 miniplate.

*Chapel Time HUM 442*: This is the very first M.I. Hummel clock. Production limited to the year 1986, in the 20th century.

The bitter conflict between Schmid and Goebel over the right to produce authentic M.I. Hummel collectibles appears to be over. Schmid will now distribute Hummel art for Goebel, and will not produce three-dimensional Hummel pieces anymore. Goebel United States, House of Global Art, and Schmid will distribute and market Hummel art in the U.S. It remains to be seen if the secondary market value of Hummel collectibles produced by Schmid will increase as a result of this agreement.

# INTRODUCTION

Even with the current popularity of posters and limited edition prints, few artists have had their art available to the general public in such profusion as Sister Maria Innocenta Hummel. Numerous adaptations of her original works have been made into ceramic figurines, postcards, prints, dolls, calendars, and various objects such as spoons and bells. The tremendous surge of popularity of Hummel figurines with collectors and investors led to rising prices until a year and a half ago. The late seventies was a time of frantic searching and buying with the demand from buyers surpassing the available number of pieces.

Although prices for Hummels had been climbing steadily, they first began to increase suddenly when a large number of investors started buying the figurines. But when the economy slowed and investors sold their Hummels in order to earn fast gains (as they did with many collectibles), the prices for Hummels slowed and finally came to a halt. Some of the Hummels—perhaps 10 to 15%—even dropped in price slightly.

But this situation is changing. As the economy improves prices for Hummels are on the increase once again. This is an excellent time for the collector to purchase the pieces he wants to add to his collection. That's why it is crucial for Hummel buyers to have a price guide that reflects the market as it presently stands.

The prices in this guide have been determined by carefully examining the current market as well as the price trends over the last year. These prices are an average of what Hummel dealers are charging across the country. With the slowing of price increases, our research has shown there is less of a fluctuation between the prices dealers are charging for any particular piece. The narrowing of price differences has been incorporated into the price ranges in this edition. This information will help you avoid paying 1981–1982 prices for the models with prices that have decreased. Also, it is very important for the collector to know the prices for models which have remained the same, including the ones which have smaller price ranges. These models have shown their ability to hold their values during a time of economical uncertainty, but with the number of avid Hummel collectors increasing every year, they can be expected to start a steady rise as the economy starts to heat up.

Whether you're an experienced hobbyist with an ever expanding collection or merely an admirer of the Hummel art, this book will deepen your understanding of these remarkable figurines. If you're a beginning collector or have collected Hummels casually—you haven't found out much about them, but you enjoy sitting them out on your shelves—you may be unaware of the interesting story behind these pieces: of Sister Maria Hummel, the artist nun who intermingled her great talent with her devotion to God; of the painstaking chore accomplished by the W. Goebel Company in adapting her works into a three-dimensional medium; and of all the complexities and ambiguities involved with the manufacturing of a larger series of objects for almost 50 years.

You might think it is a simple thing to collect Hummels, that you can just go down to a local gift shop and select some pieces that appeal to you right off the shelf. And for the beginning collector, it can be that easy. But years and years of producing these figures has led to a profusion of models, a great scarcity for some pieces, and a great deal of confusion concerning trademarks, authenticity, variations, and the availability of certain pieces.

This book attempts to clarify, as much as possible, all the areas that can befuddle collectors. Many questions remain unanswered, but for many collectors this is an added charm to collecting Hummels. Pieces not known to exist are still being discovered by alert collectors and different variations are being noted every year.

This new edition of *The Official Price Guide to Hummel Figurines & Plates* includes the latest information and pictures on the new releases as well as updated information on the older models. A number of sections have been greatly expanded to provide collectors with a more thorough coverage of the Hummel market. The extensive section on buying and selling can help the collector make decisions on where to buy, how to buy, and when to buy. Also sections on investing, collector activities, and collector terminology have been updated and enlarged. For more in-depth background on the figurines, a section on the manufacturing of Hummels has been added.

There are approximately 450 designs of Hummel figurines, but not all of these are presently in production. The numbers used to identify these pieces range from 1 to 432, not including edition pieces specially made for the members of the Goebel Collector's Club, the Annual Bells, and the rare International pieces. Not all of the numbers in this range have been used to identify a work. These are officially called *closed numbers*. For unknown reasons, the Goebel Company has decided not to release designs with these particular numbers. Recently, however, authentic Hummel pieces have been discovered with designator numbers that are supposed to be closed numbers.

Some of the 450 designs were produced in the past, but were removed from production; others have not been produced yet. Models that were released in the earlier years of manufacturing are being issued once again with the current trademark. It is not known how many of these Hummel pieces will be reissued in the future.

Some of the information here will add to your appreciation of the Hummels, such as the life story of the artist and the section on how the figurines are produced. Other sections will provide information that is crucial if you are going to collect Hummels with intelligence and caution, such as the articles on identifying authentic Hummels and on how to read the trademarks. This information coupled with the up-to-date prices here should arm you with the knowledge you need to make your collecting as fun and interesting as it can be.

## BERTA HUMMEL (SISTER MARIA I.)

Berta Hummel, the artist nun whose creative spirit lives on in Hummel figures, was born May 21, 1909, in the small Bavarian town of Massing. Her parents were prominent citizens of the town. Her father had been poor as a youth, but had become a shopkeeper, destined to be one of the most successful in Massing at the time of Berta's birth. Little is recorded of his life, except for the information that as a youth, he took an interest in art and had ambitions to become an artist. Berta's mother's name was Viktoria.

Berta's childhood was not unlike that of others in Lower Bavaria. Her inquisitive nature, exposed to the picturesque character of the land and its people, soon manifested itself into a desire to draw and sketch. This pastime was at first the object of no special notice. One can well imagine her father, Adolf, congratulating Viktoria on the fact that their daughter had adopted a refined amusement, which would keep her out of mischief. She was not, however, content to merely sit and draw. Recollections of those who knew Berta as a child are of a very active, playful, tomboy sort of girl with a decidedly outgoing personality. She put on plays for family and friends, made doll costumes, and is said to have been an avid student of German folk tales.

At the age of six, Berta was enrolled in the elementary school of Armen Schulschwestern in her hometown. Her studies there were completed at the age of twelve. She was then sent to private school at Simbach. There she boarded and was instructed by the Institute of English Sisters. It was there that Berta's artistic talents were first recognized. There were many such organizations throughout Europe before World War II whose purpose was not to prepare students for a life in religious orders, but rather to provide an atmosphere of thought and meditation for study, to improve self-discipline, and introduce religious themes into classwork. Undoubtedly her years at Simbach were the most artistically formative of her life. Sister Stephanie, one of the instructors, discussed Berta's abilities with her parents and suggested that Berta should further her studies at the Academy of Applied Arts in Munich, Bavaria's capital city. She was enrolled there in 1927, at the age of eighteen, and assigned to the Berufsfachschule, which trained artists for teaching positions in kindergartens and other schools. Because Berta Hummel related so well to children and continued as an adult to draw the kind of pictures that appealed to them, it was felt she might be well adapted to a career as teacher. Although she entered the Academy filled with enthusiasm, she was uncertain whether she would be able to fulfill the expectations others had of her talent.

The Academy instructors, including a number of professional artists, were impressed with Berta. They saw her as a kind of folk artist, not as someone who could align with the then current art movement in Germany, but who might, thanks to the public appeal of her subject matter, have a successful career as an independent painter, book illustrator, or designer. She did not concentrate exclusively on children or pastoral subjects at the Academy. Much of her work revolved around interpreting the styles of primitive masters into current subject matter, a favorite approach to teaching art in Germany at that time. The extent of her study of the works of the Old

Masters is not known, but apparently they exercised a strong influence on her work, as many of her sketches even after leaving the Academy were pre-Renaissance in concept.

While at the Academy, Berta made the acquaintance of two nuns who were also studying there. Their enjoyment of and contentment with religious life gradually had its effect on her. She contemplated her future as a sister of the Roman Catholic Church. There would be ample time for artistic pursuits, the chance to travel and teach children, and at the same time freedom from the stresses and uncertainties of making a living in a crumbling economy and a tumultuous political climate. Upon graduation from the Academy in 1931, at the age of twenty-two, Berta joined a Franciscan convent. Two years later, having completed her novitiate, her vows were taken and she became a nun. The date was August 22, 1933.

Assigned to a convent at Seissen, Berta continued sketching, turning out finished work of real artistic merit as her style became more refined. She was not by any means cloistered or closed away from the public. She taught at the convent's schools and some of her artwork was placed on public display. In 1934 her first professional art appeared (there being no record of her having sold any works prior to entering the convent) when some of her drawings were incorporated on postcards. Of course she had no ambition of profits; the vows of nuns included poverty, which meant that any monies received could not be placed to her personal use. A trust fund was established to receive royalties which subsequently were turned over for religious activities. The royalties earned by Berta Hummel would amount to millions of dollars if she were still alive today.

In 1934 Berta provided the illustrations for a pleasant little book called *The Hummel Book*, a collection of poems for children composed by Margaret Seeman. Another book, *Sketch Me—Berta Hummel*, attests to the fact that she had gained celebrity status. This work, long out of print and quite a collector's item, was issued in reprint facsimile some time ago by Robert L. Miller, a prominent Hummel collector and one of the few owners of an original copy.

In addition to the release of these two books, 1934 witnessed the beginning of her assocation with Goebel Porzellanfabrik. Franz Goebel, then in charge of the factory, convinced Berta that her drawings would be ideal subjects for ceramic figurines. An arrangement was worked out whereby the convent would have final approval and be paid for their use. The commercializing of her work in this manner did not at first appeal to Berta, but the prospect of earning money for the convent surely did. So a contract was signed, and in March, 1935, the first Hummel Figures were on the market. They came into the world with a bang. Their first appearance was at the prestigious Leipzig Trade Fair, a centuries-old merchandise fair attended by representatives of every leading German wholesale house and many foreign wholesalers and distributors. Very shortly thereafter, Hummels were on sale in German shops. Their distribution soon spread elsewhere although at first it was limited, especially when compared to the vast worldwide network of Hummel suppliers and dealers that now exists.

Sister Hummel's health began to deteriorate in the late 1930's. The Nazi regime made life hard on the convents, allocating them insufficient supplies of food and medicines. During the war her condition, long undiagnosed and attributed to overwork or strain, worsened. Finally her illness was diagnosed as tuberculosis. Although Berta survived the war, peace came too late for her health to be restored. She died at the convent, on November 6, 1946, at the age of thirty-seven. By this time Hummel art, though its production had been curtailed during the war, was known internationally. Berta died knowing she had left the Seissen convent a major legacy.

## THE POPULARITY OF HUMMELS

Small, angelic-looking children engaged in some chore or merely enjoying the delights of the world, staring with wide-eyed innocence, pensive—these characteristic traits of the Hummel figurines enchant many different people from all over the world. The serenity of these delicately-painted, ceramic figurines radiates a quiet charm of days past. At a time when gift shops bulge with an array of ceramic objects and knickknacks, more and more people are drawn to Hummels. Based on the 500 or 600 original pieces painted or sketched by Berta Hummel, numerous adaptations have been made into ceramic figurines and objects. Since the first figurines designed after her works were produced in 1935, the adaptations of Sister Maria's works have steadily grown in popularity.

Prior to World War II, the Hummels were exported to America and sold widely. During the war, the Goebel firm was unable to export the figurines, but was able to remain in operation by producing ceramic dinnerware for sale inside Germany and coffee mugs and mess hall plates for the German military.

By the time the United States Army occupied the area surrounding the location of the Goebel Company, the firm was closed down as were most of the other companies in Germany. The Goebel firm was located in a section of Germany which was cut off from its normal commercial outlets because of the political divisions made after the war.

The U.S. Military Government lifted the restrictions formerly imposed, granting the Goebel Company permission to once again produce and export its ceramic articles. Some of the most avid collectors at that time were the GIs stationed in Germany; many of them wanted to take home gifts to their families and friends which would be characteristic of Germany. Small ceramic figurines were inexpensive and looked typically German and could easily be packed away for the return trip home. Many of these were purchased at prices that were extremely low due to rates of exchange between the currency issued to GIs and German money.

When the GIs returned to the United States, the popularity of Hummels was spread even wider. Today there are clubs, numerous books, newsletters, exhibits, and festivals for the Hummel collectors. Collectors by the thousands seek out more information on new releases, newly discovered models and anything which pertains to Hummels.

## ORIGINAL ART

Over 500 original sketches and paintings that were produced by Sister Maria Innocentia Hummel still exist. Her drawings are mostly in pencil, charcoal, and artist's crayon while her paintings are in watercolor and oil. Charcoal and crayon, used separately or together, were her favorite mediums which allowed her to work with quickness and precision. She used watercolors and oils infrequently. Since Berta habitually worked with great speed, she disliked taking the time needed for the paint to dry. While at the Academy, Berta often discussed a project with her professor in the morning, then turned in the finished product that very afternoon.

Her ability to capture quickly what she saw accounts for the strong emotions her works evoke. Her pieces are based on her close observations of middle class Bavarian life in the early 20th century. Quite often, she would illustrate one moment in some particular incident which would tell a whole story about those around her. "Moonlight Return" is reported to be based on Berta's brother who had fallen asleep in a haystack after working late in a neighbor's fields. Her drawing shows him headed home upon awakening after midnight. His features portray his concern at the certain consternation of his parents.

A majority of her subjects were children who were depicted with round, cherubic faces. Her works show children playing, working, worshipping, musing, and sometimes imitating adults. Much of the charm in the Hummels derives from their capacity to suggest universal truths in a simple way, much likes the works of the American artist, Norman Rockwell. The cheerful or religious mood is emotionally inspiring—many fans of Hummels revel in the nostalgia of their childhood, recalled when viewing these pieces. For example, #166 "Boy with Bird," which shows a boy stretched out on the ground quietly contemplating a bird perched in front of him, illustrates the unique ability of a child to be continually amazed and captivated by the wonders of nature. These types of works can probably be regarded as being indirectly religious. The amazement at God's works is a sort of recognition of His divinity and goodness.

Although the facial characteristics of the children Berta illustrated are basically the same—big, wide-set eyes; a high forehead; a turned-up nose; round, chubby cheeks; a small, pursed mouth—the expressions vary greatly, representing a wide range of feelings and sentiments. It is only fair to note that the faces of children are difficult subjects to portray because of the tendency for children to have the same basic facial traits. Very young children rarely have distinctive noses and their eyes usually appear big and wide-set.

Not only are the facial expressions sensitive, but the great attention to the smallest details provides the works with warmth and interest: You respond emotionally to these details because they are ones you have seen or experienced. Part of the charisma exuding from #142 "Apple Tree Boy" results from the intensity of concentration and delight pictured on the boy's face as he carefully observes a singing bird closely perched next to him. But the naturalistic posture and the graphically depicted clothing which drapes in a genuine manner also provide the work with a sense of being realistic. The boy's posture for such a position is very lifelike. His legs hang in a fashion peculiar to small children—relaxed with the toes coming together and pointing up while his socks droop around his ankles. His arms wrap around the limbs of the tree in a typical manner and his coat flares out naturally. In fact, not only does the clothing appear to be genuinely

Bavarian, but you can practically determine the type of material of each piece of clothing that is illustrated; for example, the coat appears to be made of a light wool. These realistic touches are characteristic of all of Berta's works and lend these figurines a common flair—one that appeals to a large number of people. *(Note: These traits are not present in many of the variations of "Apple Tree Boy," especially the earlier models.)*

Some of Berta Hummel's original works are housed in her childhood home where her mother and brother still live. These are mostly works she completed prior to entering the convent in 1933. Some are housed in the Franciscan Convent at Seissen, West Germany. The convent owns most of her original works for which they hold the two-dimensional copyrights. Others were given away by Sister Hummel as gifts. Several years ago, one of her original works surfaced in St. Louis—it had been done in 1939 at the request of some young children.

Her original sketches and paintings carry her signature in a variety of forms. Usually these are found in the lower left or right corner. Normally her signature is clearly legible and reads "M.I. Hummel." Some of her works have only an initial—"H," "B," or "B" and "H" superimposed. "B. Hummel" and "M.I. Hummel" without the accent are also found on some of her works.

The only two known works with dates are "Stormy Weather," a drawing which she signed "Hummel '36," and an oil painting which she signed "B. Hummel '29." The painting of her parish church next to the river Rott in Massing is one of her most professional and sophisticated pieces accomplished prior to her entrance into the convent. It was done while she was at the Academy in Munich at the age of twenty.

So far no one has been able to find a correlation between her choice of signature and the year the work was finished, though some collectors of Hummels have noticed that many of her religious pieces are signed "M.I. Hummel." None of the non-religious subjects are signed in this manner. Most of her drawings of children are signed only "Hummel." The "Goose Girl" is the only work with the title and signature printed in block style.

Forgers have duplicated these works, so you cannot assume a signed piece is authentic merely on the basis of the signature. Before buying any work offered for sale as an original Hummel, you should have a qualified art expert examine the piece for authenticity.

# HISTORY OF THE GOEBEL FACTORY

Germany, as the seasoned collector is well aware, was the birthplace of European porcelain or "chinaware." Since the beginning of the importation of Oriental porcelain to Europe, Western potters had been attempting to duplicate this ware, trying to gain for themselves the trade that was going abroad. For nearly three centuries they experimented without success. Early in the 1700's a ware closely approximating Chinese porcelain using kaolin as its chief ingredient was achieved at Meissen. It may be of interest to collectors that this pioneer European porcelain got its first public exposure at the Leipzig Trade Fair, just as Hummels did 200 years later.

The "secret" was soon carried into other parts of Germany, and from there to France and elsewhere. By 1760 porcelain was being produced in most areas of the continent and the British Isles. Numerous large and small factories sprang up in Germany, some of them successful, others, for lack of sufficient capital or various reasons, in operation only briefly. By 1800 a tradition of porcelain-making existed in Berta Hummel's Bavaria.

The first porcelain works in the Coburg area was founded in 1765, and operated by Johann Hammann. This region was especially well suited to the manufacturing of porcelain because clays rich in the necessary sub-stances were found nearby. Surprising though it may seem today, a tourist trade for Bavarian porcelain, not to mention woodcarvings, clocks, and other items, flourished even then. The chief cities of Old Bavaria, such as Munich, were mandatory stopping places for Frenchmen, Englishmen, and others taking the grand tour. The proportion of works sold to visitors was probably as great as the proportion of works sold to natives.

As the porcelain trade increased during the 19th century, more and more people in various parts of Bavaria were encouraged to enter the business. Undoubtedly the number of people involved would have been much larger were it not for the stringent system of licensing that prevailed in many regions. It must be noted that during the 19th century Germany was not the same country, geographically speaking, that it became after World War I. Many of the regions were still controlled by local monarchies. In 1853 Franz-Detleff Goebel applied to the local magistrates at Coburg for a license to set up and operate a porcelain works factory. He was turned down, the reason given being the danger of fire from factory kilns. Some fires had indeed occurred at porcelain factories, but whether this was the true ob-jection is yet to be determined; political considerations may have been involved.

Franz-Detleff Goebel did not give up easily. He continued applying and finally, after 18 years, was given a limited license. He was authorized to establish a factory, but was forbidden to manufacture porcelain. The license restricted him to "Thuringer Ware," which included writing slates, marbles, and other incidental products, with the promise that a license for porcelain making would be forthcoming if his establishment met safety standards. When this failed to materialize after an additional eight years of waiting, he applied in 1879 to Duke Ernst II of Saxe-Coburg-Gotha for a royal privilege. The arguments he employed must have proved convincing. The Duke gave his approval, and shortly thereafter Herr Goebel built a porcelain kiln at Oeslau, just outside Coburg.

The operation was a partnership with his son, William, and was known as the F. and W. Goebel Porcelain Works. At first it did not concentrate on decorative wares, but manufactured table porcelain and assorted house-hold and gift items. After Franz-Detleff's death, greater attention was paid to figureware, though the bulk of the Goebel trade was still in dishes, pitchers, steins, and other household wares. William, an enterprising busi-nessman, enlarged the company's export activities, sending its products into many parts of Europe and America.

The late 1800's and early 1900's was a period of rapid expansion, thanks chiefly to the favorable economic conditions in Germany. The nation was experiencing vast industrial growth. Salaries were increasing and the middle classes, who were not in a position to afford porcelain 50 years earlier, could now buy it. Almost everyone who could afford to buy it, **did** buy it. At the outbreak of World War I the Goebel operation employed 400 workers. It was at this time piloted by Max-Louis Goebel, son of William and grandson of the founder.

The war proved, as might be suspected, a hindrance, but it did not put Goebel out of business. By the early 1920's the factory was operating almost at pre-war capacity. Max-Louis reasoned that it would be necessary to regain international trade cut off by export bans during the war, before new innovative lines could be introduced. It was the Art Deco era and figureware was enjoying a surge of popularity. Max-Louis was determined that Goebel would be at the forefront of figureware production, supplying imaginative, well-made, yet inexpensive items of this type to the world market.

Upon Max-Louis' death in 1929, leadership of the firm was taken over by his son Franz, his widow Frieda Goebel, and his brother-in-law Dr. Eugene Stocke. Germany was then experiencing its worst inflationary period in history, with loaves of bread costing billions of marks. The value of the mark was so low that this once-respected currency unit was now worth only a tiny fraction of a U.S. penny. Foreign trade was hampered as few countries wanted to accept German marks. As if this did not provide enough problems, the U.S. stock market crash of 1929 and its effects in Europe, which were immediately felt, made things worse. For the next six years the factory endured hard times. Its introduction of M.I. Hummel figures in 1935 proved to be the turning point, though the great commercial success of these figures did not come until after World War II.

By 1951, with Hummels selling in every country of the western world, Goebel had expanded well beyond its pre-World War I proportions. It now had 700 employees and could scarcely turn out Hummels fast enough to meet the demand. A very large proportion of its output was going to America, despite the prejudice that still existed in this country against goods made in Germany and Japan. In 1956 Franz Goebel opened an office in the U.S. and a separate doll factory in 1957. The number of workers grew to about 1,400 by 1968. The complex of Goebel factories as it now exists in Coburg/Oeslau is huge. The operation is so extensive that the company maintains its own day nursery for young children of employees.

# THE MANUFACTURING OF HUMMELS

The manufacturing of Hummel figurines, faithfully based on the original works of Sister Maria Innocentia, demands a wide combination of skills, technical knowledge, specialized equipment, carefully prepared materials, as well as a great deal of care, patience, and talent.

The craftsmen who work for the W. Goebel Company pass through a rigorous screening and training program that results in an ample supply of talented, trained artisans. When the Goebel firm began to produce Hummel figurines and other collector articles, they established a training program which includes a combination of study and practical work. Those who are hired work as apprentices for three years, studying all facets of the craft—drawing, design, mold making, and the chemistry involved in producing and painting porcelain and ceramics. Most of these craftsmen work for 30 or 40 years in the firm, eventually taking their turn at teaching apprentices.

The first step in the producing of a Hummel figure is the sculpting of a clay model based on one of Sister Maria's works which captures every detail down to the exact shade of color and all the nuances of the form. This is made by one of the sculptors, such as Gerhard Skrobek who is the present master sculptor. He uses a special compound which allows him to duplicate the most intricate designs. After completion of this figure, the Goebel firm presents it to the Siessen Convent for approval. The convent may or may not ask for minor changes to be made before giving their approval. If the convent gives its approval after the changes are made, the sculpture must then be approved by the directors of the Goebel Company. Not all of the figures that have been approved are manufactured.

After the decision has been made to proceed with production, the original mold is cut by the chief designer. This mold may include as many as 30 pieces for a complex figurine. A master mold is made for each separate piece in order to create the exact details necessary and to make it easier to remove the pieces from the mold. These two-part molds are reverse molds of plaster of paris which are in turn used to create a plaster of paris sculpture. Craftsmen then carve the fine details into these models to correspond to the original clay model. Then specially prepared acrylic resin is poured over this plaster of paris model to form another two-part reverse mold. The final piece is made by pouring a special material, called slip, into these molds.

The slip, which looks like cream, is poured into the top of the closed two-piece mold until it is completely full. The acrylic mold is porous and begins to absorb water from the slip. After twenty minutes or so, enough water has been absorbed to form a hard wall around its interior. The remaining amount of the slip is then poured out of the mold, so that the final piece is hollow.

Before 1954, the final piece was made by pouring the slip into a plaster of paris mold. These plaster molds lost details in the design after only several uses, so they had to be replaced by fresh molds frequently. Nevertheless, the walls of the molds absorbed water too quickly, resulting in an increase in the size of some of the pieces. Through the research accomplished by the Goebel Company, the acrylic resin models were developed to allow for better retention of details and size. The use of acrylic resin then became common throughout the porcelain and ceramic industry. Although it is necessary for the mold to absorb water for the hard ceramic shell to form, the acrylic resin holds its shape enough to be utilized 20 to 25 times before having to be replaced.

After these final pieces are removed from the molds, they are placed on a pallet and sent to the garnishing department. Then the various pieces are assembled and arranged to correspond with the original sculpture with the slip used as a bonding agent. After the figurine is put together, excess material and imperfections are trimmed away before letting it dry. The garnisher also perforates the figure in one or two places to prevent the figure from exploding when the steam builds up inside it during the firing process.

Before the piece is sent off to the next stage, it is examined carefully for quality. Those pieces which do not pass inspection are destroyed. Those which pass inspection are marked with the Goebel trademark.

The figures are then placed on a slow moving car which passes through a tunnel oven with a temperature of 2,100° Farenheit. Supports are added to some pieces to keep them from losing their shape in the severe heat. After this initial firing, the pieces are covered with a colored glaze which assures the glazer that each figurine has been sufficiently covered. The glaze, which is a liquid glass, coats the figure with a protective seal. The glaze becomes very hard and completely bonded to the figure after the next firing. Again, the pieces are thoroughly inspected with the imperfect ones being discarded before the remainder are sent to the decoration department.

Over four hundred people are employed in the decoration department working in teams guided by master painters. A four to five year apprenticeship is required for some of the more difficult chores performed. More than 2,000 color variations are mixed daily made of metallic oxides, pulverized glaze, and a bit of oil. One painter does not paint an entire piece; if he did, it would take him about a day to complete just one figure. But teams of painters work on the same piece in an assembly line with the more complex painting tasks left for the last painter. This allows each color to dry and set before a new color is added. The most difficult, and therefore always the last part to be painted, is the face. Capturing the correct flesh tone and facial details takes the most skill. The last artist is allowed to initial or sign the base of the figure. Starting in 1979, these final artists have placed the year of production on the base which gives collectors an accurate date when the piece was actually made.

The final firing melts the colors into the figurine, giving it a matte finish. Modern methods make the colors more impervious to fading. The final check is even more thorough than the earlier check. Some pieces are only in need of a touch up from the decorating department; others are considered to be imperfect and are destroyed. The majority are sent to the packaging department where they are wrapped and placed in protective boxes before being shipped.

# HOW TO IDENTIFY HUMMELS

Hummels are a race unto themselves with their own terminology, symbols, and markings. Their identification is really not difficult in the majority of cases. Proper identification hinges upon the markings. Once one has mastered the art of reading or understanding these markings, almost any Hummel figurine, whether old or new, figurine or other article, is readily identifiable. While the marks themselves have changed over the years, the basic system by which the factory employs them has not. It is important that anyone interested in owning or collecting Hummels be able to identify them by use of the factory markings. The uninformed owner may sell a model based on the advertised price of a specimen with current or recent trademark, when in fact it bears an old mark. This piece could have, with proper identification, been sold more profitably. It is not a hard and fast rule that obsolete trademarks are more valuable than those presently in use, but generally this is so. The price variance between seemingly identical pieces with different trademarks can be substantial. Not only the mark, but the size designator must be taken into account, as the value of models issued in more than one proportion depends very much on their size. The size should never be judged solely by measuring: Measurement of the actual specimen is of less importance compared to the size designation given on the figure's base. You should never buy Hummels from lists or advertisements whose sizes are given only by measurement.

There are a number of signs and markings to be found on Hummels, more on some specimens than others. Certain of these markings are useful toward identification and others, though they may confirm authenticity, do not help in identifying, dating, or pricing the item. For example, all Hummels carry an incised facsimile of Berta Hummel's signature. The presence of this signature is a guarantee that the work is a product of the Goebel factory and is based on an original work by Sister Hummel; but this is all it indicates. Occasionally, collectors report figurines without the signature, but these are rarely found. With some of the smaller objects which lack enough space for a signature, the company attached a label with the signature. If you find an object with one of the Goebel trademarks, but without the signature, the object is probably one of the other ceramic products manufactured by Goebel. Many people erroneously believe that any item with the Goebel trademark—especially one of the bee marks—is a Hummel. This is certainly not true; the Goebel Company produces a full line of ceramic articles which are not Hummels. It is probably unwise to pay a high price for a Hummel without the signature, because the authenticity is difficult to determine. You'd find it hard, if not impossible, to resell and get your money's worth back. For further information the other markings must be consulted.

A large Hummel model number always will be found on the underside of the base. It may or may not be accompanied by other markings. This is variously termed the figure indicator, work indicator, or, more commonly, model number. Hummels are issued in a series with a specific number assigned to each production. A collector need only check this number against a list of the works manufactured such as provided in the listings section of this book, to identify the item. If the number is 169, the work is "Bird Duet." If the number is 49, you have a specimen of "To Market." Figures that were designed to be a part of a set usually have the same model number followed by a slash and a letter. For example, two pieces which carry the same title, "Angels at Prayer," are numbered "91/A" and "91/B."

Investigation cannot end here. In addition to the basic model number, there may be a size designator. This indicates that the model was manufactured in more than one size. The size designator is represented by a slash following the model number, which is subsequently followed by another numeral, either Roman or Arabic. During the first 17 years of production—from 1935 to 1952—the first size produced was considered as the standard for that work. When the company had plans to produce a work in different sizes, it would place a slash and an "O" after the model number. For example, #51 is "Village Boy." The marking 51/0 indicates this figure is made in an original standard size, but that other sizes also exist.

If the slash is followed by a Roman numeral "I," 51/I, this piece is the next size larger than standard. Roman numeral "II" would indicate the second size larger and so on.

Sizes smaller than standard are indicated by the model followed by a slash, an Arabic numeral, slash, and a "0." "Village Boy" exists in two sizes smaller than the original that are designated by 51/2/0 (the next smaller size) and 51/3/0 (the smallest size).

It is important to note that all markings are indications of relative size. Not all Hummels are produced in a variety of sizes. If the model number is not followed by a slash and size designator, probably no other size exists, or did not exist, at the time the piece was marked. But there are exceptions. Since 1952, the "0" has not been used.

Having learned to identify the model and size, the next step is deciphering the trademark. Proper identification is very important as a factor in determining the value of each individual piece. Since the inception of its production of M.I. Hummel art, Goebel has used six basic trademarks. There are variations of some of these marks, but all fall into one of the six basic groups. These are in the order of their chronological introduction:

| | |
|---|---|
| Crown Mark (CM) | 1935—1949 |
| Full Bee | 1950—1955 |
| Stylized Bee | 1957—1960 |
| 3-line mark | 1963—1972 |
| Goebel/V (or V-G) | 1972—1979 |
| Goebel (plain) | 1979—Present |

Not every Hummel design has figurines in existence with each of the six trademarks. Only six pieces introduced early, and still in production, may be found with the six marks. Many recent additions to the line have only the Goebel/V and Goebel (plain) marks. On the other hand, some old discontinued or closed edition works exist with early marks, but not those in recent use. It will perhaps be more clearly understood if explained in the following fashion. The Goebel (plain) mark was introduced in 1979. If a number was closed out in 1965, it cannot be found with the Goebel (plain) mark, since this mark was not in use at the time of its production. By the same token, a work first produced in 1979 could not logically carry the CM mark.

It should not, however, be presumed that the introduction of one mark necessarily means the retiring of its precedessor. This is not the case. During the era of the 3-line mark, many pieces were still being stamped with the Stylized Bee. Consequently it is impossible to say, just on grounds that a certain mark was superceded in a given year, that any piece bearing that mark must date to that year or earlier.

Some Hummels carry an incised date on the underside of their base. It is important not to attach too great a significance to this date. It represents the date of copyright of the design, and has nothing to do with the date of production. Many designs were copyrighted years before they ever reached production.

There are generally other markings as well, though the rest are not of much importance. A small letter symbol, usually at the lower left of the underside of the base, is the painter's or enameler's mark. Since 1979, the final artist has placed the date on the base which eliminates any guesswork on dating these pieces. A number in the upper right, is a quality control or mold number check.

# TRADEMARKS

The study of trademarks is an integral part of Hummel collecting, not so much to identify genuine issues, but to aid in dating a particular specimen. Six different trademarks have been used on Hummels, the majority of them so similar that a close familiarity with each variation is necessary for identification. Before going any further, it should be pointed out that trademarks do not provide an infallible means of dating and should not be relied upon to the exclusion of additional evidence and study.

Trademarks sometimes overlapped; that is, two or more were in use simultaneously. This was especially true in the mid to late 1950's, since new marks were introduced in approximately 1956, 1957, and 1958. Research into the use of Hummel trademarks, though it has yielded much helpful information, is not yet complete. As long as figures continue to turn up bearing marks that are not recorded, it is evident that the full story is untold. If Goebel was in the practice of retiring one mark upon introduction of another, the matter would be simplified; but this has never been their policy.

The earliest Hummels bore the old Crown trademark used by Goebel since 1923, a dozen years before Hummels were introduced. The stylized "W.G." under the crown stands for "W. Goebel." This mark is sometimes referred to as the "Crown W.G." or the "Wide Crown" mark. In 1937, a mark was placed into use consisting of a small crown surmounting the name "Goebel," written out in script characters without capitalization of the first letter. This symbol, sometimes called the "Narrow Crown," is not documented as having been used on a genuine M.I. Hummel item. It was used on other Goebel products produced during this period.

Beginning in 1946 at the conclusion of World War II, lettering was added to the figures as required by law to indicate that the models originated in occupied West Germany, U.S. occupied zone, as opposed to East Germany, on the Soviet occupied zone. In 1949, after U.S. occupation had ceased, the Crown Mark was employed along with the lettering "West Germany" or "W. Germany" since the Russians continued to occupy East Germany. The mark can safely be taken as evidence that the piece was made between 1946 and 1948. There are various styles of this additional mark, such as "Made in U.S. Zone" and "Made in U.S.-Zone Germany."

The 1950's saw use of the "V and Bee" marks which are more familiar today than earlier markings. Goebel adopted the bee as a trademark in honor of Sister M.I. Hummel. Her childhood nickname "Das Hummels" is roughly translated to mean "bumblebee" or "busy bee." The first of the bee marks were styled naturalistically showing bands about the body, eyes, wing separations, and the like.

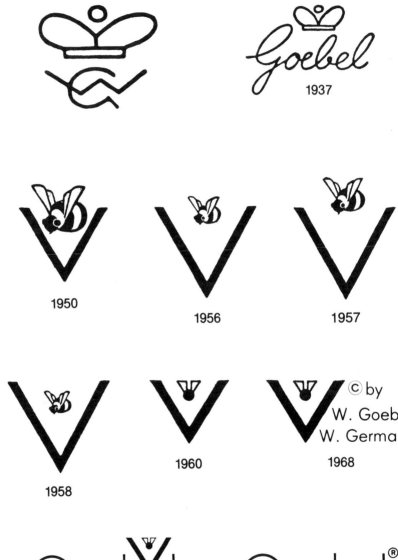

1937

1950

1956

1957

1958

1960

© by
W. Goebe
W. German

1968

1972

1979 - Current Trademark

1950. "Full Bee." First version of the bee. Naturalistic bee of large size with the letter V, filling the letter.

1956. "Small Bee." First variation of the above. Bee reduced in size within a letter V, positioned toward the top of the letter.

1957. "High Bee." Bee slightly larger than in 1956 version, positioned higher up over V.

1958. "Baby Bee." Very small bee, brought down within letter so that no portion of bee, including wings, extends above imaginary line between branches of V.

1959. "Vee Bee." Final variation of Full Bee marks. Wings become stylized forming a v within a letter V. Bee further distinguishable because of lack of eyes.

The Stylized Bee trademark was adopted for Hummels in the late 1950's. Although the exact year is not known, this trademark was in full use by 1960. It replaced the Full Bee marks which had seen more than 15 years of service. The Stylized Bee consists of nothing more than a circle with wings attached to it. Undoubtedly, Goebel considered the naturalistic bee old-fashioned and out of step with the character of 20th century German art.

1960. "Stylized Bee." Bee is drawn in stylistic form, consisting of circle surmounted by two wings. Wing tops are placed at imaginary line between branches of V.

1968. "Stylized Bee" (as above) with addition of copyright symbol and wording, "by/W. Goebel/W. Germany" placed to right of V, also known as 3-line mark.

1972. Word "Goebel" is large size, spelled out in printed rather than script characters. Stylized bee within V positioned above word, point of V between juncture of "b" and "e" in "Goebel."

1979. Word "Goebel" exactly as above but without V and bee. Small copyright symbol "R" ("registered") appears after word, enclosed within circle, positioned toward top of "l" in "Goebel."

In addition to one of these trademarks, Hummel models also bear an incised facsimile of Sister Hummel's signature, a number identifying the model in the Hummel series, and sometimes an artist's mark, which is small and inconspicuous.

It can never be said that a Hummel model must conform, so far as its markings are concerned, to an established standard. For example, some figures will occasionally be found with no trademark, yet they are undeniably Hummels. Others bear two different trademarks. Why any model should carry more than one trademark is puzzling at first, until you learn of the irregularity of Goebel's marking system and come to expect anything. Apparently, such pieces were manufactured but not immediately released and were provided with the additional marking so they would confirm to whatever mark was currently in use at the time of distribution.

As most Hummel figures are in production for a number of years, they carry over from the use of one mark to another. It cannot be presumed that specimens bearing the earliest mark are scarcest or most desirable. This may be the case but the reverse is also sometimes true, depending on circumstances. Production might have been far heavier at the outset than in subsequent production runs. With Hummels, never assume, and never take for granted.

The collector needs to keep in mind that this information continues to be updated as more data is discovered about the trademarks that was previously unknown and that figurines are still being found that have trademarks that do not conform to the dates outlined.

Sometimes the figurines were manufactured with an incised circle on the bottom of the base as a target for the trademark to be stamped into. The incised circle has no significance in determining dates or value. Also, on a few Hummel objects a sticker has been applied as the trademark if there was insufficient space for it to be stamped or incised. Prior to 1976, these decals were placed under the glaze; since then the decals have been applied over the glaze, then fired again.

# DESIGNS

## ADVERTISING PLAQUES

This is a very special and rare group of works. Advertising or store plaques are manufactured not for retail sale, but for placement in shops to attract attention and to act as an assurance that the shop sells official Hummels. There are a number of varieties of the basic advertising plaque, differing mainly in language, as Hummels are sold in many parts of the world. A standard message in a single language would hardly be suitable for all countries.

All have a small "Merry Wanderer" figure at the right side, facing left, on an oval sign mounted upright. A bee, the symbol long associated with Hummels, is looking down from the top of the plaque. The message, in whatever language, is "Genuine Hummel Figures" or "Authentic Hummel Figures." Though numbered sequentially in the regular Hummel series, they were not intended for sale to the public. This would not, of course, preclude a dealer owning such a plaque from selling it to a customer, if he elected to do so. This has obviously been done on a number of occasions. The factory's practice has been to supply these plaques without charge to its major distributors. As only a limited number are likely be given to each distributor, they have been produced in much smaller quantities than the normal retail line. They are certainly worthy additions to any Hummel collection and must be ranked in a class far higher than mere memorabilia.

## ASHTRAYS

Hummel has in current production a total of five different ashtrays, utilizing these motifs: "Let's Sing," "Singing Lesson," "Joyful," "Happy Pastime," and "Boy with Bird." Though officially classified as ashtrays, they should not be confused with the products of firms turning out two-dimensional Hummel art in which picture designs are applied to the objects. Hummel ashtrays all feature fully sculpted figures in the usual manner of models, with accessory ornamentation as well. Their coloration, contrasted to the whiteness of the bowls to which they are attached, makes a striking impres-

sion and ranks them among the most visually appealing of Hummel's miscellaneous products. It is highly doubtful that many, if any, have been put
to the use for which they were designed.

## BANKS

Hummel has to date produced only one bank, #118 "Little Thrifty." It
shows a girl reaching up to deposit a coin into a tall donation box of the
sort found in churches, and generally referred to as a "poor box." The box
is slotted at the top and will admit coins of small size. This model is provided
with a removable metal cover on the underside of the base. Though well
received by collectors, its use as a bank is probably not extensive.

## BOOKENDS

The factory has in current production six varieties of bookends, utilizing
these motifs: "Apple Tree Children," "Bookworms," "Goose Girl/Farm Boy,"
"Good Friends," "Little Goat Herder/Feeding Time," and "Playmates/Chick
Girl." The nature of bookends, being sold in sets, presents special oppor-
tunities for designing, as different figures of variations of the same figure
can be used for each bookend in a set. This has been done with all Hummel
bookends; none have identical figures on both sides. In all instances, one
figure represents a boy and the other a girl, engaged in similar activities,
with different coloring.

Hummel bookends are attractive and worthy works of art, but their use
as bookends, excepting perhaps to support very slim books of minimum
weight, is to be avoided. They are not sturdy enough to stand up to heavy-
duty use, and run the risk of injury when placed on shelves with encyclo-
pedias or even just a few heavy novels.

## BUSTS

The only bust figure ever produced by the factory is the celebrated one
of Sister M.I. Hummel, made in two sizes. It is doubtful that any further
busts will be manufactured.

## CANDY BOXES

These have been very incidental articles in the Hummel line, but as
some gift shop demand exists for candy boxes, the factory has occasionally
produced them. There have been a total of six different designs used for
candy boxes: "Happy Pastime," "Playmates," "Chick Girl," "Joyful," "Singing
Lesson," and "Let's Sing." A set of all six types can be easily assembled
as they are plentiful.

## COLLECTOR PLAQUES

These are versions of the advertising plaques released for sale to private
buyers. Identical in design to the former, they differ only in wording, as they
do not bear the words "authorized dealer." It should be noted that not all

advertising plaques carry these words either, especially the earlier ones, and that any attempted determination of the status of a plaque based on such evidence is risky. The collector plaques are quite popular, and for good reason. For years collectors wished to own the advertising plaques displayed by the dealers but, except in rare instances, were unable to do so. Collector plaques make a good, if not as scarce, substitute.

## FONTS

A variety of wall fonts, used as receptacles for holy water, have been manufactured by the factory. In all but one instance, #210 "Angel at Prayer," they are single units and the majority feature angels, often in combination with small birds or animals. It has long been the practice of devout Roman Catholics to keep holy water fonts in the home, containing water that has received a blessing from the local priest. Though this custom is more prevalent in Europe and South America than in the U.S., it is far from unknown in America. Its origin is centuries old. The Hummel fonts issued are: "Angel Duet," "Angelic Prayer," "Angel at Prayer," "Angel with Bird and Cross," "Angel with Birds," "Angel with Flowers," "Child Jesus," "Devotion," "Good Shepherd," "Heavenly Angel," "Holy Family," "Kneeling Angel," "Madonna with Child," and "Worship." "Angel with Bird and Cross" and "Angel with Birds," though similiarly titled, are entirely different designs. Hummel fonts show considerable imagination and creativity. Some are provided with full backgrounds, which vary in contour; others consist of the figure only, plus the water receptacle. The bowls, too, are designed in a number of different shapes.

## LAMP BASES

It could hardly have been anticipated, when the first Hummel figurines were placed on sale in 1935, that the factory would one day be incorporating Sister Hummel's designs into lamp bases. This has been successfully done, both artistically and commercially. It is quite likely that lamp bases will continue to be a standard item in the production line. The nine designs so far employed have been: "Apple Tree Boy," "Apple Tree Girl," "Culprits," "Out of Danger," 'Good Friends," "Just Resting," "She Loves Me," "To Market," and "Wayside Harmony." They are referred to as lamp bases rather than lamps, as they are sold with or without shades. In all cases, the stems represent tree trunks and are surmounted by brass or plastic sockets. The figure or figures are either placed beside the tree, shown seated upon a limb, or climbing the trunk.

## MUSIC BOXES

The factory has thus far marketed just two music boxes, #388/M and #392/M. Both are titled "Little Band." These boxes are two versions using the same figurines—one with a candleholder and one without. Whether or not music boxes are ideal vehicles for Hummel art is open to debate. Being mechanical objects, their secondhand value is naturally influenced by their operating condition. The market for them is larger than might be at first imagined, as buyers include music box collectors, who do not normally take an interest in Hummels.

## INTERNATIONAL FIGURINES

An area of collecting Hummels which continually fascinates hobbyists is that of rare figurines. Like the pursuit of variations, rarities offer the collector the possiblity of uncovering an exciting find. In the last ten years, rare Hummels not known to exist have been found by a number of alert collectors.

One of the most remarkable finds in the last few years was that of what is now called the international figures. These figures began coming to light in 1976 when Mr. Robert L. Miller, the prominent American collector, received a postcard from a gentleman in Vienna, Austria, offering eight unusual Hummels for sale. Frequently in instances such as this, once the merchandise has been inspected, it proves to be something other than described. Miller requested that photographs be sent. The seller complied, and pictures arrived showing attractive figurines of youths in Eastern European peasant dress. It was not, of course, possible to determine, on the strength of these photos, if they were genuine Hummels. They agreed with no recorded descriptions of the factory's products, yet appeared so like Hummels that Miller was sufficiently tempted to send a check for $500.

While anxiously awaiting their delivery, he contacted Goebel in the hope of gaining information about these mysterious pieces. He was told that no such works had ever been manufactured. When they reached his hands he found that each carried the "M.I. Hummel" signature and were thus, presumably, genuine. Another call to Goebel elicited a similar response, and this time the factory agreed to search its books to see if there might be entries of "closed numbers" for these designs. A letter was subsequently received from Goebel stating that, indeed, the eight figures were official products, prepared in the early days of World War II. They were part of a project to release figurines of youths in regional European costume, both for the international market and, in certain cases, special promotion within countries represented by the costumes. The eight Miller figures, wearing Hungarian dress, had apparently been designed as the result of an agreement with a Hungarian distributor. Subsequent to this find, more native costume figures belonging to the same series have turned up, all different and all representing factory samples never actually marketed. They consist not only of ones with Hungarian dress, but also of various other European costumes.

The reason for their non-production was presumably the escalation of the war. This had become the largest and costliest undertaking by the factory as far as Hummels were concerned. To release two dozen or more fresh figures, requiring the investment of a considerable sum of money and depending upon favorable international relations that would allow normal trade, was simply not considered wise. With many of its chief purchasing nations on the Allied side, and thereby cut off from distribution, Goebel decided to ride out the war with models already in production. Not only were the foreign costume figures shelved, but also a number of other designs. They were not resurrected after the war. Goebel did not again operate at full capacity until 1948, by which time the majority of pre-war and early war designs were nearly a decade old and forgotten. Many of the Goebel employees had escaped elsewhere during the war; some had lost their lives. There was no desire to look back.

There is much speculation as to whether the total of native costume figures so far brought to light is complete or whether additional specimens await discovery. The latter is, of course, a distinct possibility. Even though the factory professes to own no further samples, it is obvious from the Miller specimens that some of these figures went into private hands.

One of the difficulties facing researchers and those who wish to catalogue the factory's products is that the "closed number" designations never received names. Therefore, names must be devised for identification purposes, and judgements must be made regarding the countries of origin represented by each figure. As most of the territories involved border each other and employ similar modes of dress, this is no easy task. There is really no substantial difference between Serbian and Slavic costume, nor Slovak and Czech; and the outfits worn by Bulgarian peasants would not be out of place in Latvia, Estonia, or a number of other countries that could be mentioned. For the sake of clarity, national origins have been assigned to all these specimens by those responsible for the discovery and study of these figures.

It will be noticed that **some of the poses** are duplications of, or are similar to, standard Hummel designs, altered only in the matter of dress. One of the Bulgarian costumed girls is a close approximation of #199 "Feeding Time;" a Bulgarian boy playing a flute is a close cousin to #85 "Serenade," and so forth. The most obvious reemployment of a standard design occurs with #824, a "Merry Wanderer" in what has been termed Swedish attire.

But some of the International figures are unique and have no matching counterparts in the regular Hummels series. The Goebel firm reserved the numbers from 800 to 999 for these International figures. So there may well be another 175 of this set still waiting to be found.

There is still much to be learned about these beautiful articles. For example, one figurine #947 has the slash and "0" which normally indicates that a figurine is the standard size for that particular model. This marking usually means that various sizes of that same model were to be produced in the future. So there is the possiblity of uncovering not only more of these figurines, but ones in different sizes.

## PLATES

Beginning in 1971, the factory initiated a series of annual plates still in progress. #264 "Heavenly Angel," the first plate, went on sale with a modest suggested retail price of $25 and could in fact be bought for as little as $20 from some dealers. It sells today for $675 to $700.

All Hummel Annual Plates are a standard 7½" in diameter. This has been a point of criticism, as some collectors consider this too small a size to make an attractive display, or to compare favorably with other commemorative plates on the market which are generally around 10". Designs are simple, with figures in low relief and lightly molded.

A limited number of the first plate, "Heavenly Angel," were produced for distribution as gifts to workers at the Goebel factory in Germany and bear a German inscription. These preceded the production of the standard retail version. The occasion was the 100th anniversary of the firm, which had been in operation long before Hummels. The retail version was tested in the United States only, being the activity center for plate collecting, and not released for general sale abroad. Beginning the following year, 1972, the plates had international distribution through the usual dealers who sell Hummels.

## WALL PLAQUES

The typical Hummel plaque is of small size, less than 6" × 6" square, with a design in relatively low relief. Artistically, the best Hummel wall plaque is "Vacation Time" in which the figures, an Alpine boy and girl at a window, are well modeled and the coloration presents a pleasing contrast between light and dim tones. Many of the designs used for plaques are identical to existing models. These usually are based on the more popular pieces. Others have been adapted from figurines, but some, like #323 "Merry Christmas," are totally unique in design.

## WALL VASES

Wall vases produced by the factory are in fact plaques designed to give the appearance of vases, and intended to be hung on a wall. They feature three-dimensional figures superimposed upon the vase ground which invariably is white and serves as an attractive backdrop. See #360A, #360B, and #360C.

# VARIATIONS

## COLOR UNIFORMITY

Since all Hummel figures are hand painted, it is natural and inevitable that some variation should be apparent in coloration from one specimen to the next. In an effort to maintain the highest level of uniformity, the factory's practice is to mix all colors every day, from which each artist is apportioned quantities for his use. Differences in shades can occur because of slight differences from day to day.

## FREAKS

In addition to intentional major variations in the design or color of models, minor differences are sometimes found which generally are referred to collectively as "freaks." Usually, these involve the use of a color different than the standard. It is easy to see that color varieties can occur much more readily than model or sculptural varieties, because each specimen is hand painted whereas the casting is done from common molds.

The blue eyed version of #204 "Weary Wanderer" is an example of a notable freak. This is, on the whole, not a very scarce figurine, but only two specimens are known to exist with blue eyes. When hundreds of figures are being painted daily, it is understandable that occasionally a wrong color is used. In such instances the inspector is supposed to destroy these pieces. Being human, he may fail to notice the variation and the figure gets boxed and sent off into circulation.

## REVERSE MOLD VARIATION

There is an operation in which a model, generally comprising two figures on a common base, is reissued in reversed format, the figures having traded positions or accessories. For example in #218, "Birthday Serenade," a boy and girl are shown, the boy playing a flute and the girl playing a concertina. The reversed mold variation has the boy playing the concertina, the girl playing the flute. The designation is a misnomer, in that molds cannot physically be reversed. Designs can be reversed, but this requires fashioning a new mold.

Hummel collectors, like collectors in general, are an inquisitive breed. They have put forth, quite often, several questions: Why have reverse mold variations been manufactured? What purpose do they serve? What is the motive behind them? These are indeed good questions. Several reasons for this variation can be offered.

(a) Reversing the mold might be resorted to in the case of a model regarded as well designed, but which is not selling as anticipated.

(b) In the case of "Birthday Serenade," it may have been concluded that the flute is a somewhat more feminine instrument than the concertina.

## REVISIONS

Revisions in design are not uncommon to Hummel models. They have occurred more frequently with numbers in production for a long period of time, but can also be found in fairly recent works as well, such as #340 "Letter to Santa Claus." The motive for revision is not always readily apparent; nor is the alteration in design likely to win unanimous approval of collectors and Hummel fans.

The switch from matte to textured finish, carried out in wholesale quantities in the 1970's, had some basis in artistic theory: It was believed that if clothing and accessories in a model were textured, the skin would appear by contrast to be more lifelike. This is undeniable, but whether or not the result is a more handsome or more pleasing model on the whole is a matter of debate. There is some feeling that textured finishes were introduced on Hummel figures because of the extensive use of texturing on Italian and Spanish porcelain figures being distributed in America. Hummels are not textured so strongly as these works.

Other variations include the tilting of heads from one direction to another, shifting of arms or legs, and revisions in clothing styles or patterns. Revisions sometimes eliminate old detail without introducing new detail. This is the case with "Letter to Santa Claus," in which the new version has less color and less modeling work.

## UNRECORDED VARIATIONS

It occasionally happens that specimens of Hummel models are discovered with unrecorded variations. Generally, these are of a minor nature, but major finds are made from time to time. An unrecorded variant may be a figurine that normally wears a blue hat but which is found with a green one; arms or legs positioned differently; or a trademark not previously believed to be used on that edition.

The cause of these variations can often be blamed on human error: A worker not faithfully carrying out his instructions. In some instances, the variant may be in the nature of an early production type that was soon altered to the standard form, or an effort at experimentation that was not intended to reach the market.

## REISSUED HUMMELS

Since the first Hummels were produced in 1935, the Goebel firm has added more than four hundred designs to the series. Some of these models have been manufactured continuously since the first piece was issued. Other models were issued for only a short period of time, then discontinued for one reason or another. Some of these models were produced for such a short period of time that very few of them are known to exist. Some models have only five or ten specimens left. Most of these carry high values because of their scarcity. These are the pieces which many collectors avidly search for year after year, and will pay large sums for when they finally find them. Some of these have sold for more than $8,000.

During the great scarcity of many Hummels in the late 1970's due to the overwhelming demand from the growing numbers of collectors, rumors abounded that the Goebel firm would reissue about 50 models that had not been produced for years. These rumors were soon followed up by fact: The 1978 German and Canadian catalogs listed most of these discontinued pieces as being available in very limited numbers at reasonable prices (on the same level as comparable Hummel pieces). Many sold for about $100 from the dealers. It wasn't long before these pieces were circulating in the United States at prices tremendously higher than when they were first released. Still, these prices were much less than the prices for these models with the older trademarks. In the following two years, the same reissues were released in the United States.

When collectors discovered they could buy a reissued model at a much lower price, the prices for the older pieces either stagnated or actually decreased. Many collectors were willing to pay high prices for scarce pieces either because they were particularly fond of a design or because they enjoyed seeking out hard-to-find items. Regardless of their reasons for paying high prices for discontinued pieces, their enthusiasm for these old pieces waned when the reissued pieces became available. Some collectors were content to own a favorite model they previously couldn't find; others just couldn't get excited about pieces that were no longer rare.

Today, the Goebel Company's intentions for reissues are unknown. This has kept the Hummel collectors wary—some are fearful that the high values they paid for their rare pieces will crumble. This is a possibility. Also, without any assurance from the Goebel firm that the reissues will be in limited numbers, collectors are not inspired to buy them in the hope that they, too, will become scarce in the future.

If the reissued models differed from the older models markedly, collectors might feel less concern. Unfortunately, the differences for the most part are minor and difficult to discern unless a specimen of the reissued and the older model are sitting side by side. The most obvious differences are the trademarks. The reissued models carry the "Goebel" or the "Goebel Bee" trademarks, but there are some exceptions. Some collectors have reported finding several reissued models with the "Three-Line Mark" and even the "Stylized Bee with V" trademarks. Other differences include color variations—or minor modification in the design. For example, the reissued model of #13 "Meditation" doesn't have any flowers in the basket like the older model does, and the texture of the birthday cake in the reissued "Happy Birthday" is bumpy as opposed to the swirled appearance for the older model.

There is disagreement over which models have been reissued, so it is imperative that the collector be alert when buying old trademarks. Unscrupulous individuals could alter the trademarks on the reissued models in order to sell these pieces for the higher prices that are obtainable with the older models. The best way to avoid this type of problem is to buy from reputable sources and to arm yourself with as much knowledge as possible.

# NEW RELEASES

Except for its annual items, such as plates, the factory adheres to no fixed schedule of new releases, nor is advance publicity given on such releases. New additions to the line can be made either by the production of newly designed models or placing "open number" designations into distribution. As the factory has a wealth of such open numbers at its disposal, it could conceivably supply the market with new releases for decades without doing any further designing. This, however, is not likely to be done, because many open number designations will probably never be released for various reasons and it would be considered bad merchandising if the factory failed to place new designs before the public occasionally. The best source of information on new releases is the annual price list published by House of Goebel, 350 Fellowship Road, Moorestown, New Jersey 08057. In the future, the Goebel firm intends to announce as soon as possible their intentions of releasing new models and discontinuing others in order to aid collectors. In 1981 and 1982, the Goebel firm released a number of new models, some which were completely new designs whereas the others had previously been open numbers. The new releases were: #343 "Christmas Song," #350 "On Holiday," #351 "The Botanist," #352 "Sweet Greetings," #376 "Little Nurse," #394 "Timid Little Sister," #414 "In Tune," and #415 "Thoughtful." The 1983 new releases were: #188 "Celestial Musician," #309

"With Loving Greetings," #432 "Knit One, Purl One," #276 "M.I. Hummel" Annual Plate, 1983, and #705 "M.I. Hummel" Annual Bell, 1983.

The special edition issue for Goebel Collector's Club for 1982–83 is #421 "It's Cold." Also, a 4½" model was released of #396 "Ride Into Christmas." The special edition issue for 1983–84 is #422 "What Now?"

These questions are often asked: "When is the best time to buy newly released Hummels? Should they be bought immediately or is one likely to gain some price advantage by waiting?" There is one answer which can apply in all situations. Generally, the new Hummels tend to sell for higher prices, that is closer to the suggested list, when first issued and drop down slightly thereafter. This is due to the rush of demand from persons who habitually buy every new issue. Once they have been satisfied, demand levels out. However, there is always a danger that by waiting, a golden opportunity may be missed. The Hummel a collector intends to buy in the future may no longer be readily available, and will require a search before it can be obtained. This is especially true if the source of supply is a small local dealer who carries only a modest stock.

# RARITIES

Rarity, in regard to almost any collectible item, is a complex matter. With Hummels it is perhaps a bit more so. Some figures which are not rare as a class, are quite scarce when found with certain markings. Many early models have been placed back into production, creating a situation in which the work itself is plentiful but original examples may be rare.

It is natural enough to confuse price with rarity and to assume that the highest priced Hummels are those of which the fewest specimens are known to exist. This is generally true in the case of "discontinued" models but does not apply to those in current production. The price given for #141/X "Apple Tree Girl," is $7,500. This is neither an old nor a rare model. Yet its valuation is as high as, if not higher than, early models of which only one or two specimens are recorded. Its size, of course, is a major determining factor. "Apple Tree Girl" stands 32" high, more than three times taller than most Hummels of the 1930's and 1940's.

In the formulative years of the Hummel enterprise, its wares were offered on a different basis than today to a public which bought for different reasons. Nobody was collecting Hummels until after World War II. They may have been collecting in the sense of buying Hummels as they came out and placing them on a cabinet shelf as attractive decorations. They were not the Hummel enthusiasts who buy today. They did not treat Hummels as a serious hobby and certainly not as an investment. They did not try to own one specimen of every Hummel in circulation. They bought what appealed to them, and if another manufacturer brought out a model they liked better, they bought it instead. Hummel was not a magic word then. It was not found throughout the pages of collector magazines. Antiques dealers did not handle Hummels. In fact, traditionalists in porcelain collecting took a dim view of Hummels, regarding them in a category far below Meissen, Derby, Sevres, and other figureware.

The factory made no effort to cater to collectors, investors, or others. As collector demand for Hummels gradually grew, it became apparent that there were customers willing to spend large sums of money on the hobby. This encouraged retail price increases, which almost surely would not have come about if demand had remained with gift shop browsers and impulse buyers, and the production of extraordinary models, such as the 32″ "Apple Tree Girl," whose sales appeal lay mainly in the fact that they represented prime collectors' items and lucrative investments. Without any question, a model such as "Apple Tree Girl" would have a difficult time selling at $7,500 if it did not bear the Hummel name. This is not a criticism of the model in any way; "Apple Tree Girl" is an extremely good Hummel. Simple business logic shows that in an era when even the finest 200-year-old chinaware figures seldom realize five-figure prices, a newly manufactured model, regardless of quality or any other consideration, could not hope to bring that kind of money merely as an object d'art.

The old rare Hummels are in a position of having to catch models such as "Apple Tree Girl" in price. After starting off at very low prices, increases of even 50% or 100% per year, during the years of Hummel collectibility, have failed to place them in that range. It would be foolish to presume that even the most sought after Hummels advance steadily at this pace. When an item exists in just a handful of specimens, years pass with no recorded sales. When a sale finally occurs, it may be for double the last amount; but that could have been five or six years earlier, in which event the increase is more in the neighborhood of 20% annually. Just as these rare models advance in price, so do the recent ones which were originally expensive. These specimens usually appreciate at a slower pace, so that the relation of price to rarity does not become equitable. The factory holds the key; it controls this situation just as much as do collectors and dealers. If it elected to issue a model limited to ten specimens and ask $50,000 for each specimen, there is no doubt that the ten would be quickly sold. They would be instant collectors' items and, in the opinion of many, attractive investments.

Lost Hummels have turned up. Usually, one single specimen is found, not a carton or carload. When they do turn up, it is usually not in a shop, basement, or warehouse, but in the possession of a private individual, who knew nothing of its rarity or value.

The value of a unique Hummel, a model of which only one specimen is recorded, is dependent upon no other specimens being located. Because Hummels are of modern origin, the chance of another specimen coming to light is always a possibility. Even early collectors' items believed unique are occasionally stricken from that category. This does not mean that the appearance of a second specimen will necessarily lessen the market value. It may, and it may not, depending on circumstances. Generally, the specimen previously thought to be unique reposes in a well-known collection, from which it is not likely to depart until the owner's death, and maybe not even then. The item has received great publicity and many Hummel collectors would like to own it, but they cannot buy it out of this collection. When the newly discovered second specimen is announced for sale, eager competition awaits it, and the price may be driven up higher than it was believed to be worth when unique.

The relative rarity of ordinary Hummels, those not in the unique category or approaching it, is difficult to judge, owing in part to the factory's practice of not issuing limited numbered editions. Production quantities in most instances are not known even approximately. Even if they provided the quantities of each item in existence, it would be necessary to know the number lost or destroyed over the years.

Generally, unique specimens, or those of extreme rarity, have resulted from the manufacture of experimental models which were not placed into ordinary circulation.

## HUMMEL COLLECTIBLES

### CALENDARS

Publication of Hummel calendars began without any intention of their becoming collectors' items, or even with much confidence that they would find a large circle of buyers among the public. Today, a quarter century after their introduction, some of the earlier editions are scarce and are deemed prime Hummel collectibles.

Since 1951, Goebel has published Hummel calendars. The first year, only a German edition was released. In the following year, the first U.S. edition was published which was based on the 1951 German edition. Each year, a new version of the German edition is issued; but, the U.S. edition continues to be based on the German edition from the preceding year.

In recent years Hummel awareness has encouraged preservation of these calendars, as well as all other material related to the factory. When the issuing of calendars began, in the early 1950's, they were not treated as articles which might eventually appreciate in value. Some old Hummel calendars have been rescued out of the "slush boxes" in antiquarian bookshops, where they were mixed among miscellaneous backdate magazines, and other odds and ends. In situations such as this, a sharp browser can generally secure them for a very inexpensive price.

Hummel calendars published by the factory have all, up to the present, been vertically rectangular, with a spiral top and a hole punched near the top for hanging. All depict examples of Hummel models, but without advertising messages of any kind. The full color printed covers could be considered collectors' items in themselves. At the very least they are worth framing if found detached from the calendar itself. No better photography work has been done on Hummels than the pictures adorning these calendar covers.

A point of great interest, and one which seems not to have been investigated with the enthusiasm it deserves, is that the models depicted sometimes vary from those in the standard production line in certain details. There seems no doubt that they were specially designed for use in calendar photography. If this is the case, one can only wonder about their subsequent fate. Are these special models put away in the factory's vault? Have any reached public hands? Is there just a single sample specimen? If that is so, they constitute an extremely desirable class of variations for which collectors would give huge sums. None of these specimens have ever been seen on the market.

Calendar models invariably differ from standard production models in having the Hummel name on the front, rather than the back of the base. This provides a ready means of identifying them, without the necessity of studying small details or seeking out minor variations. So far as variations in color are concerned, there is no question but that calendar models are frequently specially colored to enhance their suitability for photography. The differences in color are not, however, always so extreme as they may appear by comparing calendar covers against the standard production models. Color as seen on a model can differ quite a bit from the shades and tones produced in a photograph, depending on photography and printing methods. Colors can be lightened or darkened in a photo, and the use of colored lenses can alter one color of a subject without materially affecting others.

**Values.** Prices on calendars can vary drastically, because much higher values are paid for ones felt to possess more artistic merit than the others. But, generally, calendars from the 1950's sell for $70 or higher, with some of the earlier ones selling for as much as $100. The calendars from the early 1960's are valued at $60 with prices decreasing to $30 for issues from the late 1960's. Values range from $5 to $50 for ones from the 1970's with values decreasing for the later issues.

**Other Publishers.** Hummel calendars are published by the Goebel firm; however, a number of other organizations have brought out calendars featuring Hummel art. These include Josef Muller/Verlag Ars Sacra and Emil Fink, of Germany. This is all quite legitimate as these firms own rights to the reproduction of original sketches by Berta Hummel into two-dimensional Hummel art. On the calendars of these publishers you will not find photographs of Hummel models, the right of commercial use of pictures of models being retained by Goebel, but rather reproductions of drawings, and watercolors. They are sold in various parts of the world and, like Goebel's calendars, issued in a number of different languages. So far Schmid Brothers has been the only American publisher of Hummel calendars.

The foreign language Hummel calendars are hard to find in the U.S. Though printed in substantial quantities, they simply do not reach the American market in large numbers. It is sometimes necessary for an American collector to wait a year or more after the issue of a calendar to lay hands upon one in a foreign language.

**Standards of Condition.** The collector who has initiative and does not object to searching should have no real difficulty finding mint or near mint specimens of all Hummel calendars from the 1960's and 1970's. Those of the 1950's are much more difficult to get in a high grade of condition. On publication of these early editions, the majority of specimens fell into the hands of noncollectors who took no special pains to treat them with care. They were used in the normal manner of calendars, frequently marked with notations, circled dates and the like. Certainly a 1952 or 1953 edition would be prized even in mediocre condition. A 1960's or 1970's edition in such condition would have very little value.

The following table of condition definitions applies to calendars only—not other paper Hummel collectibles.

*MINT.* As issued, fresh, bright, having the appearance of being unhandled.

*FINE.* Not defective in any way, no notations or markings, but shows some evidence of use or handling. Possibly some soiling.

*VERY GOOD.* No major defects, some soiling, perhaps a few penciled notations.

*GOOD.* Soiled, creased, marked with notations.

*AVERAGE.* Pages torn or heavily annotated in ink. Cover intact.

## EPHEMERA

Ephemera collecting is becoming increasingly widespread in the Hummel hobby. It has not yet reached the point when Hummel memorabilia is hunted down by collectors with the enthusiasm of Coca-Cola or Disney items, but in a very short time this may be the case. "Ephemera" is not easily defined. The exclusion or inclusion of any particular item is a matter of personal choice. Old letterheads of the Goebel firm, envelopes, postal cards, newspaper and magazine advertisements, and distributors' brochures are examples of what might be collected by an enthusiast of Hummel ephemera. Ranking at the top of the list would be original letters written by Berta Hummel. These, while not impossible to locate, are very scarce, owing to her short life and the fact that her work in a religious order did not allow for extensive social activity. By all means, preserve whatever Hummel ephemera or memorabilia that turns up. It may not be of much value today, but future generations will almost certainly take a keen interest in it.

## GREETING CARDS

Publication of greeting cards carrying designs reproduced from sketches or watercolors by Sister Hummel has been extensive, and is largely the work of two German firms: Ars Sacra/Josef Muller and Emil Fink. These corporations acquired publication rights to many of Sister Hummel's artworks and have endeavored to use them for a variety of products. Hummel greeting cards are in no sense rare and their status as collectors' items, at present, is merely an adjunct to the collection of figurines and other three-dimensional art. They are in demand, however, and the possiblity is good that early ones could, in time, achieve a moderate value. Their distribution has been more extensive in Europe than America. Collectors prefer specimens in mint condition without inscribed messages.

## SPOONS

A new Hummel product, which collectors may not have seen as yet, is a series of collector spoons manufactured by Ars Sacra. These spoons are in silver plate.

Each spoon bears a different Hummel motif on the handle. The series consists of twelve pieces and is available as a set or individually. Suggested retail price for each spoon is $12.95; for the set of twelve, $139.50.

The following is a list of the motifs used on the spoon handles:

| | |
|---|---|
| "School Boys" | "Playmates" |
| "School Girls" | "Little Scholar" |
| "Farewell" | "Stormy Weather" |
| "Chick Girl" | "Rainy Day" |

"Just Resting"        "Not for You"
"Mischief Maker"    "School Girl"

In addition to the above-mentioned series, a Christmas spoon was issued bearing "Christmas Angel."

## STITCHERY

Stitchery kits using exact copies of Sister Hummel's artwork have been available to interested parties for several years. These kits are manufactured by Paragon Needlecraft, operating on a license obtained from Ars Sacra in Munich, West Germany.

The kits are designed to use cross-stitch and are made of polyester/cotton material with an exact copy of an original Hummel drawing stamped on one side. Finished kits are in an oval or circular shape and come with or without a frame. All kits include the necessary colored yarn and instructions. Newer kits include crewel. Still others utilize the popular latchhook method and come complete with colored yarn cut to the proper length. Some of the latch-hook models make wall hangings up to 16″ × 27″. Prices for the various kits range from $10 to $60.

## T-SHIRTS

In 1979 a T-shirt was produced for sale carrying a printed likeness of "Merry Wanderer" and the wording "Happiness is a Hummel." Made of 50% polyester, it was available in blue, white, yellow, red, beige, and other colors. The retail price was $5.95. Though not a Hummel factory product, it is possible this item might interest collectors.

# PSEUDO–HUMMELS

Almost from the outset of Hummel's popularity, rival makers brought out figurines of similar type. In fact, far more imitative specimens exist than those of the real thing. Sometimes they copied the whole figure, but more often they borrowed details and added others of their own, the result being a kind of hybrid that could be easily mistaken for a Hummel.

A distinction must be drawn between pseudo-Hummels and outright fakes. The pseudo-Hummels or imitations were not fakes as they did not bear falsified or fraudulent markings. They were not designed to fool informed buyers who insisted on having a Hummel. Rather they were aimed at the general public in the theory that if Hummelware was finding a large market, some buyers would undoubtedly purchase works of a closely akin type without regard to markings or point of origin. In this belief, they were more or less correct. For many years, pseudo-Hummels were retailed internationally, especially in American dime stores. They filled a certain need of supplying low budget Hummel fanciers with something they could easily afford. It is surely not a cause of shame to collect pseudo-Hummels if that is one's wish; but to acquire them in the belief one is buying Hummels is another matter.

Some beginning Hummel collectors fall into the trap of buying imitations because their knowledge is limited. They do not realize that the word "Hummel" is not a generic designation for figurines of cherubic children or other Hummel specialties. Hummels are the product of a single corporation. Hummel is, in effect, a trade name, and can legally be used only by the Goebel corporation. For another firm to make a Hummel would be similar to General Motors making Chrysler autos. Another error made by beginners is the assumption that thousands of genuine Hummels exist, and that no complete account of the total is available. Goebel has produced only about 450 articles in its entire history. Previously unrecorded Hummels do turn up occasionally, but these instances are rare.

Hummels must be bought with a certain amount of caution by using any reference material available to check out designs, sizes, and marks.

## COLOR FAKES

Though uncommon, color fakes of Hummels do exist and are a sufficiently serious problem to deserve the collector's attention. It is an old adage in the world of collectors' items that anything worth faking, will be faked sooner or later. Hummels are not especially good targets for the usual variety of faking—manufacturing a totally spurious facsimile. However, there are a number of examples in the factory series of models that are relatively common and inexpensive in one color, but rare in another color. The model itself is identical, only the coloring differs. A good example is #42 "Good Shepherd." The usual variety with a pale rust robe is not by any means rare; even with the Crown Mark it sells for under $300. The very same figure, with the same markings but a pale violet robe, is worth a four-digit price.

It is not a difficult matter for a skilled faker to strip off the existing color and replace it with another. The new color is not likely to agree perfectly with that of a genuine figurine, but this does not deter the faker's effort. He assumes that the purchaser has neither seen an original or will not be able to locate a genuine specimen for comparison. By the time the truth is discovered, the counterfeiter has disappeared. As Hummel collecting gains greater publicity and prices go higher, more counterfeiting of this sort will be attempted. For an investment of $50 to $100 plus a few days of work, the counterfeiter stands to reap a large profit.

There is no sure safeguard against fakes. It can only be suggested that the collector refrain from buying rare or costly Hummels until a thorough knowledge of the subject is acquired. A collector should not rely solely on knowledge gained from books. The experience of handling and observing actual specimens is invaluable. Hummels must not be bought from unknown sellers. A collector must be especially cautious of discounts and bargains. These ploys are often used by fakers to encourage customers to make a hasty and unwise decision.

It is sometimes assumed by uniformed collectors that a model consisting of many color variations, in which the change of just one color constitutes a rarity, is not likely to be faked. They reason that the faker, in subjecting the figurine to a bleach bath for removal of one color, will remove the others.

He is not apt to have success in replacing all of them with any degree of accuracy. This is overconfident thinking. No bleach bath is needed if the faker is skilled. He need only brush on a strong solvent over the desired area, and in this way remove a single color without affecting other colors in the least.

## OTHER ADAPTATIONS OF HUMMEL ART

The art work of Sister Maria Hummel continues to gain in popularity as the proliferation of pieces developed from her works garner more and more collectors. This would not be possible without the many adaptations that have been derived from her works: Only 500 or 600 of her original drawings and paintings exist. Without these numerous adaptations, knowledge and enjoyment of her artistic achievements would be limited. Instead, most admirers can own and display in their own homes some representation of her work.

Although the United States Customs office defines the Hummels as original works of art, some people would argue that this is not a correct description. But there are lithographs that have been adapted from an artist's works without the artist being involved in the execution of the print except to give his final approval and sign and number the prints. This was certainly the case with many of the lithographs made of Norman Rockwell's works. The prices paid for these pieces indicate that they are valued regardless of their status. Such is the case with Hummels. Sister Maria's works were rendered into other art mediums by professional artists with her suggestions used to modify the pieces until she was satisfied with the final piece. Usually, figurines or statues that are cast from clay models created by a professional sculptor are considered by many experts to be original multiple art works, even if they are derived from another artist's works in another medium. But if a figurine is derived from another figurine, then it is considered a reproduction.

Most collectors of Hummels are not concerned whether these pieces are adaptations or reproductions. They enjoy the Hummels and are willing to pay high prices for their favorite ones. This in itself is sufficient to rank the Hummels as "collectible art."

Of the numerous adaptations based on Sister Maria's works, the Goebel Company's are the most numerous and the best known, but there are other companies who have reproduced ceramic figurines adapted or reproduced from her works also. Some of these companies have manufactured a variety of articles depicting Hummel art. They have made postcards, calendars, spoons, needlecraft works, candles, bells, Christmas ornaments, and even jigsaw puzzles. Goebel produced different types of Hummel items, too, such as dolls, bells, and functional articles.

Some collectors enjoy adding these articles to their collection of figurines produced by the Goebel Company. They feel these items add variety and flare to their displays. And there isn't any harm in this, but you will find that the quality of these vary. Amid these many companies, there have been disputes and court cases determining who owned the copyrights to Sister

Maria's works. Some of these pieces are deemed authorized adaptations like the Goebel pieces; others were possibly authorized while some are not passed off as Hummels, but are so duplicative of the Hummels that they are referred to as Hummel-like.

## MEL FIGURINES

A very small, but interesting series of items was discovered just a few years ago. The Mel figurines were produced by the Goebel firm, but were not included in their regular series or given the authentic M.I. Hummel signature. During the early 1940's a small number of clay models which were designed from original drawings by Sister Maria were apparently not approved by the Siessen Convent. Since it was against their contract to issue these as part of their regular series, they used the last three letters of Hummel—Mel—to indicate these as unauthorized figurines. It is not known why the firm felt it was permissible to issue pieces which did not have the convent's final approval or whether there was some other type of agreement.

Presently, Mel figurines numbered one through seven are known to exist. The first three of these were later remodeled by Gerhard Skrobeck, the present master sculptor, and approved by the Convent. Subsequently, these same pieces have become part of the regular Hummel series as numbers 115, 116, and 117.

As with the many Hummel variations, collectors find the discovery of such figurines just another challenging and interesting aspect to a fascinating hobby. The discovery of more Mel figurines looms as an exciting possibility—anyone who uncovers one of these will have probably found a rare and valuable piece.

## HUMMEL-LIKE FIGURINES

It is important for collectors to become aware of Hummel-like figurines, which are not authentic pieces by the Goebel Company. But sometimes on the secondary market, these figurines are offered fraudulently to collectors as authentic Hummels. When you have become very familiar with Hummels, these figurines, for the most part, won't fool you. None of the Hummel-like figurines match the Goebel Company's high quality of achievement in re-creating the artistic realism and subtleties of Sister Maria's work.

There are two companies, Arnart and NAPCO, presently importing figurines which are not authentic Hummels, but are so much like Hummels in subject matter, details, coloration, and modeling techniques, that they are placed in the class of Hummel-like figurines. Both of these companies import these figurines from Japan.

Arnart Import of New York has imported a set of figurines titled "Original Child Life Series." The older ones are stamped with the Arnart crown trademark superimposed over "Arnart Fifth Ave.—handpainted." The current pieces have just the Arnart trademark. Some have ony two crossed arrows with "designed by Erick Stauffer" stamped on the base. Most of these are selling for much less than Hummels—anywhere between 10% to 25% the values for comparable Hummel pieces.

NAPCO stands for the National Potteries of Cleveland. Their series, which is titled "Our Children," also consists of the same characteristics that are associated with Hummels. Many of these pieces show children engaged in activities normally done by adults, dressed in clothing which looks very European. Yet some of their figurines bear no resemblance to the Hummels.

The NAPCO pieces are identified by their model numbers which are incised on the bottom of the base. These are four digit numbers preceded by the letter "C." Some of them still have a trademark which is a large foil "N." These pieces are somewhat more popular than the ones imported by Arnart although they sell for the same modest sums.

There are other Hummel-like figurines which are available in gift shops and at secondary sources. If a collector knows how to identify a Hummel produced by the Goebel firm correctly (see the section on identification) and is familiar with the high-quality appearance of Hummels, Hummel-like items should present no problem. But be aware that there are those who will try to pass these off as authentic Hummels either from ignorance or the desire to defraud you. (See sections under "Terminology" for information on Beswick, Dubler, and Schmid Brothers.)

# BUYING AND SELLING

Many people who are attracted to Hummels and decide to start collecting them are usually surprised by the hurdles that the avid hobbyists encounter. You would think that a collectible that is still being manufactured and shipped on a regular basis to the United States would be readily available, but this is not always the case. The beginning collector who isn't yet seeking specific pieces for his collection faces very little difficulty: He can always find something that he likes well enough to add to his collection. But as the number of Hummels he owns grows, he will find it a little more difficult to obtain Hummels that fit into the scheme of his collection or that are not duplicates of what he already has. And the larger his collection becomes, the more selective he will become about what pieces he wants to add, which further increases his difficulty.

During the later 1970s many speculators who saw the growing interest in Hummels with their rising prices snatched up many of the available pieces with the anticipation of selling them later when the prices had risen even more. These speculators bought so many pieces that the demand for Hummels far outweighed the supply. As with most commodities, when demand surpasses supply, the prices for such items increase. And as the price tags grew even more, more speculators were enticed into investing in Hummels which created a scarcity of these items. Thus, many hobbyists were unable to find the pieces they wanted. An advertisement of newly-received Hummels or sometimes just a rumor of new Hummels being available would initiate a flurry of potential customers crowding into shops.

Today, the market is not as competitive and difficult as it was in the late 1970's. Apparently not as many investors are buying Hummels now, but the number of hobbyists continues to grow at a steady pace which keeps the market for the figurines very brisk. Buyers cannot expect to purchase the Hummels they want when they want them, and can rarely expect to buy them at the prices they want.

The increased demand for Hummels is coupled with a limited supply. Only a certain number of newly-released works are available because of the manner in which the Hummels are produced and distributed. The figurines are made in batches and are distributed by allocation because of the time it takes to produce each item. Just the hand painting of each item alone is a very time-consuming process because it is done with great care. If one artist painted an entire figure, it would take him a day to paint just one. The painting plus the painstaking process of molding and garnishing limits the number of Hummels that can be produced each year. So only a small number of the possible designs can be manufactured at any given time. When you realize that Hummels are sold worldwide with their popularity increasing in Europe, you can understand why dealers have a limited number of figurines.

Usually, the dealer does not know which models he will receive unless he uses part of his allocation to order special pieces. Otherwise, the distributor (there are presently only three in the U.S.) determines what pieces the dealer will receive. This further complicates the dealers task of filling the needs of his customers: He can't obtain as many pieces as he wants no matter how many customers he has and he often can't get the particular pieces he knows his customers want to buy.

Few dealers have more than 100 Hummels at any one time. It is not unusual to find dealers with no more than 25 Hummels in their stocks. Some may go for weeks without any Hummels until they receive their next allocation. Obviously, many dealers cannot sell Hummels exclusively; in fact, many run gift shops which offer other currently manufactured collectibles. There are possibly 30 to 40 dealers across the country with sizable inventories of Hummels. The few dealers with large inventories—ranging from several hundred to over a thousand—build their supplies from several sources besides their allocation. Some carry the most recently released items as well as previously owned objects. These dealers supplement their domestic allocations of recently released pieces by buying directly from Germany. Such a dealer will demand a higher payment for these in order to off-set the extra costs he pays for packaging, shipping, and duty. Ten percent above the market value for these items is reasonable. Of course, many dealers buy Hummels from the public, flea markets, and through auctions if they carry previously owned pieces. But this supply is also limited. When you realize that Hummel figurines are not only breakable, but quite heavy objects, you'll understand why so many of them have been broken beyond repair. If they are dropped on a hard surface, the damage is usually too extensive for restoration. Also, the earliest pieces were made 47 years ago and it is quite common for collectible items to become scarcer the older they are even if they aren't highly fragile. With the passage of time, you can expect a certain number of collectibles to be damaged and lost—and this was doubly true for the early Hummels which were manufactured in a war-ridden country.

## BUYING

Before purchasing any Hummels, you would be wise to familiarize yourself with the different characteristics of these objects in order to save time and money. You can avoid the hassle of paying too much for an item, or purchasing an item which isn't what you thought it was, or of owning a figurine that you later don't find suitable for your collection (after you've accumulated a number of them) by taking the time now to fully understand the different aspects involved in buying.

You need to be knowledgeable about how to identify a Hummel made by the W. Goebel Company, how to read the various marks on a Hummel, how to interpret the trademarks, and how to evaluate the innumerable variations and deviations of Hummels. These topics are discussed completely in other sections in this book. The section on identification will help you discern a Hummel made by the Goebel Company from Hummel objects made by other companies (some are authorized and some are not) and Hummel-like objects. Although there would be no harm in buying such items, you wouldn't want to buy one thinking you were purchasing an authentic Hummel—particularly since the values are rarely as high as the Hummels. Presently, fakes and forgeries are not plentiful, but you should not let yourself become lackadaisical. As prices for Hummels increase, you can expect an increase in the number of fakes and forgeries. This has been true with most collectibles—the higher the values, the more fakes there will be on the market.

Since the trademark can have a great bearing on the value, you will need to study this information thoroughly. You'll need to know which trademarks are the oldest, because Hummels bearing trademarks which are no longer being used are the most difficult to find and generally more expensive. Usually the older the trademark, the more valuable the piece, but this is not always the case. Some pieces that are older are more plentiful than more recent pieces, either because more were originally produced or because fewer were lost and damaged. If this occurs then they are not as scarce as a newer model, and the older piece will be less valuable since the demand for it will be less. Either of these factors can make a more recent trademark more valuable than an older trademark. But normally, an older trademark for the same model will be more expensive. For example, the #7 "Merry Wanderer," in a 6″ to 6½″ size, ranges in price from $65 to $425 depending on the trademark. With the most current trademark— the "Goebel"—this model sells for around $65. Yet the model with the oldest trademark—the "Crown Mark"—carries a price tag of $300 to $425.

Another factor which influences the value of a Hummel is its size. The larger the piece, the greater the value with models of the same trademark. Thus, a 7″ model of the "Merry Wanderer" with a "Goebel" trademark sells for more than a 6″ model with the same trademark; but a smaller model with an older trademark may or may not sell for more. The 6″ model of the "Merry Wanderer" with the "Crown Mark" trademark sells for $345 more than the 7″ model with the "Goebel" trademark; whereas, a 6″ model with a "Full Bee" trademark sells for less than a 7″ one with the more current "Goebel" trademark. This varies from model to model.

Since size is so important, you should be prepared to measure a figurine before buying it, since many people measure these objects either carelessly or incorrectly. The majority of Hummels are under 12″, so a foot long ruler will suffice unless you plan to purchase one of the bigger variations. You will need either another ruler or a flat, hard object. In order to get a reliable measurement, place the figurine on a flat, firm surface. Then, stand a ruler beside it. By placing another ruler or another flat object horizontally across the highest point of the figurine, you will have an accurate measurement at the point where the two rulers touch. Make sure to place the horizontal ruler at the highest point on the object, even if it is just a tip of a hat or a ruffled strand of hair.

One of the most exciting areas for the more advanced collector is that of variations and deviations. This area can cause great confusion for the beginner, but the experienced hobbyist perceives the variations as a challenge: Undiscovered variations continue to be uncovered—and their rarity gives these works breath-taking prices. Many collectors search extensively for these rarities, savoring the possession of a fairly unique variation.

By being informed, the beginner will not mistake a common variation of a particular model for a scarce variation of the same model; otherwise, he is liable to end up paying a huge price for a common piece. For the listings, you'll see that the great rarity—#947 "Goose Girl with Serbian Costume" is very scarce and possibly sells from somewhere between $8,000 and $12,000. But, the #47 "Goose Girl," which obviously had the same casting mold, has a price range from $50 to $775 depending on the size and the trademark. This is, of course, an extreme case. But, nevertheless, the person who uncovered the first Serbian "Goose Girl" had to be knowledgeable enough to know that this was a unique variation of a very common piece. This was a fairly easy difference to discern, but some scarce variations differ so slightly from the common variations that only the most observant will catch such deviations. For example, the model number 47/ 0 of the "Goose Girl" in a 5¼″ size sells for $68 to $370. But some pieces which have a blade of grass between the goose and the girl place these particular pieces in the "very scarce" category which means there are probably as few as 100 to 1000 specimens of this specific variation.

The condition of a piece is of great importance to the value, and is easier for the beginner to determine than with many other collectibles, such as coins or stamps. With such items, condition is broken down into many gradations, each with different values. Condition is not that complex with Hummels. Nevertheless, before buying a piece, you should make a careful examination in a good light. Turn the piece slowly in your hands, looking at it from various angles. While looking for any flaws, you should keep variations and deviations in mind also. Uniform fading which is fairly common on pieces manufactured prior to 1952 does not detract from the value of these early pieces. But if you detect patches of fading which were probably caused by exposure to direct sunlight, the work is not worth the full market value. Obviously, the more extensive the fading the more it affects the price. Hairline cracks, small nicks or chips, and any signs of repair may be very difficult, if not impossible, to detect. Check carefully around the base and on small components of the figure, such as fingertips or small accessories, because these are the parts most likely to sustain damage that is not noticeable.

Many restorations are so well done that most collectors are unable to detect them through a visual inspection. Although you may not have access to elaborate equipment, you should know that long-wave ultraviolet and X-ray can be used to determine if a piece has been repaired. Long-wave ultraviolet can detect most restorations, but X-rays are probably the only infallible manner. Despite the difficulty of finding signs of repair, you should make whatever effort you can to discover any before buying a piece: generally, an expertly repaired piece will be worth only half the regular market price for a mint condition piece. This does vary though, depending on the availability of the model. The more scarce a restored piece, the closer its value will be to the mint price. The degree of damage and how well it was repaired will also influence the price.

Another area you need to be knowledgeable on is the recent practice of reissuing some of the older pieces that were thought to be permanently out of production. The reissuing of an older model may influence the value of the models with older trademarks. With the changes in production, these reissues should differ enough from the older ones to be considered variations. Besides, many collectors are interested in obtaining pieces with the older trademarks only. It really depends on just how many people are seeking a particular piece and whether they will be satisfied with a reissued one. The reissues can be expected to affect the market for these pieces initially, but the continual growth of the hobby will still leave most of these in a difficult-to-find category.

The best procedure for the beginning collector is to find a local outlet for Hummels. If there are no sizable dealers, you might try gift shops and antique shops. Your first visit should be to just browse. Take your price guide with you and a note pad and pencil. Take note of how many pieces the dealer has and how many different designs he has. This could be a good indication as to how well he'll be able to fill your collecting needs in the future; besides, it may indicate whether the dealer just happens to have a few Hummels or is a serious dealer. Also, note the condition of the items he has—Are they in mint condition? Are they dusty or stuck in some remote corner of the shop? These points might help you decide whether you will be satisfied when dealing with such an operator. Next, compare his prices to the ones listed in the book. If his prices are 20% or even 15% percent more, you should look elsewhere. If you can engage the proprietor in conversation, ask him whether he carries both newly-released and previously-owned pieces; ask him which trademarks he carries and whether he has any variations. From these questions, you should be able to tell (if you've done your homework) if he will be a reliable and knowledgeable dealer. Once you've found a reputable dealer, limit yor purchases to him until you develop more expertise. A good dealer wants to keep you coming back and will accomplish this with good service. Most of these dealers will stand behind what they sell to you, so you can be assured that you are getting what you paid for.

Eventually, as your collection grows in size, you'll be interested in obtaining specific pieces which your dealer won't have available. As you become more and more selective in your choices, you will no longer be satisfied with designs that are readily available and common. When you begin to look for particular pieces, it could easily take up to three months to find the piece you want if you work with only one dealer. A special order—that is, a piece that the dealer orders for you which is not part of his domestic allocation—could take even longer. So you will probably find it necessary to expand your choices unless you're exceptionally patient. As you branch out to use other sources, collecting Hummels will present more of a challenge. You can buy Hummels through mail order from dealers, from individuals, at gift shops, auctions, through mail bids, and secondary sources, such as flea markets, garage sales, charity bazaars, and secondhand stores. All of these involve some risks—quite often, the sellers for these sources know very little about Hummels except that they are expensive, so you must base your buying price entirely on your price guide and what knowledge you've acquired. Also, you are more likely to encounter unscrupulous people who are unconcerned about making you a satisfied customer. But the advantages to buying through secondary sources certainly outweigh the disadvantages. Not only will you be able to fill in what pieces you are seeking, but you are more likely to secure some bargains along the way, which is rarely the case with established dealers.

Probably the most sensible source for the new collector who is ready to branch out is a reputable dealer that offers a mail order service. Again, take your time evaluating the persons you decide to deal with. It could save you problems in the long run. You can check several issues of publications that carry dealers' ads, such as *The Antique Trader, Collector' News, The Plate Collector*, or any number of magazines and newspapers devoted to antiques and collectibles. Look the ads over with care; you can learn a lot about a dealer by what he includes or doesn't include in his ad, and by the physical appearance of the ad. Since there is no standard method for describing Hummel figurines, these ads can often be confusing and sometimes misleading. So don't hesitate to write or call a dealer for more specific information—most of them will try to be as helpful as possible. If the dealer provides the model number, but doesn't mention the trademarks or the sizes, you should realize that this is insufficient information. Try to find ads which provide enough of the necessary information so you can tell exactly which piece or variation they are offering to sell. Also, the ad should have some mention of the condition of each item. The term "good quality" may or may not indicate the piece is in the best of condition. Also, watch out for such words as "excellent" or "very good." In general usage, these terms would mean objects that are of high quality, but in the language of collectibles, these terms often describe articles that show signs of aging or wear and tear.

You'll need to check any terms of sale mentioned. Only deal with people who offer the seller a full refund if they're unsatisfied with the sale. This stipulation will protect you if you should receive a piece which is not in the condition acceptable to you or does not meet your approval. A time limit of three to four days is not unreasonable. Most ads will indicate acceptable forms of payment. If you don't want to encounter any delay, a money order is probably the quickest means, since most dealers will not ship the piece to you until your check has cleared. Some of them may accept charge cards, but you may have to inquire about this. If you show yourself to be a reliable and regular customer, the dealer will become less stringent about waiting before your check clears.

When you've narrowed your choices of dealers down to four or five, you might want to check through different issues of the same publication. Dealers who have run ads over a period of time with the same periodical probably are reputable; otherwise, dissatisfied customers would have had plenty of time to complain to the publication. Most of the bigger publications which cover antiques and collectibles refuse to run ads from dealers who have gained a reputation as not giving satisfactory service to their readers.

Instead of listing the pieces that they have for sale, some dealers will request want lists. Since most dealers don't know which pieces they will have available from one month to the next, many of them prefer taking want lists instead of running large ads listing their entire stock or publishing their own lists which are sent out to prospective customers. Although the lists can be helpful (they are usually obtainable by writing the dealer— either free or for a nominal fee), the want lists are especially effective for the more advanced collectors.

Your want lists should include your name, address and phone number, plus a full description of what pieces you want. Indicate the models you want by name and model number. If you are looking for a particular trademark, size, or variation include this information, also. The dealer will check his stock. If he has the piece or pieces, he'll inform you of his prices and terms of sale. Obviously, you should not list a large number of articles you're not seriously intending to purchase. This type of list will discourage the dealer from helping you or taking you seriously. It would be much better to list several pieces that you want and maybe several alternatives if these are not available.

If the dealer doesn't have any of the pieces that you want, he'll probably inform you that he has placed your list in his file. Then, if the dealer receives a piece that is on your want list, he will contact you. As to whether he will keep the piece for you until he hears from you depends on whether or not you've been a long-standing customer of his. This really varies from dealer to dealer. Sometimes, the dealer will know of another dealer or a collector who has the piece for sale and can secure it for you. He may charge you a commission for such a sale, so be sure to find out beforehand. The more dealers you work with, the greater the chance you will have of finding the pieces you want.

One of the more exciting ways to obtain Hummels is through auctions. Thousands of Hummels are sold through auctions every year—ranging from the very common to very rare. Most beginners are afraid to try bidding at an auction if they've never done so before, but it isn't as difficult as you might think if you come properly equipped and know what to do. You might want to attend an auction just as a spectator first, in order to get a feeling of what happens.

The best source for finding auctions will be your local newspaper. Try looking under the art and antique section for a listing of auctions. Most of these will be estate auctions and will only list several of the larger articles that will be on sale. Sales of antique or gift shop inventories that are closing down are not very frequent, but offer great potential for the Hummel collector. You can either go to the presale exhibit or call the auctioneer to ask him if any Hummels are included. Most small auctions won't have a catalog, but it is worth finding out if they do since these can be a good source of information for the prospective bidder. Usually, you will run into the same problem that you do with mail order: The information will be insufficient. But still, the catalog could give you a clue to which models are available and give you enough information so that you will be able to determine whether you'll want to attend the sale. The major auction houses, especially those which specialize in art objects and have sold many Hummels in the past, will list more complete data. Presently, the only auctions which are completely of Hummels are mail-bid sales. So, most of the auctions you can attend will have a variety of objects of sale. You may feel that your chances for winning a bid are practically non-existent when there are so few Hummels available. But look at it this way—there will probably be very few people present who are interested in buying the Hummels.

Before the bidding starts, there will be a presale exhibit. Sometimes, this occurs the day before the sale, but arriving early on the day of the sale should give you enough time. Be sure to go prepared to a presale with a notepad, a pencil, two rulers, and this price guide. If you see an item which interests you, take your time to examine it with great care. Notice the condition and any identification marks. You will be allowed to handle any objects for sale, so check the base for the incised facsimile of the Hummel signature, the trademark, model number, size designators, and other marks. Be wary of an item with a small slash on the base. Presently, it is not known conclusively what the slash indicates. But on most ceramic articles, such a slash would indicate that the piece was a second. The Goebel Company claims that seconds of Hummels were not released either to the general public or to employees. Still, collectors speculate that employees took some of the imperfect specimens home with them and over the years some of these have entered the general market. So you would probably be better off avoiding such pieces, as they could very well have some flaw which would make them worth less than you paid.

After you have noted the marks, condition and determined an accurate measurement (this is very important at auctions sales, because most objects are often measured in a hurry and quite often without the knowledge as to how Hummels should be measured), consult this price guide. Remember: There are many variations of some models. You need to determine exactly which variation you're considering to buy. The difference in value can be considerable. Then, you need to determine just how much you are intending to bid. How much you are willing to pay for a piece will depend on how eager you are to own a particular piece, how long you've been looking for it and how likely you are to find it again. If you want to bid under book price, that's fine. It can be exciting to purchase a fine piece at a bargain, but you shouldn't feel foolish if you're willing to bid over book price. If it's a difficult model to locate, you may find that when the next opportunity arrives to buy it the book price will have increased beyond the price for which it sold. Whatever you decide on for your highest bid depends on your circumstances, the scarcity of the piece, and your willingness to spend.

Once you've decided on your highest bid for a particular piece, jot it down and plan to stick with this figure regardless of your feelings later on. This will prevent any errors or indiscretions on your part during the heat of competitive bidding. And don't think you can't become infected with the fever of competition. Auctioneers depend on the competitiveness of bidders to drive the prices up. Even the most experienced bidders succumb to their feelings at the moment if they don't set up limitations beforehand and stick to them. Also, you should do this for every piece you intend to bid for and not let yourself bid for any item which you did not include in your notepad. During the bidding, an item may look much more attractive to you or you may suddenly feel that you overlooked the perfect piece. This is not too likely, and besides, you won't really know what you're bidding on.

Quite often, Hummels can be purchased at bargain prices at auctions, but there are many cases of pieces selling well above the market price. It all depends on a variety of circumstances. If the sale is big, chances are that the Hummels will sell for more because collectors and dealers are more likely to be present.

But don't let the presence of numerous dealers discourage you from bidding. You may very well outbid the dealers without overextending your plans. Most dealers will drop out of the bidding when 50% of the retail market value is reached. Since the dealer must leave himself enough margin to cover his costs and still make a profit, he needs to purchase his pieces well below the retail price. Occasionally, you will see a dealer bid higher than this. In such cases, the dealer usually has a customer who has authorized him to purchase the piece at a certain price or he has a waiting customer he knows he can sell the piece to immediately at a profit. Besides, many of the dealers present at an auction may not even be interested in Hummels. It is difficult to tell the dealers apart from the crowd at first, but after 20 or more sales, you'll be able to pick them out easily. The auctioneer often reserves the front seats for the dealers. They will bid coolly, showing no signs of emotion whether they win the bid or not.

Bidding against collectors can present a problem, depending on how many collectors are present and their circumstances. Collectors are often content to pay 80% of the retail price for a piece. If it is a difficult piece to acquire and more than one wants it badly enough, they will sometimes offer prices higher than the market level. For some collectors, money is of no concern and they will go as high as necessary to outbid everyone else. Others may have been looking for a particular piece for a long time and be prepared to pay a high price for it. Sometimes pieces that are not rare or even scarce sell for well above market price, because the bidders just couldn't stand to lose the bid. Don't let yourself fall into this trap. You'll only regret it later. So, be very cautious and prepared to drop out of the bidding against avid collectors.

If you are successful in your bid, the next consideration is how to get the piece home safely. Even if you will be taking it home in your own car, you should immediately package the piece properly. Usually, the rule with most auction houses states that you are responsible for the piece as soon as you take possession. So attend the auction prepared to package and mail (if necessary) your piece safely. Plan to place each piece in a box inside a box with plenty of cushioning material in between the boxes. Hummels are fragile and a small accident or even a quick braking of your car could mean enough damage to make the piece worthless. The auctioneer might provide you with a box, but it is best not to take a chance and count on this. Some of the big auction houses will not only package objects for you, but can mail them for you if you wish. If you have to mail it yourself, be sure to have parcel sealing tape and labels, plus twine to bind the boxes. If your purchase was for less than $200, it would be a lot less expensive to ship the piece by parcel post. If the piece is worth more, then you should send it by registered mail. Either way be sure to insure it for whatever it's worth.

If you cannot attend an auction, some auctioneers will accept mail or phone bids, but you will have to rely on any written descriptions of a piece, unless you can get more detailed information by phoning or writing. With such sales, you need to read the conditions of sale carefully. It may state that if your mail bid surpasses any floor bids, you would not be expected to pay the full amount you bid, but only the next level of advancement. This means that if you bid $300 for a piece and the next highest bid was $200, you would pay a little more than 5% of the other bid—about $225 instead of the $300. Technically, this service should be offered to all mail bidders, but it rarely is. So be sure not to assume anything. Only those terms stated in printing will be binding.

Some auctions are exclusively by mail order. In fact, this manner of purchasing Hummels is becoming increasingly more popular as more and more collectors are searching for hard-to-find articles. Again, read the terms of sale with care. As with mail orders, you must be very meticulous about including all the information that identifies the particular piece that you want. Listing just the number is foolish—you could end up with the wrong piece or a variation you don't want. Read over your bid a second time before mailing it out; any errors you make will be your responsibility. The dealer will not refund your money because you bid on a different model than you thought.

In these sales, the highest bid received first will win the bid. It may take a week or two before you hear from the auctioneer as to whether you were successful, so it is wise not to spend the money earmarked for the auction on something else. If you are limited in the amount you can spend, some auctioneers will extend the service of limiting the total purchase amount. For example, you could send in bids that total up to $500, but stipulate that you want to spend only $300. The auctioneer would automatically void any remaining bids when your total was reached. Some auctioneers will offer this service because it increases their chance to make more sales and at higher prices.

Private parties—either collectors or persons disposing of a deceased relative's estate—can be a source of great bargains, but the risks are much greater than with most other sources. A collector or private party may be unwilling to guarantee satisfaction and may be more likely to misjudge the condition. Quite often, a private party will have only several pieces he wants to dispose of and will know very little about them. His ad may not include trademarks or other pertinent information, because he doesn't realize it is of importance. Obviously, such persons may be willing to sell their pieces for well under the market price either because of ignorance or experience. Collectors can also be a great supply of bargains. Sometimes they must sell their collections quick in order to raise cash for an emergency. They don't have the time to wait for a good offer in such cases. You would be wise to avoid any mail-bid sales which list only a post office box number. At least if a phone number or address is printed you have a better chance of not being swindled. Some of these sales do not offer refunds, in which case you should not send in a bid.

Bargains on Hummels can be found in gift shops, and through second-hand stores, but this depends on circumstances. It is rare to get a bargain in an antique shop. Usually, the dealer knows exactly how much he needs to sell an item for in order to make a profit; and quite often, he bought the piece at a certain percentage of the market price with the anticipation of selling it at the market value. So unless you make a large purchase, you won't get a discount that is more than 5%. But with these other outlets, the situation may be different. Sometimes gift shop proprietors don't know enough about the Hummel trademarks. They could easily place a price tag on a scarce variation that would be appropriate for a more common variety. Browse around enough to examine most of the trademarks; if the shop advertises that it has older trademarks available, don't bother. Sometimes the prices at gift shops can be much higher than market value, so don't purchase anything without being completely informed. Gift shops at airports can have prices that are considerably higher, because many buyers come in looking for gifts and will purchase items without knowing the values, just knowing that Hummels are generally expensive. Christmas time is also a good time to avoid gift shops as these articles are sometimes marked up then.

These same problems hold true when buying at flea markets and other such sources. The buyer may not know the worth of what he is selling which gives you the opportunity of finding great bargains. But again, you could find prices well above market value or pieces which are inferior in condition. Your chances for buying a fake or altered piece are greatly increased, also. Few of these sources offer a refund if you find out later that the piece is fraudulent. So, these sources offer a challenge and a risk for the adventurous collector.

Regardless of the sources you use for buying your Hummels, the more you know about Hummels, the better chance you have of being satisfied with your purchases. Even by fully arming yourself with sufficient knowledge you can still find that you have been swindled or left with a piece you don't want. Don't let this sour you on collecting. This is part of the risk that is involved in collecting any objects—even the objects in well-established hobbies, such as coins and stamps. There are few collectors of any objects who have not been unhappy for one reason or another with their purchases. Just learn from the mistakes and continue to sharpen your buying skills.

## SELLING

There may come a time when you will want to or need to sell your Hummels—either a few pieces or an entire collection. Just as in buying, there are various avenues open to you, each with its advantages and disadvantages. Your circumstances and how many items you have to sell may dictate the method you choose. If you are forced to sell your items quickly because you need to raise the cash in a hurry, you should anticipate a loss, though this is not always the case. Anytime you have to sell a collectible of any type quickly, you dramatically decrease your chances of selling the item at a profit or breaking even. It takes time to sell a collectible—time to shop around for an eager buyer who is willing to pay close to book price or higher. To sell a collectible at a profit, you normally need to hold on to an article for years (to let it appreciate enough in value) and to sell it at your leisure.

The most common ways to sell Hummels are to a dealer outright or on consignment, through an auction, to private collectors by advertising (either with a stated price or with a mail bid), and by answering want ads. The easiest way to sell Hummels is through an auction, but this method is suitable only for large collections; in fact, many auctioneers will not want to handle just a few pieces unless you have very valuable ones.

Although auctions are ideal for selling with very little effort, they can also be the riskiest. You never really know just how much you will receive; even auctioneers' estimates are sometimes drastically off. Some of the highest and the lowest prices for Hummels were paid at auctions. The amount realized depends on a number of factors, some of which you have no control over. With an outdoor sale, poor weather usually means a poor turnout which makes the competition mild. And lack of competition results in low selling prices. The time of day your pieces are sold could make a big difference, too. For example, early in the day, bidders may not be warmed up yet: they may bid cautiously at first until they get caught up in the competitiveness. Yet, late in the day, many bidders may have already gone home or depleted their bidding money. The extent of advertising, the availability of catalogs, and the size of the sale will greatly alter the number of prospective buyers. A quiet little auction in the country will not draw as many buyers as a well-advertised auction in a large city.

Before turning your pieces over for an auction sale, you might find out how much is spent for advertising and whether they publish a catalog. If they have catalogs, examine them for clarity, attractive designs, and any other signs that indicate the auction house runs a successful sale. Also, ask them how many other articles, and what type of items will be included in the auction. Not only would you be better off with a large sale, but one which offers articles similar to your Hummels. Not many Hummel collectors will attend an auction selling mostly furniture or automobiles. You are more likely to obtain a higher price for a Hummel at an art auction or one which features other limited edition collectibles.

Another important factor over which you have no control is the competitiveness which can develop inexplicably between two or more bidders. The challenge of winning a bid can drive people to offer prices well above market value. This happens most frequently when two collectors have been looking for the same piece and are willing to pay a high price to obtain it.

If you decide to place your articles for sale at an auction, the auctioneer will ask you to sign a contract. Read it with care: it will state the date of the sale, commissions, any other charges (some will require you to pay a percentage of the advertising costs) that will be deducted from the selling price, whether the auctioneer will take the responsibility for damage or loss (almost all of them will, but this is too important not to know for sure), and a time limit for your payment which will normally be 30 to 45 days. Occasionally, you will receive an advance on the sale at the time you sign the contract, but it normally would be only a small portion of the anticipated amount. Once you sign a contract, you will not be allowed to renege on it.

You can have your pieces auctioned with a reserved price which means the auctioneer places a minimum for which they can sell. This will protect you from disappointing results due to poor weather, a small turnout, or lack of interest from the bidders. But most auctioneers will either refuse or discourage a set price since they feel an unreserved auction will draw more bidders. If you are allowed to set reserves, don't set them too high as this will discourage many bidders from participating.

If you're in a great hurry to raise cash, selling to a dealer is the quickest method, but you will be disappointed if you expect to receive the full value for your articles. Buying from the public is the best source of collectibles for antique dealers. But before you take the time to pack your Hummels off to a shop, you should call to find out if they carry limited edition collectibles in ceramic. Some dealers will have little interest in such items, so you would just be wasting your time. If they are an authorized Hummel dealer, you should also find out if they are interested in previously-owned Hummels. Some handle only newly-released pieces.

Try to arrange to visit the shop at the hours they're least likely to be busy. Pack each Hummel separately and carefully—not only for protection, but to impress the dealer with the idea that you value your pieces. If he thinks you inherited them and just want to get rid of them in a hurry, he'll assume he can buy them from you at a bargain. It's probably best not to appear to be overly eager or anxious about obtaining immediate cash for the same reason. With a large collection, you could take in just several pieces; then, if the dealer is interested in the entire collection, he may very well visit your home to give you an estimate of his buying price.

You'll have greater success for a satisfactory sale when you can take your time. Get estimates from a number of dealers—their offers can vary greatly. You never know if a dealer has a Hummel customer eager to purchase the pieces you have or whether he has only a few customers for ceramic figurines. There can be numerous reasons why one dealer will offer you a low price while another will offer you considerably more. One dealer might have exceeded his budget for buying from the public or be overstocked at the moment. Another might have a low inventory and be looking for something to fill his shelves. You never can know until you've taken the time to talk to them and received an estimate. Their offers will reflect their particular business and their clientele.

Just remember: You may have to pay 80% to 100% of the market value for a piece, but a dealer couldn't do that and stay in business. He will rarely offer you more than 50% to 60% of book price. And you will rarely receive a better percentage from a dealer by trying to haggle with him, because he has usually figured out just how much he must make on his articles in order to pay his overhead and still make a small profit.

If it irks you to receive only half of the book price for your Hummels, you could place them with a dealer on consignment. This is a much slower method, but you will receive a higher price. If you don't mind waiting months or even years for your pieces to sell, you can set the price yourself. Make sure you know the market value of your Hummel before you agree on a selling price. If you agree to let a dealer sell an item for $100 when it is really worth $200, he could easily sell it for the $200 and pocket the extra $100 without you ever being the wiser.

You should insist upon a written agreement which stipulates the selling price, how long you agree to leave it on consignment, the amount for his commission (which will probably be about 20%), and how much he will insure your item from damage or theft. Your regular insurance will not cover your piece when it is in a dealer's shop. Also, it doesn't do you much good if the pieces is worth $500 and he'll only insure it for $200.

If you are determined to obtain full book value on your Hummels, advertising in a collector's publication with national distribution is an effective method, but one which can be very time-consuming. You will probably get faster results than if you place your items on consignment with a dealer, but you must expect to put in quite a bit of effort. By reaching a large, but select, readership, you will increase your chances for some excellent sales. But even if you sell your articles at full book price, you will have expenses which will detract from your profit.

Except for the most common pieces, most articles that are priced at market values or slightly under will sell immediately after the publication comes out—some by telephone perhaps even that very afternoon. Common pieces that you price below market value will probably be snatched up quickly, also. Some items may take weeks to sell; whereas, some pieces will not attract any offers at all.

You can choose to either state prices for each piece or offer to take mail bids. Either way, be sure to state your terms of sale out clearly and fully. You will need to list enough information so that the readers can determine exactly which pieces and which variations you have. List the names, the model numbers, the sizes, colors (for color variations that have different values), and the trademarks. You will attract a greater response if your ad is easy to read, includes all necessary information, and looks professional. Many advertisements are poorly written because the advertiser was trying to save space (and thus, advertising money) or was just plain careless. You can try to conserve space and still present a professional-looking ad. If you have a number of pieces of the same size, group them under a head indicating the size. The same method can be done with other important traits. If all of your pieces are in top condition, you can just state that once in the ad; but if most of your pieces are in top condition with some in less than mint, you could place asterisks next to those works and state that the asterisks indicate pieces in less than mint condition. Experiment with what you will include in your ad; try writing it in several different ways. If you leave out some crucial information, such as your address (which has been done by professionals, so don't think that you couldn't be that foolish), you will have had the cost of an ad without the benefits. This will cut into the profit you will make on selling your Hummels.

As the checks arrive, deposit them in your bank account and allow for ten days to make sure they clear before shipping any pieces off. It might be a good idea to state this stipulation in your ad. With money orders and drafts, you will not need to wait. Duplicate checks which arrive late or bids that didn't win should be returned immediately. You should expect to receive inquiries as well as offers to buy by phone and by mail. So keep a full list of all pertinent information handy to the phone. And make sure you have enough time set aside to answer the written queries. You may receive requests for photographs, so if you're willing to take on this added expense, be prepared ahead of time.

Be sure to double pack each piece—place it in a box inside a box—with plenty of cushioning material. You should insure the piece, since the buyer will certainly ask for a refund if the article arrives in unsatisfactory condition. Most buyers will not make a purchase unless they have the right for a full refund if they are dissatisfied with the piece. Three to four days after receiving the item should be sufficient. Be sure to spell out this time limitation in your terms of sale.

Another alternative is to advertise in a local publication. This is the most likely manner for receiving a high price with few expenses, but it is probably the least likely to occur. This could be even more time-consuming than placing an ad in a national publication since you'll probably receive numerous calls, many from dealers who will offer you prices well below retail values. Also, you will have a number of browsers—there are people who fill their leisure hours by merely window shopping at sales with no intentions of buying. This also increases the risk of theft and takes up a lot of your time.

Some collectors sell their Hummels by answering want ads in national collector publications. Usually, these ads are run by people who are looking for specific pieces. They quite often receive offers from people selling pieces at very low prices who are trying to dispose of their Hummels quickly and easily. But sometimes, these advertisers are searching for scarce or rare pieces that they have been unable to find and are willing to pay well above book price for such items.

# INVESTMENT

As in buying any art, you should elect to buy Hummels because you enjoy them. Investment should not be your main consideration. If you buy mainly for investment, you'll be tempted to sell if prices don't increase enough or are temporarily stagnant. You'll have no reason to hold on to the Hummels except for the possibility that they will begin to increase in value sufficiently in the near future. You will have the choice of selling at a loss, or possibly breaking even, or holding on to objects you care nothing about.

If you really like Hummels, you'll keep them long enough to let the values appreciate, so you can probably sell them at a profit (if you should need to or want to). Meanwhile, you'll have had the pleasure of enjoying them for years. The longer you keep them, the greater the chances are that you can sell them at a profit.

But just as in buying other objects, investing in Hummels can be risky. Many collectors have made satisfactory profits from their Hummels; other have actually lost money in terms of buying power. It all depends on the demand and supply of particular pieces. Many collectors bought a piece they liked in the 1950's for a mere $10, then watched in amazement as its increasing scarcity drove the price up to several hundred dollars. In these cases, the appreciation of the model outstripped inflation considerably and yielded the owner a worthwhile investment. But whether this will occur in the future, and if it does which pieces will appreciate enough, is unknown.

Hummels do hold their value—you probably can rely on their values to start increasing again, because their high prices are attained from the large numbers of collectors who want them. The needs of collectors exceed the actual number of available Hummels. Unlike investors, collectors will not sell their Hummels in great numbers at the same time because the figurines are not appreciating sufficiently; thus, causing the supply to increase substantially. Most collectors hold on to the majority of their pieces. Their collections, all or part of them, become available on the market either because of death, a great need for cash, or an altering of their collection. The number of these types of sales are never enough to swamp the market with Hummels. The demand for Hummels continues to increase while the supply continues to decrease, which in turn increases the price. You have no worry about a figurine you bought at $200 selling for less in two or three years if you bought it at a fair price.

But to make a profit from Hummels on a predictable or regular basis, you would have to become a dealer which would enable you to purchase Hummels at wholesale. As a collector, you will have to buy most of your Hummels at retail prices and sell them at wholesale. Even if you manage to sell your items to another collector for the full book price, you will have to deduct the costs for advertising, shipping, and insuring from your total selling price.

You might think that if you cleared more money than you paid for it, that you have made a profit. This is not necessarily true. In order to invest successfully, you need to receive more in buying power than you spent. With the continual loss of value in money because of inflation, you could lose money by ignoring this fact. Inflation is probably here to stay; an average yearly increase of 10% can be expected to occur. With such a yearly increase, an item which sells for $100 would be selling for at least $150 in five years. If you bought a Hummel figurine for a $100 today and sold it for $150 in five years, you would be merely breaking even. Anything over $150 would be a profit. But considering that you would probably have to sell the Hummel at wholesale, you would profit only if the retail price had tripled. (This doesn't even take into account that money invested in Hummels could be earning interst at a rate higher than inflation in some other type of investment—which would mean you would lose out by having your money tied up in Hummels.)

Your best bet for investing is to acquire pieces that will appreciate considerably more than inflation—which are the older trademarks, especially the Crown Marks. Unless you find a scarce or rare piece at a bargain price, you are better off selecting pieces between $500 and $1,000. There are so few sales for the rarities that it is difficult to determine a value for many of them, and besides, most collectors cannot afford the pieces with the big price tags. So it is difficult to predict how much prices for such items will go up. In the medium price bracket, more buyer activity will help establish average market values and make these values go up faster.

No one knows how prices will be affected on the models that are currently being reissued. Some collectors will not be willing to pay high prices for a piece just because it has an older trademark; they may be content to buy a reissued model with a current trademark at a much lower price. If this becomes a trend among collectors, this would lessen the demand for the older trademarks which in turn would lessen the amount they will appreciate.

So, you should not hesitate to buy Hummels out of fear that you'll lose money. By following the market and paying reasonable amounts for your pieces, you should expect to own pieces that are worth more than you paid. But you should buy Hummels as valuable art that is to be enjoyed, not some commodity you can resell for a sure-fire profit.

# CARE, DISPLAY, AND REPAIR

## CLEANING TECHNIQUES

Hummels, like most things in the world, get dirty. Usually the problem is nothing worse than an accumulation of surface dust and discoloration caused by microscopic particles of airborne soot and other pollutants. It is an established fact that Hummels maintained in locations where the air is heavily laden with pollutants become soiled much faster, and require more frequent cleaning, than those where the air is cleaner. Their surface is of such nature that it attracts these particles and they accumulate at a rapid pace. They become covered with an inky substance. More often than not, this leads to a quick, harsh remedy by the collector, which may cause irreparable damage to the item. It is better to clean Hummels periodically in a careful, safe fashion before they are in need of a major cleaning.

Occasionally a piece is encountered in which the problem goes beyond mere dust or soot. It may be stained by ink, paint, or something else resistant to removal. In this event, a professional restorer should be consulted. Removing the stain without hurting the underlying color may be impossible, but with his chemicals and methods of operation, a restorer can do more good and less harm than an amateur. The charge for services of this kind is not excessive, but it may be necessary, depending on his location, to ship the item.

In the case of common surface grime, a good washing will do the trick. A proper "bath" can be administered to Hummels by anyone without danger or risk, by following these outlined procedures. First, before any attempt is made at bathing, brush away loose dust and large particles. If this step is neglected the bathing job will only be more difficult. Do not use a common dustcloth or any device of this kind, but an unused soft artist's brush. A ½" camel's hair brush suits the purpose very well. Go over the figure's entire surface, including the base and underside of the base, brushing gently at every area whether or not it appears to need brushing. The brush will quickly become soiled and will need repeated wiping with a dry cloth. Do not use stiff brushes as they can scratch. Tiny brushes may cause problems as the metal ferrule, into which the hairs are secured, may strike the surface.

The next step is the bath. Make up a cleansing solution using warm water into which a few drops of baby shampoo have been stirred. A slight foam should be created. Use a brush similar to the one used in the first operation. Dip it into this mixture and begin brushing the entire surface of the model, top to bottom, frequently dipping the brush into clean water along the way. If a number of models are bathed at the same time, it will probably be necessary to discard the solution after one or two and make a fresh batch. Never work from the base upward, but always from the top down, as the water will run along the model and cause streaking. The model should not be brushed so vigorously as to work up a lather, though it is not harmful if a weak soap is used. One good reason for not doing this is that the soapier a model gets, the slipperier it becomes, and it may become difficult to handle. There is not much satisfaction to be taken in a spotlessly washed model that lies broken on the floor.

The model must then be rinsed. This is done by dipping it into a basin of clear warm water, lifting it out, replacing the water, and dipping again. To facilitate rinsing, the model may be gently agitated in the water. When cleaning large models, the basin or pot must be correspondingly large. With huge models, washing can be done in a bathtub so long as the sides and bottom of the tub are cushioned to guard against breakage in case of bumping.

Afterwards, all that remains is to let the model dry out. This can be speeded up by subjecting it to currents of warm air from a hand held hair drier. Do not let this machine get closer than a foot from the specimen, and under no circumstances turn the switch to "Hot."

Be careful about where specimens are left to dry. Windowsills by opened windows are not advisable, as a strong current of air could knock them down. Do not leave them near a stove or source of extreme heat.

## DAMAGED OR REPAIRED SPECIMENS

As is the case with all works of art made from baked clay, Hummels are not very sturdy. They will break if dropped. Slight injuries can also result in breakage, depending on the point of impact, the figure's size and other considerations. A sharp blow from a carelessly directed table knife could crack away a small detail from a figure placed on the table for decoration, or cause a chip or scratch. Obviously, the larger figures, which have thicker walls, are less prone to damage from this sort of accident, but are no less vulnerable to injury by dropping.

Hummels do not shatter like glass, rather they generally break into several large pieces. Thanks to the texture and opaqueness of the ware, they often can be mended together by an expert so successfully as to defy detection except under the most rigid examination. Every Hummel collection contains some repaired specimens whose repairs have yet to be noticed. The total quantity of repaired Hummels in circulation being bought by the general public and by collectors is undoubtedly greater than most authorities realize or are willing to admit. This is not just true of early pieces. Collectors often have a habit of carefully scrutinizing old Hummels for repairs or damage in the belief that, having existed longer and passed through a number of hands, they are more apt to have suffered injury. This is simply not the case. A recent or new Hummel is no less likely to be damaged and/or repaired than one made thirty or forty years ago. Damage in **shipment** is just as common as domestic damage. Any dealer receiving a damaged shipment should, morally and ethically, not attempt to have repair work performed and sell the pieces as undamaged. Rather, the dealer should collect whatever insurance is carried. Sadly this is not always done, with the result that many mended Hummels, of all ages and ranges of price, are to be found. Unless the repair is sloppy or otherwise readily apparent, they are nearly always sold successfully. The dealers are all well aware of this. While some are too honorable or reputation-conscious to attempt such deceptions, others are not. The buyer's enjoyment of such a specimen is likely to end when he attempts to sell his collection and discovers the flaw. By then it is too late to ask recourse from the dealer; the owner is stuck, and his financial loss could amount to thousands of dollars.

It is most important to determine the condition of a Hummel prior to purchase. Few dealers will take back a specimen after selling it, as it could have been switched or damaged while in the purchaser's possession.

The buyer is limited in the type of examination which can reasonably be carried out in a shop, auction house, or most other places of sale. He will not have the opportunity to use x-ray apparatus, which generally provides the most conclusive evidence of condition. However, he should still do a fairly good checking job. A pocket magnifier, of X5 or X6 power should be used to study the figure along its natural points of breakage. Every piece of figureware has points or junctures at which it is most likely to break in the event of injury. The place where an outstretched arm meets the shoulder is a common point of breakage. Heads are much more likely to snap off at the neck than break at the face. Accessory decorations are extremely vulnerable and should be given extra attention as they are often thin and delicate and will be broken by accidents of a really minor nature that do not harm the figure's primary component. Petals of a flower, the tip of a staff or cane, and other small details are in the high-risk category. Signs of dried glue or similar substance are most obvious. If the repair has been well executed, however, glue will not be visible. Hairline markings at each point of possible breakage will indicate repair. No such lines are present in mint condition specimens. They may be very difficult to detect, especially if the surface has been painted over to hide them. Repaired chipping is also quite common and can easily pass unnoticed. The chipped area is usually filled in with plaster of paris or another product of that type, then painted over. Holding a figure sidewise to a light may reveal areas of uneven paint, or alterations in the surface that would lead to a suspicion of repair.

Certainly, well-repaired Hummels are not worthless any more than is a repaired painting or postage stamp. Their value is less than if perfect, but they still have a value. A repaired specimen is worth largely what can be obtained for it, which depends mostly on the seller's luck in finding the right buyer. As a general rule it can be assumed that the more plentiful, lower value Hummels are worth proportionately **less** when repaired than more valuable issues. Some collectors don't want repaired specimens, even of very rare Hummels, while other are pleased to get a near perfect piece at a large discount. There are a few persons who would like to own a $2,000 or $3,000 specimen, but cannot afford the price. Nearly everyone, however, can afford the inexpensive Hummels in perfect condition, so there is little market for seconds.

The extent and nature of repairs must be taken into account to arrive at a fair price. Certainly a specimen from which a thumb was snapped off and replaced ought to be worth more than one on which the head is replaced. When repairs are extensive or noticeable with casual observation, the piece is next to valueless unless it is very rare.

## DISPLAY

The display of his collection is a matter which the serious hobbyist should not regard lightly. Much more is involved than simply making an attractive presentation or rendering the pieces easily accessible. A well-displayed collection takes into account *safety*, both immediate and long-term, and makes provisions for the material's safeguard against theft, fire and other hazards. It is untrue that for a collection to be properly safeguarded in the home, it must be displayed in a manner that reduces viewability or visual appeal. Arriving at the best method of display will require some planning, but the effort is well repaid.

The size and relative value of the collection is the most important factor. A large collection and little available display space is quite common with Hummelites and in all cases can be overcome. Collections of hundreds of pieces have been successfully stored and displayed in one room apartments, without giving the appearance of overcrowding.

The natural tendency is to place Hummels all about the house, wherever a decorative touch seems called for, on tables, bureau tops, mantlepieces, along kitchen counters, and on various shelves. This is not, however, a recommended approach. The more scattered the collection, the more prone it will be to accidents of one kind or another. This is especially true if pets or small children are about, in which case special precautions must be taken.

The safest place for Hummels, so far as breakage is concerned, is in a case or on wall shelving. The advantages and disadvantages of cases versus open wall shelves could be debated endlessly. Both have much in their favor, and both have certain points against them. It boils down mostly to a matter of choice, and of course to the consideration of whether the walls will support shelving. Plaster walls, generally found in old apartment buildings and certain other residences, are not ideal for shelving. The installation is a difficult bit of work; long screws must be driven into the studs or wooden supports behind the plaster, which first must be located by knocking and listening for a hollowing sound. For the reader who undertakes such a project, it is suggested that they consult a home handyman book. Unless space is at an absolute premium, short shelves are much more preferable than long ones as there is less risk with short shelves of having too much weight on them. Wall shelving will seldom support more than about ten pounds per shelf.

Having pets in your home is one of the circumstances in which cases, fronted with glazed glass doors, may be the better choice. Hummels are attractive in cases or cabinets. They are less apt to get dusty, and most types of accidents to which they would be vulnerable are no longer a danger. They do, however, present a better target for burglars in cases, as the average burglar entering a home in search of valuables will automatically conclude that anything kept behind glass must be worth stealing. Otherwise, a Hummel collection worth tens of thousands is apt to be overlooked in favor of a $200 television set, unless the burglar knows something about Hummels. When buying a case for use in displaying Hummels, one with adjustable shelving is desirable. With adjustable shelving, the top space can be made 6″ to accommodate models of the smallest size, and graduate up to a lower shelf of 15" or so. This will still not be sufficient for every Hummel, but most of the factory's products could be readily displayed in such a case. Old display cases once used in shops are not usually handsome pieces of furniture, but are ideal for display, as they frequently have glass sides and are equipped with one or more lighting fixtures.

## EFFECTS OF AGE

It is normally presumed by the general public that porcelain undergoes no material change from growing old; that a century old porcelain figure is the same today as when originally purchased. But the passing of time does take its toll upon porcelain. Chiefly, this involves the fading or alteration of colors. Certain colors will merely wash out with age, growing gradually less intense. Others tend to transmute themselves into different shades. Green often takes on a purple tone. Owners are partially responsible for this as the conditions under which porcelain is stored are very much to blame. Objects exposed to constant sunlight or excessive heat will invariably fade much faster than others. A lighted display cabinet should not be kept lit constantly but only on occasion. Otherwise, heat will build up inside the cabinet especially if there are glazed doors and no opportunity for ventilation. The older Hummels are more subject to fading and color alterations than the new, as the factory began in the mid-1950's to use improved paint, which supposedly is fade resistant. Only time will tell if it possesses the properties claimed. When colors have darkened with age, this is often not a matter of alteration, but a simple overlay of dirt and grime that can be cleaned away.

## PACKING

Even if one is not a dealer, it occasionally happens that a Hummel figure must be sent through the mail. If properly and securely packed, this can be done with little risk. Damage in transit is nearly always the result of weak, insufficient, or amateurish packing, rather than some accident which occurred along the way. If a Hummel is not well packed, it cannot help but be broken under the weight of hundreds of pounds of other packages and mail, even if nobody treats the parcel carelessly.

First, a proper inner box must be obtained. This should be at least two inches larger than the figure on all sides, but preferably not more than four inches larger. It must be a strong box, sturdily made, its floor held fast with strong staples, its sides good and firm. It must have flaps which, when closed, entirely cover the top, not leaving any uncovered area. Best by far are boxes with very long flaps which make a two-layer covering over the top. If the box flaps can be easily bent with the fingers, the box is unsuitable. They should be so sturdy that bending requires the exertion of very great pressure.

Once the box has been found, line the bottom with shredded paper or bits of sponge, up to a depth of about one inch. Wrap the model in many layers of tissue paper or florist's paper, seal with cellotape, and gently insert it into the box, positioning it so that some space is left all around. The box must now be filled to the brim with more cushioning material. It should be packed in tightly all around the model, and there should be enough in the box so that some slight pressure is necessary to close the flaps. Seal up the flaps with parcel sealing tape, going all around the box in two directions.

This box, all sealed up, does not go into the mail; it goes into a larger box, of the same general specifications, and is protected by cushioning material just as was the model in the first box. This second box is not only securely sealed with tape, but tied with good strong twine—at least 30 pound breaking strength. The address should not be affixed by means of a label which could be torn off inadvertantly, but written directly on the box along with the return address. It is not a bad practice to address the interior box, too, just in case of mishap.

## REPAIR TECHNIQUES

The best advice that can be given for the mending of broken figures or other models is to seek professional aid. A professional restorer, having the patience and experience which the amateur may not have, is more likely to perform the job satisfactorily. Nevertheless, many persons do elect to carry out their own repair work and, for their benefit, the following advice is presented on a strictly "at your own risk" basis.

By far the most common damage to Hummel figures involves heads or arms breaking off. An arm will generally break off at the elbow if bent, at the shoulder if straight. Heads break off at the neck. Success in making an acceptable repair will depend to some degree upon whether the break is "clean," that is, if the arm or head or other component has merely sep- arated from the figure or whether shattering or powdering has occurred. Luckily, in most instances the break is quite clean. Shattered breaks are primarily the result of a figure being dropped from a height on a tile or concrete floor. Before beginning any repair effort, line up the detached component to the figure and examine it carefully to determine if any small pieces are missing. If not, this is a more or less simple repair, which should be successful with correct procedure.

Choice of glue is important. A well-handled repair effort, that might other- wise yield perfect results can be spoiled by using the wrong glue. Never resort to the use of just any glue in the house because it happens to be handy. The tendency, when a figure breaks, is for the owner to take leave of his senses temporarily and become so anxious to have it fixed that he uses any product at hand. This is especially true when the accident occurs on a Sunday or holiday, and the owner cannot bear waiting until the hard- ware shop opens and proper glue can be obtained. He is beset with the desire to right his wrong at once. By all means, wait! Patience will be well rewarded.

Paste glues are not suitable for this kind of operation. Any glue of a white color or glue sold in a squeeze bottle is to be avoided. These glues are simply not strong enough to make a permanent bond using the small quantity to which one is restricted in this kind of repair work. Cement glue, preferably of the tube variety, is the only satisfactory one. This glue is clear in color, is very odorous, and it dries rapidly. It is sometimes referred to as model-maker's glue. It should not be applied directly from the tube, as would normally be done in other situations, but with an artist's brush. Do not load up the brush. Take just a very small quantity of glue on the brush tip. Both the component and the place of attachment must be coated with glue.

When brushing use inward rather than outward strokes, and keep strokes short. It is neither necessary nor desirable to carry glue totally out to the perimeter, as the pressure of rejoining may force it outward, resulting in an overflow. Even lightly applied glue can overflow in this fashion.

After application of the glue, the piece must be gently but firmly set into position. Now comes the tricky part. It must be held with pressure until fully dry to achieve a firm bond. Holding it by hand is not recommended; a clamp must be devised. As commercially sold clamps designed for woodworking projects are useless in this kind of situation, a homemade one must be relied on. It may consist of loose fitting rubber bands, elastic cotton, or a device to which small weights such as fishing line weights are attached.

Drying time is not always easy to estimate. Do not place too much faith in statements by the glue manufacturer. Glue advertised to fully dry in thirty minutes may take an hour or two in humid conditions. It is far better to wait longer than necessary than to unclamp a model and discover that a bond has not yet been achieved. Do not test the bond by putting pressure on the reattached component. It will always be somewhat weaker than if no break had occurred.

## INSURING

As you are gradually acquiring more Hummels, you probably are assuming that your homeowner's policy sufficiently insures your growing collection. You would be wise to take several steps to fully protect your collection as it grows beyond a few pieces. Most homeowner's policies will not cover a Hummel collection fully—and they rarely cover breakage or appreciation.

Many Hummel owners are uninformed as to the actual value of their collections; they just remember that they paid certain prices for particular pieces or that they have their receipts. The longer you've had your pieces the more outdated the prices are that you paid for them. So, those prices are of no service in determining the present value of your collection. Not only has inflation made these pieces worth more, but Hummels have continued to appreciate in value faster than the rate of inflation. Plus, when the rush of investors bought up many of the available Hummels in the late 1970s, the prices rose sharply.

In order to insure and protect your collection completely, you should take a full inventory of each piece, noting names, model numbers, trademarks, and their current values. Any distinctive characteristics that would identify it as being the particular piece you own are also of value. You will need to make three copies of your inventory—one for your insurance company, one to place in a safety deposit box, and one to keep in your home files as a handy reference. This inventory should be updated regularly or anytime you've made a number of purchases.

To aid you in this project, the House of Collectibles has published *The Official Collector's Journal.* You will find in this book special inventory forms which will allow you to record each item in your collection in minute detail. Also included are forms for recording the names of dealers, collectors, clubs, museums, and reference materials. Value development charts provide space for keeping track of investment value. Complete information is also given on appraisal, taxes, insurance, buying and selling, and the importance condition plays in determining the value of dozens of specific collectible items. Once you have recorded the information on the forms included in *The Collector's Journal*, you can be assured that you have correctly cataloged your collection.

In the last few years, more and more people are placing identification numbers on such values as their photographic equipment, firearms, or bicycles. In case of theft, their particular piece, if found, can be returned to them. Without an identification number there is no way the police can confirm that an article is yours. This holds true with Hummels, too. It is worth the effort to mark each one you own. You can easily mark the bottoms of your Hummels either with your social security number or a special number that you use for cataloging your pieces. There are special engravers which can be used; many of these are available at hardware stores—just be sure they are safe to use on ceramic objects. You could use diamond point pencils which make permanent marks or use an invisible marking pen which makes marks that are visible under ultraviolet light only. Of course, this information should be added to your inventory. *The Official Collector's Journal* also contains detailed information on marking your collection.

You should obtain insurance for the total value of your collection. Determine the market value of each item you own, then add these prices up for the total value. Many insurance companies will accept appraisals by owners if they use an authoritative, current price guide for collections that are worth less than $20,000. For more valuable collections, most companies will require an expert appraiser or experienced dealer to evaluate it. Appraisals can cost as much as $50 to $100 per hour. Thus, an appraisal for a $10,000 collection could cost between $200 and $300.

Besides protection from vandalism and robbery, you should have coverage for breakage. A special clause covering breakage will cost somewhat more, but it is very important since that is the most common hazard for Hummels. Also, you may be able to get coverage for any new purchases made while your policy is in force. Usually, this is limited, based on a percentage of the total worth of your collection—the normal amount is about 20%. A few policies will cover any pieces that are being shipped, or moved, or are placed on exhibit. You may find it difficult to obtain this type of coverage. If so, check with a number of different companies. Some which specialize in insuring fine art galleries, antique dealers, or museums might offer these services.

Some insurance companies will request photographs of your entire collection. Even if they don't, a photographic inventory is an excellent idea: It provides visual proof of the extent of your collection. Although you may consider taking photographs of all pieces as a bothersome task, you'd feel differently if you lost all or part of your collection: Photos are helpful in receiving a fair settlement from your insurance company. The I.R.S. will allow you to deduct an uninsured loss, but the amount allowed will depend on having pictures of such items. Without pictures, you may not be allowed to claim the loss.

The least expensive and easiest manner to photograph your collection would be to line up enough figurines to fill a picture on a table in front of a window. This will reflect light on the shadowed side of the figurine.

You can use an inexpensive camera, such as a miniature Instamatic, but you can't take pictures from any closer than three feet without causing blurring. If you have a close-up lens, you could take photos of the marks on the bottom of the pieces as well.

## ACTIVITIES FOR THE COLLECTOR

The popularity of Hummels has spawned a number of related activities for the collector. These various activities can heighten your enjoyment of your collection as well as widen your knowledge and aid you in resolving any problems you encounter. Presently, there are Hummel clubs, festivals, publications, and even a look-alike contest.

There are two large clubs you might want to join. The Hummel Collectors' Club was founded years ago by two avid hobbyists, Dorothy Dous and her daughter, Tammy. Membership costs $15 a year. Members receive a newsletter which covers information about new releases, price trends, any upcoming Hummel activities and other topics of interest to collectors. The club offers a unique service which you may be forced to use if you badly damage one of your pieces: They have a spare parts bank for Hummels. If you have a broken model that needs a completely replaced arm or accessory, the bank may have just the portion you need. You can obtain more details or send for a sample of their newsletter by writing to Hummel Collectors' Club, Box 257, Yardley, Pennsylvania 19067.

The Goebel Collectors' Club is sponsored by the Goebel Company. But this club differs from the Hummel Collectors' Club in that it is for anyone who collects any of the Goebel ware, including Hummels. Membership is $15 annually. Members receive a publication which is issued quarterly. Special limited edition pieces are made available each year to members only. Six of these special editions have been Hummels. More information can be obtained by writing to: Goebel Collectors' Club, 105 White Plains Road, Tarrytown, New York 10591.

If you get a chance to visit the Goebel Collectors' Club home office in Tarrytown, you'll enjoy seeing the interesting prototypes or designs from the factory in Germany. Sometimes they exhibit rare and unusual pieces, such as when they displayed the international pieces in 1979.

There are several places where collectors can view some of the most outstanding collections in the world. Obviously, the Goebel factory in Rodental, West Germany offers the largest display of Hummels which are currently being produced. Pieces that are no longer in production are rarely displayed at the factory, but they have been shown several times in the United States.

In 1979, The Franciscan Convent in Siessen, West Germany opened a museum. Their display contains many of Sister Maria's original works, including the only scupture done by her. Some of the drawings displayed are pieces that have not been rendered into other art mediums.

The original works from her early days were grouped together for a traveling exhibit which was in the United States from the fall of 1980 to the spring of 1982. These forty works show the development of Berta Hummel's artistic abilities. There is a possibility that this exhibit will be brought back to the United States in the near future.

Every year, on the second weekend in June, a festival is held just for Hummel collectors in Eaton, Ohio. Most of the top Hummel dealers and collectors attend the festival which has a large auction as the culminating event. Seminars and films are provided to further educate collectors on how the figurines are made, how to repair them, and other important information.

Another impressive exhibit is the one currently at the Caravelle Hotel located in Rosemont, Illinois, a suburb of Chicago. Besides being very large, this collection includes some very rare pieces.

Several activities offer collectors an opportunity to win exciting prizes by using their imaginations and creativity. Every year there is a Hummel Figurine Look-Alike Contest. You can enter by sending a photograph of a child between two and ten years old who is dressed and posed to represent one of the Hummel figurines. You can get entry blanks from your Hummel dealer. There are a number of prizes with two grand winners receiving $1,000 each, plus a painted portrait of the child by a leading artist.

There is also an annual essay contest on a selected topic. These are to be of 200 words or less. The grand winner receives an all-expense paid weekend for two in Tarrytown, New York—the location of the club's headquarters and museums.

## GLOSSARY

### AIR HOLES

Air holes can be found in many Hummel models. They are not defects but were placed there purposely, to provide ventilation during the firing process when the model was heated in a kiln. Without these passages for air escapement, extremely hot air would build up inside the model to such degree that it could become volatile, with cracking or breaking a strong possibility. The holes are normally so small and placed so strategically that they will go unnoticed by casual observers. They can be located only if you make the effort to seek them out.

### ANNUAL PLATE

Since 1971, the Goebel Company has issued a yearly plate, the first one depicting the design of #21 "Heavenly Angel," released to commemorate the 100th anniversary of the Goebel firm. Rendered as a bas-relief on the plate, the themes are taken from some of the most popular Hummel Figurines.

### ARTIST'S MARK

This can be a signature, initials, or symbol used by one of the master painters. The master painter is allowed to apply his mark to the base of a figurine on which he has completed the painting, normally after painting the face which is the most difficult task and is finished last.

## BABY BEE

This was the trademark used by the Goebel firm in 1958. It is a small bee inside a large "V."

## BESWICK

The Beswick Company of England is another firm which produced its own versions of Hummels while claiming they had copyrights to Sister Maria's original works. Very little is known as to the circumstances or the materials used in producing these figurines. Beswick has since then been bought by the Royal Doulton Company of England which has no records of any agreements or contracts which gave the company the rights to adapt her works. As with the Dubler figurines, these Hummels were manufactured in order to capture the public's desire for such items during the war, and possibly it was felt that the copyrights owned by a Germany company did not need to be honored during a time of war with their nation.

The Beswick pieces, which are scarce, were only uncovered in the last few years. Presently, only eleven designs are known to exist. The quality surpasses that of the Dubler figurines—the material used appears to be of a higher quality, possibly ceramic. These adaptations reflect the original works of Sister Maria more closely than the Dubler works. In fact, they come closer to the quality of the Goebel figurines, but can be easily distinguished by the knowledgeable collector. These are probably authentic pieces in that they were rendered from original works and not from the Goebel figurines. Some of these are very much like some of the figurines made by the Goebel Company. But the Beswick figurines are identified by the information on their bases. Model numbers are incised into the base with the Beswick trademark (which reads "Beswick England," set in a circle), the term "Hummel Studios" and a facsimile of the M. I. Hummel signature are stamped in black. The signature looks different from the one incised on the Goebel figurines: It appears rough and crude.

The rarity of these pieces and their superior quality to the Dubler pieces have given the few that have been sold very high values. There is probably more collector interest in these than in the Dubler products.

## BISQUE

This term is used for ceramic which has been fired, but not glazed. These usually are white in appearance.

## CLOSED EDITION

This term is used by the Goebel Company to indicate a model which they will no longer produce and have no intentions of producing in the future.

## CLOSED NUMBER

A "closed number" designation refers to a design or sample model that has never been authorized for release. There can be many reasons for an item to be withheld from production by the factory, the most obvious being lack of official approval of the design by the Seissen Convent. Even though some items have been classified as a "closed number" by the factory, some genuine examples are known to exist.

## COLLECTOR'S PLAQUE

These are slight modifications of the special plaques that were made for Hummel dealers to display to indicate that they were authorized dealers. The collector's plaque doesn't have "authorized dealer" stamped on it.

## COLOR FAKES

These are figurines which are authentic Hummels, but which have had their original color tampered with in order to make the piece appear to be a scarce color variation. Certain color variations are much more valuable than others because of their scarcity. Unscrupulous individuals can alter common models, then sell them at the higher prices at which the uncommon variations sell.

## CROWN MARK

This includes two of the trademarks used by the Goebel Company, during the early years of the production of Hummels. There is the "Wide Crown" and the "Narrow Crown." This mark appears on the Hummels as well as their other products made before 1950.

## CURRENT MARK

This is the term used to indicate the trademark currently being used by a company. Presently, the Goebel Company is using the "Goebel" trademark.

## CURRENT PRODUCTION

When a Hummel is designated as being in "current production," the logical assumption would be that the work is being made at the factory, sent off to distributors, and offered in retail shops. As used by Hummel, "current production" merely means the item has not been retired or discontinued. It may not actually be in production; it could be standing by, in a state of limbo, and it could very well continue in this fashion for years. Goebel has never adhered to a policy of keeping any specific group of models in continuous production over an extended period of time. The factory's operation is inconsistent, turning out a quantity of one model, then putting the mold aside to await public reaction. If sales warrant, the model's production is resumed. Since public reaction cannot generally be measured in a short length of time, the factory is careful not to make any hasty determinations. And if it should make an incorrect determination and remove from "current production" any model in which interest is subsequently shown, the factory has the option of making a reinstatement.

## DEALER'S PLAQUE

These are advertising plaques which the Goebel Company distributed to their dealers without charge. There are a number of varieties of this plaque with written messages in different languages which read "Genuine

Hummel Figures" or "Authentic Hummel Figures." The "Merry Wanderer" motif is used and the symbol long associated with Goebel, the bee, is placed at the top of the plaque.

## DISCONTINUED

When a Hummel is referred to as "discontinued," this may mean that the model itself is no longer in production or merely that specimens of the size mentioned are discontinued. However, many "discontinued" Hummels have been reissued by the factory. Generally, when a size has been discontinued but other sizes of the same model remain in production, it does not become as valuable as if the whole edition were discontinued.

## DOUBLE CROWN

This term refers to a figurine which carries two of the "Crown Marks." Usually one of the marks is incised and the other is stamped, but some figurines have been found with both trademarks incised. These models were produced between 1935 and 1938.

## DOUGHNUT BASE

The term popularly used to designate the underside of bases of some Hummel models, it consists of a circular shape within a circular shape and gives the suggestion of a doughnut.

## FONT

These fonts were designed as receptacles for holy water. There are many different wall fonts in the Hummel series. Devout Roman Catholics have often kept fonts in their homes, especially in Europe. The Hummel fonts usually include angel motifs with small animals and birds. Some of these consist of a figure and the container for the water; others include contoured backgrounds as well.

## FULL BEE

This is the trademark used by the Goebel Company from 1950 to 1955. This was the first form of the bee trademark that was used and it has a number of variations. These can occur either incised or stamped on a figure.

## GOEBEL BEE

This is the trademark used by the Goebel Company between 1972 and 1979. This mark includes the firm's name, with W. Germany under it and the stylized bee with V placed over the "bel" of Goebel.

## GREEK CROSS

Greek cross symbols appear frequently on Hummels, usually in the form of small decorations (often in gold) on the robes of angels, Madonnas and the like. The Greek cross differs from the conventional or Roman cross in that both bars are of equal length and cross at their centers, not two-thirds upward as in Roman crosses.

## HIGH BEE

This is the trademark used by the Goebel Company in 1957. This shows a bee inside the large V like the other bee trademark, but this one differs in that the wings of the bee are placed higher than the top of the V.

## HUMMEL REGISTRY

A notations book, published by Tandem of Torrency, California, the registry is for use by Hummel collectors in keeping records of items they buy, sell, swap, etc.

## HUMMELWERK

This is an American subsidiary of the Goebel firm which distributes Hummels in the United States.

## MODEL

The word "model," when used in reference to Hummel figures, indicates a figure or other item (plaque, candleholder, font, etc.) There is, of course, a secondary use of the word, to indicate the working model from which such a figure has been produced.

## MODEL ASSEMBLY

As with porcelain figureware in general, Hummel models are assembled from separately cast components. The number of components varies depending upon the model's size and intricacy. The job of attaching them together is carried out by a skilled artisan known as a garnisher. Traditionally, the title of this work was "model repair," but this has been discontinued in most parts of the world as it suggests restoration of damaged specimens.

## MOLD GROWTH

This is a theory which attempts to explain the differences in sizes of the same models. Sometimes these size differences vary as much as a half an inch. It is thought that when the final working molds used were of plaster of paris they absorbed so much water during each casting that the working mold became larger with each pouring. Since 1954, the working molds have been made of acrylic resin which eliminates the possibility of mold growth.

## MULTIPLE FIGURE MODELS

There are models consisting of a number of figures upon a common base, not to be confused with sets (such as the Nativity Sets), which may comprise many separate figures. When Hummels were first issued in 1935, it would probably not have been believed that the factory would one day be producing models comprising half a dozen figures. Certainly at that early time it would have been unwise to do so, without the network of eager buyers that now await every new release.

There is no law that a porcelain figurine must represent just one or two individuals, and the factory has shown laudible ambition since the 1950's in attempting a number of complex productions. Without exception, all have been artistic successes and have enjoyed good public response. So far the greatest number of figures included in a Hummel model has been seven in #347 "Adventure Bound," a work of exceptional quality.

The argument that multiple-figure models are not typically Hummel is without foundation; they are not typical of the factory's early work, but Sister Hummel frequently sketched such composition, and final word on what is or is not typically Hummel must rest with her art. Multiple figure models are not produced in quantities as large as single figures, because of their higher price. Thus they are automatically more scarce than most issues in line.

## NARROW CROWN

This is one of the "Crown Marks" used by the Goebel company as one of their trademarks from 1937 to 1949.

## OPEN EDITION

This term includes Hummel figurines which are either currently produced or will be in production in the near future.

## OPEN NUMBER

An "open number" designation refers to a model planned for release which has not yet been released. Models are constructed and assigned a number, but may not be officially released for years. Some Hummels have remained in the limbo of open designations for a quarter century, without either being released or canceled. The reasons for this in each separate instance are known only to the factory, and information is virtually impossible to obtain. One possibility is that the Seissen Convent which reserves final approval of each design may request minor changes and the factory, rather than make such changes immediately, prefers to busy itself with new designs. There is also the likelihood that merchandising considerations play a part. If a model is deemed to be very similar to one already in distribution, it may be withheld for a time.

## OVERSIZE

A model that is larger than the size indicated by the designator on bottom of the base is considered "oversize."

Oversize can also refer to Hummels produced in sizes larger than normal for Hummels as a class. These are usually around 30″.

## PACKAGING, FACTORY

The packaging department of the Goebel factory packs each model separately in specially fitted styropor boxes, a variety of styofoam that is lightweight and durable and provides maximum protection against damage in transit.

## RODENTAL

Rodental is the town in West Germany where the W. Goebel factory (Goebel Porzellanfabrik) is located. The company has been established there since its founding in 1871 and has operated continuously except for an interruption during World War II.

## SCHMID BROTHERS.

In the late 1960's, Schmid Brothers, Inc., received the exclusive rights to adapt works from the original art done by Sister Maria prior to her entry into the Siessen Convent. This permission was granted to them through Sister Maria's mother, Viktoria Hummel.

Before gaining rights to create her works, Schmid Brothers were distributors of the Hummels manufactured by Goebel. For years, this company was the only distributor in the United States. During the 1960's, Goebel set up their own branch of distribution, ending Schmid's distributorship. This led to legal action taken by Schmid Brothers against the Goebel Company. Schmid supposedly won a sizable settlement from Goebel. Still, Schmid continued distributing Hummel lithographs from the publishers of her two-dimensional works in Germany.

In 1971, Schmid Brothers released a limited edition Christmas plate with a rendition of one of Sister Maria's drawings called "Angel with Candle." In that same year, Goebel issued a Christmas plate with the same exact design. Since both plates were obviously derived from the same original work, lawsuits and counter lawsuits erupted. The German Supreme Court ruled that Sister Maria's mother, Viktoria Hummel, did hold the rights to any original works done by her daughter prior to her entrance into the Siessen Convent; but the Convent held the rights to all the works she did while she was a nun. This decision was reached in 1974.

Since 1971, Schmid has continued to issue a yearly Christmas plate. In 1972, they began a Mother's Day plate series. The most popular of these plates is "Moonlight Return" which is the 1977 plate. This is the same as the figurine produced by the Goebel Company called "On Secret Path" (386). This same theme has been utilized on many items. Collectors like to include a lithograph of this scene which has been signed by the artist's brother, Adolf. According to her family, Adolf was the subject of Sister Maria's drawing.

Schmid manufactures numerous other types of articles by using lithographs or decalcomania transfers applied to surfaces. Some of these are produced on a yearly basis as the plates are, such as bells, candles, Christmas ornaments, and cups. For a while, the firm expanded their production to include novelty items such as music boxes and musical key chains.

Many collectors of the Hummels produced by Goebel enjoy adding these to their collections of figurines, especially if a motif on a Schmid article matches one of their figurines. But these novelty items have been discontinued and are available in varying quantities depending on the numbers that were originally produced.

## SETS

It has been a long-standing practice of the factory to issue some of its figures in sets which consist of two or more pieces. The largest set is #214 the "Nativity Set," which has 14 figures. In all instances, the components of a set are available separately, as well as collectively. Generally, the value of a complete set is higher than the combined values of each individual piece, but not to a marked degree. It should be pointed out that some figures which by subject, size, or style appear related and which are collected often as "sets" were not issued as such. The three musicians, frequently referred to as "The Little Band" or "Child Band" comprising #389, #390, and #391, were separate releases, but are often sold as a set. In such instances the value as a set should not be higher than the combined individual values.

## SIZES

Size has always been a major consideration to the Hummel collector. Models can vary considerably in value because of size. Differences are sometimes slight, sometimes great. In any discussion of size a distinction must be drawn between size gradations, acknowledged by the factory to represent separate and distinct issues, and sizes which merely vary haphazardly. The latter is a tough class of specimens to define.

Sizes of figures always refer to height. Base size, or width, is never indicated. The highest point, whether or not it happens to be the chief object of interest, is always measured. In #71 "Stormy Weather," two children stand beneath an umbrella. The size is the total height to the umbrella's top, **not** to the heads of the children. By the same token, if a figure holds a pole, the model's height will be that of the pole if it extends above the figure's head. Sizes of wall plaques, fonts and other works not classifiable as figures are usually given with the shorter side indicated first.

## SLASH

Occasionally, Hummel figurines will have a slash on their base. It is not known what this mark indicates, but normally factories place this on items which are considered to be seconds. The Goebel Company claims that all imperfect specimens have always been destroyed. But it is surmised that some imperfect items were taken home by employees of the firm and eventually found their way into the hands of collectors.

## SMALL BEE

This is the trademark used by the Goebel Company in 1956. This differs from the previous bee mark in that the bee is much smaller.

## STAMPED

Some of the marks on the bases are stamped instead of incised. Some of the trademarks have been found stamped on the bases, but usually important information, such as the facsimile of Sister Maria's signature and the model number are incised.

## STANDARD SIZE

This is the first size that was produced of each model. All other sizes of that particular model are considered to be variations in size. The standard sizes for different models vary, but usually these are the smaller figurines. Standard sizes are usually indicated by a slash and a "0" following the model number, but for models which the Goebel firm had no plans to produce in various sizes, there are no designators except the model number.

## STYLIZED BEE

This is the trademark used by the Goebel Company in one form or another between 1957 and 1972. This differs from the previous bee marks in that the bee between the V is only a representation of a bee. It is merely a black circle with two triangles for wings. Because the term "W. Germany" appears either below it or to the right of it, this mark is sometimes called the "One Line Mark."

## THREE LINE MARK

This is one of the trademarks used by the Goebel Company between 1964 and 1972. This is called the "Three Line Mark" because of the three lines of writing which are to the left of the stylized bee with V.

## U.S. ZONE—GERMANY

This term was stamped on the base of all of the figurines produced during the period following World War II. At that time, the U.S. Military Government required that all such products be marked with "U.S. Zone—Germany." There have been some items made during this period which were not marked with this phrase. These markings occur in a variety of forms, such as in squares, ovals, and variously shaped strips.

## VEE BEE

This is the trademark used by Goebel Company in 1959. This differs from the preceding bee marks in that the wings of the bee form a V.

## WHITE OVERGLAZE

This type of figurine appears white and shiny because it was not painted and glazed as most of the figurines are, but was covered with a white glaze.

## WIDE CROWN

This is the most common of the "Crown Marks" used in the early years of the production of Hummels. This mark, which was stamped or incised on the bases of figurines, was used from 1935 to 1949.

# THE PRICES IN THIS BOOK

*The Official Price Guide to Hummel Figurines and Plates* offers the collector thousands of current prices for as many models and their variations as possible. Some models listed or described in this book have no prices either because pricing information is unavailable or because it is insufficient. Prices are not given for some models or variations because the items are too rare. Many of these pieces are so rare that they are never offered for sale and when they are the one-time sale is indicative of its worth to one collector only. Sometimes these rare pieces are bought for a very low price because the seller is unaware of its rarity and value; other times an exorbitant price is paid because of the willingness of a wealthy collector.

A price range is given for each variation. This range shows the lowest and highest selling prices for this particular piece at the time this book was compiled. Usually, the more expensive the piece, the larger the price range. These prices are retail selling prices—what dealers sell these items for to the public. Prices were determined by averaging the prices of actual sales or sale offers from across the country. Sales at secondary sources, such as flea markets and garage sales, which can be much higher or much lower, were not included in the averaging of prices.

These prices should be used as guidelines, not as set laws. Just as in buying other articles, you can find differences in prices by shopping around. You will discover prices much higher and much lower than these averages, but these will be exceptions, not the rule. It is not unusual for very high or very low prices to be paid at auctions. Also, the prices that dealers charge will vary depending on their volume of business, their overhead, and the type of customers they have. A dealer who pays high rent for an attractively situated shop may have to charge more to meet his high overhead; another dealer may have such a large number of customers that he can afford to make a smaller margin of profit on each piece, so his prices may be lower.

Also, a 20% to 30% variation from these prices might indicate a changing trend for that particular piece, especially if you keep encountering prices consistently higher or lower. In fact, you should remain aware of any fluctuations in prices as this may affect your strategy as to what you'll purchase and when.

These prices are those at which dealers sell Hummels to the public. Dealers will not buy Hummels from you at these prices. In order to meet their overhead expenses and still make a profit, dealers buy at wholesale— which is about 50% to 60% of the retail price. This can vary, too, due to a dealer's circumstances.

# Recommended Reading . . .

*The Official Price Guide to Hummel Figurines and Plates is
designed for the novice as well as the seasoned collector. Information on price trends, industry development, investing, and
collecting techniques such as care and repair, storage, or
building a collection is written in a way a beginning hobbyist will
understand, yet gives specific details and helpful hints the hard-
core collector will find useful.*

This guide also offers up-to-date
prices for both rare and common collectibles that are available in the current
secondary market. This guide will give
any collector confidence when determining what articles to purchase at what
price. With the knowledge gained from
this guide, a collector will move from
flea market to auction house with ease
knowing which items are "hot" and
which articles are definitely overpriced.

As your interest in collecting grows,
you may want to start a reference library
of your favorite areas. For the collector
who needs more extensive coverage of
the collectibles market, The House of
Collectibles publishes a complete line of
comprehensive companion guides
which are itemized at the back of this
book. They contain full coverage on buying, selling, and caring of valuable articles, plus listings with thousands of
prices for rare, unusual, and common
antiques and collectibles.

*$11.95-4th Edition, 597 pgs., Order #266-3*

The House of Collectibles recommends *The Official Price Guide to
Collector Plates,* fourth edition, as the companion to this guide.

- *Over 18,700 current collector values*—The most complete listing of all U.S.
  and Foreign plate manufacturers and distributors in print!
- **COMPARE CURRENT MARKET VALUES WITH THE ORIGINAL ISSUE PRICE —**
  Our special price column will enable you to spot the best investment potential
  in one glance!
- **INVESTMENT REVIEW —** Certain types of plates, artists and manufacturers
  are more valuable . . . learn which ones are and why!
- **EVERY KNOWN COLLECTOR PLATE, FROM 1895 TO DATE —** Each plate
  listing includes title and series, the original release date, designing artist, pro-
  duction methods used, quantities issued, issue price and the current value
  price range.
- **EXPANDED GALLERY OF ARTISTS —** Read about the legendary artists
  who create collector plates including tributes to the late Ted De Grazia and
  Frances Hook.
- **FULLY ILLUSTRATED.**

*Available from your local dealer or order direct from:*
*THE HOUSE OF COLLECTIBLES, see order blank*

## HOW TO USE THIS BOOK

*The Official Price Guide To Hummel Figurines and Plates* contains the most complete listings of Hummels, covering models currently in production as well as closed number and open number models. Although many rare pieces are listed, the greatest rarities, such as the International pieces and the Mel pieces, are not. These are one-of-a-kind pieces which are offered for sale only once in a while making their values difficult to determine.

All models are arranged in this book numerically according to the mold or model number which is normally found on the bottom of the base of each piece. If you don't know the model number for a particular piece, an index at the front of the book lists the pieces alphabetically by their titles.

Each listing has a complete description of the pieces and a background sketch of its production. All the different sizes and trademarks for each piece are listed. The model number is given, followed by size designators if there are any. In order to find the correct listing for a particular piece, you must be sure that the trademark and the size on the piece match the listing exactly. If you are unfamiliar with the various Hummel trademarks or size designators, you will want to read the sections "How To Identify Hummels" and "Trademarks," so you'll be able to understand the listings properly.

## 1  PUPPY LOVE

Figurine in current production. A boy playing a violin with a small dog at his feet. This figure, long in production, exists in both an "old" and a "new" style, the result of redesigning which altered minor characteristics but introduced no major changes. The boy is dressed in a white shirt, suspendered trousers and a brownish short jacket which is unbuttoned and hangs open and loose. His shoes are brown, brownish black, or black. The rolled cuffs of his trousers lie about his shoe tops. He wears a narrow brimmed black Tyrolean or Bavarian style hat, pulled down close to the crown. His violin is wood grained in a light brown color suggesting maple, and the bow is white and black. Slung over his right shoulder is a green leather carrybag or pouch and a black umbrella with a pale brown curved handle.

The dog is not modeled in sufficient detail to identify breed, but appears to be a type of terrier. He is looking at the boy attentively with one ear pointed upward, supposedly to catch the music. The dog varies in color from dark brown mixed with maroon and henna to a brown and rust combination to almost white with highlights of reddish brown.

**1** Puppy Love

In the old version, the boy's head is inclined forward, his eyes seemingly fixed on the fingers of his left hand which manipulate the violin strings. In the new version, his head is turned toward the right shoulder and he appears to gaze upon the ground or into space, as if being captivated by the music. In the old version, two rather long strands of hair fall across his forehead, one of which touches his right eyebrow; in the new version, there is but one long strand, wider than the two in the old version and it does not touch his eyebrow. Its placement is more toward the left side of his forehead. A significant and easily discernible alteration is that in the new version he wears a blue necktie, while in the old there is no necktie. The eyes may seem to be open slightly wide in the old version, but this is merely an optical illusion resulting from the tilt of the head. The base is a white oval for both versions.

| | Price Range | |
|---|---:|---:|
| ☐ 1, trademark CM, 5″–5¼″ | 345.00 | 385.00 |
| ☐ 1, trademark Full Bee, 5″–5¼″ | 245.00 | 275.00 |
| ☐ 1, trademark Stylized Bee, 5″–5¼″ | 145.00 | 175.00 |
| ☐ 1, trademark 3-line mark, 5″–5¼″ | 95.00 | 125.00 |
| ☐ 1, trademark Goebel/V, 5″–5¼″ | 80.00 | 100.00 |
| ☐ 1, trademark Goebel, 5″–5¼″ | 77.50 | 90.00 |

## 2 LITTLE FIDDLER

Figurine in current production. Essentially the same figure as in #1 "Puppy Love," but without the dog. In models produced since 1972, the head is inclined to the right, as in the revised version of #1, but not identical to it. #2 faces the viewer more fully, the chin thrust outward. The modeling of the hair differs from both the old and new versions of "Puppy Love" in that "Little Fiddler' has more hair than either of these two. A number of long strands fall toward the left side of his face, while short, thick strands cover the right side. His facial coloring is stronger, his cheeks rosier. Prior to 1972, the face was less highly colored and the head did not incline as sharply. The hat is always brown. "Little Fiddler" was previously called "Violinist" or "The Wandering Fiddler." In 1984 the first miniature Hummel figurine was introduced by Goebel. It is a 3″ high version of "Little Fiddler," #2/4/0. This mini-figurine is the first issue in the "Little Music Makers" series of four and is the companion to the "Little Fiddler" mini-plate #466 which is 4″ in diameter.

| | | |
|---|---:|---:|
| ☐ 2/0, trademark CM, 5¾″–6″ | 375.00 | 460.00 |
| ☐ 2/0, trademark Full Bee, 5¾″–6″ | 225.00 | 245.00 |
| ☐ 2/0, trademark Stylized Bee, 5¾″–6″ | 145.00 | 160.00 |
| ☐ 2/0, trademark 3-line mark, 5¾″–6″ | 110.00 | 120.00 |
| ☐ 2/0, trademark Goebel/V, 5¾″–6″ | 105.00 | 120.00 |
| ☐ 2/0, trademark Goebel, 5¾″–6″ | 94.50 | 105.00 |
| ☐ 2/I, trademark CM, 7½″ | 700.00 | 770.00 |
| ☐ 2/I, trademark Full Bee, 7½″ | 550.00 | 610.00 |
| ☐ 2/I, trademark Stylized Bee, 7½″ | 350.00 | 385.00 |
| ☐ 2/I, trademark 3-line mark, 7½″ | 300.00 | 330.00 |

**2** Little Fiddler (Brown Hat)

| | | Price Range | |
|---|---|---|---|
| ☐ 2/I, trademark Goebel/V, 7½".................... | | 195.00 | 220.00 |
| ☐ 2/I, trademark Goebel, 7½"...................... | | 185.00 | 200.00 |
| ☐ 2/II, trademark CM, 10¾"–11".................... | | 1900.00 | 2090.00 |
| ☐ 2/II, trademark Full Bee, 10¾"–11" ............. | | 1500.00 | 1650.00 |
| ☐ 2/II, trademark Stylized Bee, 10¾"–11".......... | | 950.00 | 1045.00 |
| ☐ 2/II, trademark 3-line mark, 10¾"–11" .......... | | 800.00 | 880.00 |
| ☐ 2/II, trademark Goebel/V, 10¾"–11"............. | | 730.00 | 800.00 |
| ☐ 2/II, trademark Goebel, 10¾"–11"............... | | 630.00 | 690.00 |
| ☐ 2/III, trademark CM, 12¼"...................... | | 2800.00 | 3080.00 |
| ☐ 2/III, trademark Full Bee, 12¼"................. | | 1900.00 | 2090.00 |
| ☐ 2/III, trademark Stylized Bee, 12¼" ............. | | 1500.00 | 1650.00 |
| ☐ 2/III, trademark 3-line mark, 12¼"................ | | 900.00 | 990.00 |
| ☐ 2/III, trademark Goebel/V, 12¼" ................. | | 780.00 | 850.00 |
| ☐ 2/III, trademark Goebel, 12¼".................... | | 680.00 | 740.00 |
| ☐ 2/4/0, trademark Goebel, 3"..................... | | — | 39.00 |

## 3 BOOKWORM

Figurine in current production. Baseless figure of a young girl, three to five years of age, seated on the ground reading a book. This has frequently been referred to as one of the more lifelike and charming of Hummel models, since the absence of a base adds to its realism and appeal. It is also quite intricate in detail and coloration. The girl has an open picture book across her outstretched legs. On one of the open pages there appears a likeness of a duck; on the other, two flowers. Her right hand points to the flowers, while her left index finger points to her cheek. Not at all cherubic, the figure has a serious, meditative expression.

**3** Bookworm

The girl wears a greenish long-sleeved, high-collared dress touched with highlights of pinkish brown, and adorned with red and yellow concentric circles. Over the dress she wears a bib type garment, varying in tone from deep rust to a cream yellow with suggestions of orange. Dotted at various points on the bib are small circular decorations. She has western style brown shoes intended to represent leather. Her stockings, reaching nearly to the knee, are vertically ribbed and adorned with bands of pastel blue, red and yellow. She wears a muted red ribbon in her hair, which is worn in a modified "page boy."

The book is an item of great interest as it is by far the finest representation of a book ever to appear in a Hummel model. It is shaped to closely resemble the contour of a soft cover book when held open. An effort was made, through the use of varying colors and gradations of size, to suggest pages. The colored drawings appearing on the opened leaves are most attractively executed; the duck in yellow and orange, and the flowers in orange, blue, and a very light pastel blue bordering on white. "Bookworm" is a most captivating work, and one of the factory's most successful. "Bookworm" was earlier referred to as "Little Bookworm."

|  | Price Range | |
|---|---|---|
| ☐ 3/I, trademark CM, 5½".......................... | 645.00 | 715.00 |
| ☐ 3/I, trademark Full Bee, 5½" ..................... | 445.00 | 500.00 |
| ☐ 3/I, trademark Stylized Bee, 5½"................ | 275.00 | 310.00 |
| ☐ 3/I, trademark 3-line mark, 5½" ................. | 195.00 | 225.00 |
| ☐ 3/I, trademark Goebel/V, 5½".................... | 145.00 | 170.00 |
| ☐ 3/I, trademark Goebel, 5½"...................... | 140.00 | 160.00 |
| ☐ 3/II, trademark C-M, 8"........................... | 1375.00 | 1550.00 |
| ☐ 3/II, trademark Full Bee, 8"...................... | 1150.00 | 1350.00 |
| ☐ 3/II, trademark Stylized Bee, 8" ................. | 975.00 | 1200.00 |
| ☐ 3/II, trademark 3-line mark, 8" .................. | 895.00 | 985.00 |
| ☐ 3/II, trademark Goebel/V, 8" .................... | 725.00 | 795.00 |
| ☐ 3/II, trademark Goebel, 8" ...................... | 630.00 | 700.00 |
| ☐ 3/III, trademark CM, 9"–9½".................... | 2850.00 | 3200.00 |
| ☐ 3/III, trademark Full Bee, 9"–9½" ............... | 2075.00 | 2295.00 |
| ☐ 3/III, trademark Stylized Bee, 9"–9½"........... | 1075.00 | 1175.00 |
| ☐ 3/III, trademark 3-line mark, 9"–9½" ............ | 895.00 | 995.00 |
| ☐ 3/III, trademark Goebel/V, 9"–9½"............... | 775.00 | 855.00 |
| ☐ 3/III, trademark Goebel, 9"–9½"................. | 680.00 | 745.00 |

## 4 LITTLE FIDDLER

Figurine in current production. Identical to #2 "Little Fiddler" except with a black hat.

|  | | |
|---|---|---|
| ☐ 4, trademark CM, 4¾"–5½"...................... | 350.00 | 385.00 |
| ☐ 4, trademark Full Bee, 4¾"–5½".............. | 200.00 | 220.00 |
| ☐ 4, trademark Stylized Bee, 4¾"–5½" .......... | 150.00 | 165.00 |
| ☐ 4, trademark 3-line mark, 4¾"–5½".......... | 100.00 | 110.00 |
| ☐ 4, trademark Goebel/V, 4¾"–5½" .............. | 82.00 | 90.00 |
| ☐ 4, trademark Goebel, 4¾"–5½" ................ | 72.00 | 80.00 |

## 5 STROLLING ALONG

Figurine in current production. This model utilizes a basic theme often repeated in Hummel figures of the strolling child, who appears again as "Merry Wanderer," "Globe Trotter," and in a variety of other guises. There are two basic variations of "Strolling Along" which are so slight that they are almost imperceptible. In the older or original version, the eyes glance to the rear; newer specimens have eyes facing more or less directly forward at the viewer. The stroller is a young boy accompanied by a terrier dog. The boy is in full stride, his left foot forward with its heel planted on the base, but the toe pointed upward as if caught in stop action. This impression of suspended animation is used repeatedly in Hummelware and is considered one of its more creative qualities.

Snappily dressed, the boy wears a green short jacket with the tail billowing behind him, a tan vest, and trousers of light greyish brown. His shoes are brown. His hat is dark grey or black. Over his left shoulder he carries

**5** Strolling Along

a reddish-orange umbrella with ochre handle. The expression on this model's face has been variously described as wonderment, surprise, or curiosity; the collector can make his own interpretation. His mouth and eyes are both opened wide. He has long henna hair combed downward at the side with a lock protruding from his hat. Between the old and new models the dog varies more than the boy. In the older version it looks upward and ahead; in the revision it looks upward to its master, a difference which can be spotted without difficulty. The dog's color also varies, both in shade and intensity. In the new version the dog usually has a brownish rust upper body with lightly-colored legs and lower torso. The tail invariably points upward. The dog is positioned on the outer side of the Stroller, closer to the viewer, and obscures the boy's right shoe.

| | Price Range | |
|---|---|---|
| ☐ 5, trademark CM, 4¾″–5½″ ...................... | 350.00 | 385.00 |
| ☐ 5, trademark Full Bee, 4¾″–5½″ ................. | 185.00 | 200.00 |
| ☐ 5, trademark Stylized Bee, 4¾″–5½″ ............ | 145.00 | 160.00 |
| ☐ 5, trademark 3-line mark, 4¾″–5½″ .............. | 65.00 | 80.00 |
| ☐ 5, trademark Goebel/V, 4¾″–5½″ ................ | 82.00 | 90.00 |
| ☐ 5, trademark Goebel, 4¾″–5½″ .................. | 72.00 | 80.00 |

## 6  SENSITIVE HUNTER

Figurine in current production. Previously known as "Timid Hunter," this model shows a boy in Tyrolean outfit carrying a rifle, gazing down upon a rabbit. Though no official explanation has ever surfaced for the name change, it was apparently an effort to avoid offending animal lovers. "Sensitive Hunter" refrains from shooting the rabbit because he takes pity on it, while the "timid" hunter may have other reasons. This seems a minor point, but it demonstrates the extent to which art must regulate itself by public opinion.

"Sensitive Hunter" is an attractive composition because the colors in the boy's costume are in such contrast to the reddish orange of the rabbit. The boy stands with his feet together and knees slightly bent, looking down at the rabbit and seeming to gaze directly into the rabbit's eyes. He wears an outfit that has become associated with Tyrolean mountaineering: Short pants, known as lederhosen, a long-sleeved shirt, suspenders, a Tyrolean feathered hat, and high boots with socks. The lederhosen are deep green, somewhat darker in back than in front. The shirt is rather billowy and of a light mint green with areas of white and light spots of reddish orange, which

**6** Sensitive Hunter

**New Style**　　　　**Old Style**

are more pronounced on the back. The suspenders are reddish, and the hat is forest green with a grained effect. The boots are a leathery brown, and the socks are light henna with touches of ochre and orange for highlight. The gun is a walnut brown and depicted simply as a stick with no effort to indicate a steel barrel or any other metal furnishings. It is carried by a brown shoulder strap representing leather.

There is an old and revised version of this design, which differ in only one major respect: In the old version, the suspenders holding the lederhosen are H-shaped in the back, while the new type has crossed suspenders. This difference can be seen only from the back; from the front both versions are identical. In 1982, this model was again redesigned.

| | Price Range | |
|---|---|---|
| ☐ 6/0, trademark CM, 4¾" | 350.00 | 385.00 |
| ☐ 6/0, trademark Full Bee, 4¾" | 250.00 | 275.00 |
| ☐ 6/0, trademark Stylized Bee, 4¾" | 180.00 | 200.00 |
| ☐ 6/0, trademark 3-line mark, 4¾" | 100.00 | 110.00 |
| ☐ 6/0, trademark Goebel/V, 4¾" | 82.00 | 90.00 |
| ☐ 6/0, trademark Goebel, 4¾" | 72.00 | 80.00 |
| ☐ 6/I, trademark CM, 5½" | 950.00 | 1045.00 |
| ☐ 6/I, trademark Full Bee, 5½" | 550.00 | 600.00 |
| ☐ 6/I, trademark Stylized Bee, 5½" | 200.00 | 220.00 |
| ☐ 6/I, trademark 3-line mark, 5½" | 150.00 | 165.00 |
| ☐ 6/I, trademark Goebel/V, 5½" | 105.00 | 115.00 |
| ☐ 6/I, trademark Goebel, 5½" | 94.50 | 105.00 |
| ☐ 6/II, trademark CM, 7½" | 1400.00 | 1540.00 |
| ☐ 6/II, trademark Full Bee, 7½" | 800.00 | 880.00 |

| | Price Range | |
|---|---|---|
| ☐ 6/II, trademark Stylized Bee, 7½" ................ | **400.00** | **440.00** |
| ☐ 6/II, trademark 3-line mark, 7½".................. | **320.00** | **350.00** |
| ☐ 6/II, trademark Goebel/V, 7½".................... | **275.00** | **300.00** |
| ☐ 6/II, trademark Goebel, 7½"..................... | **175.00** | **200.00** |

## 7 MERRY WANDERER

Figurine in current production. Of all the Hummel figures, the "Merry Wanderer" is undoubtedly best known internationally to the general public. This is due to its extensive manufacturing in a great variety of sizes and its use in Hummel advertising and on store plaques. There is no disputing the fact that a whole collection could be built around "Merry Wanderer" and its variations. Taking into account size and trademark varieties and changes in design, dozens of figurines in this motif exist. In size they range all the way from 6" up to the huge leviathans of 32". It is one of only three Hummel designs to be produced in an oversize version, attesting to its popularity and to the legions of collectors who will take a "Merry Wanderer" in whatever size, shape, or format it may be encountered.

The "Merry Wanderer" is intended to typify a free spirit: He is perhaps a youth off to school, or a sightseer, or simply an adventurer. He is not running away from home, as some have mistakenly chosen to interpret the design (Hummel has another figure for that). He carries in his left hand a satchel, in his right an umbrella, jauntily thrust over his shoulder. He wears long trousers somewhat flared at the cuff, a vest, and a short jacket. On his head is a narrow-brimmed hat similar to that worn by the fiddler in

**7** Merry Wanderer

"Puppy Love." His head is tilted backward slightly and the expression on his face is one of placid determination. His brown hair is combed downward on the left side of his face and a shock on his forehead is swept toward the right. The satchel he carries is an old fashioned European type still manufactured in which two wooden rods run through loops at the top to provide stability.

The figure's base is rectangular. There is an important base variation among the "Merry Wanderer" models as some of the old version 7/I models have a double base, which consists of one rectangular platform atop another of slightly larger dimensions. An important change was introduced in "Merry Wanderer" in 1972, which by then had been in production a long while. In size 7/II or 7/2 the finish was altered from the traditional matte to textured and the copyright date was incised into the base. The next larger size, 7/III, was revised in 1978 to conform in texture to 7/II, but did not have the incised copyright date.

"Merry Wanderer" is an ideal model for collectors, especially beginning collectors, because it is readily available in shops everywhere, and its many variations afford the collector a great deal of research.

|  | Price Range | |
|---|---|---|
| ☐ 7/0, trademark CM, 6″–6¼″ | 450.00 | 495.00 |
| ☐ 7/0, trademark Full Bee, 6″–6¼″ | 300.00 | 330.00 |
| ☐ 7/0, trademark Stylized Bee, 6″–6¼″ | 200.00 | 220.00 |
| ☐ 7/0, trademark 3-line mark, 6″–6¼″ | 150.00 | 165.00 |
| ☐ 7/0, trademark Goebel/V, 6″–6¼″ | 110.00 | 120.00 |
| ☐ 7/0, trademark Goebel, 6″–6¼″ | 100.00 | 110.00 |
| ☐ 7/I, trademark CM, 7″ | 900.00 | 990.00 |
| ☐ 7/I, trademark Full Bee, 7″ | 800.00 | 880.00 |
| ☐ 7/I, trademark Stylized Bee, 7″ | 700.00 | 770.00 |
| ☐ 7/I, trademark 3-line mark, 7″ | 250.00 | 275.00 |
| ☐ 7/I, trademark Goebel/V, 7″ | 195.00 | 215.00 |
| ☐ 7/I, trademark Goebel, 7″ | 185.00 | 205.00 |
| ☐ 7/II, trademark CM, 9½″ | 1900.00 | 2090.00 |
| ☐ 7/II, trademark Full Bee, 9½″ | 1600.00 | 1760.00 |
| ☐ 7/II, trademark Stylized Bee, 9½″ | 1200.00 | 1320.00 |
| ☐ 7/II, trademark 3-line mark, 9½″ | 900.00 | 990.00 |
| ☐ 7/II, trademark Goebel/V, 9½″ | 730.00 | 800.00 |
| ☐ 7/II, trademark Goebel, 9½″ | 630.00 | 690.00 |
| ☐ 7/III, trademark CM, 11¼″ | 2450.00 | 2900.00 |
| ☐ 7/III, trademark Full Bee, 11¼″ | 2000.00 | 2200.00 |
| ☐ 7/III, trademark Stylized Bee, 11¼″ | 1100.00 | 1210.00 |
| ☐ 7/III, trademark 3-line mark, 11¼″ | 90.00 | 990.00 |
| ☐ 7/III, trademark Goebel/V, 11¼″ | 800.00 | 880.00 |
| ☐ 7/III, trademark Goebel, 11¼″ | 680.00 | 750.00 |
| ☐ 7/X, trademark Goebel/V, 32″* | 13000.00 | 14300.00 |
| ☐ 7/X, trademark Goebel, 32″* | 13000.00 | 14300.00 |

*NOTE. The "suggested list price" on this model is $12,390.00, although a sale at this figure has not been verified. Apparently the item is wholesaled by Goebel at a figure which permits dealers to discount sharply. It is unlikely that any well-informed buyer, knowing that 7/X can be obtained at discounts of 10–30%, would pay the full $12,390.00. It is equally unlikely that a non-Hummel collector would buy 7/X at all.

## 8 BOOKWORM

Figurine in current production. Previously known as "Little Bookworm." Identical to #3 except in reduced size.

|  | Price Range | |
|---|---:|---:|
| □ 8, trademark CM, 4"–4½" ........................ | 445.00 | 500.00 |
| □ 8, trademark Full Bee, 4"–4½" .................. | 295.00 | 325.00 |
| □ 8, trademark Stylized Bee, 4"–4½"............... | 195.00 | 225.00 |
| □ 8, trademark 3-line mark, 4"–4½" ............... | 145.00 | 170.00 |
| □ 8, trademark Goebel/V, 4"–4½" ................. | 95.00 | 115.00 |
| □ 8, trademark Goebel, 4"–4½" ................... | 88.00 | 95.00 |

## 9 BEGGING HIS SHARE

Figurine in current production. "Begging his Share" is considered by some to be one of the more overly cute models in the Hummel line. It shows a boy in short pants, shirt and his father's slippers. He is holding a cake on a platter while a black terrier-type dog stands before him on hind legs begging for a portion.

There were two distinct variations of this model. In the original design, the cake is hollowed out in the center to permit insertion of a small candle,

**9** Begging His Share

the intention being that the figure could serve as a table ornament for birthday celebrations. In the revised style the hole is not present. There is an additional slight difference, not important for means of identification but which should be noted. In the old type, the boy's head is tilted somewhat to his left side, so that he looks more directly at the dog. In the restyling this was altered so that he gazes forward and seems to take little notice of the dog's presence.

This is quite a colorful figure available in many size variations. Exactly what type of cake is represented is a matter of some argument. Its sloping shape with fluted sides, and its coloration of buff yellow intermixed with deep brownish red along the edges, suggests a rumcake; but taking into account the massive variety of Bavarian cakes that exist, one hesitates to draw conclusions. The boy has on large red slippers intended to represent leather. His socks, which reach below the knee, are pastel yellow. The shorts are red, and the plaid shirt has predominant colors of blue and yellow. The front of his hair is brushed upward and toward his right temple. The dog is black. Both figures are contained on an oval base.

| | Price Range | |
|---|---|---|
| ☐ 9, trademark CM, 5¼"–5¾" ..................... | 445.00 | 500.00 |
| ☐ 9, trademark Full Bee, 5¼"–5¾", with hole for candle............................................ | 345.00 | 390.00 |
| ☐ 9, trademark Full Bee, 5¼"–5¾"................ | 295.00 | 335.00 |
| ☐ 9, trademark Stylized Bee, 5¼"–5¾", with hole for candle......................................... | 245.00 | 280.00 |
| ☐ 9, trademark Stylized Bee, 5¼"–5¾" ............ | 195.00 | 225.00 |
| ☐ 9, trademark 3-line mark, 5¼"–5¾", with hole for candle......................................... | 120.00 | 140.00 |
| ☐ 9, trademark 3-line mark, 5¼"–5¾".............. | 105.00 | 125.00 |
| ☐ 9, trademark Goebel/V, 5¼"–5¾" ............... | 95.00 | 115.00 |
| ☐ 9, trademark Goebel, 5¼"–5¾" ................. | 88.00 | 105.00 |

# 10  FLOWER MADONNA

Figurine in current production. One of the Hummel figurines continuously produced for the longest time is "Flower Madonna" which was introduced in 1935, the first year of Hummel production. In these 47 years it has undergone a number of alterations providing the collector with quite a formidable challenge. A complete collection of "Flower Madonna" representing every size, color, and trademark would be no small accomplishment.

"Flower Madonna" is a figure of the Virgin Mary with the Christ Child. She is seated with an open book on her lap. The Christ Child stands, supported by her right arm, with his feet upon the book. A small bird is perched on the book. In her left hand the Virgin holds a flower, thereby supplying the title for the model. Her robe is adorned with a raised series of dots resembling flowers.

This is, of course, an ancient theme. Rendered by sculptors for more than a thousand years the theme presents both opportunity and restrictions to designers. No great liberty can be taken without risk of destroying the

**10/Old**     **10** Flower Madonna     **10/New**

solemn nature of the subject; yet to merely copy and repeat old versions of the theme is uncreative. The Madonna and Child was a favorite subject of Berta Hummel's for sketching. She left behind numerous examples of Madonna and Child drawings, of which the design for "Flower Madonna" was neither the finest nor the best known. That distinction would undoubtedly belong to the half length version incorporated as #48 "Madonna Plaque," styled in a fashion suggestive of Italian primitive of the 13th and 14th centuries. "Flower Madonna" is, however, an imaginative rendering of a full length Madonna and Child. The Madonna has a youthful but not entirely childlike face, more or less in the traditional manner. The child is depicted not as an infant but a as child approximately two years of age. He is given an animated expression and a sense of physical motion. So memorable is this production that its modeler, Rheinhold Unger, became somewhat of a celebrity as a result of having executed it. Hummel modelers rarely achieve notoriety.

There are two distinct and important size variations of "Flower Madonna." From its inception in 1935 until 1956 it was produced in a standard size of 7¾" and 9½". The mold was then remade in 1956 in a larger size, resulting in the standard being increased to 11"–13". So far, valuations for sizes within these ranges of variations have not been established. When the old mold was being used, specimens as tall as 14" were advertised, larger than any actually recorded. Whether such specimens were manufactured or merely announced with the intent to manufacture, is not known, but the latter would appear the more likely probability. In 1982, the 13" model, numbered 10/III, was temporarily withdrawn from production. The Goebel firm claims that this size will be reinstated in the future.

"Flower Madonna" has been made in both colored and uncolored versions. The uncolored has a cream overglaze referred to as an ivory finish and is fashioned after the tradition of Bavarians in the late Middle Ages who carved Madonnas from walrus ivory. The colored versions have comprised finishes referred to as pastel blue and brown with variations. The pastel blue tends toward violet. Brown may be a misnomer, however, as the color contains enough red pigment to be called pale rust or pinkish brown. Hummel collectors should be aware of the fact that any color designations found in books are mostly carry-overs of old applications, from the days when any color resembling brown was called brown for the sake of simplification. Today, only the cream overglaze finish and pastel blue are being produced. The other variations of brown have been discontinued and are considered quite valuable with prices ranging in the low- to mid-thousands.

There is also a difference to be noticed in the halo. In the old version, the Madonna wears a natural open halo surrounding the crown of her head. The back of her head can be seen when the model is viewed from behind. The current version has a closed halo more closely approximately a hat. It is indeed a most impressive composition. It was formerly known as "Sitting Madonna with Child."

| | **Price Range** | |
|---|---|---|
| ☐ 10/I, white overglaze, trademark CM, 7¾"–9½" | 345.00 | 390.00 |
| ☐ 10/I, white overglaze, trademark Full Bee, 7¾"–9½" | 295.00 | 335.00 |
| ☐ 10/I, white overglaze, trademark Stylized Bee, 7¾"–9½" | 115.00 | 140.00 |
| ☐ 10/I, white overglaze, trademark 3-line mark, 7¾"–9½" | 95.00 | 115.00 |
| ☐ 10/I, white overglaze, trademark Goebel/V, 7¾"–9½" | 75.00 | 95.00 |
| ☐ 10/I, white overglaze, trademark Goebel, 7¾"–9½" | 70.00 | 85.00 |
| ☐ 10/I, brown, trademark CM, 7¾"–9½" | 795.00 | 885.00 |
| ☐ 10/I, brown, trademark Full Bee, 7¾"–9½" | 770.00 | 850.00 |
| ☐ 10/I, brown, trademark Stylized Bee, 7¾"–9½" | 245.00 | 280.00 |
| ☐ 10/I, brown, trademark 3-line mark, 7¾"–9½" | 160.00 | 190.00 |
| ☐ 10/I, pastel blue, trademark CM, 7¾"–9½" | 345.00 | 390.00 |
| ☐ 10/I, pastel blue, trademark Full Bee, 7¾"–9½" | 255.00 | 290.00 |
| ☐ 10/I, pastel blue, trademark Stylized Bee, 7¾"–9½" | 155.00 | 185.00 |
| ☐ 10/I, pastel blue, trademark 3-line mark, 7¾"–9½" | 120.00 | 140.00 |
| ☐ 10/I, pastel blue, trademark Goebel/V, 7¾"–9½" | 95.00 | 115.00 |
| ☐ 10/I, pastel blue, trademark Goebel, 7¾" | 100.00 | 115.00 |
| ☐ 10/III, white overglaze, trademark CM, 11"–13" | 405.00 | 455.00 |
| ☐ 10/III, white overglaze, trademark Full Bee, 11"–13" | 230.00 | 255.00 |
| ☐ 10/III, white overglaze, trademark Stylized Bee, 11"–13" | 175.00 | 205.00 |

**Price Range**

| | | |
|---|---:|---:|
| ☐ 10/III, white overglaze, trademark 3-line mark, 11″–13″ | **145.00** | **180.00** |
| ☐ 10/III, white overglaze, trademark Goebel/V, 11″–13″ | **135.00** | **170.00** |
| ☐ 10/III, white overglaze, trademark Goebel, 11″–13″ | **140.00** | **170.00** |
| ☐ 10/III, brown, trademark CM, 11″–13″ | **2570.00** | **2920.00** |
| ☐ 10/III, brown, trademark Full Bee, 11″–13″ | **1545.00** | **1955.00** |
| ☐ 10/III, brown, trademark Stylized Bee, 11″–13″ | **405.00** | **495.00** |
| ☐ 10/III, brown, trademark 3-line mark, 11″–13″ | **300.00** | **350.00** |
| ☐ 10/III, pastel blue, trademark CM, 11″–13″ | **595.00** | **665.00** |
| ☐ 10/III, pastel blue, trademark Full Bee, 11″–13″ | **395.00** | **445.00** |
| ☐ 10/III, pastel blue, trademark Stylized Bee, 11″–13″ | **270.00** | **305.00** |
| ☐ 10/III, pastel blue, trademark 3-line mark, 11″–13″ | **270.00** | **305.00** |
| ☐ 10/III, pastel blue, trademark Goebel/V, 11″–13″ | **245.00** | **280.00** |
| ☐ 10/III, pastel blue, trademark Goebel, 11″–13″ | **250.00** | **280.00** |

## 11  MERRY WANDERER

Figurine in current production. Identical in design and coloration to #7 "Merry Wanderer."

| | | |
|---|---:|---:|
| ☐ 11/2/0, trademark CM, 4¼″ or less | **300.00** | **330.00** |
| ☐ 11/2/0, trademark Full Bee, 4¼″ or less | **175.00** | **195.00** |
| ☐ 11/2/0, trademark Stylized Bee, 4¼″ or less | **125.00** | **140.00** |
| ☐ 11/2/0, trademark 3-line mark, 4¼″ or less | **50.00** | **65.00** |
| ☐ 11/2/0, trademark Goebel/V, 4¼″ or less | **80.00** | **90.00** |
| ☐ 11/2/0, trademark Goebel, 4¼″ or less | **65.00** | **75.00** |
| ☐ 11/2/0, trademark CM, larger than 4¼″ | **350.00** | **385.00** |
| ☐ 11/2/0, trademark Full Bee, larger than 4¼″ | **180.00** | **200.00** |
| ☐ 11/2/0, trademark Stylized Bee, larger than 4¼″ | **150.00** | **165.00** |
| ☐ 11/2/0, trademark 3-line mark, larger than 4¼″ | **90.00** | **100.00** |
| ☐ 11/2/0, trademark Goebel/V, larger than 4¼″ | **80.00** | **90.00** |
| ☐ 11/2/0, trademark Goebel, larger than 4¼″ | **72.50** | **82.50** |
| ☐ 11/0, trademark CM, 4¾″ or less | **500.00** | **550.00** |
| ☐ 11/0, trademark Full Bee, 4¾″ or less | **250.00** | **275.00** |
| ☐ 11/0, trademark Stylized Bee, 4¾″ or less | **200.00** | **220.00** |
| ☐ 11/0, trademark 3-line mark, 4¾″ or less | **180.00** | **200.00** |
| ☐ 11/0, trademark Goebel/V, 4¾″ or less | **85.00** | **95.00** |
| ☐ 11/0, trademark Goebel, 4¾″ or less | **72.00** | **80.00** |
| ☐ 11/0, trademark CM, larger than 4¾″ | **550.00** | **595.00** |
| ☐ 11/0, trademark Full Bee, larger than 4¾″ | **250.00** | **275.00** |
| ☐ 11/0, trademark Stylized Bee, larger than 4¾″ | **150.00** | **165.00** |
| ☐ 11/0, trademark 3-line mark, larger than 4¾″ | **100.00** | **110.00** |
| ☐ 11/0, trademark Goebel/V, larger than 4¾″ | **82.00** | **90.00** |
| ☐ 11/0, trademark Goebel, larger than 4¾″ | **72.50** | **82.50** |

## 12  CHIMNEY SWEEP

Figurine in current production. "Chimney Sweep" has been known as "Smoky" and "Good Luck." The model is intended to represent a chimney sweeper of the 19th century. This was a thriving trade over 100 years ago, when fires provided the only means of heat in German villages. Many a youth was saved from starvation or the workhouse by taking a broom and hiring himself out as a chimney cleaner. This youthful Hummel figure is not at all idealized but is very realistic, since the job of chimney sweep was often handled by boys under ten years of age. The Hummel "Chimney Sweep" has been made in two basic sizes: 12/2/0 approximately 4" and 12/1 approximately 5½", but there are variations to be encountered.

"Chimney Sweep" is attired in a leather oversuit buttoning at the front. The basic color is black, with lightened areas (such as the knee) to provide highlight and contour. Over one shoulder he carries the usual tools of the trade: A rope and a brush. The other arm holds a short step ladder. He wears a red tie and a black woolen cap. His eyes are open wide gazing directly at the viewer, his cheeks and lips are floral red, and his hair is somewhat tousled. He stands on a circular base.

**12** Chimney Sweep

**Price Range**

| | | |
|---|---|---|
| ☐ 12/2/0, trademark CM, 4"–4¼"................... | **114.00** | **126.00** |
| ☐ 12/2/0, trademark Full Bee, 4"–4¼".............. | **98.00** | **112.00** |
| ☐ 12/2/0, trademark Stylized Bee, 4"–4¼"......... | **68.00** | **82.00** |
| ☐ 12/2/0, trademark 3-line mark, 4"–4¼".......... | **48.00** | **62.00** |
| ☐ 12/2/0, trademark Goebel/V, 4"–4¼"............. | **38.00** | **52.00** |
| ☐ 12/2/0, trademark Goebel, 4"–4¼"............... | **39.00** | **46.00** |
| ☐ 12/I, trademark CM, 5½"–6½" ................... | **348.00** | **372.00** |
| ☐ 12/I, trademark Full Bee, 5½"–6½dp ............ | **248.00** | **275.00** |
| ☐ 12/I, trademark Stylized Bee, 5½"–6½".......... | **124.00** | **148.00** |
| ☐ 12/I, trademark 3-line mark, 5½"–6½" .......... | **98.00** | **112.00** |
| ☐ 12/I, trademark Goebel/V, 5½"–6½" ............. | **70.00** | **82.00** |
| ☐ 12/I, trademark Goebel, 5½"–6½" ............... | **55.00** | **81.00** |

## 13 MEDITATION

Figurine in current production. "Meditation" is one of the more collectible Hummels in the present series since it is produced in four basic sizes and has many design variations. This model previously went by the name of "The Little Messenger." It portrays a little girl in traditional peasant dress, holding a letter in her right hand and carrying a basket on her left arm. The original and long-produced version had flowers in the basket. In 1978 the motif was redesigned and the basket was left empty, presumably to be used for display of artificial flowers or other decoration.

**13** Meditation

Clear evidence is furnished in "Meditation" that the model is intended to represent yesteryear, rather than the present or even the recent past, as the letter is closed with sealing wax. This method of letter sealing became obsolete in the mid-1800s, so it can be presumed that the figure is designed as a period piece of the first half of the 19th century. She wears a white blouse, a black or bluish grey jumper, and a salmon-colored apron with washes of rust brown. Her brown shoes are a clog type with a low heel. Her hair is strawberry blonde, with some slight variation from specimen to specimen. She gazes upward with lips parted, as if in fixed thought, with the index finger of her left hand pointed toward her chin. The basket is of wicker with circular banding around its circumference. It is scarcely discernable that the girl wears hair ribbons when viewed from the front, but these can be readily observed from the back. Some variations have occurred in the design of these ribbons.

|  | Price Range | |
|---|---|---|
| ☐ 13/2/0, trademark Full Bee, 4¼" ................ | 155.00 | 180.00 |
| ☐ 13/2/0, trademark Stylized Bee, 4¼" ............ | 105.00 | 125.00 |
| ☐ 13/2/0, trademark 3-line mark, 4¼" .............. | 75.00 | 95.00 |
| ☐ 13/2/0, trademark Goebel/V, 4¼" ................ | 60.00 | 80.00 |
| ☐ 13/2/0, trademark Goebel, 4¼" .................. | 55.00 | 65.00 |
| ☐ 13/0, trademark CM, 5¼"–5¾" ................... | 295.00 | 335.00 |
| ☐ 13/0, trademark Full Bee, 5¼"–5¾" ............ | 245.00 | 280.00 |
| ☐ 13/0, trademark Stylized Bee, 5¼"–5¾" ........ | 175.00 | 205.00 |
| ☐ 13/0, trademark 3-line mark, 5¼"–5¾" ......... | 120.00 | 140.00 |
| ☐ 13/0, trademark Goebel/V, 5¼"–5¾" ............ | 85.00 | 95.00 |
| ☐ 13/0, trademark Goebel, 5¼"–5¾" ............... | 77.50 | 115.00 |
| ☐ 13/II, trademark CM, 7"–7¼" .................... | 2995.00 | 3295.00 |
| ☐ 13/II, trademark Full Bee, 7"–7¼" ............... | 2200.00 | 3085.00 |
| ☐ 13/II, trademark Stylized Bee, 7"–7¼" ........... | 2195.00 | 2425.00 |
| ☐ 13/II,trademark Goebel/V, 7"–7¼" ............... | 245.00 | 280.00 |
| ☐ 13/II, trademark Goebel, 7" ...................... | 200.00 | 225.00 |
| ☐ 13/2, trademark CM, 7"–7¼" .................... | 2070.00 | 2280.00 |
| ☐ 13/2, trademark Full Bee, 7"–7¼" ............... | 2070.00 | 2280.00 |
| ☐ 13/2, trademark Stylized Bee, 7"–7¼" ........... | 1770.00 | 1980.00 |
| ☐ 13/2, trademark Goebel/V, 7"–7¼" .............. | 155.00 | 180.00 |
| ☐ 13/2, trademark Goebel, 7"–7¼" ............... | 160.00 | 180.00 |
| ☐ 13/V, trademark Full Bee, 13½"–14" ............. | 2595.00 | 2865.00 |
| ☐ 13/V, trademark Stylized Bee, 13½"–14"......... | 1595.00 | 1765.00 |
| ☐ 13/V, trademark 3-line mark, 13½"–14" .......... | 1195.00 | 1325.00 |
| ☐ 13/V, trademark Goebel/V, 13½"–14" ........... | 745.00 | 830.00 |
| ☐ 13/V, trademark Goebel, 13½"–14" .............. | 680.00 | 745.00 |
| ☐ 13/5, trademark Full Bee, 13½"–14" ............. | 3695.00 | 4075.00 |
| ☐ 13/5, trademark Stylized Bee, 13½"–14"......... | 3695.00 | 4075.00 |
| ☐ 13/5, trademark 3-line mark, 13½"–14" .......... | 3695.00 | 4075.00 |
| ☐ 13/5, trademark Goebel/V, 13½"–14" ........... | 420.00 | 465.00 |
| ☐ 13/5, trademark Goebel, 13½"–14" .............. | 425.00 | 465.00 |

## 14 A AND B  BOOKWORM BOOKENDS

Set of bookends in current production. The set comprises one figure of a boy and another of a girl, similarly posed. Both are seated on the ground, without bases, reading books that rest on their laps. The girl is a duplication in design and coloration of #3 and #8 "Bookworm," except that the open pages in her book, colored in those models, are now in black and white. To facilitate their use as bookends, these figures can be filled with sand through an opening at the base, which is plugged with other plastic or cork. As far as their use as bookends is concerned, owners should exercise reasonable caution. Since they measure only 5½″ high, they are not suitable as stabilizers for books of folio size, nor a shelf full of unbound periodicals, catalogues, or other volumes that persistently refuse to stand upright. Damage is invited if they are used in these situations. Therefore, it is better not to use them as bookends at all.

As the girl bookworm has already been described in detail (see Hummel #3 above), comments shall be confined to her companion. His attire is similar to hers, except that he wears short trousers, and the color combination of his shirt and bib is reversed, with green atop orange instead of orange atop green. His shoes are black and his socks are chiefly pale violet with bands of light ochre yellow. The soles of his shoes are a lighter shade than the girl's, tending toward yellow with a slight addition of brown. His hair is closely cropped, except in front where it is combed down to frame his forehead. The boy bookworm is available only as part of the set. This design was never manufactured as a separately sold figure. Values are given for the set. Some specimens have a gold paper sticker with the wording "75 Years Goebel." At one time this set had been made in a nine-inch size, but this oversized version is extremely scarce and little information is available on it.

**14/A**          **14** Bookworms          **14/B**

|  | Price Range | |
|---|---|---|
| ☐ 14/A and 14/B, trademark CM, 5½".............. | 800.00 | 880.00 |
| ☐ 14/A and 14/B, trademark Full Bee, 5½"......... | 600.00 | 660.00 |
| ☐ 14/A and 14/B, trademark Stylized Bee, 5½" .... | 400.00 | 440.00 |
| ☐ 14/A and 14/B, trademark 3-line mark, 5½"...... | 280.00 | 310.00 |
| ☐ 14/A and 14/B, trademark Goebel/V, 5½"........ | 220.00 | 245.00 |
| ☐ 14/A and 14/B, trademark Goebel, 5½".......... | 190.00 | 210.00 |
| ☐ 14/A-III and 14/B-III, trademark CM, 9"........... | 2150.00 | 2365.00 |
| ☐ 14/A-III and 14/B-III, trademark Full Bee, 9" ..... | 2150.00 | 2365.00 |
| ☐ 14/A-III and 14/B-III, trademark Stylized Bee, 9" | 2150.00 | 2365.00 |
| ☐ 14/A-III and 14/B-III, trademark 3-line mark, 9" .. | 2150.00 | 2365.00 |

## 15 HEAR YE, HEAR YE

Figurine in current production. Previously designated "Night Watchman," "Hear Ye, Hear Ye" is a figure of a watchman sounding a horn. Because of the great detail of its accessories, this figurine ranks as one of the more complicated Hummels. Its costume is representative of the earlier or mid portion of the 19th century. The night watch was maintained in virtually all German and other European towns and villages from the later Middle Ages until fairly recent times, and it is still occasionally maintained as a tourist

**15** Hear Ye, Hear Ye

attraction. The watchman patrolled alone in small towns, but often with assistants or deputies in cities. There were a number of duties to which the watchman attended. Few persons owned clocks or watches, so he announced the hour. He looked about for unlocked gates and notified property owners of this neglect. If suspicious persons were observed in the streets, he called for the constable. Since streets were not lighted, he carried a lantern, and also usually a club or baton to be used in emergencies against man or beast. He was not otherwise armed. Sometimes, as in the case of "Hear Ye, Hear Ye," he was provided with a horn to announce his presence. In general, he looked after the safety and comfort of the villagers. "Hear Ye, Hear Ye" is attired in what was termed, during this period, a greatcoat whose primary color is blue and highlighted with yellow and brown. The pocket flap and lapel trim is in yellow orange, and the inner side of the coat is red. He wears a yellow cream scarf and greyish brown boots. In his left hand he holds a long stick which touches the ground. In his right he holds a ram's horn trumpet to his lips. Dangling on his left arm is a lantern which is dark brown with a yellow and red interior designed to represent the glow and flame of a candle.

There are both old and new versions of this model which are so similar that a casual observer, viewing the two side by side, would probably not take any notice of the difference. The basic change is in the left hand. The watchman wears gloves of the mitten variety. In the old version, the outlines of his fingers can be seen in the left hand. They have disappeared in the redesign. The theory that this inconspicuous feature simply wore away in the mold cannot be correct as the redesigned version bears additional slight differences which could not have resulted in this fashion.

|  | Price Range | |
|---|---|---|
| ☐ 15/0, trademark CM, 5″–5¼″ ..................... | 395.00 | 425.00 |
| ☐ 15/0, trademark Full Bee, 5″–5¼″ ............... | 195.00 | 240.00 |
| ☐ 15/0, trademark Stylized Bee, 5″–5¼″ ........... | 145.00 | 175.00 |
| ☐ 15/0, trademark 3-line mark, 5″–5¼″............. | 120.00 | 145.00 |
| ☐ 15/0, trademark Goebel/V, 5″–5¼″ ............... | 95.00 | 120.00 |
| ☐ 15/0, trademark Goebel, 5″–5¼″ ................. | 88.00 | 115.00 |
| ☐ 15/I, trademark CM, 6″–6¼″..................... | 495.00 | 555.00 |
| ☐ 15/I, trademark Full Bee, 6″–6¼″ ............... | 295.00 | 325.00 |
| ☐ 15/I, trademark Stylized Bee, 6″–6¼″ ........... | 170.00 | 200.00 |
| ☐ 15/I, trademark 3-line mark, 6″–6¼″ ............ | 130.00 | 155.00 |
| ☐ 15/I, trademark Goebel/V, 6″–6¼″................ | 105.00 | 130.00 |
| ☐ 15/I, trademark Goebel, 6″–6¼″................. | 65.00 | 90.00 |
| ☐ 15/II, trademark CM, 7″–7½″..................... | 995.00 | 1105.00 |
| ☐ 15/II, trademark Full Bee, 7″–7½″................ | 705.00 | 765.00 |
| ☐ 15/II, trademark Stylized Bee, 7″–7½″ ........... | 395.00 | 445.00 |
| ☐ 15/II, trademark 3-line mark, 7″–7½″............. | 295.00 | 335.00 |
| ☐ 15/II, trademark Goebel/V, 7″–7½″ ............... | 215.00 | 245.00 |
| ☐ 15/II, trademark Goebel, 7″–7½″ ................. | 185.00 | 205.00 |

## 16 LITTLE HIKER

Figurine in current production. "Little Hiker" was formerly known as "Happy Go Lucky." The personification of an Alpine traveler, this figure wears lederhosen, suspenders, a smartly styled jacket, an oversized bowtie, a cap, knee socks, and shoes. There are no redesigns to contend with and no other variations that have any reported influence on value.

This is a softly colored model. The lederhosen are black and highlighted in violet. The jacket is pale blue with a criss-cross pattern of red streaks. The suspenders are maroon, and his stockings are an off-white with minute touches of brown and yellow. The bow tie is red, and the shoes are brown with areas of pale highlights. In his right hand he holds a walking stick colored dark brown. His left hand is thrust deeply into his pocket. His head is turned upward and, with a sense of wonder on his face, he appears to be gazing upon a mountain or other high object. His face is colored with great realism and without the tinges of yellow that are so often included in the faces of Hummels. This coloring seems to be a detraction, in the opinion of many, despite the fact that this may be in keeping with the appearance of classic porcelain.

**16** Little Hiker

| | Price Range | |
|---|---|---|
| ☐ 16/2/0, trademark CM, 4¼″ or smaller ........... | **220.00** | **240.00** |
| ☐ 16/2/0, trademark Full Bee, 4¼″ or smaller ...... | **120.00** | **140.00** |
| ☐ 16/2/0, trademark Stylized Bee, 4¼″ or smaller | **100.00** | **110.00** |
| ☐ 16/2/0, trademark 3-line mark, 4¼″ or smaller ... | **70.00** | **80.00** |
| ☐ 16/2/0, trademark Goebel/V, 4¼″ or smaller ..... | **54.00** | **65.00** |
| ☐ 16/2/0, trademark Goebel, 4¼″ or smaller ....... | **44.00** | **55.00** |
| ☐ 16/I, trademark CM, 5½″–6″...................... | **350.00** | **385.00** |
| ☐ 16/I, trademark Full Bee, 5½″–6″ ............... | **250.00** | **275.00** |
| ☐ 16/I, trademark Stylized Bee, 5½″–6″ ............ | **150.00** | **175.00** |
| ☐ 16/I, trademark 3-line mark, 5½″–6″ ............. | **110.00** | **120.00** |
| ☐ 16/I, trademark Goebel/V, 5½″–6″................ | **97.00** | **110.00** |
| ☐ 16/I, trademark Goebel, 5½″–6″................. | **77.50** | **90.00** |

## 17  CONGRATULATIONS

Figurine in current production. "Congratulations," very long in production, exists in both an original and redesigned state. While the differences are readily apparent, they could very well pass unnoticed. The model is of a

**New Style**    **17** Congratulations    **Old Style**

young girl who wears a short blue shift style dress dotted with red ornaments and highlighted with areas of yellow or light ochre. In the old style she wears no socks or she could be wearing long colorless cotton stockings that might be mistaken for bare legs. In the redesigned version, bulky socks with circular ribbing have been added in light yellow, pastel brown, and dark brown. The old style has shortly cropped hair; in the revision, her hair has gotten a bit longer and more stylish, tending to give the figure an older appearance. In both instances the hair is carrot-colored. Coloration of the shoes varies slightly. In her right arm she carries a flower pot containing flowers with a bird perched atop them. In the other hand she carries a small trumpet.

|  | Price Range | |
|---|---|---|
| ☐ 17/0, trademark CM, 5½"–6" .................... | **295.00** | **335.00** |
| ☐ 17/0, trademark Full Bee, 5½"–6" ............... | **195.00** | **225.00** |
| ☐ 17/0, trademark Stylized Bee, 5½"–6" .......... | **170.00** | **195.00** |
| ☐ 17/0, trademark 3-line mark, 5½"–6" ............ | **145.00** | **170.00** |
| ☐ 17/0, trademark Goebel/V, 5½"–6" .............. | **75.00** | **90.00** |
| ☐ 17/0, trademark Goebel, 5½"–6" ................ | **60.00** | **80.00** |
| ☐ 17/2, trademark CM, 7¾"–8¼" .................. | **6995.00** | **7695.00** |

## 18  CHRIST CHILD

Figurine in current production. "Christ Child," was originally known as "Christmas Night." A representation of the Christ Child lying upon a blanket on a straw bed, this figurine was not designed as a component in a nativity set but rather for individual sale. Its use in nativity sets has been extensive in combination with accessory figures by other manufacturers. The later Hummel nativity sets feature a Christ Child modeled very closely after #18. The obvious question to be raised is: Why would this figure be placed on the market by itself, as it would surely appear out of place if displayed alone? This is easily explained by the fact that, in Europe, a long standing tradition was to carefully preserve and hand down nativity models from one generation of a family to the next. In the course of doing this, some figures would be lost or broken and need replacement. Hence, for well over a hundred years there has been a thriving trade in individual nativity figures throughout the continent. "Christmas Child" is certainly a worthy addition to any set, whether its other figures are primarily antique or modern.

The Christ Child was a subject frequently sketched by Berta Hummel and its representation as a model seemed mandatory from the outset of Hummel production. "Christ Child," unlike some produced by other makers, is a solid one-piece construction; the child cannot be removed from its bed. This is indeed a valuable feature as it reduces the risk of accident, or the separation of components which can occur when nativity models are stored away after Christmas.

There are several variations. The old version measures approximately 3¾" × 6½", while the redesigned type is 3¼" × 6". It should be noted in measuring that the bed is measured and not the figure itself. Measurements sometimes encountered in lists giving a width of only two inches, do not represent variant sizes, but are the result of measuring across the figure only, which is an error. During the early period of production, the model was available both painted, as is the current version, and in a cream overglaze. The cream overglaze specimens did not have extensive sales and are rare today. They must have existed until the motif was redesigned as some examples in the smaller size are known. As for designing differences between the smaller and larger types, these are subtle but well worth the collector's attention. In the painted specimens, blankets are identical, but the straw on the bed of the smaller version varies somewhat with its sharply contrasting tones of light and dark brown, whereas the straw in the larger type is a more uniform shade. The head tilts slightly more toward the right side in the larger version. Minor differences of skin color will be observed from specimen to specimen, but do not represent different types.

|  | Price Range | |
|---|---|---|
| □ 18, trademark CM, 3¾"–6½".................... | 250.00 | 275.00 |
| □ 18, trademark Full Bee, 3¾"–6½"............... | 180.00 | 200.00 |
| □ 18, trademark Stylized Bee, 3¾"–6½"........... | 120.00 | 135.00 |
| □ 18, trademark 3-line mark, 3¼"–6"............... | 80.00 | 90.00 |
| □ 18, trademark Goebel/V, 3¾"–6"................ | 75.00 | 85.00 |
| □ 18, white overglaze trademark Goebel, 3¼"–6" | 55.50 | 65.00 |
| □ 18, white overglaze, trademark CM, 3¾"–6½"... | 400.00 | 440.00 |
| □ 18, white overglaze, trademark Full Bee, 3¾"–6½" ........................................ | 350.00 | 385.00 |
| □ 18, white overglaze, trademark Stylized Bee, 3¾"–6½" ........................................ | 300.00 | 330.00 |
| □ 18, white overglaze, trademark 3-line mark, 3¾"–6½" ........................................ | 250.00 | 270.00 |

## 19 PRAYER BEFORE BATTLE

Closed number designation. This was the original design for "Prayer Before Battle." It portrays a boy with hands clasped in prayer, holding a flagstaff, standing beside a hobbyhorse. The model was executed by A. Moller, one of the Hummel factory modelers, after a sketch by Berta Hummel, on June 20, 1935. When turned over to the Seissen Convent for final approval, as had been the arrangement with all the other Hummel models, it was rejected and not placed into production. Goebel, not one to give up easily, made alterations, resubmitted "Prayer Before Battle," and this time won acceptance. The result was #20 (below), a favorite through many years of production. There are no known examples or photographs of #19.

## 20 PRAYER BEFORE BATTLE

Figurine in current production. After rejection of the initial design (see above), "Prayer Before Battle" was finally accepted for production by the Seissen Convent. The theme is typically Hummel: A child placed in an adult situation with strong emotional overtones. The origin of this subject has its roots in the Middle Ages. Before entering into battle, it was customary for

**20** Prayer Before Battle

soldiers to recite certain prayers and, in the case of a "holy mission," such as the Crusades, receive blessings.

"Prayer Before Battle" is quite an effective composition showing a child in the role of a soldier and his toy wooden horse in the role of his mount. The child is attired in a short, whitish green shirt tinged with pink and decorated with circular ornaments composed of yellow within bold outlines. He has on brown boots of heavy oxhide and ribbed socks of pastel grey blue. He carries in his left arm a wooden stick to which is attached a white and blue flag, symbolic of the staff and standard borne by medieval knights. At his left side is a small trumpet colored yellow to suggest brass. The horse is a light creamy brown, its head held downward and its eyes shut. It wears a black bridle and has a blackish brown mane and tail.

|  | Price Range | |
|---|---|---|
| ☐ 20, trademark CM, 4″–4½″ ..................... | 345.00 | 385.00 |
| ☐ 20, trademark Full Bee, 4″–4½″.................. | 195.00 | 225.00 |
| ☐ 20, trademark Stylized Bee, 4″–4½″ ............. | 145.00 | 175.00 |
| ☐ 20, trademark 3-line mark, 4″–4½″............... | 95.00 | 125.00 |
| ☐ 20, trademark Goebel/V, 4″–4½″................. | 75.00 | 95.00 |
| ☐ 20, trademark Goebel, 4″–4½″ .................. | 72.00 | 80.00 |

## 21 HEAVENLY ANGEL

Figurine in current production. "Heavenly Angel" is considered one of the more typical Hummel designs. It is one of the most confusing Hummel figures to collect. There are so many size variations which do not correspond with the factory's four basic sizes of 4½", 6", 6¾", and 8¾", that it is nearly impossible to collect a specimen of each variation. This figure was also produced at one time with a white overglaze finish. These specimens are quite scarce and, of course, are worth much more than the same model in color.

"Heavenly Angel" is the only model in the entire Hummel series of more than 400 pieces to use a fractional size designator, 21/0½. Unfortunately the factory prints it as 21/0/1/2, leading to considerable bewilderment on the part of beginning collectors who are unaware of the practice. The reason for this fractional numeration is that the intermediate 6" size (actually 5¾"–6½") was inserted into the series after 21/0 and 21/I were already in production. Nothing seemed more logical than to term the newcomer 21/0½.

"Heavenly Angel" is a figure of a youth with wings, dressed in a long, flowing gown and holding an oversized candle. At first glance it appears a simple composition and is a good example of a Hummel whose artistic

**21** Heavenly Angel

merits are largely missed by casual observation. Note the tilt of the head; the direction in which the hair blows; the horizontal slant of the candle flame; the manner in which the skirt of the gown billows outward. "Heavenly Angel" is being buffeted about by a strong wind and looks apprehensively at her candle, in fear that it will be extinguished. This sense of motion is difficult to successfully capture in a work of porcelain, just as it is difficult in a woodcarving or most other forms of three-dimensional art. It is easy to exaggerate, but when exaggerated, the effect is usually lost. There are only about a dozen Hummel figures in which motion in an important component; "Heavenly Angel" is by far one of the best. It must be admitted, however, that the smaller sizes, especially 21/0, convey this feeling of motion somewhat better than the larger.

The angel's gown is pale green intermixed with white and ornamented with a number of yellow five pointed stars. Her shoes are brown, and her hair is reddish brown. The wings are handsomely modeled and colored, the chief colors being yellow and pink but highlighted with a few strokes of red. The candle is pure white with a drop of wax rolling down from the top. She stands on an elevated base whose center is composed of a circular platform.

| | Price Range | |
|---|---:|---:|
| ☐ 21/0, trademark CM, 4″–4¾″ | 210.00 | 230.00 |
| ☐ 21/0, trademark Full Bee, 4″–4¾″ | 150.00 | 165.00 |
| ☐ 21/0, trademark Stylized Bee, 4″–4¾″ | 100.00 | 110.00 |
| ☐ 21/0, trademark 3-line mark, 4″–4¾″ | 60.00 | 70.00 |
| ☐ 21/0, trademark Goebel/V, 4″–4¾″ | 52.00 | 60.00 |
| ☐ 21/0, trademark Goebel, 4″–4¾″ | 42.00 | 50.00 |
| ☐ 21/0½, trademark CM, 5¾″–6½″ | 350.00 | 385.00 |
| ☐ 21/0½, trademark Full Bee, 5¾″–6½″ | 250.00 | 270.00 |
| ☐ 21/0½, trademark Stylized Bee, 5¾″–6½″ | 150.00 | 165.00 |
| ☐ 21/0½, trademark 3-line mark, 5¾″–6½″ | 100.00 | 110.00 |
| ☐ 21/0½, trademark Goebel/V, 5¾″–6½″ | 80.00 | 95.00 |
| ☐ 21/0½, trademark Goebel, 5¾″–6½″ | 70.00 | 85.00 |
| ☐ 21/I, trademark CM, 6¾″–7¼″ | 395.00 | 455.00 |
| ☐ 21/I, trademark Full Bee, 6¾″–7¼″ | 275.00 | 315.00 |
| ☐ 21/I, trademark Stylized Bee, 6¾″–7¼″ | 245.00 | 280.00 |
| ☐ 21/I, trademark 3-line mark, 6¾″–7¼″ | 145.00 | 170.00 |
| ☐ 21/I, trademark Goebel/V, 6¾″–7¼″ | 95.00 | 115.00 |
| ☐ 21/I, trademark Goebel, 6¾″–7¼″ | 88.00 | 100.00 |
| ☐ 21/II, trademark CM, 8½″–8¾″ | 1195.00 | 1325.00 |
| ☐ 21/II, trademark Full Bee, 8½″–8¾″ | 795.00 | 885.00 |
| ☐ 21/II, trademark Stylized Bee, 8½″–8¾″ | 395.00 | 445.00 |
| ☐ 21/II, trademark 3-line mark, 8½″–8¾″ | 295.00 | 335.00 |
| ☐ 21/II, trademark Goebel/V, 8½″–8¾″ | 205.00 | 225.00 |
| ☐ 21/II, trademark Goebel, 8½″–8¾″ | 184.00 | 205.00 |

## 22  ANGEL WITH BIRDS

Wall font in current production. Also known as "Seated Angel" or "Sitting Angel." This is a small, highly-colored font, and is quite a pleasing composition. The angel is wingless and might readily be termed child or youth except that she wears a halo. She wears a reddish gown extending to slightly above her knees, and brown shoes. Her blonde hair, touched with

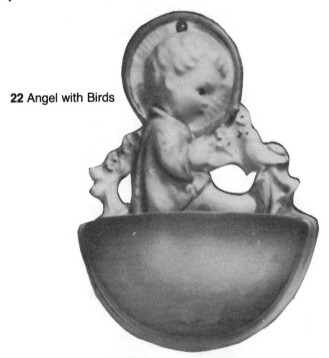

**22** Angel with Birds

red, is curly and swept back. One hand is not visible. With the other hand she points to a blue and red flower. Four other similar flowers are included in the design. A yellow canary perches on her right shoe, gazing up at her with its beak parted in song. The halo, of moderate size, is basically a cream white, outlined in the same shade of red as the angel's gown.

The smaller version, 22/0, was discontinued in 1977. There are a number of bowl shapes.

|  | Price Range | |
|---|---|---|
| ☐ 22/0, trademark CM, 3″–4″ ..................... | 200.00 | 220.00 |
| ☐ 22/0, trademark Full Bee, 3″–4″ ................. | 150.00 | 160.00 |
| ☐ 22/0, trademark Stylized Bee, 3″–4″ ............. | 100.00 | 110.00 |
| ☐ 22/0, trademark 3-line mark, 3″–4″ ............... | 50.00 | 60.00 |
| ☐ 22/0, trademark Goebel/V, 3″–4″ ................ | 28.00 | 35.00 |
| ☐ 22/0, trademark Goebel, 3″–4″ .................. | 23.00 | 28.00 |
| ☐ 22/1, trademark CM, 3½″–4⅞″ .................. | 500.00 | 520.00 |

|  | **Price Range** | |
|---|---|---|
| ☐ 22/I, trademark Full Bee, 3½″–4⅞″ .............. | **300.00** | **320.00** |
| ☐ 22/I, trademark Stylized Bee, 3½″–4⅞″......... | **250.00** | **270.00** |

## 23 ADORATION

Figurine in current production. "Adoration" has been produced in two basic sizes, to which the numbers 23/I and 23/III refer. The former ranges in overall height from 6½″ to 7″, while the latter is fairly uniform at 8¾″ to 9″. Rare versions of both sizes exist in cream overglaze. These were manufactured briefly in the years when Hummel attempted to style its works in the manner of classic porcelain. They did not meet with great public approval and were discontinued. Sales of these cream overglaze specimens occur so seldom that it is impossible to provide accurate price guidelines. There does not appear to be any reliable information on the marks that they carry. It can be safely assumed that after having been out of production a long while, these do not exist with marks any more recent than the Stylized Bee. In 1978, the smaller version was restyled with a textured finish. The original name was "Ave Maria."

"Adoration" presents a departure from the usual type of Hummel model

**23** Adoration

since it consists of figures within a fully composed setting. It represents a boy and a girl standing before a religious shrine to which a plaque of the Madonna and Child is affixed. Although the smallest component in the overall composition, this plaque is of significant interest. Delicately modeled and superbly colored, the plaque is an artwork in itself. It is positioned on a canopied mount supported by a wooden column and set against a railing to form a kind of altar. It would have been easy to show the plaque as a woodcarving and escape the need for delicate coloration. Instead the factory chose to portray it as enameled with striking results. The Madonna wears a reddish cloak, and the Child is attired in pale salmon mixed with pink. He clings to her and she supports him with both hands, one at his shoulders, one at his thighs. Halos radiate from the heads of both with white and red rays.

The girl appears to be several years older than the boy and a good deal taller. She wears her hair in braids, plaited with flowers. The boy is smartly dressed in short blue trousers, a plaid jacket, brown shoes, and white socks banded with pastel colors. The boy holds a small spray of flowers; the girl has her hands together in prayer. The girl's gaze is fixed on the plaque. The boy studies a floral garland which is attached to the support column. A few flowers are on the ground. The woodwork is simple enough, but an attractive shingled effect is on the plaque's canopy. "Adoration," despite being on the market for a long time, is essentially a scarce model. It has simply not been turned out in large quantity because of a higher than general retail price and limited public demand.

| | Price Range | |
|---|---|---|
| ☐ 23/I, trademark CM, 6¼"–7" .................... | 645.00 | 665.00 |
| ☐ 23/I, trademark Full Bee, 6¼"–7" ............... | 395.00 | 415.00 |
| ☐ 23/I, trademark Stylized Bee, 6¼"–7" ........... | 245.00 | 255.00 |
| ☐ 23/I, trademark 3-line mark, 6¼"–7" ............ | 195.00 | 215.00 |
| ☐ 23/I, trademark Goebel/V, 6¼"–7" ............... | 160.00 | 180.00 |
| ☐ 23/I, trademark Goebel, 6¼"–7" ................. | 155.00 | 170.00 |
| ☐ 23/II, trademark Full Bee, 7½"–8" ............... | 2095.00 | 2300.00 |
| ☐ 23/III, trademark CM, 8¾"–9" ................... | 945.00 | 1095.00 |
| ☐ 23/III, trademark Full Bee, 8¾"–9" .............. | 895.00 | 945.00 |
| ☐ 23/III, trademark Stylized Bee, 8¾"–9" .......... | 745.00 | 765.00 |
| ☐ 23/III, trademark 3-line mark, 8¾"–9" ........... | 345.00 | 365.00 |
| ☐ 23/III, trademark Goebel/V, 8¾"–9" ............. | 245.00 | 275.00 |
| ☐ 23/III, trademark Goebel, 8¾"–9" ............... | 165.00 | 190.00 |

## 24 LULLABY

Candleholder in current production. "Lullaby" was formerly known as "Cradle Song." There are two basic sizes with slight variations. There are also some minor differences in the reservoir into which the candle fits, but these are merely points to be noted by the collector who demands owning one of every existing variety. These differences play no part in value determination. "Lullaby" depicts an angel playing a mandolin beside the Christ Child. The Child lies, as in the nativity sets, upon a blanket on a bed of straw, and is swaddled in violet. The angel wears a blue robe and has white

**24** Lullaby

wings with red tips. Both figures have blonde hair, the angel's tending somewhat more to red. It definitely appears to be a boy angel. "Lullaby" is an essentially pleasing composition and is also manufactured as a statuette without a candleholder (see #262 "Heavenly Lullaby").

The larger version, 24/III, was discontinued for some years but was reinstated in 1978. In 1982 this size was again temporarily withdrawn from production. Although older specimens are quite scarce and are demanding premium prices, their value is likely to decrease as more and more current 24/III models come on the market.

|  | Price Range | |
|---|---|---|
| ☐ 24/I, trademark CM, 3½″ × 5″−5½″ .............. | 320.00 | 350.00 |
| ☐ 24/I, trademark Full Bee, 3½″ × 5″−5½″ ......... | 280.00 | 310.00 |
| ☐ 24/I, trademark Stylized Bee, 3½″ × 5″−5½″ ..... | 180.00 | 200.00 |
| ☐ 24/I, trademark 3-line mark, 3½″ × 5″−5½″ ...... | 120.00 | 135.00 |
| ☐ 24/I, trademark Goebel/V, 3½″ × 5″−5½″ ......... | 90.00 | 100.00 |
| ☐ 24/I, trademark Goebel, 3½″ × 5″−5½″ ........... | 77.00 | 90.00 |
| ☐ 24/III, trademark CM, 6½″−8¾″ ................. | 1600.00 | 1760.00 |
| ☐ 24/III, trademark Full Bee, 6½″−8¾″ ............ | 1200.00 | 1320.00 |
| ☐ 24/III, trademark Stylized Bee, 6½″−8¾″ ........ | 550.00 | 600.00 |
| ☐ 24/III, trademark Goebel/V, 6½″−8¾″ ........... | 350.00 | 385.00 |
| ☐ 24/III, trademark Goebel, 6½″−8¾″ .............. | 285.00 | 300.00 |

## 25  ANGELIC SLEEP

Candleholder in current production. "Angelic Sleep" is similar in subject to #24 "Lullaby" above. Instead of serenading the Christ Child, the angel in this model bends over to observe him in sleep. Other details such as color, hair style, and position of the candleholder have been altered. The candle receptable is attached toward the head of the Christ Child rather than the foot. The angel's hair appears to be curlier in this model than in "Lullaby."

Although brown is the basic color of "Angelic Sleep," there is such a variety of tints and tones that this figure can hardly be regarded as a "brown model." The straw bedding is a pinkish brown. The Christ Child's wrapping is done in pink with some dark overstrokes. The angel's cloak is a reddish brown with dark brown round the cuffs. The angel's cloak is a reddish brown with dark brown round the cuffs. It has circular decorations placed at intervals here and there. The angel's wings have been transformed to a combination of pale brown and purple with highlights of red and blue.

"Angelic Sleep" in the usual colored version is not especially scarce, but a rare variety does exist in white overglaze. There is no reliable pricing information on this model.

**25** Angelic Sleep

| | Price Range | |
|---|---|---|
| ☐ 25, trademark CM, 3½″ × 5″–5½″ ................. | 395.00 | 445.00 |
| ☐ 25, trademark Full Bee, 3½″ × 5″–5½″ ............ | 245.00 | 280.00 |
| ☐ 25, trademark Stylized Bee, 3½″ × 5″–5½″ ....... | 175.00 | 205.00 |
| ☐ 25, trademark 3-line mark, 3½″ × 5″–5½″ ........ | 95.00 | 115.00 |
| ☐ 25, trademark Goebel/V, 3½″ × 5″–5½″ .......... | 90.00 | 110.00 |
| ☐ 25, trademark Goebel, 3½″ × 5″–5½″ ............ | 80.00 | 95.00 |

## 26  CHILD JESUS

Wall font in current production. "Child Jesus" features a representation derived from the "Infant of Prague," a figure of the Christ Child standing with hands raised in benediction. It is natural that this subject, widely known in America but even more familiar in Europe, would be sketched by Berta Hummel.

There are two color varieties; one in which the child wears a bright red robe; in the other, pale blue. The blue-robed specimens are considerably less common. There are also some specimens of the larger size in which the bowl has a scalloped edge along the font. These, too, are scarce. A

**26** Child Jesus

combination of the blue robe with scalloped bowl would be quite a collector's item.

The composition itself is simple, its most striking feature the large modernistic halo worn by the Christ Child. In a rich yellow color, the halo is suspended from his head by means of wide flat rays with an almost pinwheel appearance. The robe is decorated with miniature Greek crosses (that is, crosses of which the bars are of equal length and cross at the center). In the red-robed specimens these crosses are gold, and in the blue specimens they are white.

| | Price Range | |
|---|---|---|
| ☐ 26/0, trademark CM, 2¾″ × 5¼″ .................. | 160.00 | 175.00 |
| ☐ 26/0, trademark Full Bee, 2¾″ × 5¼″ ............. | 110.00 | 120.00 |
| ☐ 26/0, trademark Stylized Bee, 2¾″ × 5¼″ ........ | 60.00 | 70.00 |
| ☐ 26/0, trademark 3-line mark, 2¾″ × 5¼″ .......... | 40.00 | 50.00 |
| ☐ 26/0, trademark Goebel/V, 2¾″ × 5¼″ ............. | 25.00 | 35.00 |
| ☐ 26/0, trademark Goebel, 2¾″ × 5¼″ .............. | 17.50 | 25.00 |
| ☐ 26/I, trademark CM, 3¼″ × 6″ .................... | 550.00 | 600.00 |
| ☐ 26/I, trademark Full Bee, 3¼″ × 6″ ............... | 350.00 | 385.00 |
| ☐ 26/I, trademark Stylized Bee, 3¼″ × 6″ ........... | 250.00 | 275.00 |

## 27 JOYOUS NEWS

Figurine and candleholder; only the figurine is in current production. The original version of "Joyous News" was a candleholder, but this feature was abandoned along the way. Never one of the more popular Hummels, this is a scarce model in all its varieties and trademarks. There is conflicting opinion as to whether "Joyous News" was produced with the 3-line trademark. It is sometimes found listed with 3-line mark in reference books, but this could well be the result of assumptions on the part of authors without tangible evidence. Until its existence is verified, its production will remain questionable. Just what its value might be, if a genuine specimen were offered for sale, is difficult to speculate. There is no doubt that it would be worth a minimum of $1000 as the other trademarks for which a number of specimens exist are in that price range or higher priced. How much higher than $1000 is anyone's guess.

"Joyous News" is a representation of a seated herald blowing a trumpet. He is not an earthly herald, but an angelic one, with a pair of wings sprouting from his back. The concept of herald angels was founded upon the medieval assumption that duties discharged on earth would have their counterparts, and counterpart officers to execute them, in heaven. The medieval herald actually originated in the ancient world but was most prevalent during the time of the Crusades. He rode the streets sounding his horn and informing the citizens of whatever the king or local official wished. Nothing unfavorable to the government was ever announced, unless it chanced to be a case of having no choice such as Huns banging down the walls of the city.

"Joyous News" is obviously reporting good news. The model is dressed in an outer garment combining shades of brown and salmon pink. Slung over his left shoulder is a green leather pouch. He wears a typically medieval pageboy type haircut and has brownish shoes tinged with red violet. His wings are a mixture of yellow, red, and dull blue. The trumpet is yellow and his cloak is adorned with small white stars. The figure does not rest upon a base but directly on the ground; the wings render him useless as a bookend, a task for which he might otherwise be well suited. There is a slight variation in the hairstyle between the larger and smaller versions, and, of course, the small one is readily identified by the presence of the candleholder. This is nothing more than a bowl, shaped in basket fashion and placed alongside the figure on the ground. It is suitable for use with a candle of very small size.

|  | Price Range | |
|---|---|---|
| ☐ 27/I, trademark CM, 2¾″ ...................... | 545.00 | 605.00 |
| ☐ 27/I, trademark Full Bee, 2¾″ .................... | 445.00 | 500.00 |
| ☐ 27/I, trademark Stylized Bee, 2¾″................ | RARE | |
| ☐ 27/III, trademark 4½″ × 4¾″ ..................... | 2195.00 | 2455.00 |
| ☐ 27/III, trademark Full Bee, 4½″ × 4¾″ ........... | 1795.00 | 1985.00 |
| ☐ 27/III, trademark Stylized Bee, 4½″ × 4¾″........ | 1095.00 | 1205.00 |
| ☐ 27/III, trademark Goebel/V, 4½″ × 4¾″ .......... | 255.00 | 290.00 |
| ☐ 27/III, trademark Goebel, 4½″ × 4¾″ ............ | 94.50 | 110.00 |

## 28  WAYSIDE DEVOTION

Figurine in current production. "Wayside Devotion" is similar in theme to #23 "Adoration," in that it features a pair of children at a religious shrine. The posing, detailing, coloration, and accessory details are quite different, however. It is a somewhat less sombre composition, with more vivid coloring. The prayer theme has been downplayed so that neither child has his hands at prayer. The central component is a tall, canopied wooden shrine into which is set a likeness of the crucifixion. The crucifixion is represented as a marble sculpture of moderate size, well executed in traditional style. At its base is a spray of reddish flowers with black centers. Placed at right angles to the supporting column are two roughly hewn wooden logs made into a makeshift fence on which the children sit. The boy plays a flute while the girl holds flowers. Two sheep are at their feet. The boy wears a wide-brimmed Alpine hat with a feather, a purple jacket, an orange shirt, and short green lederhosen. His shoes are brown and his white socks are ribbed with bands of coloring. The girl wears a red kerchief on her head, a green blouse, and a red skirt. Her brown shoes are tinted with tones of purple and her socks are similar to those of her companion. The flowers she holds are yellow with red centers. The sheep, pure white with additions of pale brown for tonal contour, are modeled in a naturalistic manner. The crucifixion's canopy, unlike the one in "Adoration," is not shingled, but composed of two lengths of wood mitred together. For its fine coloration (one of the best specimens of Hummel brushwork) and its realism as an Alpine scene, "Wayside Devotion" surely ranks among the best in Hummel Art.

"Wayside Devotion" was formerly known as "The Little Shepherd." It has been manufactured in two sizes, 28/II (basic height to the top of canopy is 7½″) and 28/III (8½″), with variations to be encountered in both. The rarest versions of this model are in cream overglaze, which were manufactured for a brief while and then discontinued.

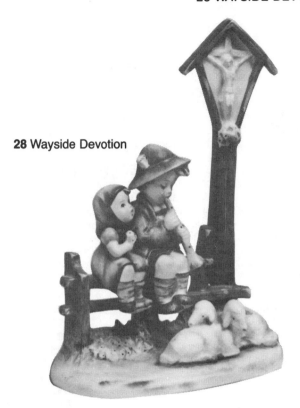

**28** Wayside Devotion

|  | **Price Range** | |
|---|---|---|
| ☐ 28/II, trademark CM, 7"–7½" .................... | 750.00 | 820.00 |
| ☐ 28/II, trademark Full Bee, 7"–7½" .............. | 450.00 | 470.00 |
| ☐ 28/II, trademark Stylized Bee, 7"–7½" .......... | 300.00 | 330.00 |
| ☐ 28/II, trademark 3-line mark, 7"–7½" ........... | 225.00 | 250.00 |
| ☐ 28/II, trademark Goebel/V, 7"–7½" .............. | 180.00 | 200.00 |
| ☐ 28/II, trademark Goebel, 7"–7½" ................ | 165.00 | 185.00 |
| ☐ 28/2, trademark CM, 7"–7½" ..................... | 500.00 | 550.00 |
| ☐ 28/2, trademark Full Bee, 7"–7½" ............... | 450.00 | 495.00 |
| ☐ 28/2, trademark Stylized Bee, 7"–7½" ........... | 350.00 | 385.00 |
| ☐ 28/2, trademark 3-line mark, 7"–7½" ............ | 250.00 | 270.00 |
| ☐ 28/2, trademark Goebel/V, 7"–7½" ............... | 180.00 | 195.00 |
| ☐ 28/III, trademark CM, 8½"–8¾" .................. | 900.00 | 990.00 |
| ☐ 28/III, trademark Full Bee, 8½"–8¾" ............ | 650.00 | 715.00 |
| ☐ 28/III, trademark Stylized Bee, 8½"–8¾" ........ | 500.00 | 550.00 |
| ☐ 28/III, trademark 3-line mark, 8½"–8¾" ......... | 400.00 | 440.00 |
| ☐ 28/III, trademark Goebel/V, 8½"–8¾" ............ | 280.00 | 310.00 |
| ☐ 28/III, trademark Goebel, 8½"–8¾" .............. | 231.00 | 250.00 |

## 29 GUARDIAN ANGEL

Wall font, closed edition. "Guardian Angel" is a holy water font composed of an angel kneeling atop a waterbowl. Although a very traditional representation, this item never proved to be very popular. This was due in part to the fact that the angel's wings are extremely fragile. Complaints were regularly received from retailers who reported shipments arriving with wings broken. It was taken out of production in the 1960s and, as a result of having been subsequently redesigned as #248 (see below) with strengthened wings, it is not likely that "Guardian Angel" will be reinstated into the line.

There are three basic sizes, designated as 29, 29/0, and 29/I, all of which are fairly uniform with little reported variation.

The angel kneels in a modified three-quarter profile, facing her right. She is wearing a long robe of crimson orange, studded with greek crosses, over an inner garment of bright yellow. Her hair is reddish brown. She holds her hands in prayer. It is interesting to note that the facial characteristics, unlike those common to most Hummel angels, suggests an adult woman rather than a young girl. In the redesigning as #248, the figure is transformed into a youth.

|  | Price Range | |
| --- | --- | --- |
| ☐ 29, trademark CM, 2½″ × 5¾″ | 1495.00 | 1645.00 |
| ☐ 29, trademark Full Bee, 2½″ × 5¾″ | 1295.00 | 1435.00 |
| ☐ 29, trademark Stylized Bee, 2½″ × 5¾″ | 795.00 | 885.00 |
| ☐ 29/0, trademark CM, 2⅞″ × 6″ | 1495.00 | 1655.00 |
| ☐ 29/0, trademark Full Bee, 2⅞″ × 6″ | 1295.00 | 1435.00 |
| ☐ 29/0, trademark Stylized Bee, 2⅞″ × 6″ | 1095.00 | 1205.00 |
| ☐ 29/I, trademark CM, 3″ × 6⅜″ | 1995.00 | 2195.00 |
| ☐ 29/I, trademark Full Bee, 3″ × 6⅜″ | 1695.00 | 1875.00 |
| ☐ 29/I, trademark Stylized Bee, 3″ × 6⅜″ | 1095.00 | 1205.00 |

## 30 A AND B  BA-BEE RINGS

Wall plaques (set of two) in current production. It may be stretching things slightly to refer to the "Ba-Bee Rings" as wall plaques; they are really more in the nature of novel ornaments designed for wall hanging. Both praise and criticism have been heaped upon them. Some have referred to the "Ba-Bee Rings" as the most novel, original, and charming creations ever produced by the factory. Others have said that they are too out-of-keeping with the Hummel tradition to deserve a place in the line. But good, bad, or indifferent, there is one indisputable thing to be said of them—they sell. "Ba-Bee Rings" are bought not only by Hummelites, but also by the general public, largely for the decoration of nurseries and children's rooms. For this purpose they are probably not surpassed by anything on the market. As for their status as works of art, that is for the collector to judge. It may, however, be pointed out to critics that they are entirely representative of Sister Hummel's work. She delighted in sketching heads of infants, and the "Ba-Bee Rings" rings are easily as fine a model of such sketches as the factory has produced.

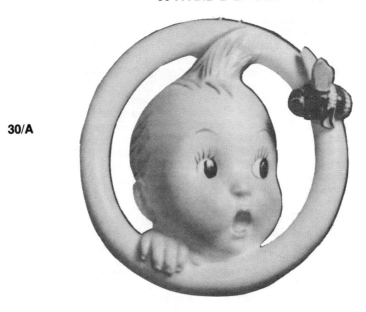

**30/A**

**30** Ba-Bee Rings

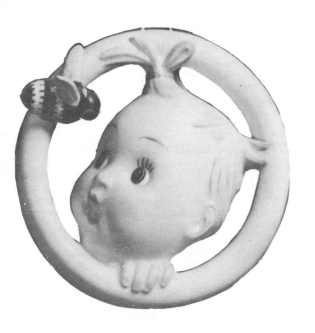

**30/B**

These are circular rings of medium thickness, open at the center, and half molded to give the impression of tubes. Within each is the head of a baby and one small hand resting upon the inner portion of the ring. Along the upper portion of the ring is perched a very naturalistically modeled bee; not the bee in Hummel's old trademarks but rather a big, handsome, three-dimensional creature who seems as lifelike as the porcelainmaker's art could render him. Thus the name "Ba-Bee."

"Ba-Bee Rings" are intended to be sold in sets of two, with a right and left model. They are essentially identical, except that the face in the left model faces toward the viewer's right, with the bee on the right hand side, and vice versa. There is not much description that can be given of the infant, but to observe that his hair (of which there is little) points upward in a shock at the top of his head. Its color varies from red blonde to almost pure red. His eyes are open in amazement at the bee. His lips are cherry red.

"Ba-Bee Rings" were formerly referred to as "Hummel Rings," a far less catchy designation. Only one size is now being produced, 30 A and B, measuring 4¾" × 5". There was at one time a larger size, 30/I A and B, whose dimensions were 5¼" × 6". A single set of "Ba-Bee Rings" is known to exist with the rings colored red. That these were not merely cast from the standard mold and painted differently is readily apparent from a design variation in the right model: The hair in front is tied in a bow and two strands of hair at the back touch the ring. It is not possible to give a price estimate for this rare type.

|  | Price Range | |
|---|---|---|
| ☐ 30/0, A and B, trademark CM, 4¾" × 5" . . . . . . . . . | 495.00 | 605.00 |
| ☐ 30/0, A and B, trademark Full Bee, 4¾" × 5" . . . . . | 345.00 | 390.00 |
| ☐ 30/0, A and B, trademark Stylized Bee, 4¾" × 5" | 175.00 | 200.00 |
| ☐ 30/0, A and B, trademark 3-line mark, 4¾" × 5" | 145.00 | 170.00 |
| ☐ 30/0, A and B, trademark Goebel/V, 4¾" × 5" . . . . | 115.00 | 140.00 |
| ☐ 30/0, A and B, trademark Goebel, 4¾" × 5" . . . . . . | 90.00 | 105.00 |
| ☐ 30/I, A and B, trademark CM, 5¼" × 6" . . . . . . . . . . . | RARE | |
| ☐ 30/I, A and B, trademark Full Bee, 5¼" × 6" . . . . . | RARE | |
| ☐ 30/I, A and B, trademark Stylized Bee, 5¼" × 6" | RARE | |

## 31 SILENT NIGHT WITH BLACK CHILD

Candleholder, discontinued. This group of four figures on a base with candleholder is one of very few controversial productions of the factory. It was introduced about 1935 and includes among the figures a representation of a black child which was intended to be a juvenile version of one of the Moorish wise men who brought gifts to the Christ Child. It was discontinued after producing a relatively limited number, possibly (an unconfirmed theory) because of the Nazi government's racial viewpoints. Consequently, it is a rare piece, with only one specimen definitely known to exist. There is no information on the quantity manufactured, nor has it been established whether any actually reached sale. It was reinstated later as #54 under the name "Silent Night" with the black child changed to white. "Silent Night with Black Child" represents an angel plus two additional figures and the Christ Child on a shallow partially scalloped base, intended to suggest straw of the stable, which includes the candle holder and measures 3½″ × 5″. The price stated below should be taken as a rough suggestion only; there are no sales upon which firm guidelines can be drawn.

**Price Range**

☐ 31, trademark CM, 3½″ × 5″ . . . . . . . . . . . . . . . . . . . . .     **6000.00 +**

## 32 LITTLE GABRIEL

Figurine in current production. "Little Gabriel" is a representation of the archangel sounding his trumpet. It has been produced in three basic sizes, each of which has a number of variations. The old series, now discontinued but not rare because it was long in production, comprised the size designators 32/0 and 32/I, the former standing 5″ to 5½″ and the latter 5¾″ to 6″. The current model, which uses the designation 32 without a slash, is being made in a 5″ size. "Little Gabriel" is considered one of the better standard sellers in the Hummel line.

**32** Little Gabriel

The model is one of Hummel's "basic brown," as they have come to be termed, but with sufficient color highlights to avoid monotony. Gabriel stands at attention, holding his trumpet with both hands to his lips. He wears a rust red short gown, shoes that may range from a slight beige to deep chocolate brown, and has a green pouch bag slung over his shoulder. His wings are pastel brown touched with yellow and have crimson tips. Gabriel's haircut is a pageboy at the sides, falling down in tousled strands at the front.

|  | Price Range | |
|---|---:|---:|
| ☐ 32/0, trademark CM, 5″–5½″ | 300.00 | 330.00 |
| ☐ 32/0, trademark Full Bee, 5″–5½″ | 180.00 | 200.00 |
| ☐ 32/0, trademark Stylized Bee, 5″–5½″ | 110.00 | 120.00 |
| ☐ 32/0, trademark 3-line mark, 5″–5½″ | 80.00 | 90.00 |
| ☐ 32, trademark Goebel/V, 5″–5½″ | 65.00 | 75.00 |
| ☐ 32, trademark Goebel, 5″–5½″ | 55.00 | 60.00 |
| ☐ 32/I, trademark CM, 5¾″–6″ | 1600.00 | 1760.00 |
| ☐ 32/I, trademark Full Bee, 5¾″–6″ | 1250.00 | 1375.00 |
| ☐ 32/I, trademark Stylized Bee, 5¾″–6″ | 100.00 | 1100.00 |
| ☐ 32/I, trademark 3-line mark, 5¾″–6″ | 900.00 | 990.00 |

## 33  JOYFUL

Ashtray in current production. Ashtrays have never been a major item in the Hummel line but the factory has designed them well. "Joyful" is certainly among the best. As is common with all Hummel ashtrays, the tray itself is plain without painting or modeling. It has a three-dimensional figure attached to it. When viewed as a whole, this model forms a cohesive composition.

There are really two figures in "Joyful": A youth strumming a mandolin, and a small canary bird who perches on the tray's rim. The boy wears a greyish gown with a texture which suggests wool, and a red collar. He wears brown shoes. The mandolin, sometimes referred to in descriptions as a guitar or lute, is white with green strings and brown highlights. The youth gazes down as if to study the movement of his fingers on the strings; his mouth is open slightly. The canary has its beak opened in song with an expression of true joy on its face. The tray is circular with a protruding cigarette rest, at the side opposite the figures compartmented for two cigarettes. There are some variations to be found in the design of the tray, but essentially this is a very basic model to collect. There is just a single size, a single size designator, and no old discontinued types.

| | | |
|---|---:|---:|
| ☐ 33, trademark CM, 3½″ × 6″ | 345.00 | 390.00 |
| ☐ 33, trademark Full Bee, 3½″ × 6″ | 175.00 | 200.00 |
| ☐ 33, trademark Stylized Bee, 3½″ × 6″ | 125.00 | 150.00 |
| ☐ 33, trademark 3-line mark, 3½″ × 6″ | 95.00 | 115.00 |
| ☐ 33, trademark Goebel/V, 3½″ × 6″ | 70.00 | 90.00 |
| ☐ 33, trademark Goebel, 3½″ × 6″ | 65.00 | 75.00 |

## 34 SINGING LESSON

Ashtray in current production. Reference works sometimes refer to "Singing Lesson" as similar to "Joyful" (see #33 above). Although the basic theme may be similar, sufficient changes have been made to qualify this as an entirely original model. Instead of sitting alongside the tray, the boy is seated on its rim. He no longer plays a mandolin nor any instrument. His attire is totally different from that worn in "Joyful" and the bird is not a canary but a black crow. While "Singing Lesson" might not evoke the same kind of sentimental emotion as its predecessor it is unquestionably as fine a piece of art.

The figure is smaller than in #33 and snappily dressed in a yellow plaid jacket, russet orange trousers, brown shoes with a mixture of purple, and a conical Tyrolean hat with a yellow feather. The hat is generally green at the crown with a brown brim. It is probably best, however, that we make no strict rules regarding color since "Singing Lesson" is often found, especially with the Crown and Full Bee marks, in color variations. The crow is an absolute delight; not too realistic but perfect for the setting. The cigarette rest is divided up into three compartments, the central one being somewhat longer.

**34** Singing Lesson

|  | Price Range | |
|---|---|---|
| ☐ 34, trademark CM, 3½″ × 6¼″ .................... | 345.00 | 390.00 |
| ☐ 34, trademark Full Bee, 3½″ × 6¼″ ............... | 205.00 | 235.00 |
| ☐ 34, trademark Stylized Bee, 3½″ × 6¼″ .......... | 145.00 | 170.00 |
| ☐ 34, trademark 3-line mark, 3½″ × 6¼″ ............ | 105.00 | 125.00 |
| ☐ 34, trademark Goebel/V, 3½″ × 6¼″ .............. | 95.00 | 115.00 |
| ☐ 34, trademark Goebel, 3½″ × 6¼″ ............... | 80.00 | 95.00 |

## 35 GOOD SHEPHERD

Wall font in current production. As with most Hummel wall fonts that have remained in production over a long period of time, the bowl has varied in design but the shepherd remains today just about as he was in the Crown trademark era. The standard "Good Shepherd" is 35/0, measuring 2½″ × 4¾″. Formerly, a larger version was also made, designated 35/I and measuring 2¾″ × 5¾″. This was discontinued in the mid to late 1960s, but there is talk of it being reinstated.

"Good Shepherd" is a likeness of a boy holding a shepherd's crook in his left hand. Slung across his back is a young sheep with its feet dangling down upon each of his shoulders. He holds onto the sheep's front leg with

**35** Good Shepherd

his right hand. Another sheep stands at his feet and gazes upward; the eyes of the two sheep appear to meet. The shepherd is dressed in a long blue-white gown set with a number of small knobs which at first may mistakenly be presumed to be buttons, but are merely decorations. Two flowers appear near the shepherd's feet. The shepherd's expression has been termed angelic, and there is also a touch of weariness.

|  | Price Range | |
|---|---|---|
| ☐ 35/0, trademark CM, 2½″ × 4¾″ . . . . . . . . . . . . . . . . | 150.00 | 170.00 |
| ☐ 35/0, trademark Full Bee, 2½″ × 4¾″ . . . . . . . . . . . . | 75.00 | 85.00 |
| ☐ 35/0, trademark Stylized Bee, 2½″ × 4¾″ . . . . . . . | 35.00 | 45.00 |
| ☐ 35/0, trademark 3-line mark, 2½″ × 4¾″ . . . . . . . . . | 30.00 | 40.00 |
| ☐ 35/0, trademark Goebel/V, 2½″ × 4¾″ . . . . . . . . . . . | 25.00 | 35.00 |
| ☐ 35/0, trademark Goebel, 2½″ × 4¾″ . . . . . . . . . . . . . | 17.50 | 25.00 |
| ☐ 35/I, trademark CM, 2¾″ × 5¾″ . . . . . . . . . . . . . . . . . | 350.00 | 670.00 |
| ☐ 35/I, trademark Full Bee, 2¾″ × 5¾″ . . . . . . . . . . . . | 300.00 | 320.00 |
| ☐ 35/I, trademark Stylized Bee, 2¾″ × 5¾″ . . . . . . . . | 150.00 | 170.00 |

## 36 ANGEL WITH FLOWERS

Wall font in current production. "Angel with Flowers" is often, and more correctly, referred to as "Child with Flowers." It is presently made in only one size, 3¼″ × 4¼″. Earlier, it was also available in a slightly larger version measuring 3½″ × 4½″. Because the sizes were so similar, it was considered unnecessary to continue offering both.

The figure does not kneel, nor is she at prayer. She sits, with her legs forward, atop the font, holding a flower, which she gazes at pensively. She wears a blue cloak and black shoes; her hair is a light red sandy color. She has red lips and a reddish tint to her cheek. The accessory decoration of this model is simple. It is comprised of three reddish flowers growing upon pale green stems. There is a flowerless stem behind the figure. The font itself is a half oval, basically white with subdued fluting at the upper front. The figure's oversized halo is a creamy beige with suggestions of yellow.

| ☐ 36/0, trademark CM, 3¼″ × 4¼″ . . . . . . . . . . . . . . . . | 135.00 | 160.00 |
|---|---|---|
| ☐ 36/0, trademark Full Bee, 3¼″ × 4¼″ . . . . . . . . . . . . | 95.00 | 115.00 |
| ☐ 36/0, trademark Stylized Bee, 3¼″ × 4¼″ . . . . . . . | 40.00 | 55.00 |
| ☐ 36/0, trademark 3-line mark, 3¼″ × 4¼″ . . . . . . . . . | 30.00 | 45.00 |
| ☐ 36/0, trademark Goebel/V, 3¼″ × 4¼″ . . . . . . . . . . . | 20.00 | 35.00 |
| ☐ 36/0, trademark Goebel, 3¼″ × 4¼″ . . . . . . . . . . . . . | 17.50 | 25.00 |
| ☐ 36/I, trademark CM, 3½″ × 4½″ . . . . . . . . . . . . . . . . . | 345.00 | 390.00 |
| ☐ 36/I, trademark Full Bee, 3½″ × 4½″ . . . . . . . . . . . . | 305.00 | 325.00 |
| ☐ 36/I, trademark Stylized Bee, 3½″ × 4½″ . . . . . . . . | 155.00 | 180.00 |
| ☐ 36/I, trademark 3-line mark, 3½″ × 4½″ . . . . . . . . . . | 95.00 | 115.00 |

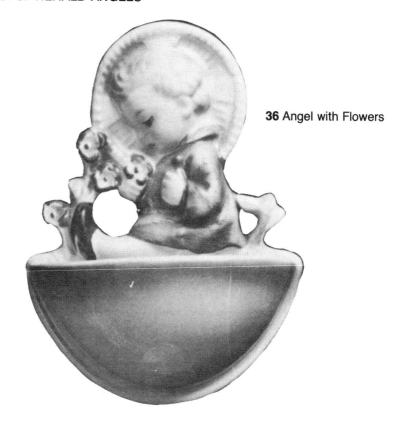

**36** Angel with Flowers

## 37 HERALD ANGELS

Candleholder in current production. A number of variations are to be noted in "Herald Angels," sometimes referred to as "Angel Band." The composition consists of three angels who are seated around the candle receptacle playing musical instruments. One plays an accordion, another a mandolin or lute, and the third a trumpet. They are arranged in a clockwise fashion; that is, the outstretched legs of each one points toward the back of the next angel. Because of the small physical dimensions of this model, a certain clarity is sacrificed both in the sculpturing and coloration but, unless one is a trained observer, it is not likely to be noticed. The angels all wear similar cloaks: one colored pastel blue, the second brown, and the third white with areas of green and brown highlights. The trumpeter carries a green satchel over her shoulder. All have sandy blonde hair worn in somewhat different fashions. The wings are brown with red tips and traces of blue or green.

These figures were also manufactured separately as candleholders, as #38, #39, and #40 (see below), with the intent that they would be utilized in sets. Among the smallest Hummels, their appeal has extended into the realm of collectors of miniatures.

The chief variation between old and new specimens is in the candle receptacle. This is shaped as a bowl and placed at the center of the circle formed by the three figures. In the early version the bowl is considerably taller than in the later version. Also, occasionally there is a variation in placement of the figures. The normal clockwise arrangement is accordion player, mandolin player, and horn player, but, as the figures were modeled and cast separately from the base and had to later be attached, the order could easily be changed intentionally or unintentionally. Specimens now being manufactured have a somewhat wider base than previously.

|  | Price Range | |
|---|---|---|
| ☐ 37, trademark CM, 2¾″ × 4″ ..................... | 550.00 | 600.00 |
| ☐ 37, trademark Full Bee, 2¾″ × 4″ ................ | 280.00 | 310.00 |
| ☐ 37, trademark Stylized Bee, 2¾″ × 4″ ........... | 160.00 | 175.00 |
| ☐ 37, trademark 3-line mark, 2¾″ × 4″ ............. | 120.00 | 135.00 |
| ☐ 37, trademark Goebel/V, 2¾″ × 4½″ ............. | 94.00 | 100.00 |
| ☐ 37, trademark Goebel, 2¾″ × 4½″ ............... | 84.00 | 95.00 |

## 38 ANGEL, JOYOUS NEWS WITH LUTE

Candleholder in current production. "Joyous News with Lute" is an adaptation of one of the figures in #37 "Herald Angels." There are three sizes which vary only slightly from each other. The candle receptacle in the smallest of these three sizes measures 0.6 centimeters. In the other two sizes it has a diameter of one full centimeter. The Roman numeral before the size designator represents the size of the candle receptacle, I being the smaller and III being the larger. #38 is generally sold in conjunction with #39 and #40 as a set, but will occasionally be sold separately.

|  | Price Range | |
|---|---|---|
| ☐ I/38/0, trademark CM, 2″–2¼″ ................... | 120.00 | 140.00 |
| ☐ I/38/0, trademark Full Bee, 2″–2¼″ ............. | 85.00 | 105.00 |
| ☐ I/38/0, trademark Stylized Bee, 2″–2¼″ ......... | 50.00 | 70.00 |
| ☐ I/38/0, trademark 3-line mark, 2″–2¼″ .......... | 25.00 | 40.00 |
| ☐ III/38/0, trademark CM, 2″–2¼″ ................. | 145.00 | 170.00 |
| ☐ III/38/0, trademark Full Bee, 2″–2¼″ ........... | 95.00 | 115.00 |
| ☐ III/38/0, trademark Stylized Bee, 2″–2¼″ ....... | 55.00 | 70.00 |
| ☐ III/38/0, trademark 3-line mark, 2″–2¼″ ........ | 35.00 | 50.00 |
| ☐ III/38/0, trademark Goebel/V, 2″–2¼″ .......... | 30.00 | 45.00 |
| ☐ III/38/0, trademark Goebel, 2″–2¼″ ............. | 23.00 | 30.00 |
| ☐ III/38/I, trademark CM, 2¾″ .................... | 295.00 | 335.00 |
| ☐ III/38/I, trademark Full Bee, 2¾″ ............... | 245.00 | 280.00 |
| ☐ III/38/I, trademark Stylized Bee, 2¾″ ........... | 145.00 | 170.00 |
| ☐ III/38/I, trademark 3-line mark, 2¾″ ............ | 120.00 | 140.00 |

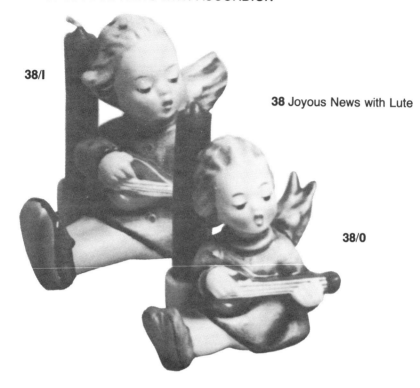

**38/I**

**38** Joyous News with Lute

**38/0**

## 39 ANGEL, JOYOUS NEWS WITH ACCORDION

Candleholder in current production. "Joyous News with Accordion" (a concertina, but Hummel terminology, once having taken root, carries on forever) is, like #38, an adaptation of one of the figures from the larger candleholder "Herald Angels."

| | Price Range | |
|---|---|---|
| ☐ I/39/0, trademark CM, 2″–2¼″................... | 125.00 | 140.00 |
| ☐ I/39/0, trademark Full Bee, 2″–2¼″.............. | 100.00 | 110.00 |
| ☐ I/39/0, trademark Stylized Bee, 2″–2¼″......... | 55.00 | 60.00 |
| ☐ I/39/0, trademark 3-line mark, 2″–2¼″.......... | 40.00 | 45.00 |
| ☐ III/39/0, trademark CM, 2″–2¼″................. | 130.00 | 145.00 |
| ☐ III/39/0, trademark Full Bee, 2″–2¼″............. | 100.00 | 110.00 |
| ☐ III/39/0, trademark Stylized Bee, 2″–2¼″........ | 55.00 | 60.00 |
| ☐ III/39/0, trademark 3-line mark, 2″–2¼″.......... | 45.00 | 50.00 |
| ☐ III/39/0, trademark Goebel/V, 2″–2¼″............ | 35.00 | 40.00 |
| ☐ III/39/0, trademark Goebel, 2″–2¼″.............. | 23.00 | 28.00 |
| ☐ III/39/I, trademark CM, 2¾″..................... | 250.00 | 275.00 |

**39** Joyous News with Accordion

|  | Price Range | |
|---|---|---|
| ☐ III/39/I, trademark Full Bee, 2¾" ................. | 220.00 | 240.00 |
| ☐ III/39/I, trademark Stylized Bee, 2¾" ............. | 150.00 | 165.00 |
| ☐ III/39/I, trademark 3-line mark, 2¾" .............. | 120.00 | 130.00 |

## 40 ANGEL, JOYOUS NEWS WITH TRUMPET

Candleholder in current production. Like #38 and #39, "Joyous News with Trumpet" is a separately produced version of a figure appearing in #37 "Herald Angels." She is sometimes called "Angel with Horn." This figurine must not be confused with the rare discontinued candleholder of #27 "Joyous News." It is important to note the difference in the placement of the candle receptacle in both specimens. In #27 it is attached to the angel's left knee and in #40 it is attached to the angel's right hip. This difference may mean thousands of dollars to the buyer or seller.

|  | Price Range | |
|---|---|---|
| ☐ I/40/0, trademark CM, 2"–2¼" .................... | 125.00 | 150.00 |
| ☐ I/40/0, trademark Full Bee, 2"–2¼" ............. | 75.00 | 95.00 |

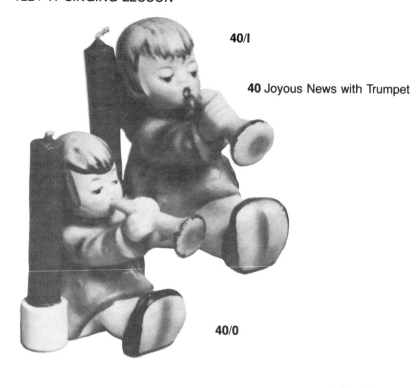

**40/I**

**40** Joyous News with Trumpet

**40/0**

| | Price Range | |
|---|---|---|
| ☐ I/40/0, trademark Stylized Bee, 2″–2¼″ .......... | 40.00 | 55.00 |
| ☐ I/40/0, trademark 3-line mark, 2″–2¼″ ........... | 35.00 | 50.00 |
| ☐ III/40/0, trademark CM, 2″–2¼″ ................. | 120.00 | 135.00 |
| ☐ III/40/0, trademark Full Bee, 2″–2¼″ ............ | 95.00 | 115.00 |
| ☐ III/40/0, trademark Stylized Bee, 2″–2¼″......... | 55.00 | 70.00 |
| ☐ III/40/0, trademark 3-line mark, 2″–2¼″ ......... | 35.00 | 50.00 |
| ☐ III/40/0, trademark Goebel/V, 2″–2¼″ ........... | 25.00 | 40.00 |
| ☐ III/40/0, trademark Goebel, 2″–2¼″ .............. | 23.00 | 32.00 |
| ☐ III/40/I, trademark CM, 2¾″...................... | 255.00 | 280.00 |
| ☐ III/40/I, trademark Full Bee, 2¾″ ................ | 195.00 | 225.00 |
| ☐ III/40/I, trademark Stylized Bee, 2¾″ ............ | 145.00 | 170.00 |
| ☐ III/40/I, trademark 3-line mark, 2¾″ ............. | 45.00 | 60.00 |

## 41  SINGING LESSON

Figurine, closed number designation. This model, of which no examples have been recorded, is said to be based upon #34 "Singing Lesson Ashtray," without the ashtray (refer to #34 above for details). Produced in 1935, it was apparently never placed on sale for reasons which can only be speculated. The piece may have been rejected by the convent.

## 42 GOOD SHEPHERD

Figurine in current production. "Good Shepherd" figurine is similar in design to #35 "Good Shepherd Holy Water Font," except that it represents a somewhat older child. The subject is known to have been a favorite of Sister Hummel's, and though she may not have personally observed shepherds in the Bavarian countryside, there were surely images of them to be found in Seissen.

This is an uncomplicated composition. The shepherd cradles a sheep over his shoulders. In his left hand he holds a crook. He gazes down upon a sheep at his feet. The usual coloration of the shepherd's robe, which reaches down to his shoes, is a pale rust, though listings invariably refer to it merely as brown. The figure was at one time produced with a pale violet robe; such specimens, when genuine, are extremely scarce and command stiff premiums. Regardless of the color, the robe is decorated with a series of Green crosses.

An earlier version of "Good Shepherd" was in 7½" size (actually 7¼" to 7¾"); this has been discontinued and is quite rare. By all means, when buying a specimen of the larger size, **take a careful measurement**. If it stands less than 7½" high, it is probably best regarded as an oversized example of the standard size with a fraudulently altered designator. There is also the danger of color counterfeiting. Beware!

**42** Good Shepherd

|  | Price Range | |
|---|---|---|
| ☐ 42/0, trademark CM, 6¼″–6½″ .................. | 300.00 | 330.00 |
| ☐ 42/0, trademark Full Bee, 6¼″–6½″ .............. | 250.00 | 275.00 |
| ☐ 42/0, trademark Stylized Bee, 6¼″–6½″ ......... | 150.00 | 165.00 |
| ☐ 42/0, trademark 3-line mark, 6¼″–6½″ ........... | 85.00 | 95.00 |
| ☐ 42, trademark Goebel/V, 6¼″..................... | 75.00 | 85.00 |
| ☐ 42, trademark Goebel, 6¼″...................... | 66.00 | 72.00 |
| ☐ 42/I, trademark CM, 7¼″–7¾″ .................. | 5000.00 | 5500.00 |
| ☐ 42/I, trademark Full Bee, 7¼″–7¾″ .............. | 3200.00 | 3520.00 |
| ☐ 42/I, trademark Stylized Bee, 7¼″–7¾″ .......... | 3000.00 | 3300.00 |

## 43  MARCH WINDS

Figurine in current production. Stylistically one of the finest Hummel figures, "March Winds" represents a boy bundled against the elements, and being buffeted by a strong wind. It is a perfect presentation of a well-known situation. Every detail in the model reflects the wind's effects, as the youth looks over his shoulder, wondering whether to continue or return home. (An interesting note to point out is that the kind of winters known to Sister Hummel in Bavaria are comparable to those of North Dakota, Minnesota, and northern New England.)

**43** March Winds

The boy thrusts his hands deep into his trouser pockets. He wears long woolen leggings, but they seem to be of little help. His scarf, the top of his woolen hat, and the shock of hair that falls from his hat are blown backward by the wind. He plants his feet solidly and inclines slightly forward to avoid suffering the same fate. The only bit of mystery about this figure is why he ventured out-of-doors without a coat, jacket, or some kind of substantial protection. He wears nothing over his shirt. The shirt is white with red plaid striping. The knee length trousers are a deep rich green. His hat and scarf are red, his hair a sandy brown, and his shoes a walnut color.

There is one slight difference between old and new versions of "March Winds," recognizable only by paying particular attention. In the early type, the boy's gaze is fixed backward with his head turned more to the shoulder, while in currently produced specimens he faces directly toward the observer when viewed in profile. There are minor size variations, the older specimens generally being a fraction of an inch taller.

| | Price Range | |
|---|---|---|
| ☐ 43, trademark CM, 4¾"–5½"..................... | 245.00 | 280.00 |
| ☐ 43, trademark Full Bee, 4¾"–5½" .............. | 145.00 | 170.00 |
| ☐ 43, trademark Stylized Bee, 4¾"–5½" .......... | 90.00 | 110.00 |
| ☐ 43, trademark 3-line mark, 4¾"–5½" ........... | 70.00 | 90.00 |
| ☐ 43, trademark Goebel/V, 4¾"–5½".............. | 60.00 | 75.00 |
| ☐ 43, trademark Goebel, 4¾"–5½"................ | 55.00 | 65.00 |

## 44A  CULPRITS

Lamp base in current production. "Culprits" was the first lamp base in the Hummel line. It was produced to test public reaction in 1935 (the copyright date is incised into the base) followed the next year by its companion piece, #44B "Out of Danger" (see below). Though often sold as a pair, #44A and #44B are separate productions.

"Culprits" depicts a boy clinging to the trunk of a tree. He is looking down at a schnauzer type dog on the ground which is attempting to climb the tree. It would be easy to draw a mistaken conclusion about the subject of this work. It might appear that the boy has climbed the tree in an effort to escape the dog. This, however, is not the case. He climbed the tree for the purpose of dislodging one of its apples. He has succeeded in doing this and an apple is on the ground. The boy is caught in a predicament and pondering his next move, while his arms and legs begin to grow weary of clasping the tree trunk. A handsome composition, "Culprits" is enameled in rich colors. The apple thief wears a blue shirt with red plaid striping, red short pants, ankle length yellow socks, and brown shoes. His hair is sandy blonde. The dog is mahogany-colored. Older specimens of "Culprits" have a half-inch larger base with a small opening at the top for the electrical switch.

**44A** Culprits

| | Price Range | |
|---|---|---|
| ☐ 44/A, trademark CM, 8½"–9½" ................. | 550.00 | 600.00 |
| ☐ 44/A, trademark Full Bee, 8½"–9½" ............. | 400.00 | 440.00 |
| ☐ 44/A, trademark Stylized Bee, 8½"–9½" ........ | 350.00 | 385.00 |
| ☐ 44/A, trademark 3-line mark, 8½"–9½" .......... | 255.00 | 280.00 |
| ☐ 44/A, trademark Goebel/V, 8½"–9½" ............ | 225.00 | 247.00 |
| ☐ 44/A, trademark Goebel, 8½"–9½" .............. | 205.00 | 225.00 |

## 44B  OUT OF DANGER

Lamp base in current production. "Out of Danger" is the companion piece to #44A "Culprits" (see above). Measurements and general design are the same except that in "Out of Danger" a girl, rather than a boy, is stuck in the tree. She climbed the tree in an effort to escape a dog similar in appearance to the one in "Culprits." Although the dog does not appear to be frightening, he grips one of her shoes between his teeth. She sits on a tree branch viewing him with an expression of mild disgust. She wears a rust

**44B** Out of Danger

red bonnet tied beneath the chin, a bluish-white dress, with a red plaid apron, and only one shoe. A few pink flowers with black centers adorn the tree, while other flowers, somewhat larger and of a reddish-brown color, grow at its base.

This model was copyrighted in 1936 and is often sold as a set in combination with #44A. The same general comments made about #44A can be applied to it.

| | Price Range | |
|---|---|---|
| ☐ 44/B, trademark CM, 8½″–9½″ .................. | 495.00 | 605.00 |
| ☐ 44/B, trademark Full Bee, 8½″–9½″ ............. | 395.00 | 445.00 |
| ☐ 44/B, trademark Stylized Bee, 8½″–9½″ ......... | 345.00 | 390.00 |
| ☐ 44/B, trademark 3-line mark, 8½″–9½″ .......... | 275.00 | 320.00 |
| ☐ 44/B, trademark Goebel/V, 8½″–9½″ ............ | 220.00 | 245.00 |
| ☐ 44/B, trademark Goebel, 8½″–9½″ .............. | 205.00 | 230.00 |

## 45 MADONNA WITH HALO

Figurine in current production. Of the numerous Hummel Madonnas, #45 "Madonna with Halo" and its counterpart, #46 "Madonna without Halo" (see next page) are probably the best known and the best sellers. These are sometimes referred to as "Madonna Praying," but the more traditional designations (and those now adopted by the factory) of "Madonna with

Halo" and "Madonna without Halo" are considerably less confusing. These models are each made in three basic sizes with numerous variations. The tallest "Madonna with Halo" is more than 16 inches, making this the largest model in the line next to the oversized versions of "Apple Tree Boy," "Apple Tree Girl" and "Merry Wanderer." Both the 45/III and the 45/III/6 models were discontinued in 1982.

Many experiments have been made in the coloring of this figure. It is also produced in a white overglaze. The two larger sizes were temporarily discontinued during the 3-line mark era, but reinstated in the late 1970s. It could hardly be said that they were ever off the market, as production had been so extensive prior to discontinuation that dealers had no difficulty supplying specimens to their customers.

The model is stylized with the Madonna or Virgin shown as a young woman with reddish hair. Regardless of the robe color, the base is always yellow, except, of course, in the white or cream overglaze version.

The price of this figure is extremely low in light of its size. Compare its price with the 10 inch "Apple Tree Girl" (listed at $500 in the 1981 Hummel catalogue). This is surely due to its lack of complexity, as it can be produced with fewer molds than can other large works. The "W" following the size designator indicates white overglaze.

**45** Madonna with Halo

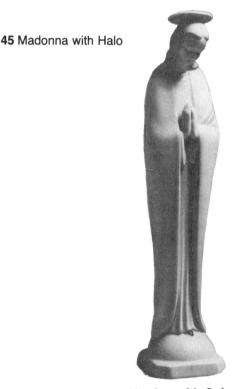

**White Version**

**Version with Color**

| | Price Range | |
|---|---|---|
| ☐ 45/0, trademark CM, 10¼"–10½" .............. | 200.00 | 220.00 |
| ☐ 45/0, trademark Full Bee, 10¼"–10½" .......... | 125.00 | 145.00 |
| ☐ 45/0, trademark Stylized Bee, 10¼"–10½" ...... | 75.00 | 85.00 |
| ☐ 45/0, trademark 3-line mark, 10¼"–10½" ........ | 65.00 | 75.00 |
| ☐ 45/0, trademark Goebel/V, 10¼"–10½" .......... | 47.00 | 55.00 |
| ☐ 45/0, trademark Goebel, 10¼"–10½" .......... | 42.00 | 52.00 |
| ☐ 45/0/W, trademark CM, 10¼"–10½" ............ | 65.00 | 70.00 |
| ☐ 45/0/W, trademark Full Bee, 10¼"–10½" ........ | 100.00 | 110.00 |
| ☐ 45/0/W, trademark Stylized Bee, 10¼"–10½".... | 80.00 | 90.00 |
| ☐ 45/0/W, trademark 3-line mark, 10¼"–10½" ..... | 55.00 | 60.00 |
| ☐ 45/0/W, trademark Goebel/V, 10¼"–10½" ...... | 35.00 | 40.00 |
| ☐ 45/0/W, trademark Goebel, 10¼"–10½" ........ | 26.50 | 32.50 |
| ☐ 45/I, trademark CM, 11¼"–12" .................. | 150.00 | 165.00 |
| ☐ 45/I, trademark Full Bee, 11¼"–12" .............. | 110.00 | 120.00 |
| ☐ 45/I, trademark Stylized Bee, 11¼"–12" ......... | 90.00 | 100.00 |
| ☐ 45/I, trademark 3-line mark, 11¼"–12" .......... | 55.00 | 60.00 |
| ☐ 45/I, trademark Goebel/V, 11¼"–12" ............ | 40.00 | 45.00 |
| ☐ 45/I, trademark Goebel, 11¼"–12" .............. | 31.50 | 36.50 |
| ☐ 45/1/W, trademark CM, 11¼"–12" ................ | 250.00 | 275.00 |
| ☐ 45/1/W, trademark Full Bee, 11¼"–12" .......... | 180.00 | 200.00 |
| ☐ 45/1/W, trademark Stylized Bee, 11¼"–12" ...... | 120.00 | 135.00 |
| ☐ 45/1/W, trademark 3-line mark, 11¼"–12" ....... | 90.00 | 100.00 |
| ☐ 45/I/W, trademark Goebel/V, 11¼"–12" .......... | 85.00 | 95.00 |
| ☐ 45/I/W, trademark Goebel, 11¼"–12" ............ | 31.50 | 36.50 |
| ☐ 45/III, trademark CM, 16¼"–16¾" .............. | 500.00 | 550.00 |
| ☐ 45/III, trademark Full Bee, 16¼"–16¾" .......... | 350.00 | 385.00 |
| ☐ 45/III, trademark Stylized Bee, 16¼"–16¾"...... | 150.00 | 165.00 |
| ☐ 45/III, trademark 3-line mark, 16¼"–16¾" ....... | 125.00 | 137.50 |
| ☐ 45/III, trademark Goebel/V, 16¼"–16¾ .......... | 120.00 | 135.00 |
| ☐ 45/III, trademark Goebel, 16¼"–16¾" .......... | 105.00 | 115.00 |
| ☐ 45/III/W, trademark CM, 16¼"–16¾"............. | 250.00 | 275.00 |
| ☐ 45/III/W, trademark Full Bee, 16¼"................ | 150.00 | 165.00 |
| ☐ 45/III/W, trademark Stylized Bee, 16¼"–16¾" ... | 110.00 | 120.00 |
| ☐ 45/III/W, trademark 3-line mark, 16¼"–16¾"..... | 95.00 | 105.00 |
| ☐ 45/III/W, trademark Goebel/V, 16¼"–16¾"....... | 85.00 | 95.00 |
| ☐ 45/III/W, trademark Goebel, 16¼"–16¾"......... | 70.00 | 80.00 |

## 46 MADONNA WITHOUT HALO

Figurine in current production. Identical to the preceding except without a halo. Sometimes found incorrectly marked 45. Both the color and white versions of the largest size, models 46/III and 46/III/W, were temporarily discontinued.

| | | |
|---|---|---|
| ☐ 46/0, trademark CM, 10¼"–10½" ................ | 220.00 | 240.00 |
| ☐ 46/0, trademark Full Bee, 10¼"–10½" ........... | 150.00 | 165.00 |
| ☐ 46/0, trademark Stylized Bee, 10¼"–10½" ...... | 100.00 | 110.00 |
| ☐ 46/0, trademark 3-line mark, 10¼"–10½" ........ | 75.00 | 85.00 |

**46** Madonna without Halo

| | Price Range | |
|---|---|---|
| ☐ 46/0, trademark Goebel/V, 10¼″–10½″ . . . . . . . . . | **55.00** | **60.00** |
| ☐ 46/0, trademark Goebel, 10¼″–10½″ . . . . . . . . . . . | **42.00** | **47.50** |
| ☐ 46/0/W, trademark CM, 10¼″–10½″ . . . . . . . . . . . . | **65.00** | **71.50** |
| ☐ 46/0/W, trademark Full Bee, 10¼″–10½″ . . . . . . . | **125.00** | **137.50** |
| ☐ 46/0/W, trademark Stylized Bee, 10¼″–10½″ . . . . | **100.00** | **110.00** |
| ☐ 46/0/W, trademark 3-line mark, 10¼″–10½″ . . . . . | **80.00** | **90.00** |
| ☐ 46/0/W, trademark Goebel/V, 10¼″–10½″ . . . . . . . | **55.00** | **60.00** |
| ☐ 46/0/W, trademark Goebel, 10¼″–10½″ . . . . . . . . . | **45.00** | **50.00** |
| ☐ 46/I, trademark CM, 11¼″–12″ . . . . . . . . . . . . . . . . . | **270.00** | **300.00** |
| ☐ 46/I, trademark Full Bee, 11¼″–12″ . . . . . . . . . . . . . | **180.00** | **200.00** |
| ☐ 46/I, trademark Stylized Bee, 11¼″–12″ . . . . . . . . | **125.00** | **137.50** |
| ☐ 46/I, trademark 3-line mark, 11¼″–12″ . . . . . . . . . | **100.00** | **110.00** |
| ☐ 46/I, trademark Goebel/V, 11¼″–12″ . . . . . . . . . . . | **62.50** | **68.75** |
| ☐ 46/I, trademark Goebel, 11¼″–12″ . . . . . . . . . . . . . | **52.50** | **57.50** |
| ☐ 46/1/W, trademark CM, 11¼″–12″ . . . . . . . . . . . . . | **160.00** | **175.00** |
| ☐ 46/1/W, trademark Full Bee, 11¼″–12″ . . . . . . . . . | **120.00** | **132.00** |
| ☐ 46/1/W, trademark Stylized Bee, 11¼″–12½″ . . . . | **100.00** | **110.00** |
| ☐ 46/1/W, trademark 3-line mark, 11¼″–12½″ . . . . . | **75.00** | **85.00** |
| ☐ 46/1/W, trademark Goebel/V, 11¼″–12″ . . . . . . . . . | **41.50** | **45.50** |
| ☐ 46/I/W, trademark Goebel, 11¼″–12″ . . . . . . . . . . . | **31.50** | **35.00** |
| ☐ 46/III, trademark CM, 16¼″–16¾″ . . . . . . . . . . . . . | **550.00** | **500.00** |
| ☐ 46/III, trademark Full Bee, 16¼″–16¾″ . . . . . . . . . | **350.00** | **385.00** |

| | Price Range | |
|---|---|---|
| ☐ 46/III, trademark Stylized Bee, 16¼″–16¾″ ...... | 250.00 | 275.00 |
| ☐ 46/III, trademark 3-line mark, 16¼″–16¾″ ....... | 200.00 | 220.00 |
| ☐ 46/III, trademark Goebel/V, 16¼″–16¾″ ......... | 150.00 | 165.00 |
| ☐ 46/III, trademark Goebel, 16¼″–16¾″ ........... | 105.00 | 115.00 |
| ☐ 46/III/W, trademark CM, 16¼″–16¾″.............. | 275.00 | 300.00 |
| ☐ 46/III/W, trademark Full Bee, 16¼″–16¾″........ | 175.00 | 190.00 |
| ☐ 46/III/W, trademark Stylized Bee, 16¼″–16¾″ ... | 125.00 | 137.00 |
| ☐ 46/III/W, trademark 3-line mark, 16¼″–16¾″..... | 100.00 | 110.00 |
| ☐ 46/III/W, trademark Goebel/V, 16¼″–16¾″....... | 85.00 | 95.00 |
| ☐ 46/III/W, trademark Goebel, 16¼″–16¾″......... | 70.00 | 80.00 |

## 47  GOOSE GIRL

Figurine in current production. One of the more familiar Hummels, "Goose Girl" is considered to be representative of the factory's best work. It has certainly been among the best sellers over a long period of time. The demand for this piece is such that even today, long after Hummel discontinued multi-size production of many of its old designs, "Goose Girl" continues to be made in three editions: 47/3/0, 47/0, and 47/II.

**47** Goose Girl

The subject is a pair of hungry-looking geese approaching a young girl who holds her hands behind her back as if teasing the birds before feeding them. The geese are exceptionally well modeled. They can be compared favorably with natural history designs of the chief European porcelain factories of the 18th century. The girl wears a white short-sleeved blouse, a dark brown jumper, a yellow apron with red polka dots, and brown clogs. She has a red kerchief with white polka dots pulled around her head. The base of this model is textured and colored to represent grass. The largest size, 47/II, was restyled around 1972.

|  | Price Range | |
|---|---|---|
| ☐ 47/3/0, trademark CM, 4"–4¼" | 315.00 | 345.00 |
| ☐ 47/3/0, trademark Full Bee, 4"–4¼" | 180.00 | 200.00 |
| ☐ 47/3/0, trademark Stylized Bee, 4"–4¼" | 125.00 | 140.00 |
| ☐ 47/3/0, trademark 3-line mark, 4"–4¼" | 85.00 | 105.00 |
| ☐ 47/3/0, trademark Goebel/V, 4"–4¼" | 75.00 | 86.00 |
| ☐ 47/3/0, trademark Goebel, 4"–4¼" | 66.00 | 73.00 |
| ☐ 47/0, trademark CM, 4¾"–5¼" | 445.00 | 498.00 |
| ☐ 47/0, trademark Full Bee, 4¾"–5¼" | 365.00 | 408.00 |
| ☐ 47/0, trademark Stylized Bee, 4¾"–5¼" | 185.00 | 215.00 |
| ☐ 47/0, trademark 3-line mark, 4¾"–5¼" | 120.00 | 135.00 |
| ☐ 47/0, trademark Goebel/V, 4¾"–5¼" | 105.00 | 125.00 |
| ☐ 47/0, trademark Goebel, 4¾"–5¼" | 90.00 | 105.00 |
| ☐ 47/II, trademark CM, 7"–7½" | 995.00 | 1095.00 |
| ☐ 47/II, trademark Full Bee, 7"–7½" | 675.00 | 750.00 |
| ☐ 47/II, trademark Stylized Bee, 7"–7½" | 395.00 | 445.00 |
| ☐ 47/II, trademark 3-line mark, 7"–7½" | 275.00 | 315.00 |
| ☐ 47/II, trademark Goebel/V, 7"–7½" | 245.00 | 280.00 |
| ☐ 47/II, trademark Goebel, 7"–7½" | 200.00 | 225.00 |

## 48 MADONNA PLAQUE

Wall plaque in current production. This plaque, a simple but strong study of the Madonna and Child, has been manufactured in three sizes, the largest of which is discontinued. Model #48/V, the largest wall plaque ever produced by the factory, was never manufactured extensively and is rare today, regardless of what trademark it carries.

Though the basic version is colored, "Madonna Plaque" was made in cream overglaze during the early years of production. These specimens are extremely scarce. The Madonna wears an orange gown and has reddish brown hair. Neither she nor the child has a halo, but beams of light radiate from the head of each. The child is shown as a very young infant. The figures are in medium bas-relief and set into an arched recess. The frame is generally cream overglaze.

| | | |
|---|---|---|
| ☐ 48/0, trademark CM, 3¼" × 4¼" | 320.00 | 350.00 |
| ☐ 48/0/W, trademark CM, 3¼" × 4¼" | 170.00 | 185.00 |
| ☐ 48/0, trademark Full Bee, 3¼" × 4¼" | 120.00 | 145.00 |
| ☐ 48/0/W, trademark Full Bee, 3¼" × 4¼" | 80.00 | 90.00 |
| ☐ 48/0, trademark Stylized Bee, 3¼" × 4¼" | 62.50 | 68.75 |

**48** Madonna

|  | Price Range | |
| --- | ---: | ---: |
| ☐ 48/0, trademark 3-line mark, 3¼" × 4¼"......... | 52.50 | 57.75 |
| ☐ 48/0, trademark Goebel/V, 3¼" × 4¼"........... | 62.50 | 68.75 |
| ☐ 48/0, trademark Goebel, 3¼" × 4¼".............. | 52.50 | 57.75 |
| ☐ 48/II, trademark CM, 4¾" × 5¾"................. | 750.00 | 825.00 |
| ☐ 48/II/W, trademark CM, 4¾" × 5¾" ............. | 1550.00 | 1700.00 |
| ☐ 48/II, trademark Full Bee, 4¾" × 5¾"............ | 400.00 | 440.00 |
| ☐ 48/II/W, trademark Full Bee, 4¾" × 5¾" ......... | 1500.00 | 1650.00 |
| ☐ 48/II, trademark Stylized Bee, 4¾" × 5¾" ....... | 200.00 | 220.00 |
| ☐ 48/II, trademark 3-line mark, 4¾" × 4¾"......... | 135.00 | 150.00 |
| ☐ 48/II, trademark Goebel/V, 4¾" × 5¾"........... | 110.00 | 120.00 |
| ☐ 48/II, trademark Goebel, 4¾" × 5¾".............. | 94.50 | 105.00 |
| ☐ 48/V, trademark CM, 8¾" × 10¾"................ | 1700.00 | 1870.00 |
| ☐ 48/V/W, trademark CM, 8¾" × 10¾".............. | 2000.00 | 2200.00 |
| ☐ 48/V, trademark Full Bee, 8¾" × 10¾" .......... | 1500.00 | 1650.00 |
| ☐ 48/V/W, trademark Full Bee, 8¾" × 10¾" ....... | 1250.00 | 1375.00 |
| ☐ 48/V, trademark Stylized Bee, 8¾" × 10¾" ...... | 800.00 | 1100.00 |

## 49  TO MARKET

Figurine in current production. "To Market" is a figure showing a boy and girl standing together on an oval base. The girl is carrying a basket over her left arm and both are gazing ahead with an attitude of wonderment.

No less than four editions have been manufactured of this popular design, of which three continue in production. Model #49, 6¼"–6½", has been discontinued. In the smallest size, 49/3/0, the girl's basket is always empty. In the larger sizes it contains a bottle. The largest size is moderately scarce with the old trademarks. It was taken out of production for a number of years during the 1960s and 1970s and this set off a flurry of collecting activity.

The girl wears a white short-sleeved blouse, a charcoal grey or black jumper, yellow apron with red polka dots, brown shoes, white and orange socks. She has red ribbons in her braided hair. Her companion has a brownish jacket, white shirt, brown lederhosen with suspenders, tall tan hiking boots, and socks that are chiefly pastel gray. The girl has reddish hair and the boy has blonde. Slight differences will be observed in the positioning of the heads.

**49** To Market

| | Price Range | |
|---|---|---|
| ☐ 49/3/0, trademark CM, 4″ | **295.00** | **330.00** |
| ☐ 49/3/0, trademark Full Bee, 4″ | **220.00** | **250.00** |
| ☐ 49/3/0, trademark Stylized Bee, 4″ | **145.00** | **175.00** |
| ☐ 49/3/0, trademark 3-line mark, 4″ | **95.00** | **120.00** |
| ☐ 49/3/0, trademark Goebel/V, 4″ | **80.00** | **100.00** |
| ☐ 49/3/0, trademark Goebel, 4″ | **77.50** | **85.00** |
| ☐ 49/0, trademark CM, 5″–5½″ | **495.00** | **555.00** |
| ☐ 49/0, trademark Full Bee, 5″–5½″ | **295.00** | **335.00** |
| ☐ 49/0, trademark Stylized Bee, 5″–5½″ | **195.00** | **225.00** |
| ☐ 49/0, trademark 3-line mark, 5″–5½″ | **145.00** | **175.00** |
| ☐ 49/0, trademark Goebel/V, 5″–5½″ | **125.00** | **155.00** |
| ☐ 49/0, trademark Goebel, 5″–5½″ | **115.00** | **125.00** |
| ☐ 49/I, trademark CM, 6¼″–6½″ | **1495.00** | **1655.00** |
| ☐ 49/I, trademark Full Bee, 6¼″–6½″ | **1100.00** | **1350.00** |
| ☐ 49/I, trademark Stylized Bee, 6¼″–6½″ | **595.00** | **665.00** |
| ☐ 49/I, trademark 3-line mark, 6¼″–6½″ | **395.00** | **445.00** |
| ☐ 49, trademark Goebel/V, 6¼″–6½″ | **295.00** | **335.00** |
| ☐ 49, trademark Goebel, 6¼″–6½″ | **240.00** | **270.00** |

## 50  VOLUNTEERS

Figurine in current production. "Volunteers" has been produced in three basic sizes, of which there are a number of variations. The standard model,

**50** Volunteers

50/0, is generally listed at 5½" but will be found in sizes ranging up to 6". The smaller version, 50/2/0, is listed at 5" but smaller specimens going down to 4¾" will be noted. Of the larger 6½" version, 50/I, examples up to 7" are found. There is also a discontinued version, 50, which generally measures 7" and may be reinstated, although at the time of this writing, no definite word has been received. The latest Hummel catalogue lists only 50/0, 50/2/0, and 50/I.

"Volunteers" is a figure of two boys marching off to war. One is playing a drum while the other is holding a toy rifle over his shoulder. They march in synchronized step, each having a leg extended forward. The rifle bearer looks upward and ahead, while the drummer looks down at his drum. If they seem to be doing the goose step, one need only be reminded that this model was introduced during the Nazi regime, when infantry marching of this type was in vogue. They both wear short trousers. The rifle bearer has a green jacket and brown military style cap. The other boy wears a white shirt and is hatless. The drum is red and white.

|  | Price Range | |
|---|---|---|
| ☐ 50/2/0, trademark CM, 4¾"–5" ................. | 500.00 | 550.00 |
| ☐ 50/2/0, trademark Full Bee, 4¾"–5" ............. | 400.00 | 440.00 |
| ☐ 50/2/0, trademark Stylized Bee, 4¾"–5" ........ | 180.00 | 200.00 |
| ☐ 50/2/0, trademark 3-line mark, 4¾"–5" .......... | 125.00 | 137.50 |
| ☐ 50/2/0, trademark Goebel/V, 4¾"–5" ............. | 115.00 | 125.00 |
| ☐ 50/2/0, trademark Goebel, 4¾"–5" .............. | 105.00 | 115.00 |
| ☐ 50/0, trademark CM, 5½"–6" .................... | 750.00 | 825.00 |
| ☐ 50/0, trademark Full Bee, 5½"–6" ............... | 500.00 | 550.00 |
| ☐ 50/0, trademark Stylized Bee, 5½"–6" ........... | 300.00 | 330.00 |
| ☐ 50/0, trademark 3-line mark, 5½"–6" ............ | 200.00 | 220.00 |
| ☐ 50/0, trademark Goebel/V, 5½"–6" .............. | 175.00 | 192.50 |
| ☐ 50/0, trademark Goebel, 5½"–6" ................ | 136.50 | 150.00 |
| ☐ 50, trademark CM, 7" ........................... | 1500.00 | 1650.00 |
| ☐ 50, trademark Full Bee, 7" ...................... | 1000.00 | 1100.00 |
| ☐ 50/I, trademark CM, 6½"–7" ..................... | 1100.00 | 1210.00 |
| ☐ 50/I, trademark Full Bee, 6½"–7" ................ | 850.00 | 935.00 |
| ☐ 50/I, trademark Stylized Bee, 6½"–7" ........... | 500.00 | 550.00 |
| ☐ 50/I, trademark 3-line mark, 6½"–7" ............. | 350.00 | 385.00 |
| ☐ 50/I, trademark Goebel/V, 6½"–7" ............... | 250.00 | 275.00 |
| ☐ 50/I, trademark Goebel, 6½"–7" ................. | 240.00 | 265.00 |

## 51 VILLAGE BOY

Figurine in current production. "Village Boy" varies considerably in size. The figure is described in lists and literature at anywhere from 3¾" to 8", but there are in fact only four basic sizes. All others are variations.

The largest size, 51/I, was discontinued in the mid to late 1950s, then reinstated late in the 1970s. Current Hummel lists give the size as 7¼". 51/I is not likely to be found with the 3-line trademark used during the years it was out of production. It is found in lists with the Stylized Bee mark although an actual specimen theoretically should not exist because this

**51** Village Boy

number was taken out of production before the use of the Stylized Bee mark.

During the 1930s, when this model was introduced, a number of Hummels carried similar baskets, the intention being that purchasers would fill them with artificial flowers or other decorations. While current versions of these early models still retain the baskets, they have since been deemed unnecessary and phased out on new productions. It was once thought this might be a selling point, but Hummels are so avidly bought today as objects d'art and collectors items that such accessories are no longer needed.

"Village Boy" is a figure of a smug-looking youth holding an empty wicker basket over one arm.

The boy is dressed in a brown jacket with suggestions of olive, deep brown short trousers, black boots, white socks edged in dark brown, and a white shirt with brown suspenders. A red bow tie completes the outfit. "Village Boy" holds his jacket lapel with his left hand while his right hand is thrust into his trouser pocket. His head is turned three-quarters to the viewer's right.

| | Price Range | |
|---|---|---|
| ☐ 51/3/0, trademark CM, 4″ ......................... | **145.00** | **175.00** |
| ☐ 51/3/0, trademark Full Bee, 4″ ................... | **95.00** | **115.00** |
| ☐ 51/3/0, trademark Stylized Bee, 4″ .............. | **170.00** | **200.00** |

| | Price Range | |
|---|---|---|
| ☐ 51/3/0, trademark 3-line mark, 4".................. | **45.00** | **75.00** |
| ☐ 51/3/0, trademark Goebel/V, 4".................... | **40.00** | **60.00** |
| ☐ 51/3/0, trademark Goebel, 4"..................... | **39.00** | **46.00** |
| ☐ 51/2/0, trademark CM, 5"......................... | **125.00** | **155.00** |
| ☐ 51/2/0, trademark Full Bee, 5".................... | **145.00** | **175.00** |
| ☐ 51/2/0, trademark Stylized Bee, 5" ............... | **95.00** | **120.00** |
| ☐ 51/2/0, trademark 3-line mark, 5"................. | **60.00** | **80.00** |
| ☐ 51/2/0, trademark Goebel/V, 5".................... | **55.00** | **75.00** |
| ☐ 51/2/0, trademark Goebel, 5"..................... | **55.00** | **61.00** |
| ☐ 51/0, trademark CM, 6"–6¾" ..................... | **405.00** | **445.00** |
| ☐ 51/0, trademark Full Bee, 6"–6¾"................. | **275.00** | **315.00** |
| ☐ 51/0, trademark Stylized Bee, 6"–6¾" ........... | **170.00** | **200.00** |
| ☐ 51/0, trademark 3-line mark, 6"–6¾"............. | **145.00** | **160.00** |
| ☐ 51/0, trademark Goebel/V, 6"–6¾" .............. | **95.00** | **115.00** |
| ☐ 51/0, trademark Goebel, 6"–6¾" ................. | **88.00** | **95.00** |
| ☐ 51/I, trademark CM, 7¼"–8"...................... | **695.00** | **775.00** |
| ☐ 51/I, trademark Full Bee, 7¼"–8" ................ | **395.00** | **445.00** |
| ☐ 51/I, trademark Stylized Bee, 7¼"–8"............ | **295.00** | **335.00** |
| ☐ 51/I, trademark Goebel/V, 7¼"–8"................ | **115.00** | **140.00** |
| ☐ 51/I, trademark Goebel, 7¼"–8".................. | **110.00** | **125.00** |

## 52 GOING TO GRANDMA'S

Figurine in current production. There are three basic sizes with numerous variations and a number of style changes in this old favorite. Model #52, 6¼", has been discontinued, while the other two models are still in production. 51/I was discontinued for a time, but has been reinstated.

"Going to Grandma's" is a model of two girls of about equal size, whose arms are laden with various gifts. One girl carries a cornucopia, filled with candies or similar articles in the smaller models, but empty in the large size. It was considered a good receptacle for artificial flowers. The other girl holds a dish filled with soup or porridge from which the handle of a spoon protrudes, and a basket containing a bottle of wine or mineral water. The first girl has a red dress, white socks, and red shoes. Her companion is wearing a white dress with green sleeves and ornamented with red semicircles. Her shoes are dark brown and her socks are tinted with brown. Both wear red hair ribbons. The dish is green, its contents a pastel pinkish-brown.

It is important to note the base. All large size models have a rectangular base, as do the earlier small models. However, the later versions of 52/0 have an oval base. It is not difficult, even without inspection of the mark, to distinguish the age of a specimen of 52/0.

| | Price Range | |
|---|---|---|
| ☐ 52/0, trademark CM, 4½"–5"..................... | **500.00** | **550.00** |
| ☐ 52/0, trademark Full Bee, 4½"–5"................ | **400.00** | **440.00** |
| ☐ 52/0, trademark Stylized Bee, 4½"–5" ........... | **250.00** | **275.00** |
| ☐ 52/0, trademark 3-line mark, 4½"–5"............. | **150.00** | **165.00** |
| ☐ 52/0, trademark Goebel/V, 4½"–5" .............. | **110.00** | **120.00** |

**52** Going to Grandma's

| | Price Range | |
|---|---|---|
| ☐ 52/0, trademark Goebel, 4½″–5″ ................. | 100.00 | 110.00 |
| ☐ 52/I, trademark CM, 6″–6¼″ ..................... | 1300.00 | 1450.00 |
| ☐ 52/I, trademark Full Bee, 6″–6¼″ ................ | 800.00 | 880.00 |
| ☐ 52/I, trademark Stylized Bee, 6″–6¼″ ........... | 600.00 | 660.00 |
| ☐ 52/I, trademark Goebel/V, 6″–6¼″ ............... | 500.00 | 550.00 |
| ☐ 52/I, trademark Goebel, 6″–6¼″ ................. | 240.00 | 265.00 |
| ☐ 52, trademark CM, 6¼″ ......................... | 1500.00 | 1650.00 |

## 53 JOYFUL

Figurine in current production. "Joyful" is a figure, seated without a base, of a girl playing a stringed musical instrument which looks like a banjo. She wears a violet gown decorated with red polka dots and a red collar. Her shoes are red and her hair is sandy blonde.

In addition to its production as a figurine this design is also sold as a candy box (see #III/53 below). Since its inception "Joyful" has been man-ufactured in one basic size only, but variations have been considerable—up to three-quarters of an inch.

| | | |
|---|---|---|
| ☐ 53, trademark CM, 3½″–4¼″ .................... | 295.00 | 330.00 |
| ☐ 53, trademark Full Bee, 3½″–4¼″ .............. | 145.00 | 175.00 |

53 Joyful

| | Price Range | |
|---|---|---|
| ☐ 53, trademark Stylized Bee, 3½"–4¼" .......... | **75.00** | **95.00** |
| ☐ 53, trademark 3-line mark, 3½"–4¼ ............. | **55.00** | **75.00** |
| ☐ 53, trademark Goebel/V, 3½–4¼" ............... | **50.00** | **70.00** |
| ☐ 53, trademark Goebel, 3½–4¼" ................ | **44.00** | **56.00** |

## III/53  JOYFUL

Candy box in current production. The candy box version of "Joyful" in a bowl style was introduced in 1936. The bottom is rounded duplicating the shape of a cereal bowl. The lid is concave and fits inside the rim of the dish. It was altered in 1964 to a jar style and the original type was discontinued. The jar style has flat sides and a flat bottom. The lid is flush with the sides of the jar and of the same diameter. It is produced today in jar style only. The bowl type measures 6½", the jar 5¾".

| | Price Range | |
|---|---|---|
| ☐ III/53, trademark CM, 6½" ....................... | **295.00** | **335.00** |
| ☐ III/53, trademark Full Bee, 6½" ................. | **175.00** | **195.00** |
| ☐ III/53, trademark Stylized Bee, 5¾" or 6½" ...... | **95.00** | **115.00** |

**Candy Bowl**          **Candy Jar**

|  | Price Range | |
| --- | --- | --- |
| ☐ III/53, trademark 3-line mark, 5¾"................ | 65.00 | 85.00 |
| ☐ III/53, trademark Goebel/V, 5¾".................. | 45.00 | 58.00 |
| ☐ III/53, trademark Goebel, 5¾".................... | 44.00 | 51.00 |

## 54  SILENT NIGHT

Candleholder in current production. "Silent Night" is the revised version of #31 (see above) in which the child on the left was black—the first and only example of a black child in the Hummel series which has now been made white.

There are some color variations in this multi-figure grouping, but generally the colors are as follows: Figure #1 wears a blue gown over which is a yellow apron with check design. Her shoes are a brownish orange. Figure #2 wears a green gown tinted with a creamy beige. Figure #3 is that of the Christ Child and he is wrapped in violet swaddling clothes. Figure #4 of a winged angel is dressed in a light red gown. She has gray wings with touches of red and blue. The composition rests upon a textured base designed to represent straw.

A very rare example of this model has been verified with the Crown trademark and a black child, the same as in #31. In this specimen, however, she is wearing shoes instead of being shoeless as the black figure is in #31. Since it is the only known sample, its value cannot be accurately determined.

**54** Silent Night

| | Price Range | |
|---|---|---|
| ☐ 54, trademark CM, 3½″ × 4¾..................... | **520.00** | **575.00** |
| ☐ 54, trademark Full Bee, 3½″ × 4¾ ............... | **300.00** | **330.00** |
| ☐ 54, trademark Stylized Bee, 3½″ × 4¾″ ......... | **220.00** | **240.00** |
| ☐ 54, trademark 3-line mark, 3½″ × 4¾″........... | **135.00** | **150.00** |
| ☐ 54, trademark Goebel/V, 3½″ × 4¾″............. | **110.00** | **120.00** |
| ☐ 54, trademark Goebel, 3½″ × 4¾″ ............... | **100.00** | **110.00** |

## 55 SAINT GEORGE

Figurine in current production. Formerly entitled "St. George and the Dragon," this uncharacteristic Hummel is a presentation of a theme long classified as a favorite in religious art. Whether the medieval legend of St. George slaying the dragon is strictly true, or whether it might have been a bear or other less sensational animal, is hardly important. St. George became a folk hero of Britain. Artists there and across the European continent painted, sculpted, etched, and otherwise portrayed his likeness for nearly a thousand years. Paintings of St. George and the Dragon are found in illuminated manuscripts as old as the 10th century A.D. It was not until the late Middle Ages (1350–1500), however, that this legend and its pictorial representations reached great heights.

Nearly everyone engaged in religious art has taken a go at St. George at one time or another. It would have been a very natural subject for Sister Hummel's brush or pencil. Obviously she drew a St. George, as #55 is based upon her conception. However, no record of her drawing has yet been discovered. Its whereabouts is known only to Goebel, which has not released any information. Robert Miller, one of the foremost Hummel authorities among the ranks of private collectors, speculates that the drawing might be on a church wall which has hindered publishers from reproducing it.

There is mixed emotion about the Hummel "St. George." It is missing from many collections whose owners prefer to concentrate on the child theme figurine. On the other hand, "St. George" appeals to some buyers who are not Hummel enthusiasts. Neither its subject nor its modeling are suggestive of typical Hummels. Those unfamiliar with the piece discover its origins only by inspecting the underside of the base.

The model shows the Saint on horseback, raising his sword in preparation to strike a blow upon the dragon. The dragon writhes on the sculpture's base beneath the hooves of St. George's rearing horse. This is the typical presentation of the subject, not changed very much in a thousand years. The chief criticism against this version is its rather static appearance that is without the feeling of motion demanded by its subjects. St. George seems to be merely posing, and his horse too closely resembles a chess piece. The dragon is the most effectively presented component of the piece. Another shortcoming, though it may be chalked up to artistic license, is that the Saint is too large in proportion to his horse, and his upper body is too long for his legs. The coloration is basically white with highlights ranging from pastel brown to reddish brown. Only one size has been produced. There has been no style revision but early specimens are found with a dark-colored saddle, which has changed to pastel in recent and current production.

|  | Price Range | |
|---|---|---|
| ☐ 55, trademark CM, 6¾"............................ | 895.00 | 995.00 |
| ☐ 55, trademark Full Bee, 6¾" ...................... | 495.00 | 555.00 |
| ☐ 55, trademark Stylized Bee, 6¾"................. | 295.00 | 335.00 |
| ☐ 55, trademark 3-line mark, 6¾" .................. | 195.00 | 215.00 |
| ☐ 55, trademark Goebel/V, 6¾".................... | 165.00 | 195.00 |
| ☐ 55, trademark Goebel, 6¾"...................... | 144.00 | 165.00 |

## 56/A CULPRITS

Figurine in current production. The figurine version of the lamp base issued as #44/A (see above), to which the reader should refer for information on design and coloration. Issued as a companion piece to #56/B "Out of Danger." At the outset of production "Culprits" was marked 56, not 56/A. This model has been restyled.

|  | Price Range | |
|---|---|---|
| ☐ 56/A, trademark CM, 6¼″–6¾″ ................. | 500.00 | 550.00 |
| ☐ 56/A, trademark Full Bee, 6¼″–6¾″ ............. | 300.00 | 330.00 |
| ☐ 56/A, trademark Stylized Bee, 6¼″–6¾″ ......... | 155.00 | 170.00 |
| ☐ 56/A, trademark 3-line mark, 6¼″–6¾″ ......... | 135.00 | 150.00 |
| ☐ 56/A, trademark Goebel/V, 6¼″–6¾″............. | 120.00 | 135.00 |
| ☐ 56/A, trademark Goebel, 6¼″–6¾″.............. | 105.00 | 115.00 |

## 56/B OUT OF DANGER

Figurine in current production. The figurine version of the lamp base issued as #44/B (see above), to which the reader should refer for information on design and coloration. The restyling has resulted in the girl's eyes being downcast instead of fully open.

**56/B** Out of Danger

**56/A**

**56/B**

| ☐ 56/B, trademark CM, 6¼″–6¾″ ................. | 495.00 | 555.00 |
|---|---|---|
| ☐ 56/B, trademark Full Bee, 6¼″–6¾″ ............. | 295.00 | 335.00 |
| ☐ 56/B, trademark Stylized Bee, 6¼″–6¾″ ......... | 150.00 | 175.00 |
| ☐ 56/B, trademark 3-line mark, 6¼″–6¾″ .......... | 130.00 | 155.00 |

**Price Range**

☐ 56/B, trademark Goebel/V, 6¼"–6¾"............. **115.00** **140.00**
☐ 56/B, trademark Goebel, 6¼"–6¾".............. **105.00** **120.00**

## 57  CHICK GIRL

Figurine in current production. "Chick Girl" was formerly known as "Little Chick Girl." If a list were ever made of the ten all-time Hummel favorite designs, "Chick Girl" would surely be included among them. There are three size designations of which two, 57/0 and 57/1, are still in production. Model 7, 4⅜", is a discontinued designation and such specimens are rare but do exist. Price information on this model cannot be reported since verification has not been received. There is a distinct variation in design to be noted between the large and small size. In the former, three chicks are found in the girl's basket, but there are only two in the smaller version. There are also some differences in the base underside, with use of the quarter, plain, and doughnut styles recorded.

"Chick Girl" is a figure of a girl kneeling to place a bit of food in the mouth of an anxious-looking chick. The basket containing additional chicks is at her left side resting on the model's base. She wears a white short-sleeved dress, a reddish maroon vest, and a skirt in a mixture of pink and pale

**57** Chick Girl

salmon. Her shoes are brown. All of the chicks are bright canary yellow with brown wingtips. A red flower with four petals and a black center is on the ground in front of the basket.

|  | Price Range | |
|---|---|---|
| ☐ 57/0, trademark CM, 3½"........................ | 300.00 | 320.00 |
| ☐ 57/0, trademark Full Bee, 3½" .................. | 175.00 | 185.00 |
| ☐ 57/0, trademark Stylized Bee, 3½" .............. | 125.00 | 135.00 |
| ☐ 57/0, trademark 3-line mark, 3½" ............... | 95.00 | 105.00 |
| ☐ 57/0, trademark Goebel/V, 3½"................... | 75.00 | 85.00 |
| ☐ 57/0, trademark Goebel, 3½".................... | 66.00 | 75.00 |
| ☐ 57/I, trademark CM, 4¼" ....................... | 500.00 | 520.00 |
| ☐ 57/I, trademark Full Bee, 4¼" .................. | 300.00 | 320.00 |
| ☐ 57/I, trademark Stylized Bee, 4¼"............... | 200.00 | 215.00 |
| ☐ 57/I, trademark 3-line mark, 4¼" ............... | 150.00 | 160.00 |
| ☐ 57/I, trademark Goebel/V, 4¼" ................. | 110.00 | 120.00 |
| ☐ 57/I, trademark Goebel, 4¼" ................... | 110.00 | 120.00 |

## III/57  CHICK GIRL

Candy box in current production. The candy box version of "Chick Girl" was introduced in 1936 in a bowl style. The bottom is rounded duplicating the shape of a cereal bowl. The lid is concave and fits inside the rim of the dish. It was altered in 1964 to a jar style, and the original was discontinued. The jar style has flat sides and a flat bottom. The lid is flush with the sides of the jar and of the same diameter. It is produced today in the jar style only. The bowl type measures 6¼", the jar 5".

| ☐ III/57, trademark CM, 6¼"....................... | 495.00 | 555.00 |
|---|---|---|
| ☐ III/57, trademark Full Bee, 6¼".................. | 445.00 | 500.00 |
| ☐ III/57, trademark Stylized Bee, 5" or 6¼" ........ | 135.00 | 160.00 |
| ☐ III/57, trademark 3-line mark, 5"................. | 115.00 | 140.00 |
| ☐ III/57, trademark Goebel/V, 5" ................... | 105.00 | 115.00 |
| ☐ III/57, trademark Goebel, 5" ..................... | 100.00 | 115.00 |

## 58  PLAYMATES

Figurine in current production. "Playmates," originally known as "Just Friends," shows a boy and three pet rabbits. It is a simple figure which becomes complex only because of variations in design and color from the smaller to larger size. It may be a cause for wonder what the motivation might be to produce two separate sizes varying only one-quarter inch.

Situations similar to this occur with a number of other Hummels. The best explanation that can be given for their manufacture is that by increasing the size of a figure by one-quarter inch in height, the overall size of the figure also changes. When viewed side by side, the two models appear to vary much more than one-quarter inch in size. If the size difference between the two figures was even so much as an inch in height, the smaller figure would in fact be half the overall size of the larger. This is not simply a case of optical illusion.

**58** Playmates

The boy wears a blue jacket, green trousers, brown boots, and yellow socks. He has a green Tyrolean cap decorated with a pastel green band and a red, white, and blue feather. In the small version, 58/0, the ears of one of his rabbits point outward at a right angle from the figure. In the larger version they stand slightly more upward. Two of the three rabbits are contained in a wickerwork basket, which in the smaller size is solid brown with light brown highlights, and in the larger contains areas of yellow, green, and red. There are other slight differences which may be imperceptible to casual observation, such as the boy's head is turned just a bit more to his left in the smaller version. Quarter, plain, and donut style bases have added to the variation.

|  | Price Range | |
|---|---|---|
| ☐ 58/0, trademark CM, 4″ | 300.00 | 335.00 |
| ☐ 58/0, trademark Full Bee, 4″ | 175.00 | 195.00 |
| ☐ 58/0, trademark Stylized Bee, 4″ | 125.00 | 145.00 |
| ☐ 58/0, trademark 3-line mark, 4″ | 95.00 | 115.00 |
| ☐ 58/0, trademark Goebel/V, 4″ | 75.00 | 85.00 |
| ☐ 58/0, trademark Goebel, 4″ | 66.00 | 75.00 |
| ☐ 58/I, trademark CM, 4¼″ | 500.00 | 550.00 |
| ☐ 58/I, trademark Full Bee, 4¼″ | 300.00 | 330.00 |
| ☐ 58/I, trademark Stylized Bee, 4¼″ | 200.00 | 220.00 |
| ☐ 58/I, trademark 3-line mark, 4¼″ | 150.00 | 170.00 |
| ☐ 58/I, trademark Goebel/V, 4¼″ | 110.00 | 130.00 |
| ☐ 58/I, trademark Goebel, 4¼″ | 100.00 | 110.00 |

## III/58  PLAYMATES

Candy box in current production. The candy box version of "Playmates" was introduced in 1936 in a bowl style at 6¾". The bottom is rounded, duplicating the shape of a cereal bowl. The lid is concave and fits inside the rim of the dish. This model was altered in 1964 to a jar style, the original having been discontinued. This version has flat sides and a flat bottom. The lid is flush with the sides of the jar and of the same diameter. It measures 5½".

|  | Price Range | |
|---|---|---|
| ☐ III/58, trademark CM, 6¾" | 495.00 | 555.00 |
| ☐ III/58, trademark Full Bee, 6¾" | 445.00 | 500.00 |
| ☐ III/58, trademark Stylized Bee, 5½"–6¾" | 135.00 | 160.00 |
| ☐ III/58, trademark Goebel/V, 5½" | 105.00 | 125.00 |
| ☐ III/58, trademark Goebel, 5½" | 100.00 | 115.00 |

## 59  SKIER

Figurine in current production. That Hummel should issue a figurine of a skier is natural enough, since the factory is situated very close to some of the prime skiing areas of the world. One might wonder why, however, there are no models of bobsledders, skaters, or other participants in winter sports. The only explanation could be that Sister Hummel failed to include them in her sketches.

59 Skier

As originally issued, "Skier" had wooden balance rods. These were later altered to metal or plastic. The intrepid Alpinist, ready to tackle the steepest slope, wears a dark blue or black ski suit, red muffler, red woolen cap, brown shoes, and reddish gloves or mittens. If the concept of a 6- or 7-year-old skiing seems extraordinary, it should be realized that in Bavaria children are frequently taught to ski at an even earlier age. The figure stands on a sloping base colored and textured to suggest a snowbank. There is one basic edition only, but the size can vary by as much as an inch.

|  | Price Range | |
|---|---|---|
| ☐ 59, trademark CM, 5″–6″ | 400.00 | 440.00 |
| ☐ 59, trademark Full Bee, 5″–6″ | 300.00 | 330.00 |
| ☐ 59, trademark Stylized Bee, 5″–6″ | 150.00 | 170.00 |
| ☐ 59, trademark 3-line mark, 5″–6″ | 125.00 | 145.00 |
| ☐ 59, trademark Goebel/V, 5″–6″ | 100.00 | 120.00 |
| ☐ 59, trademark Goebel, 5″–6″ | 88.00 | 100.00 |

## 60/A AND B FARM BOY & GOOSE GIRL

Set of bookends in current production. This bookend set features representations of #47 and #68, (see above and below) each mounted on a wooden base. The reader should refer to the listings for these numbers for descriptions of the designs. This set was introduced in September, 1936, and has proved a popular item in the Hummel line.

**60/B** Goose Girl          **60/A** Farm Boy

| | Price Range | |
|---|---|---|
| ☐ 60/A and 60/B, trademark CM, 4¾"............... | 995.00 | 1105.00 |
| ☐ 60/A and 60/B, trademark Full Bee, 4¾"......... | 645.00 | 720.00 |
| ☐ 60/A and 60/B, trademark Stylized Bee, 4¾".... | 445.00 | 498.00 |
| ☐ 60/A and 60/B, trademark 3-line mark, 4¾"...... | 345.00 | 390.00 |
| ☐ 60/A and 60/B, trademark Goebel/V, 4¾"........ | 245.00 | 280.00 |
| ☐ 60/A and 60/B, trademark Goebel, 4¾".......... | 220.00 | 245.00 |

## 61/A AND B  PLAYMATES & CHICK GIRL

Set of bookends in current production. This set of bookends uses designs #58 and #57, to which the reader should refer for further information on design and color.

| | | |
|---|---|---|
| ☐ 61/A and 61/B, trademark CM, 4¾"............... | 1000.00 | 1100.00 |
| ☐ 61/A and 61/B, trademark Full Bee, 4¾"......... | 650.00 | 715.00 |
| ☐ 61/A and 61/B, trademark Stylized Bee, 4¾".... | 450.00 | 495.00 |
| ☐ 61/A and 61/B, trademark 3-line mark, 4¾"...... | 350.00 | 385.00 |
| ☐ 61/A and 61/B, trademark Goebel/V, 4¾"........ | 250.00 | 275.00 |
| ☐ 61/A and 61/B, trademark Goebel, 4¾".......... | 220.00 | 240.00 |

## 62  HAPPY PASTIME

Ashtray in current production. "Happy Pastime" presents a girl seated alongside an ashtray with a black bird perched on the ashtray's rim. The "happy pastime" may be bird-feeding, or it might be whistling along with the bird, as the girl appears to be doing. Her lips are open and her head

**62** Happy Pastime

upraised in the same attitude as the bird's. She wears a white harlequin type dress with puffed sleeves and ornamental red dots. Some specimens show faint traces of yellow highlights on the dress and others do not. She has a black vest, a black skirt with a salmon-colored apron, and she wears a kerchief of deep violet, the ends of which are crimson. The bird has a canary physique, but its black color suggests it may be intended as a different species.

This model has been in production many years with virtually no changes except for a slight alteration in the tray's contour. Specimens bearing the old Crown Mark have the Hummel signature on the back of the tray. Later examples show it on the girl's back. It should be noted that the horizontal measurement of this model extends from the skirt tip (on the viewer's left) to the edge of the cigarette rest; thus from the stated size it may seem to be larger than it actually is.

|  | Price Range | |
|---|---|---|
| ☐ 62, trademark CM, 3½″ × 6¼″ .................... | 375.00 | 425.00 |
| ☐ 62, trademark Full Bee, 3½″ × 6¼″ ............... | 245.00 | 280.00 |
| ☐ 62, trademark Stylized Bee, 3½″ × 6¼″ .......... | 175.00 | 205.00 |
| ☐ 62, trademark 3-line mark, 3½″ × 6¼ ............ | 115.00 | 140.00 |
| ☐ 62, trademark Goebel/V, 3½″ × 6¼ ............... | 95.00 | 115.00 |
| ☐ 62, trademark Goebel, 3½″ × 6″ ................. | 80.00 | 95.00 |

## 63 SINGING LESSON

Figurine in current production. The "Singing Lesson" theme, used for jars and bowls by Hummel, is presented here as a figurine. It shows a seated boy with a canary bird perched on his foot. The boy looks directly at the bird and raises a finger as if in instruction. The work is small in size, measuring only 2¾″ to 3″ high, and ranks among those models referred to as quaintly appealing. The old name for "Singing Lesson" was "Duet." The new name is not inappropriate, as canaries from the Bavarian region of Germany (known commonly as Hartz Mountain canaries) are celebrated for their vocal abilities and can be taught by whistling if one has patience and skill.

The boy wears a green short jacket, a white shirt, salmon pink trousers with crosswork shading in green at the legs, light beige shoes, and a green Tyrolean style felt cap with a feather. In his right hand he holds a horn to his side. A number of molds have been used for this model, with some variations to be noticed in the attitude of the boy's head and the position of his hand. Generally speaking, the subject has been more successfully executed on jars and bowls than figurines.

| ☐ 63, trademark CM, 2¾″–3″ ..................... | 245.00 | 280.00 |
|---|---|---|
| ☐ 63, trademark Full Bee, 2¾″–3″ ................. | 145.00 | 175.00 |
| ☐ 63, trademark Stylized Bee, 2¾″–3″ ............. | 95.00 | 125.00 |
| ☐ 63, trademark 3-line mark, 2¾″–3″ .............. | 70.00 | 90.00 |
| ☐ 63, trademark Goebel/V, 2¾″–3″ ................ | 55.00 | 75.00 |
| ☐ 63, trademark Goebel, 2¾″–3″ .................. | 55.00 | 70.00 |

**63** Singing Lesson

## III/63 SINGING LESSON

Candy box in current production. The "Singing Lesson" candy box was introduced in 1937 during the Crown trademark period and has remained in continuous production since then. Its design has been unchanged except for a slight alteration in the contour of the lid. In 1964 it was changed from a bowl style, measuring 5¾" to a jar style, measuring 4¾". CM specimens are becoming increasingly hard to find. They would probably be a good deal more valuable were it not for the fact that candy boxes are not as enthusiastically collected by Hummel hobbyists as figurines.

| | Price Range | |
|---|---:|---:|
| ☐ III/63, trademark CM, 5¾" | 500.00 | 550.00 |
| ☐ III/63, trademark Full Bee, 5¾" | 450.00 | 495.00 |
| ☐ III/63, trademark Stylized Bee, 4¾"–5¾" | 350.00 | 385.00 |
| ☐ III/63, trademark 3-line mark, 4¾" | 125.00 | 137.50 |
| ☐ III/63, trademark Goebel/V, 4¾" | 110.00 | 120.00 |
| ☐ III/63, trademark Goebel, 4¾" | 90.00 | 100.00 |

**III/63** Singing Lesson

## 64 SHEPHERD'S BOY

Figurine in current production. "Shepherd's Boy" is a variation of a common Hummel theme. It is common, not because of a lack of imagination on the factory's part, but because Sister Hummel frequently sketched this subject. Her many drawings allow it to be presented in a variety of attitudes. Here the boy holds a baby sheep in his arms, at chest height, while a larger sheep, presumably its parent, stands at the boy's feet. There is sensitivity and good coloration in this model. The boy wears a three-quarter length jacket of muddy green and orange trousers with large pastel areas. Oversized brown slippers are worn over white socks. An olive Tyrolean hat with a wide sunbrim is worn on his head. He also sports the traditional bowtie. His hair is brown, combed down and shaped in pageboy fashion at the sides with loose locks falling at the front. The figures stand on a plain oval base.

Originally "Shepherd's Boy" was known as "The Good Shepherd" which

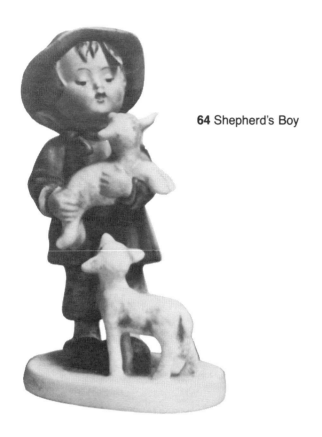

**64** Shepherd's Boy

was dropped as it seemed to suggest a religious personage. There have been numerous variations in the model, chiefly in the attitude of the boy's head and the positioning of his hands. The current version has a textured finish. "Shepherd's Boy" has been officially manufactured in only one size, but specimens as short as 5½", and as tall as 6¼" are encountered, the larger ones having greater bulk and weight. Though not specifically intended as such, "Shepherd's Boy" is often used as a nativity accessory.

|  | Price Range | |
|---|---|---|
| ☐ 64, trademark CM, 5½"–6¼" .................... | 395.00 | 445.00 |
| ☐ 64, trademark Full Bee, 5½"–6¼" ............... | 320.00 | 355.00 |
| ☐ 64, trademark Stylized Bee, 5½"–6¼" .......... | 170.00 | 200.00 |
| ☐ 64, trademark 3-line mark, 5½"–6¼" ........... | 120.00 | 150.00 |
| ☐ 64, trademark Goebel/V, 5½"–6¼" .............. | 95.00 | 115.00 |
| ☐ 64, trademark Goebel, 5½"–6¼" ................ | 88.00 | 106.00 |

## 65 FAREWELL

Figurine in current production. Three different basic sizes of "Farewell" have been sold. Only one is still in production. The present set #65 does not conform with older versions bearing the same number, however, and is technically a different edition. The old set #65, 4¾" to 5" high, is listed as a closed edition. The present version stands 4¾" with no variations yet reported. Other closed edition designations are 65/0, and 65/1, 4½"–4⅞". The closed edition 65/0 is extremely rare.

"Farewell" is a seated figure of a girl waving goodbye with a red hand-kerchief. Over her right arm she holds an empty basket, in her right hand a yellow and brown flower. By her side, a small lamb rests upon the ground. She wears a white puffed-sleeved blouse, a maroon vest and kerchief, a white skirt with touches of various highlight hues, dark brown shoes, and socks of orange and yellow. On the ground are several red flowers with dark centers.

**65** Farewell

| | Price Range | |
|---|---|---|
| □ 65/0, trademark CM, 4" | **RARE** | |
| □ 65/0, trademark Full Bee, 4" | **RARE** | |
| □ 65, trademark CM, 4¾"–5" | 325.00 | 400.00 |
| □ 65, trademark Full Bee, 4¾"–5" | 200.00 | 275.00 |
| □ 65, trademark Stylized Bee, 4¾"–5" | 130.00 | 160.00 |
| □ 65, trademark 3-line mark, 4¾"–5" | 100.00 | 125.00 |
| □ 65, trademark Goebel/V, 4¾"–5" | 70.00 | 90.00 |

| | Price Range | |
|---|---|---|
| ☐ 65, trademark Goebel, 4¾"...................... | 70.00 | 90.00 |
| ☐ 65/I, trademark CM, 4½"–4⅞" .................. | 360.00 | 440.00 |
| ☐ 65/I, trademark Full Bee, 4½"–4⅞" .............. | 230.00 | 320.00 |
| ☐ 65/1, trademark Stylized Bee, 4½"–4⅞" ......... | 140.00 | 170.00 |
| ☐ 65/1, trademark 3-line Bee, 4½"–4⅞"............ | 115.00 | 130.00 |
| ☐ 65/1, trademark Goebel/V, 4½" 4⅞".............. | 100.00 | 120.00 |

## 66 FARM BOY

Figurine in current production. "Farm Boy" was previously known as "Three Pals." The bookend #60/A depicts this same figure of a youth in short trousers standing alongside two pigs. This is not really designed as a farmyard vignette, as the boy wears street dress. He is apparently a farm child standing on the grounds in his Sunday best. The boy wears a sombre expression which could indicate concern over the pigs' fate at the butcher's hands.

"Farm Boy" is a neatly executed, well-colored model. The boy's attire comprises a natty gray blue cutaway jacket with brown plaid striping, a white shirt, black lederhosen with suspenders, and a circular maroon skull-cap. There are a number of size variations, though "Farm Boy" has been produced in only one standard size. The shoes on older specimens are somewhat larger than will be observed in the current design.

**66** Farm Boy

|  | Price Range | |
|---|---|---|
| ☐ 66, trademark CM, 5″–5¾″ ...................... | 220.00 | 355.00 |
| ☐ 66, trademark Full Bee, 5″–5¾″ .................. | 155.00 | 235.00 |
| ☐ 66, trademark Stylized Bee, 5″–5¾″ ............. | 85.00 | 140.00 |
| ☐ 66, trademark 3-line mark, 5″–5¾″ .............. | 75.00 | 100.00 |
| ☐ 66, trademark Goebel/V, 5″–5¾″ ................ | 60.00 | 90.00 |
| ☐ 66, trademark Goebel, 5″–5¾″ .................. | 65.00 | 90.00 |

## 67 DOLL MOTHER

Figurine in current production. "Doll Mother," formerly called "Little Doll Mother," is a figure of a girl with hands clasped in prayer standing beside a doll carriage. There are distinct variations in design and coloration which can be recognized without difficulty. These include:

**Version One:** Girl's face looks directly ahead; her body is turned in viewer's direction; there is no clear distinction between her shoe-tops and the soles of her shoes, which carry an overall pattern of lozengework.

**67** Doll Mother

**Version Two:** The girl's face tilts downward, as if looking at her praying hands or at the floor; her body is turned more toward the carriage; only the tops of her shoes bear lozengework decoration.

There are also other differences of less major proportions. By far the most stylistically alluring component of "Doll Mother" is the doll carriage, modeled to represent an antique specimen of the middle 1800s. Its underpinnings are especially noteworthy. They are made to resemble wood in the old method of construction, whereby two planks came down at right angles from the carriage and were fitted with wooden wheels attached by rods. In the portrayal of this type of article, the factory has demonstrated that their work is historically accurate.

|  | Price Range | |
|---|---|---|
| ☐ 67, trademark CM, 4¼″ × 4¾″ .................. | 495.00 | 555.00 |
| ☐ 67, trademark Full Bee, 4¼″ × 4¾″ .............. | 395.00 | 445.00 |
| ☐ 67, trademark Stylized Bee, 4¼″ × 4¾″ .......... | 195.00 | 225.00 |
| ☐ 67, trademark 3-line mark, 4¼″ × 4¾″............ | 175.00 | 205.00 |
| ☐ 67, trademark Goebel/V, 4¼″ × 4¾″ .............. | 105.00 | 125.00 |
| ☐ 67, trademark Goebel, 4¼″ × 4¾″ ................ | 94.50 | 106.00 |

## 68 LOST SHEEP

Figurine in current production. "Lost Sheep" is found in a number of sizes, designs, and color variations. #68 with decimal point size designator (68.) is rare, though not in the unobtainable category. Model #68 is a closed edition. The only versions of this model currently being produced are 68/2/0 and 68/0.

The model depicts a shepherd boy holding a sheep in his arms and is essentially a duplication of #64 (see above) but with a smaller base and lacking the additional sheep. A good deal of experimenting has been done with colors. The boy wears a long jacket, long trousers, brown slippers, and wide-brimmed Tyrolean hat. His jacket is sometimes a pastel brown with traces of maroon, sometimes an overall deep brown, or a shade midway between light and dark. The hat varies from pastel olive to brown; but nowhere on this model has greater liberty been taken than with the trousers, which range from pastel green to brown to orange. With so many variations, there is no hope of establishing values for all. It will also be noted by careful observers that the boy's head tilts toward his left on some specimens, and faces directly forward on others.

|  | Price Range | |
|---|---|---|
| ☐ 68, trademark CM, 5½″–6½″..................... | 300.00 | 320.00 |
| ☐ 68, trademark CM, brown trousers, 5½″–6½″ ... | 500.00 | 550.00 |
| ☐ 68, trademark Full Bee, 5½″–6½″................ | 250.00 | 275.00 |
| ☐ 68, trademark Full Bee, brown trousers, 5½″–6½″ ......................................... | 300.00 | 330.00 |
| ☐ 68, trademark Stylized Bee, 5½″–6½″ .......... | 250.00 | 275.00 |
| ☐ 68, trademark 3-line mark, 5½″–6½″............ | 100.00 | 110.00 |
| ☐ 68., trademark CM, 5½″–6½″ .................... | 500.00 | 550.00 |
| ☐ 68., trademark CM, brown trousers, 5½″–6½″... | 500.00 | 550.00 |
| ☐ 68., trademark Full Bee, 5½″–6½″ .............. | 350.00 | 385.00 |

**68** Lost Sheep

| | **Price Range** | |
|---|---|---|
| ☐ 68., trademark Full Bee, brown trousers, 5½"–6½" .......................................... | 450.00 | 495.00 |
| ☐ 68., trademark Stylized Bee, 5½"–6½" .......... | 250.00 | 275.00 |
| ☐ 68., trademark 3-line mark, 5½"–6½" ............. | 220.00 | 245.00 |
| ☐ 68/2/0, trademark CM, 4¼"–4½" ................... | 200.00 | 220.00 |
| ☐ 68/2/0, trademark Full Bee, 4¼"–4½" ............ | 150.00 | 165.00 |
| ☐ 68/2/0, trademark Stylized Bee, 4¼"–4½" ....... | 110.00 | 120.00 |
| ☐ 68/2/0, trademark 3-line mark, 4¼"–4½" ........ | 80.00 | 90.00 |
| ☐ 68/2/0, trademark Goebel/V, 4¼"–4½" ........... | 65.00 | 75.00 |
| ☐ 68/2/0, trademark Goebel, 4¼"–4½" .............. | 55.00 | 65.00 |
| ☐ 68/0, trademark CM, 5½" ........................... | 225.00 | 247.50 |
| ☐ 68/0, trademark Full Bee, 5½" ................... | 200.00 | 220.00 |
| ☐ 68/0, trademark Stylized Bee, 5½" ............... | 160.00 | 175.00 |
| ☐ 68/0 trademark 3-line mark, 5½" ................. | 110.00 | 120.00 |
| ☐ 68/0, trademark Goebel/V, 5½" .................... | 88.00 | 100.00 |
| ☐ 68/0, trademark Goebel, 5½" ...................... | 77.50 | 87.50 |

## 69 HAPPY PASTIME

Figurine in current production. "Happy Pastime" is a good example of a Hummel whose title could easily be interchangeable with 50 or more other models in the line. In this instance the "happy pastime" is knitting and the knitter is a young girl seated on the floor. In recent years the factory has not shown much favor for baseless figures. A great many were produced in the 1930s, and nearly all those in current production are holdovers from that era.

The posing of "Happy Pastime" is entirely naturalistic and it is an attractive Hummel work. The girl wears a white long-sleeve blouse, a black vest, black skirt, and a beige apron. Her shoes are brown tinged with shades of violet and she wears long white stockings. A red kerchief is wrapped around her head and tied beneath the chin. She holds two white bone knitting needles and her knitted work, which has not yet progressed to the point where it can be identified.

Older specimens of "Happy Pastime" tend to be slightly larger than the current edition, which would seem to belie the theory of mold growth. The same figure is also used to adorn jars and bowls (see below), and appears on the 1978 Hummel Plate.

**69** Happy Pastime

| | Price Range | |
|---|---|---|
| ☐ 69, trademark CM, 3½" ......................... | 345.00 | 390.00 |
| ☐ 69, trademark Full Bee, 3½" ..................... | 245.00 | 280.00 |
| ☐ 69, trademark Stylized Bee, 3½" ................. | 145.00 | 170.00 |
| ☐ 69, trademark 3-line mark, 3½" .................. | 95.00 | 115.00 |
| ☐ 69, trademark Goebel/V, 3½"..................... | 75.00 | 95.00 |
| ☐ 69, trademark Goebel, 3½"....................... | 66.00 | 76.00 |

## III/69  HAPPY PASTIME

Candy box in current production. The candy box version of "Happy Pastime" was introduced in 1936 in a bowl style. It was altered in 1964 to a jar style and the original was discontinued. One variation of the original style has a green edge on both the bowl and lid. It is produced today in the jar style only. The bowl type measures 6½", the jar 5¼".

| | Price Range | |
|---|---|---|
| ☐ III/69, trademark CM, 6½"......................... | 500.00 | 550.00 |
| ☐ III/69, trademark Full Bee, 6½".................... | 400.00 | 440.00 |
| ☐ III/69, trademark Stylized Bee, 5¼" or 6½" ...... | 350.00 | 385.00 |
| ☐ III/69, trademark 3-line mark, 5¼"................ | 150.00 | 175.00 |
| ☐ III/69, trademark Goebel/V, 5¼" ................. | 120.00 | 135.00 |
| ☐ III/69, trademark Goebel, 5¼" ................... | 90.00 | 100.00 |

## 70  THE HOLY CHILD

Figurine in current production. "The Holy Child" is a modified version of the traditional "Infant of Prague," wearing somewhat less ornate garments than usual. This familiar theme, known to churchgoers in all parts of the world, has been rendered by sculptors for many years.

It has been produced in one size only. The figure wears a pink or pale reddish orange long cape over a white gown trimmed in red. He holds an orb and cross, symbolic of Christianity ruling the world. It has a square base. Oversized specimens are worth a modest premium as indicated.

| | Price Range | |
|---|---|---|
| ☐ 70, trademark CM, 6¾"–7" ...................... | 295.00 | 330.00 |
| ☐ 70, trademark CM, over 7" ...................... | 295.00 | 330.00 |
| ☐ 70, trademark Full Bee, 6¾"–7"................. | 195.00 | 225.00 |
| ☐ 70, trademark Full Bee, over 7" ................. | 245.00 | 275.00 |
| ☐ 70, trademark Stylized Bee, 6¾"–7½" ........... | 120.00 | 155.00 |
| ☐ 70, trademark 3-line mark, 6¾"–7½" ............. | 80.00 | 100.00 |
| ☐ 70, trademark Goebel/V, 6¾"–7½"............... | 75.00 | 85.00 |
| ☐ 70, trademark Goebel, 6¾"–7½"................. | 68.00 | 75.00 |

**70** Holy Child

## 71 STORMY WEATHER

Figurine in current production. Since the model's introduction, "Stormy Weather" has been manufactured in a single standard size of which there are numerous variations. The current Hummel catalogue lists the figure as 6¼" and indeed the majority of recently produced specimens agree with that measurement. But the collector of old "Stormy Weathers," especially those marked with the Crown and Full Bee, will find himself in possession of models ranging from 6" to 7". That is quite a variation for a figure sold in one standard size.

"Stormy Weather" has been restyled and minor alterations will be observed between old and new. It is considered one of the more classic Hummels and is frequently used by Hummel dealers for window display. It shows two children caught in a rainstorm (which imagination must supply), standing beneath an adult-size umbrella which sufficiently protects them.

**71** Stormy Weather

This gives the boy an opportunity to get as close as possible to the girl. This is made more evident in the early version, prior to restyling, in which his head is turned more in her direction and his cheek almost pressed against her face. The restyling plays down the love angle.

The girl wears a white blouse, with a reddish maroon overdress. Her white apron is tinted with pastel yellow and ornamented with semicircular strokes of red. Her shoes vary in shade from beige to a deep mahogany brown. She wears white socks and there are red ribbons in her blonde braided hair. The boy is attired in a white shirt, a dark brown short jacket, green lederhosen, brown shoes, and white rolled down socks. In his left hand the boy carries a wooden walking stick. A red flower is on the ground. The umbrella is yellow on its outer side and a grayish blue underneath.

"Stormy Weather" was originally titled "Under One Roof." Some early specimens have a divided underbase, the division being across the width. This is basically a scarce piece. It seems never to have been in heavy production. Current specimens are divided lengthwise.

|  | Price Range | |
|---|---|---|
| ☐ 71, trademark CM, 6"–7".......................... | **745.00** | **830.00** |
| ☐ 71, trademark Full Bee, 6"–7".................... | **645.00** | **720.00** |
| ☐ 71, trademark Stylized Bee, 6"–7" ............... | **395.00** | **445.00** |
| ☐ 71, trademark 3-line mark, 6"–7"................. | **295.00** | **335.00** |

| | Price Range | |
|---|---|---|
| □ 71, trademark Goebel/V, 6″–7″ .................. | **245.00** | **280.00** |
| □ 71, trademark Goebel, 6″–7″ .................... | **200.00** | **225.00** |

## 72 SPRING CHEER

Figurine in current production. "Spring Cheer" is a figure of a girl holding a red flower in the air in celebration of nature once again enriching the earth at springtime. It is a simple theme, but collecting this model is not quite so simple. There are two distinct versions of #72, and nearly every component has been changed somewhat. In the old version, the girl clutches her right hand to her chest but the hand is empty; in the new type it holds two flowers. Other variations include:

**DRESS**—Old: Yellow with light washes of green. New: Green with yellow highlights (almost a negative/positive transposition).

**HAIR**—Old: Henna, upswept into two horn-like peaks at the front. New: Light brown, set in a less extreme style.

**SHOES**—Old: Reddish brown. New: Very pale brown.

**STOCKINGS**—Old: White with brown highlights and green stripping. New: Similar but without green striping.

**FLOWERS**—Old: Deep full red-colored over entire surface, with black centers. New: Red and white with black centers.

Perhaps the figure's face has the most notable alteration. In the old version she does not smile and has puffy cheeks. The restyling gave her a more carefree, joyous expression.

**72** Spring Cheer

**Old Style**          **New Style**

| | **Price Range** | |
|---|---|---|
| ☐ 72, trademark CM, 5″–5½″...................... | 300.00 | 330.00 |
| ☐ 72, trademark Full Bee, 5″–5½″.................. | 200.00 | 220.00 |
| ☐ 72, trademark Stylized Bee, 5″–5½″ ............. | 100.00 | 120.00 |
| ☐ 72, trademark 3-line mark, 5″–5½″............... | 75.00 | 85.00 |
| ☐ 72, trademark Goebel/V, 5″–5½″................. | 65.00 | 75.00 |
| ☐ 72, trademark Goebel, 5″–5½″ .................. | 55.00 | 65.00 |

## 73  LITTLE HELPER

Figurine in current production. "Little Helper" is a very uncomplicated, straightforward representation of a little girl holding a basket. To the non-collector and casual observer it appears unremarkable, but the facial expression of this model is one of the best ever created by Hummel. So sensitive and expressive is the face of "Little Helper" that even photographs fail to do it complete justice; the work itself must be seen to be fully appreciated. For very good reason, "Little Helper" has not undergone any major designing change in four decades. The girl is shown in the act of lifting her basket from the floor, not quite fully raised to a standing posture. She looks upward as if to ask, "What is my next task?" "Little Helper" has also been known as "Diligent Betsy" and "Little Sister."

**73** Little Helper

She wears a white short-sleeved blouse, a brown jumper with hints of mahogany, a blue apron, brown shoes, and white socks. Around her head is tied a green kerchief. Her hair is worn in braids at the sides, and tied with red ribbons. The large empty basket was considered a selling point as it could serve as a receptacle for artificial flowers. Specimens measuring as tall as 5¼″ have been reported, but this may be the result of incorrect measuring.

| | Price Range | |
|---|---:|---:|
| □ 73, trademark CM, 4″–4½″ | 245.00 | 280.00 |
| □ 73, trademark Full Bee, 4″–4½″ | 145.00 | 175.00 |
| □ 73, trademark Stylized Bee, 4″–4½″ | 95.00 | 115.00 |
| □ 73, trademark 3-line mark, 4″–4½″ | 70.00 | 90.00 |
| □ 73, trademark Goebel/V, 4″–4½″ | 60.00 | 80.00 |
| □ 73, trademark Goebel, 4″–4½″ | 55.00 | 70.00 |

## 74  LITTLE GARDENER

Figurine in current production. "Little Gardener" is a girl with a watering can sprinkling water on a flower. There has been some variation in this model, in both color and design. There is a change in the flower's size,

**74** Little Gardener

which in older specimens is much larger than in the current versions. The base, formerly oval, has been changed to round, and the girl's apron is found in a variety of colors. The apron is decorated with a series of raised dots, sometimes colored and sometimes not. Even the watering can has not escaped alteration. Older specimens generally show it plain, while in later ones the can has acquired a set of blue bands running near the top and bottom.

The girl has blonde hair combed forward at the front and tied at the crown with a ribbon. She wears a dress that varies in color from light to deep orange, being more pastel in the older versions. She has brown shoes with white socks ribbed with brown and red. Stylistically the best specimens are to be found among those with Crown Mark, where the head tilts slightly and appears to be intently studying the can and the imaginary cascade of water.

|  | Price Range | |
|---|---|---|
| ☐ 74, trademark CM, 4″–4½″ | 225.00 | 245.00 |
| ☐ 74, trademark Full Bee, 4″–4½″ | 125.00 | 135.00 |
| ☐ 74, trademark Stylized Bee, 4″–4½″ | 90.00 | 100.00 |
| ☐ 74, trademark 3-line mark, 4″–4½″ | 70.00 | 77.00 |
| ☐ 74, trademark Goebel/V, 4″–4½″ | 60.00 | 66.00 |
| ☐ 74, trademark Goebel, 4″–4½″ | 55.00 | 60.00 |

## 75 WHITE ANGEL

Wall font in current production. "White Angel" is also known as "Angelic Prayer." The two names have been used interchangeably, as #75 is still found referred to in some lists as "Angelic Prayer." The early examples of "White Angel" are considered a bit more successful artistically than the later, though differences in modeling are very minor. There are some variations in the color and construction, especially of the bowl. The older specimens have no visible hole for hanging, while this feature is present in later examples. The model depicts a half length representation of an angel with hands clasped in prayer, his head turned slightly to his right, eyes shut, and with large outspread wings.

The figure wears a light blue gown and has blonde hair tinged in some specimens, most notably early ones, with red. The wings are chiefly light pink most of the time, but are found intermixed with shades of yellow, orange, or brown on occasion. The angel is positioned against a plain background whose sides slope inward toward the bowl and whose top is surmounted by an angular roof which is colored brown with a red edge at the front.

|  | Price Range | |
|---|---|---|
| ☐ 75, trademark CM, 3¼″ × 4½″ | 135.00 | 160.00 |
| ☐ 75, trademark Full Bee, 3¼″ × 4½″ | 70.00 | 90.00 |
| ☐ 75, trademark Stylized Bee, 3¼″ × 4½″ | 39.00 | 46.00 |
| ☐ 75, trademark 3-line mark, 3¼″ × 4½″ | 29.00 | 36.00 |
| ☐ 75, trademark Goebel/V, 3¼″ × 4½″ | 24.00 | 31.00 |
| ☐ 75, trademark Goebel, 3¼″ × 4½″ | 17.50 | 23.00 |

**75** White Angel

## 76 A and B  DOLL MOTHER & PRAYER BEFORE BATTLE

Set of bookends, closed edition. This set of bookends employs designs #67 and #20, to which the reader should refer for descriptions. The set was closed out very shortly after production began. Whether any actually reached retail sale is questionable. No specimens have been traced. This set carried the Crown Mark.

## 77  CROSS WITH DOVES

Wall font, closed number. This attractive holy water font, of which only factory samples are known, was never manufactured for distribution and was listed as a closed number on October 21, 1937. While the reason for closed number models failing to reach production is seldom known, a fair guess can be made in the case of "Cross with Doves." If released, it would have been the first Hummel that failed to depict a human being, and that may well have been considered (perhaps by the Convent) too drastic a step.

It is, nevertheless, a handsome design and representative of Sister Hummel's work. The central component is a Roman or western style cross, the tips of its crossbar arched outward in modernistic fashion. It perches atop a half circle intended to represent a sunburst. The top of the cross terminates in a loop extending outward to the right, symbolic of the "P" in the word "Pax." The basic color of the cross is pale yellow. On either side of the cross is a dove with wings flapping, colored white and yellow. Their wings are streaked with red and blue. Beneath the crossbar are a pair of red modeled flowers with blue stems. The factory models of "Cross with Doves" measure 1¾″ × 6¼″. A few specimens may be in private hands, but a price cannot be accurately attempted.

## 78 INFANT OF KRUMBAD

Figurine in current production. One of the most universally known and popular Hummels, this model has more variations, taking into account sizes, differences in color and trademarks, than any other produced by the factory. "Infant of Krumbad" (Krumbad being a Bavarian town) was sketched by Berta Hummel as a nativity figure. Smaller specimens are still being used in nativity sets, but the factory has also produced "Infant of Krumbad" in nearly life size, 13¼″ to 14¼″. These huge examples are often employed in outdoor nativity displays, on church lawns and the like. The factory, however, does not manufacture accessory figures of a proportionate size, which would need to be huge. There have been nine separate and distinct editions, eight of which continue in production. Only the smallest size, 78/0, measuring 2½″, has been discontinued. This model has more variations. It was taken out of production in 1963. Consequently, it will not be found with more recent trademarks.

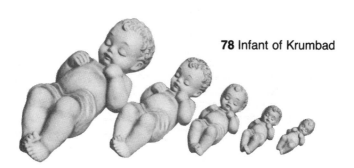

**78** Infant of Krumbad

The version of "Infant of Krumbad" most commonly seen in this country has a bisque finish of pale brown. This type was expressly produced for exportation to the U.S. It is also made in a white overglaze and an enameled edition with lifelike coloration. All sizes are manufactured in all three styles and, while one finish may be somewhat scarcer than the same trademark with a different finish, there is so far no appreciable variation in value. It would seem on the whole that the white overglaze specimens are scarcest.

In colored specimens, the coloration is pale but appealing. The child has rosy cheeks, red lips, and very fair skin. Unlike most standard representations of the Christ Child, "Infant of Krumbad" is not swaddled shoulder to toe, but has bare legs. "Infant of Krumbad" was formerly known as "In the Crib." This model has never been marketed as part of a nativity set.

|  | Price Range | |
|---|---|---|
| ☐ 78/0, trademark CM, 2¼"............................ | 210.00 | 240.00 |
| ☐ 78/0, trademark Full Bee, 2¼" .................... | 195.00 | 225.00 |
| ☐ 78/0, trademark Stylized Bee, 2¼"................ | 145.00 | 170.00 |
| ☐ 78/I, trademark CM, 2½" .......................... | 195.00 | 225.00 |
| ☐ 78/I, trademark Full Bee, 2½" ..................... | 145.00 | 170.00 |
| ☐ 78/I, trademark Stylized Bee, 2½"................. | 39.00 | 46.00 |
| ☐ 78/I, trademark 3-line mark, 2½" .................. | 31.00 | 36.00 |
| ☐ 78/I, trademark Goebel/V, 2½" .................... | 26.00 | 31.00 |
| ☐ 78/I, trademark Goebel, 2½" ....................... | 21.00 | 26.00 |
| ☐ 78/II, trademark CM, 3½".......................... | 245.00 | 280.00 |
| ☐ 78/II, trademark Full Bee, 3½" .................... | 195.00 | 225.00 |
| ☐ 78/II, trademark Stylized Bee, 3½"................ | 49.00 | 56.00 |
| ☐ 78/II, trademark 3-line mark, 3½" ................. | 39.00 | 46.00 |
| ☐ 78/II, trademark Goebel/V, 3½".................... | 29.00 | 36.00 |
| ☐ 78/II, trademark Goebel, 3½"...................... | 26.50 | 33.00 |
| ☐ 78/III, trademark CM, 4½"–5¼" ................... | 295.00 | 335.00 |
| ☐ 78/III, trademark Full Bee, 4½"–5¼".............. | 195.00 | 225.00 |
| ☐ 78/III, trademark Stylized Bee, 4½"–5¼" ........ | 49.00 | 56.00 |
| ☐ 78/III, trademark 3-line mark, 4½"–5¼".......... | 39.00 | 46.00 |
| ☐ 78/III, trademark Goebel/V, 4½"–5¼" ............ | 35.00 | 41.00 |
| ☐ 78/III, trademark Goebel, 4½"–5¼" .............. | 31.50 | 38.00 |
| ☐ 78/V, trademark CM, 7½"–7¾".................... | 495.00 | 555.00 |
| ☐ 78/V, trademark Full Bee, 7½"–7¾" .............. | 395.00 | 445.00 |
| ☐ 78/V, trademark Stylized Bee, 7½"–7¾" ......... | 145.00 | 170.00 |
| ☐ 78/V, trademark 3-line mark, 7½"–7¾".............. | 115.00 | 135.00 |
| ☐ 78/V, trademark Goebel/V, 7½"–7¾".............. | 95.00 | 115.00 |
| ☐ 78/V, trademark Goebel, 7½"–7¾"................ | 60.00 | 70.00 |
| ☐ 78/VI, trademark CM, 10"–11¼" ................. | 745.00 | 830.00 |
| ☐ 78/VI, trademark Full Bee, 10"–11¼" ............ | 495.00 | 555.00 |
| ☐ 78/VI, trademark Stylized Bee, 10"–11" ......... | 245.00 | 280.00 |
| ☐ 78/VI, trademark 3-line mark, 10"–11¼" ......... | 195.00 | 225.00 |
| ☐ 78/VI, trademark Goebel/V, 10"–11¼" ......... | 175.00 | 205.00 |
| ☐ 78/VI, trademark Goebel, 10"–11¼" ............. | 120.00 | 140.00 |
| ☐ 78/VIII, trademark CM, 13¼"–14¼".............. | 995.00 | 1105.00 |
| ☐ 78/VIII, trademark Full Bee, 13¼"–14¼"......... | 795.00 | 885.00 |
| ☐ 78/VIII, trademark Stylized Bee, 13¼"–14¼" .... | 345.00 | 390.00 |
| ☐ 78/VIII, trademark 3-line mark, 13¼"–14¼"...... | 295.00 | 335.00 |

**Price Range**

☐ 78/VIII, trademark Goebel/V, 13¼"–14¼"........  **270.00**  **295.00**
☐ 78/VIII, trademark Goebel, 13¼"–14¼"..........  **230.00**  **260.00**

## 79 GLOBE TROTTER

Figurine in current production. Another variation of the boy on the road theme, all of which are outgrowths of "Merry Wanderer." The boy in "Globe Trotter" is very similar to that in "Merry Wanderer." He appears to be about the same age and has more or less the same facial expression. Like his illustrious predecessor, he carries a red umbrella beneath his right arm. Instead of a satchel or bag, he holds a basket on his back. Both hands are thrust into his trouser pockets. "Globe Trotter" is sometimes mistakenly referred to as "Happy Traveler," a name assigned to #109 (a similar figure but without basket). The design was used for the 1973 annual plate (see #276 below).

As originally designed, in the Crown Mark period, the basket weave was in South American or Indian fashion. This was subsequently altered to European weave, as may be observed on recent specimens. Otherwise there has not been much variation in this model during its long years of production. The early Crown Mark examples normally have a brown umbrella handle, which was later changed to black. Variations will be noted in the basket interior's color, though these do not seem to follow any established pattern. The figure has been marked in just one basic size, but variations of as much as a quarter-inch are found. Usually the older specimens, especially those with Crown Mark, are the tallest. This is not a scarce piece; even the Crown Mark specimens are easily located. It has been a favorite with collectors.

**79** Globe Trotter

**Old Style**          **New Style**

There is no question that the basket was intended to be used as a receptacle by purchasers. It is quite small, but adequate enough to hold candy or artificial flowers.

"Globe Trotter" is portrayed in full stride, his left leg lifted high in a giant step. He wears a green jacket, greenish brown trousers, brown shoes, and a brown Alpine or Tyrolean style hat with narrow red band. His hair is sandy brown. The figure stands on a small circular base.

|  | Price Range | |
|---|---|---|
| ☐ 79, trademark CM, 5"–5¼" | 495.00 | 555.00 |
| ☐ 79, trademark Full Bee, 5"–5¼" | 345.00 | 380.00 |
| ☐ 79, trademark Stylized Bee, 5"–5¼" | 120.00 | 155.00 |
| ☐ 79, trademark 3-line mark, 5"–5¼" | 95.00 | 118.00 |
| ☐ 79, trademark Goebel/V, 5"–5¼" | 84.00 | 100.00 |
| ☐ 79, trademark Goebel, 5"–5¼" | 72.00 | 82.00 |

## 80 LITTLE SCHOLAR

Figurine in current production. This old favorite, found with all six marks, has undergone no change in modeling. The only major variation to be noted is that early specimens show the boy wearing brown shoes, which are black or charcoal gray in current examples. There is, however, a sharp variation

**80** Little Scholar

in sizes, from 5¼″ to 5¾″, which could hardly be accounted for by mold growth or mold shrinkage. It is apparent that a number of different molds have been used. "Little Scholar" is one of the more common of the older figures. There is no difficulty putting together a complete set of marks. The boy wears a white shirt, a blue jacket with plaid striping, brown lederhosen and suspenders, and grayish white socks. He has on a red bow tie. The base of this model is circular.

|  | Price Range | |
|---|---|---|
| ☐ 80, trademark CM, 5¼″–5¾″..................... | 325.00 | 350.00 |
| ☐ 80, trademark Full Bee, 5¼″–5¾″ ............... | 225.00 | 250.00 |
| ☐ 80, trademark Stylized Bee, 5¼″–5¾″ .......... | 150.00 | 170.00 |
| ☐ 80, trademark 3-line mark, 5¼″–5¾″ ............ | 100.00 | 120.00 |
| ☐ 80, trademark Goebel/V, 5¼″–5¾″............... | 80.00 | 90.00 |
| ☐ 80, trademark Goebel, 5¼″–5¾″................. | 72.00 | 85.00 |

## 81  SCHOOL GIRL

Figurine in current production. This model, not to be confused with #177 "School Girls," was designed as a companion piece to #82 "School Boy"

**81** School Girl

(see below). There have been three editions, although only two editions continue to be marketed. As is usual in these cases, the largest version, 81 (5⅛″–5½″), was the one to be closed out.

The smallest size, 81/2/0, depicts the girl carrying a filled basket (its contents presumably being lunch), while in larger sizes the basket is empty. In addition to the basket, "School Girl" carries a schoolbag on her back. The existence of a seven-inch specimen, listed in an old Hummel catalogue, has never been observed and is believed to be an error. The model is not rare in currently manufactured sizes.

There are some color variations. Most often, she wears a red short-sleeved dress with yellow polka dotting, a maroon vest, dark brown shoes, and gray socks. "School Girl" stands on a circular base.

| | Price Range | |
|---|---|---|
| ☐ 81/2/0, trademark CM, 4¼″–4¾″ | 245.00 | 275.00 |
| ☐ 81/2/0, trademark Full Bee, 4¼″–4¾″ | 145.00 | 175.00 |
| ☐ 81/2/0, trademark Stylized Bee, 4¼″–4¾″ | 95.00 | 125.00 |
| ☐ 81/2/0, trademark 3-line mark, 4¼″–4¾″ | 65.00 | 85.00 |
| ☐ 81/2/0, trademark Goebel/V, 4¼″–4¾″ | 55.00 | 75.00 |
| ☐ 81/2/0, trademark Goebel, 4¼″–4¾″ | 55.00 | 70.00 |
| ☐ 81/0, trademark GM, 4¾″–5¼″ | 320.00 | 360.00 |
| ☐ 81/0, trademark Full Bee, 4¾″–5¼″ | 195.00 | 225.00 |
| ☐ 81/0, trademark Stylized Bee, 4¾″–5¼″ | 120.00 | 150.00 |
| ☐ 81/0, trademark 3-line mark, 4¾″–5¼″ | 93.00 | 112.00 |
| ☐ 81/0, trademark Goebel/V, 4¾″–5¼″ | 79.00 | 91.00 |
| ☐ 81/0, trademark Goebel, 4¾″–5¼″ | 72.00 | 81.00 |
| ☐ 81, trademark CM, 5⅛″–5½″ | 345.00 | 390.00 |
| ☐ 81, trademark Full Bee, 5⅛″–5½″ | 245.00 | 280.00 |

## 82  SCHOOL BOY

Figurine in current production. "School Boy" is a figure of a boy posed with a schoolbag over his back. This model was originally known as "Little Scholar," the name now given to #80. It has also been referred to as "School Days." The largest size, 82/II, was discontinued for a time, but has been reinstated. Specimens prior to the discontinuation are rare. It is sometimes supposed that this model is produced in more than three sizes because group photos show many variations. All of them, however, belong to one or more of the numbers given below. The chief cause of confusion is 82/0, which exists in such a variety of sizes. Obviously, more than one mold was used.

"School Boy" wears a white long-sleeved shirt, dark brown trousers with matching lederhosen, charcoal gray or black shoes, white socks, and a blue Tyrolean style hat with a red and white feather. He sports a huge yellow orange bow tie and his schoolbag is fawn-colored. The model stands on a circular base.

| | | |
|---|---|---|
| ☐ 82/2/0, trademark CM 4″–4½″ | 250.00 | 275.00 |
| ☐ 82/2/0, trademark Full Bee, 4″–4½″ | 180.00 | 200.00 |

**82** School Boy

|  | Price Range | |
|---|---|---|
| ☐ 82/2/0, trademark Stylized Bee, 4″–4½″ ......... | 120.00 | 135.00 |
| ☐ 82/2/0, trademark 3-line mark, 4″–4½″........... | 80.00 | 90.00 |
| ☐ 82/2/0, trademark Goebel/V, 4″–4½″ ............. | 70.00 | 80.00 |
| ☐ 82/2/0, trademark Goebel, 4″–4½″ ............... | 55.00 | 65.00 |
| ☐ 82/0, trademark CM, 4¾″–6″ .................... | 350.00 | 385.00 |
| ☐ 82/0, trademark Full Bee, 4¾″–6″ ............... | 250.00 | 275.00 |
| ☐ 82/0, trademark Stylized Bee, 4¾″–6″ .......... | 150.00 | 165.00 |
| ☐ 82/0, trademark 3-line mark, 4¾″–6″............ | 100.00 | 110.00 |
| ☐ 82/0, trademark Goebel/V, 4¾″–6″ .............. | 85.00 | 95.00 |
| ☐ 82/0, trademark Goebel, 4¾″–6″ ................ | 72.00 | 80.00 |
| ☐ 82/II, trademark CM, 7½″........................ | 1000.00 | 1100.00 |
| ☐ 82/II, trademark Full Bee, 7½″ .................. | 800.00 | 880.00 |
| ☐ 82/II, trademark Stylized Bee, 7½″.............. | 400.00 | 440.00 |
| ☐ 82/II, trademark Goebel/V, 7½″.................. | 250.00 | 275.00 |
| ☐ 82/II, trademark Goebel, 7½″.................... | 195.00 | 215.00 |

## 83  ANGEL SERENADE WITH LAMB

Figurine in current production. Although this figure bears a title similar to #214/D "Angel Serenade" (a Nativity Set component), the composition is quite different in that the angel is standing and is accompanied by a lamb. "Angel Serenade with Lamb" was introduced in the Crown Mark period

**83** Angel Serenade with Lamb

and was produced in fair quantities until 1960, when it was either discontinued or placed into limited production. The belief that it was officially discontinued as early as 1950 is certainly mistaken, but it may have been taken off the market around 1960. It was back in full production by 1978. As normally happens with Hummels that are discontinued or believed to be discontinued, collectors flocked to buy the Crown Mark and other early specimens during the late 1960s and throughout most of the 1970s. The result is that this figure gained quite a reputation for rarity.

"Angel Serenade with Lamb" is produced in only one edition but sizes do vary, as with most Hummels that have been made for 40 or more years. The angel wears a long red gown with yellow polka dots, has brown shoes and plays a lute (sometimes referred to as a mandolin). The lamb wears a blue collar with a bell attached.

|  | Price Range | |
|---|---|---|
| ☐ 83, trademark CM, 5½"–5¾"..................... | 490.00 | 525.00 |
| ☐ 83, trademark Full Bee, 5½"–5¾" ............... | 395.00 | 425.00 |
| ☐ 83, trademark Stylized Bee, 5½"–5¾"........... | 345.00 | 380.00 |
| ☐ 83, trademark 3-linemark, 5½"–3¼" ............. | 220.00 | 240.00 |
| ☐ 83, trademark Goebel/V, 5½"–3¾"............... | 90.00 | 105.00 |
| ☐ 83, trademark Goebel, 5½"–5¾"................. | 85.00 | 95.00 |

## 84 WORSHIP

Figurine in current production. "Worship" depicts a girl seated, her hands clasped in prayer, at the base of a religious shrine. This is not the usual sort of shrine that is represented in Hummel models of this sort (see #23, #28, etc.) as a wooden structure. The shrine in "Worship" is presented as a brick or cement construction. There is no other model of this type in the Hummel line.

The report given in some reference works that "Worship" has been manufactured in as many as four different sizes is totally erroneous. This arises from the fact that the sizes given in sales lists vary considerably; but whether these represent correct or incorrect measurements, the fact is that only three editions have been marketed, one of which, 84 (5¼″), is now discontinued.

Model #84 is rare. In addition to the ordinary colored version, #84/0 was also sold for a limited time in cream overglaze. These specimens, which were originally sold only on the Belgian markets, are **extremely rare**. There is little hope of encountering them in America.

The shrine is of gothic proportions, enclosing a colored image of the Virgin Mary praying. This figure within a figure is set behind a colonnaded balcony, in a shallow niche, surmounted by a red shingled roof. The shrine is basically white with additions of black to suggest weathering. The girl wears a green jacket, red skirt, and brown shoes. She has a red kerchief tied round her head and holds an empty basket over her right arm. A Christmas Tree plus several red flowers are growing up from the base.

**84** Worship

Price Range

☐ 84/0, trademark CM, cream overglaze, 5″–5½″ | 2995.00 | 3305.00
☐ 84/0, trademark CM, 5″–5½″ .................... | 345.00 | 390.00
☐ 84/0, trademark Full Bee, 5″–5½″ ............... | 245.00 | 280.00
☐ 84/0, trademark Stylized Bee, 5″–5½″ ........... | 145.00 | 170.00
☐ 84/0, trademark 3-line mark, 5″–5½″ ............ | 98.00 | 112.00
☐ 84/0, trademark Goebel/V, 5″–5½″ .............. | 79.00 | 91.00
☐ 84/0, trademark Goebel, 5″–5½″ ................ | 68.50 | 76.00
☐ 84/V, trademark CM, 12½″–13¼″ ............... | 2995.00 | 3305.00
☐ 84/V, trademark Full Bee, 12½″–13¼″ .......... | 1995.00 | 2205.00
☐ 84/V, trademark Stylized Bee, 12½″–13¼″ ...... | 995.00 | 1105.00
☐ 84/V, trademark 3-line mark, 12½″–13¼″ ....... | 795.00 | 885.00
☐ 84/V, trademark Goebel/V, 12½″–13¼″ ......... | 745.00 | 830.00
☐ 84/V, trademark Goebel, 12½″–13¼″ ........... | 630.00 | 700.00

## 85 SERENADE

Figurine in current production. "Serenade" depicts a boy playing a piccolo or similar instrument. The often-published assertion that the instrument represents a flute is questionable because of the manner in which the boy holds it.

**85** Serenade

There has been no significant restyling but a major variation is noticeable. On some models, the boy's fingers are positioned so that the tips cover the instrument's keyholes in a natural manner; on others, the boy merely grasps the instrument with his hands clutched around it, as if it were a drinking glass. The raised finger variety occurs primarily on specimens with the Crown and Full Bee marks. "Serenade" wears a brown short jacket, white shirt, blue trousers with suspenders, black shoes, and a charcoal gray stovepipe hat. The costuming would date the subject of this figure at around 1850. It stands on a circular base.

|  | Price Range | |
|---|---|---|
| ☐ 85/0, trademark CM, 4¾"–5¼"................... | 225.00 | 245.00 |
| ☐ 85/0, trademark Full Bee, 4¾"–5¼" ............. | 175.00 | 185.00 |
| ☐ 85/0, trademark Stylized Bee, 4¾"–5¼" ......... | 95.00 | 105.00 |
| ☐ 85/0, trademark 3-line mark, 4¾"–5¼" ......... | 70.00 | 75.00 |
| ☐ 85/0, trademark Goebel/V, 4¾"–5¼"............. | 65.00 | 71.00 |
| ☐ 85/0, trademark Goebel, 4¾"–5¼"............... | 55.00 | 60.00 |
| ☐ 85/II, trademark CM, 7"–7½".................... | 950.00 | 1040.00 |
| ☐ 85/II, trademark Full Bee, 7"–7½"................ | 700.00 | 770.00 |
| ☐ 85/II, trademark Stylized Bee, 7"–7½" .......... | 250.00 | 270.00 |
| ☐ 85/II, trademark 3-line mark, 7"–7½"............ | 225.00 | 245.00 |
| ☐ 85/II, trademark Goebel/V, 7"–7½".............. | 210.00 | 230.00 |
| ☐ 85/II, trademark Goebel, 7"–7½" ................ | 195.00 | 207.00 |

## 86 HAPPINESS

Figurine in current production. "Happiness" is a likeness of a girl playing a lute or mandolin. The design was at one time referred to as "Wandersong." There are many size variations, but only one basic edition has been produced. The girl wears a red dress with white or yellow polka dots, brown shoes, gray socks, and red ribbons in her braided hair. A red flower grows on the square base.

| | | |
|---|---|---|
| ☐ 86, trademark CM, 4½"–5"...................... | 245.00 | 275.00 |
| ☐ 86, trademark Full Bee, 4½"–5".................. | 145.00 | 175.00 |
| ☐ 86, trademark Stylized Bee, 4½"–5" ............. | 95.00 | 125.00 |
| ☐ 86, trademark 3-line mark, 4½"–5".............. | 65.00 | 85.00 |
| ☐ 86, trademark Goebel/V, 4½"–5................. | 60.00 | 80.00 |
| ☐ 86, trademark Goebel, 4½"–5" .................. | 55.00 | 70.00 |

**86** Happiness

## 87 FOR FATHER

Figurine in current production. "For Father" is a figure of a boy holding a tankard in his right hand and a bunch of radishes in the other hand. This interesting composition has been the subject of a good deal of comment and study. Though the design was never again used for a Hummel product, it inspired the "Radibub" Hummel doll (boy with radishes). It has been suggested by some Americans and others unfamiliar with German traditions that radishes and ale or beer seem an unfitting gift for father. There has, however, long been a custom in Germany, especially in the Alpine region where Berta Hummel lived, of heavy snacks taken before meals. They usually consist of beverage, smoked or cured meats, and assorted raw vegetables, of which cucumbers and radishes are the favorite. At one time radishes were even given as Christmas gifts among the poor, as yogurt is today.

The gift bearer wears a long-sleeved white shirt with "V" collar, brown lederhosen with suspenders, black shoes, grayish socks, and a green Tyrolean cap with feather. "For Father" has also been called "Father's Joy."

**87** For Father

|  | Price Range | |
|---|---|---|
| ☐ 87, trademark CM, 5½"........................... | **375.00** | **395.00** |
| ☐ 87, trademark Full Bee, 5½" ..................... | **225.00** | **245.00** |
| ☐ 87, trademark Stylized Bee, 5½"................. | **150.00** | **170.00** |
| ☐ 87, trademark 3-line mark, 5½" ................. | **100.00** | **110.00** |
| ☐ 87, trademark Goebel/V, 5½"..................... | **90.00** | **100.00** |
| ☐ 87, trademark Goebel, 5½"....................... | **83.00** | **90.00** |

## 88  HEAVENLY PROTECTION

Figurine in current production. "Heavenly Protection" shows a guardian angel standing behind a boy and girl. This figure was once made in three sizes, but the large size, 88 (9¼"), has been closed out. Some specimens carry a 1961 copyright date, but its presence or absence has no bearing on the value.

"Heavenly Protection" was originally called "Guardian Angel." There is some variation in color, but basically the colors are as follows: The angel wears a white robe, and a cape colored red orange on the outside and white on the inside. She has blonde hair, no halo, and grayish wings with orange highlights. The Gretel-type girl has on a white short-sleeved blouse,

**88** Heavenly Protection

charcoal gray vest, red skirt, brown shoes, and socks that are primarily white. Her braided hair is tied with ribbons and she holds an empty basket over her left arm. Her companion has on a light blue jacket, white shirt, maroon lederhosen and suspenders, brown boots, and a reddish brown Tyrolean hat with red flower. The model is contained on an oval base.

|  | **Price Range** | |
| --- | --- | --- |
| ☐ 88/I, trademark CM, 6¼″–6¾″ ................... | 445.00 | 500.00 |
| ☐ 88/I, trademark Full Bee, 6¼″–6¾″ .............. | 320.00 | 360.00 |
| ☐ 88/I, trademark Stylized Bee, 6¼″–6¾″ .......... | 295.00 | 335.00 |
| ☐ 88/I, trademark 3-line mark, 6¼″–6¾″ .......... | 215.00 | 245.00 |
| ☐ 88/I, trademark Goebel/V, 6¼″–6¾″ ............. | 175.00 | 205.00 |
| ☐ 88/I, trademark Goebel, 6¼″–6¾″ ............... | 155.00 | 175.00 |
| ☐ 88/II, trademark CM, 8¾″–9″ .................... | 845.00 | 940.00 |
| ☐ 88/II, trademark Full Bee, 8¾″–9″ ............... | 745.00 | 830.00 |
| ☐ 88/II, trademark Stylized Bee, 8¼″–9″ .......... | 495.00 | 545.00 |

**Price Range**

☐ 88/II, trademark 3-line mark, 8¾″–9″ ............. 295.00    335.00
☐ 88/II, trademark Goebel/V, 8¾″–9″ ............... 250.00    285.00
☐ 88/II, trademark Goebel, 8¾″–9″ ................ 231.00    256.00

## 89  LITTLE CELLIST

Figurine in current production. Of the Hummels with musical instruments, "Little Cellist" is one of the favorites among collectors. The cello is attractively modeled and, in the older specimens, it is so effectively colored that it can scarcely be distinguished from wood. The coloring of newer specimens is a bit paler and the instrument does not show up as nicely.

The chief variation between the old and current style, aside from the coloration, is in the boy's eyes. In Crown Mark and other early examples, his eyes are fully open and look toward the viewer, while the present version shows them looking downward at the road. He carries a short walking stick in his right hand and the instrument is slung across his left shoulder on straps. In the old, vividly colored version he wears a yellow orange jacket, gray trousers, black shoes, and a charcoal gray derby style hat. The walking stick is black. New specimens have a paler jacket, blue trousers, light brown shoes, light gray hat, and brown walking stick. "Little Cellist" also has darker hair in the old version. With most Hummels the old trademarks are sought mainly because of scarcity or to fill out a set. In the case of "Little Cellist" there is an additional reason, since old models are visually superior.

**89** Little Cellist

**New Style**

**Old Style**

|  | Price Range | |
|---|---|---|
| ☐ 89/I, trademark CM, 5¼″–6¼″ .................. | 395.00 | 445.00 |
| ☐ 89/I, trademark Full Bee, 5¼″–6¼″ .............. | 320.00 | 360.00 |
| ☐ 89/I, trademark Stylized Bee, 5¼″–6¼″ ......... | 145.00 | 175.00 |
| ☐ 89/I, trademark 3-line mark, 5¼″–6¼″ .......... | 105.00 | 130.00 |
| ☐ 89/I, trademark Goebel/V, 5¼″–6¼″ ............. | 94.00 | 107.00 |
| ☐ 89/I, trademark Goebel, 5¼″–6¼″ ............... | 88.00 | 101.00 |
| ☐ 89/II, trademark CM, 7½″–7¾″.................. | 995.00 | 1205.00 |
| ☐ 89/II, trademark Full Bee, 7½″–7¾″.............. | 495.00 | 555.00 |
| ☐ 89/II, trademark Stylized Bee, 7½″–7¾″ ......... | 295.00 | 335.00 |
| ☐ 89/II, trademark 3-line mark, 7½″–7¾″ .......... | 245.00 | 275.00 |
| ☐ 89/II, trademark Goebel/V, 7½″–7¾″............. | 205.00 | 235.00 |
| ☐ 89/II, trademark Goebel, 7½″–7¾″............... | 195.00 | 220.00 |

## 90 A and B  EVENTIDE & ADORATION

Set of bookends, closed edition. This extremely rare set of bookends was produced briefly in the 1930s. It is sometimes listed in reference works as a "closed number" rather than a "closed edition." However, sufficient information exists to confirm that it was, if only temporarily, put into production. The edition was closed out on February 28, 1938. The motifs will readily be recognized as #23 "Adoration" and #99 "Eventide." "Adoration" is shown without the shrine. The figures are mounted on stout wooden bases. This set exists with the Crown Mark only. Since recent sale of this item cannot be verified, a speculation on price cannot be made. If found, it would undoubtedly be worth several thousand dollars.

## 91/A and 91/B  ANGELS AT PRAYER

Set of two wall fonts in current production. This set consists of one angel facing left and another facing right, both measuring 3⅜″ × 5″ including the bowl. There is an old and a restyled version, readily distinguishable. In the old version, the angels have no halos, while in the new they do. This change was made at the outset of the 3-line mark period. Thus, all sets that bear the Crown, Full Bee, and Stylized Bee marks are of the old type, while those marked 3-line, Goebel/V, and Goebel are the new variety with halo.

The angels wear red robes with pale polka dots and have bluish wings. Their hair is blonder in the new version than in the old. These figures are priced below **as a set**. When sold individually the prices are generally 40%–50% of those shown.

| ☐ 91/A and B, trademark CM, 3⅜″ × 5″............. | 225.00 | 240.00 |
|---|---|---|
| ☐ 91/A and B, trademark Full Bee, 3⅜″ × 5″........ | 200.00 | 220.00 |
| ☐ 91/A and B, trademark Stylized Bee, 3⅜″ × 5″ ... | 150.00 | 160.00 |
| ☐ 91/A and B, trademark 3-line mark, 3⅜″ × 5″ .... | 50.00 | 60.00 |
| ☐ 91/A and B, trademark Goebel/V, 3⅜″ × 5″....... | 40.00 | 45.00 |
| ☐ 91/A and B, trademark Goebel, 3⅜″ × 5″......... | 35.00 | 45.00 |

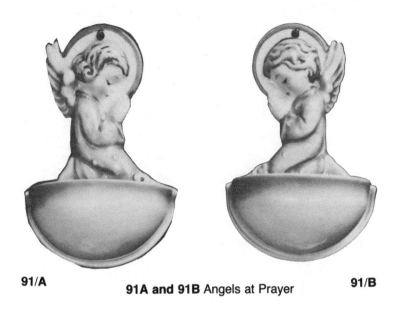

**91A and 91B** Angels at Prayer

## 92 MERRY WANDERER PLAQUE

Wall plaque in current production. It was inevitable that "Merry Wanderer," **the** symbolic Hummel, should be incorporated in a wall plaque. It is well to note, however, that #92 was designed and released in 1938, long before the "Merry Wanderer" had come into its present prominence. The plaque has been produced in one basic size, given as 4¾″ × 5″ on the current Hummel retail list, but many size variations will be noted, ranging from 4½″ × 5″ to 5″ × 5½″. Some specimens bearing the Crown Mark have a 1938 copyright date, others do not; apparently the former represent an earlier edition. The factory signature will be found on the front and back of some specimens, but only on the back of others.

The figure is not intended to be an exact duplication of the "Merry Wanderer" figurine, but is merely similar in costuming and pose. A boy walks briskly along carrying a satchel in one hand and in the other he holds an umbrella thrown across his shoulder. He wears a short green jacket, white buttoned vest, red trousers, black shoes, white socks, and a black derby style hat with narrow brim. The satchel is primarily gray with tones of pink and a few strokes of red. On the background of the beige plaque, a roadside and a house are painted in the distance. The figure is scaled to be large so that it extends vertically the entire height of the plaque, save for the frame area.

**92** Merry Wanderer

|  | Price Range | |
|---|---|---|
| ☐ 92, trademark CM, 4½″ × 5″ to 5″ × 5½″.......... | 345.00 | 390.00 |
| ☐ 92, trademark Full Bee, 4½″ × 5″ to 5″ × 5½″..... | 195.00 | 225.00 |
| ☐ 92, trademark Stylized Bee, 4½″ × 5″ to 5″ × 5½″ | 145.00 | 170.00 |
| ☐ 92, trademark 3-line mark, 4½″ × 5″ to 5″ × 5½″ | 95.00 | 115.00 |
| ☐ 92, trademark Goebel/V, 4½″ × 5″ to 5″ × 5½″.... | 85.00 | 105.00 |
| ☐ 92, trademark Goebel, 4½″ × 5″ to 5″ × 5½″...... | 68.50 | 78.00 |

## 93 LITTLE FIDDLER PLAQUE

Wall plaque in current production. The "Little Fiddler Plaque" has been a source of some confusion as one reference book lists it as discontinued, which it never has been. There are two scarce versions and one quite common one, although even the common "Little Fiddler Plaque" with early trademarks is no longer inexpensive. During the early stages of production a change was made in background design and specimens with the so-called first background did not get into wide circulation. The alteration is obvious enough when one is aware that two distinct backgrounds exist. In the scarce version, the village houses that form a backdrop to the "Little Fiddler" are portrayed in a subdued manner with pastel coloring and outlines

**93** Little Fiddler

that are hardly discernable. In the revised style, there is much greater emphasis placed on background, with the houses shown in increased detail and bolder coloration. The buildings are also larger in size, extending vertically to the plaque's entire height. There is also a cream overglaze version sought after by collectors.

The theme of a child violinist, who apparently plays in hopes of donations from passersby on the street, has been frequently employed by the factory. It is more effective on this wall plaque than other standard Hummel themes, thanks to the pleasing background which renders the scene more complete than a figurine could be. The boy is wearing an orange-red long coat (baggy and very likely a hand-me-down from an elder brother), a white shirt, grayish green trousers, a black derby style hat with narrow brim, and a prominent bow tie. He is also carrying a black umbrella with brown handle. The houses are shown in converging perspective, as if the boy were standing at the entrance to a street or walk. Buildings line both sides of the street and fade at a point roughly equal to the plaque's center, obscured by the figure. Rooftops are shown in shades of pink and red.

|  | Price Range | |
|---|---|---|
| □ 93, trademark CM, 4½″ × 5″ to 5″ × 5½″ (new style) | 350.00 | 385.00 |
| □ 93, trademark CM, 4½″ × 5″ to 5″ × 5½″ (old style) | 1500.00 | 1650.00 |
| □ 93, trademark Full Bee, 4½″ × 5″ to 5″ × 5½″ | 200.00 | 220.00 |
| □ 93, trademark Stylized Bee, 4½″ × 5″ to 5″ × 5½″ | 150.00 | 175.00 |
| □ 93, trademark 3-line mark, 4½″ × 5″ to 5″ × 5½″ | 100.00 | 110.00 |
| □ 93, trademark Goebel/V, 4½″ × 5″ to 5″ × 5½″ | 80.00 | 90.00 |
| □ 93, trademark Goebel, 4½″ × 5″ to 5″ × 5½″ | 68.50 | 75.00 |

## 94  SURPRISE

Figurine in current production. The original name of "Surprise" was "The Duet." This is one of a very few Hummel models whose name derives

**94** Surprise

exclusively from facial expression. "Surprise" shows a boy and girl looking intently at something in an attitude that may be interpreted as wonder or surprise. Some early specimens have a rectangular base; the base on all later and current examples is oval.

The boy wears a smart blue jacket, green and brown lederhosen, white shirt, suspenders, brown boots, and white socks with touches of brown. He has a Tyrolean style brown hat and orange bow tie. The girl has a white blouse with short sleeves, a black vest, a bright red skirt, red shoes, and white socks, highlighted with colored bands. She wears her henna-colored hair in braids tied with orange-red ribbons. Over her right arm she carries a wickerwork basket in shades of light and dark brown. These figures, in slightly altered poses, were also released as separate figurines; the girl as #96 "Little Shopper" and the boy as #95 "Brother." There have been three size versions of "Surprise." Model #95 (5¾") is now a closed edition and ranks as the scarcest. Specimens in which the boy wears a blue shirt instead of the standard white are also rather scarce and worth a premium over the usual values.

| | Price Range | |
|---|---|---|
| ☐ 94/3/0, trademark CM 4″–4½″.................... | **175.00** | **205.00** |
| ☐ 94/3/0, trademark Full Bee, 4″–4½″............. | **170.00** | **200.00** |
| ☐ 94/3/0, trademark Stylized Bee, 4″–4½″ ........ | **120.00** | **140.00** |
| ☐ 94/3/0, trademark 3-line mark, 4″–4½″.......... | **85.00** | **105.00** |
| ☐ 94/3/0, trademark Goebel/V, 4″–4½″............ | **70.00** | **90.00** |
| ☐ 94/3/0, trademark Goebel, 4″–4½″.............. | **66.00** | **81.00** |
| ☐ 94/I, trademark CM, 5¼″–5½″ ................... | **445.00** | **505.00** |
| ☐ 94/I, trademark Full Bee, 5¼″–5½″ ............. | **270.00** | **305.00** |
| ☐ 94/I, trademark Stylized Bee, 5¼″–5½″.......... | **170.00** | **200.00** |
| ☐ 94/I, trademark 3-line mark, 5¼″–5½″ .......... | **112.00** | **127.00** |
| ☐ 94/I, trademark Goebel/V, 5¼″–5½″ ............ | **98.00** | **122.00** |
| ☐ 94/I, trademark Goebel, 5¼″–5½″ .............. | **94.50** | **110.00** |
| ☐ 94, trademark CM, 5¾″........................... | **495.00** | **555.00** |
| ☐ 94, trademark Full Bee, 5¾″ .................... | **298.00** | **332.00** |
| ☐ 94, trademark Stylized Bee, 5¾″................ | **170.00** | **197.00** |

## 95 BROTHER

Figurine in current production. "Brother" is essentially the same youth as the boy in #94 "Surprise," to which the reader is referred for a description of his attire. His attitude is precisely the same except for the tilt of his head and facial expression, which no longer has quite the look of surprise that it carries in #94. The face appears to have gotten a bit thinner at the same time. "Brother" was once known as "Our Hero." The description of clothing coloration should be regarded as flexible. A number of variations will be found, none of which appear to exercise any great influence on value.

**95** Brother

|  | **Price Range** | |
|---|---|---|
| ☐ 95, trademark CM, 5¼″–5¾″ | 315.00 | 355.00 |
| ☐ 95, trademark Full Bee, 5¼″–5¾″ | 215.00 | 245.00 |
| ☐ 95, trademark Stylized Bee, 5¼″–5¾″ | 145.00 | 170.00 |
| ☐ 95, trademark 3-line mark, 5¼″–5¾″ | 95.00 | 115.00 |
| ☐ 95, trademark Goebel/V, 5¼″–5¾″ | 75.00 | 95.00 |
| ☐ 95, trademark Goebel, 5¼″–5¾″ | 66.00 | 76.00 |

## 96  LITTLE SHOPPER

Figurine in current production. "Little Shopper" is a virtual carbon copy of the girl in #94 "Surprise." The model has been known as "Errand Girl."

| | | |
|---|---|---|
| ☐ 96, trademark CM, 4½″–5″ | 250.00 | 270.00 |
| ☐ 96, trademark Full Bee, 4½″–5″ | 150.00 | 170.00 |
| ☐ 96, trademark Stylized Bee, 4½″–5″ | 100.00 | 120.00 |
| ☐ 96, trademark 3-line mark, 4½″–5″ | 75.00 | 85.00 |

**96** Little Shopper

| | | Price Range | |
|---|---|---|---|
| ☐ 96, trademark Goebel/V, 4½"–5"................ | · | **65.00** | **75.00** |
| ☐ 96, trademark Goebel, 4½"–5".................. | | **55.00** | **65.00** |

## 97  TRUMPET BOY

Figurine in current production. "Trumpet Boy" is a chubby, rosy-cheeked youth who stands with one hand in his trouser pocket and holds a trumpet beneath his other arm. Though listed in one size only, variations of as much as a half inch in height have been recorded. There is one genuinely scarce version of this model, stamped "Design Patent No. 116,404" on the underside of the base. Having been unable to collect any reliable information on it, we have refrained from giving prices.

The boy is dressed in a green short jacket with red plaid striping, a white shirt, green lederhosen with matching suspenders, brown boots, and grayish socks. He wears a red bandanna tie. His hair is sandy brown and closely cropped, combed forward at the sides. His lips are bright red.

**97** Trumpet Boy

| | Price Range | |
|---|---|---|
| ☐ 97, trademark CM, 4½″–4¾″.................... | 195.00 | 225.00 |
| ☐ 97, trademark CM, over 4¾″.................... | 245.00 | 280.00 |
| ☐ 97, trademark Full Bee, 4½″–4¾″ .............. | 145.00 | 170.00 |
| ☐ 97, trademark Full Bee, over 4¾″ .............. | 145.00 | 170.00 |
| ☐ 97, trademark Stylized Bee, 4½″–4¾″ ........... | 115.00 | 140.00 |
| ☐ 97, trademark 3-line mark, 4½″–4¾″ ............ | 80.00 | 100.00 |
| ☐ 97, trademark Goebel/V, 4½″–4¾″.............. | 60.00 | 80.00 |
| ☐ 97, trademark Goebel, 4½″–4¾″................ | 55.00 | 65.00 |

## 98 SISTER

Figurine in current production. "Sister" is regarded as a companion piece to #95 "Brother" (see above). "Sister" is a girl holding a pair of red flowers with dark centers in her right hand. Over her left arm she carries an empty basket. She wears a white puffy-sleeved blouse, a black jumper style dress, a white apron with decorations of red semicircles, black shoes, and white socks tinged with brown and green (there is occasionally some color variation). She has light brown hair tied at the sides in red ribbons.

"Sister" appears as the female half of Hummel's #101 "To Market" table lamp, more or less identical to this version except that in #101 she carries

**98** Sister

a bottle in her basket. Some specimens will be found with an incised 1962 copyright date.

The largest model, 98, is no longer in production. A premium is generally given for specimens of 98/2/0 standing 4¾" and for 98/0 standing 5½". There are reports of taller examples than these, bearing the 98/2/0 and 98/0 designations, which would be worth an additional 20% to 30%.

| | Price Range | |
|---|---|---|
| ☐ 98/2/0, trademark CM, 4½"–4¾" ............... | 150.00 | 170.00 |
| ☐ 98/2/0, trademark Full Bee, 4½"–4¾" ........... | 95.00 | 110.00 |
| ☐ 98/2/0, trademark Stylized Bee, 4½"–4¾" ....... | 100.00 | 120.00 |
| ☐ 98/2/0, trademark 3-line mark, 4½"–4¾" ........ | 75.00 | 85.00 |
| ☐ 98/2/0, trademark Goebel/V, 4½"–4¾" ........... | 60.00 | 70.00 |
| ☐ 98/2/0, trademark Goebel, 4½"–4¾" ............. | 55.00 | 65.00 |
| ☐ 98/0, trademark CM, 5¼"–5½" ................... | 180.00 | 200.00 |
| ☐ 98/0, trademark Full Bee, 5¼"–5½" ............. | 120.00 | 140.00 |
| ☐ 98/0, trademark Stylized Bee, 5¼"–5½" ......... | 125.00 | 145.00 |
| ☐ 98/0, trademark 3-line mark, 5¼"–5½" .......... | 95.00 | 105.00 |
| ☐ 98/0, trademark Goebel/V, 5¼"–5½" ............. | 75.00 | 85.00 |
| ☐ 98/0, trademark Goebel, 5¼"–5½" ............... | 66.00 | 75.00 |
| ☐ 98, trademark CM, 5¾" ......................... | 620.00 | 355.00 |
| ☐ 98, trademark Full Bee, 5¾" ................... | 220.00 | 240.00 |
| ☐ 98, trademark Stylized Bee, 5¾" ............... | 160.00 | 200.00 |

## 99 EVENTIDE

Figurine in current production. There is one rare version of "Eventide" in cream overglaze, which was removed from the market after very limited circulation. Otherwise, there is not much variation between the early and recent specimens in either design or coloration, though many size differences will be noted. "Eventide," a sort of meditative composition is one of the better Hummel group figurines featuring multiple components. A boy and girl sit side by side on a fence while two sheep lie recumbent on the ground beneath them. The title is apparently suggested by the fact that sheep are more likely to be in repose toward nightfall, after grazing all day.

The boy is wearing an Alpine outfit comprised of a violet jacket, white shirt, green lederhosen with matching suspenders, black or dark brown shoes, and white socks ribbed with pastel violet or brown. His hat is green with a red band, and red and yellow feather. He plays a horn. His companion is attired in a green short-sleeved dress, orange skirt, brown shoes, socks similar to his. She has a maroon kerchief over her head. The fence is modeled to give the appearance of wood. The sheep lie with their heads and shoulders together, as sheep have a habit of doing, for warmth. Some flowers and shrubbery grow up from the oval base, styled in a manner to suggest rock laden terrain.

**99** Eventide

| | **Price Range** | |
|---|---|---|
| ☐ 99, trademark CM, 4¼" × 5" ..................... | 495.00 | 525.00 |
| ☐ 99, trademark Full Bee, 4¼" × 5" ................. | 345.00 | 375.00 |
| ☐ 99, trademark Stylized Bee, 4¼" × 5" ........... | 195.00 | 225.00 |
| ☐ 99, trademark 3-line mark, 4¼" × 5" .............. | 145.00 | 165.00 |
| ☐ 99, trademark Goebel/V, 4¼" × 5" ................ | 130.00 | 150.00 |
| ☐ 99, trademark Goebel, 4¼" × 5" .................. | 125.00 | 140.00 |

## 100 SHRINE

Lamp base, discontinued. The "Shrine" table lamp is known to exist only with the Crown and Full Bee trademarks. It was produced only for a brief period and, even when in production, its distribution was limited. Speculation on the reason for a model being discontinued is always hazardous. Inasmuch as #100 was issued at about the same time as another lamp base, #101 "To Market," and both were quickly discontinued, it may be assumed that the additional cost of lamp base production was not met with sufficient public response to warrant continued manufacturing. #100 shows a boy and girl at a wayside shrine, nearly identical to #23 "Adoration" although neither the enameling nor the representation of the Madonna and Child plaque is as fine as in "Adoration." The boy is generally found with a canary yellow jacket with green plaid striping.

| | | |
|---|---|---|
| ☐ 100, trademark CM, 7½" ......................... | 5500.00 + | |
| ☐ 100, trademark Full Bee, 7½" ................... | 5500.00 + | |

## 101 TO MARKET

Lamp base, discontinued. Very few specimens were actually distributed. There is no way of knowing how many were actually made. "To Market" was listed as a closed edition on April 20, 1937. It was later revived, being redesigned and renumbered, as #223 "To Market." The model shows a girl and boy, both snappily dressed, with the girl holding a basket and standing in front of the lamp column. It is a rare example of a Hummel lamp base in which the lamp itself is not incorporated into the design (normally this is done by showing it as a tree trunk).

The boy wears a greenish jacket touched with shades of blue and interlaced with light orange pastel striping, green lederhosen and suspenders, tall brown boots, and a red neckerchief tied into a bow. The girl has a white short-sleeved blouse, black overdress, yellow apron highlighted with semicircular red ornaments, black shoes, and white socks with reddish banding at the top. Both figures are hatless. In her right hand, the girl holds a pair of crimson flowers with green centers. She wears a set of red ribbons in her braided hair. The basket she carries contains a bottle, presumably of tonic water. The lamp column is finished in cream overglaze.

| | | |
|---|---|---|
| ☐ 101, trademark CM, 7½" ......................... | 5000.00 + | |

## 102 VOLUNTEERS

Lamp base, closed edition. "Volunteers" was issued at about the same time as "Shrine," "To Market," and "Farewell" lamp bases, and was removed from production on April 10, 1937 after a short trial on the market. It was perhaps too ambitious a project. Had a single lamp base been issued it might well have been a success, but the market apparently could not absorb four at the same time. "Volunteers" utilizes a motif similar to #50 "Volunteers" of two boys marching off to war. The only known example of this lamp base is in the collection of Mr. Robert L. Miller. The lamp column is white porcelain with a brass receptacle. The two boys stand in front of the column on a white donut base. Although there is no information about its height, this specimen does bear a Double Crown Mark.

|  | Price Range |
|---|---|
| ☐ 102, trademark CM ............................... | 5500.00 + |

## 103 FAREWELL

Lamp base, closed edition. The same general remarks made about #102 "Volunteers" (see above) can be applied to "Farewell." This design was based upon #65, a farewell of a girl waving goodbye. No specimens are believed to be in circulation.

## 104 WAYSIDE DEVOTION

Lamp base, closed edition. "Wayside Devotion" was removed from production somewhat later than the four preceding closed edition lamps (see #'s 100–104 above), on March 3, 1938. Nevertheless, there are still no known specimens in circulation. The design was apparently based on #28 "Wayside Devotion," a figurine of a boy and girl at a religious shrine.

## 105 ADORATION WITH BIRD

Figurine, closed edition. #105 "Adoration with Bird" was traditionally thought to be a closed number, a number used for a model which was never placed in production, rather than a closed edition. Several years ago a specimen of this figurine was discovered and a few more have surfaced since then. A search of the factory's records disclosed that #105 was listed as a closed edition on May 24, 1938, or two and a half months after the "Wayside Devotion" lamp base had been removed from production. Consequently, it ranks among the rarest Hummels of which examples are known to exist. To date it has been found with the Crown Mark only, and considering its date of discontinuance, there should not be any Full Bee or other marks on this piece. The extent to which it was distributed and sold is not known. Quite likely it was placed on sale locally only and never exported to the

U.S. (A good search of Bavarian attics might well turn up further specimens.) The trademark is incised and stamped in blue.

Despite its rarity, "Adoration with Bird" was around long enough to undergo a mold alteration, resulting in two distinct states. The model depicts a boy and a girl, the boy considerably taller than the girl, standing beside a wooden fence. On the opposite side of the fence is a tree in which a bird perches on a branch and appears to be singing. "Adoration with Bird" has also been termed "Bird Lovers." The boy wears a yellow jacket, brightly enameled, with green or grayish green plaid striping, blue short pants, oxblood cutaway shoes, and yellow socks. He holds a bouquet of flowers of various colors. The girl wears a yellowish white short-sleeved blouse, a dark green or black vest, a salmon-colored skirt rendered in rich tones, brown shoes, and yellow socks. The color intensity varies from one specimen to another. The girl's hair is worn in braids at the sides, plaited with flowers over the crown. Herein lies the mold alteration. In the first type, the braids extend outward in a forward direction, as if swept by the wind. The second type portrays them in a more natural attitude. It is almost certain that the first type represents the earlier state. Apparently, it was changed because it was felt that there was no good reason for this windswept effect, as the remainder of the design fails to reflect it. The fence is light reddish brown and simply constructed of a wooden beam lying horizontally across a pair of uprights. The tree is thin and colored a grayish brown. No effort has been made to indicate its total height; only enough is shown to provide a suitable prop for the bird to perch upon. The bird, a canary variety, is mostly yellow with dark wings and a crimson beak. A few red flowers with black centers are on the ground. The base is rectangular.

**Price Range**

□ 105, trademark CM, 4¾" ........................ **4000.00    6000.00**

## 106  MERRY WANDERER PLAQUE

Wall plaque, closed edition. One of the rarest Hummel wall plaques, along with #107 "Little Fiddler" plaque, this was an effort to present the traditional "Merry Wanderer" theme in a plaque with a wooden frame. Its design is identical to the unframed #92 "Merry Wanderer" plaque issued in the same year (1938), differing only in the frame. It was produced in an extremely limited quantity on an experimental basis as a test of public reaction to wooden frame plaques. European wall enamels are normally unframed, a practice dating to the 16th century, and this may well have proved an influence. While the frame is pleasing enough, #106 and #107 failed to appeal to buyers. Consequently, a decision was made to continue production of the unframed variety and close out editions #106 and #107.

The official date of close was August 1, 1938. If it seems that an inordinately high number of Hummels went into closed edition ranks in 1937 and 1938 it must be remembered that the era of enthusiastic collecting had not yet begun. There was no guaranteed demand for each new design as it exists today. Many of the designs closed out in the 1930s would sell today, as there are now thousands of buyers who automatically purchase every new item the factory markets.

The frames differ on #106 and #107, the former being more sharply sloped toward the center and consisting of an unbroken plane. In #107 the frame sides are ribbed and the wood is of a slightly more yellowish color. Both were furnished with triangular shaped metal hangers.

|  | | **Price Range** |  |
|---|---|---|---|
| ☐ 106, trademark CM, 6″ × 6″...................... | | **5000.00** | **7000.00** |

## 107 LITTLE FIDDLER PLAQUE

Wall plaque, closed edition. #107 is identical to the subdued background version of #93 excepting for the wooden frame. It was listed as a closed edition on August 1, 1938.

| ☐ 107, trademark CM, 6″ × 6″...................... | | **5000.00** | **7000.00** |

## 108 ANGEL WITH TWO CHILDREN AT FEET

Wall plaque, closed number. "Angel with Two Children at Feet" was designed in 1938 but apparently never reached production. No specimens are known to be in circulation and there is no information on the design or size. Factory records do indicate that the design was for a wall plaque, probably with a wooden frame and measuring 6″ × 6″.

## 109 HAPPY TRAVELER

Figurine in current production. "Happy Traveler" is a variation on the "Merry Wanderer" theme: A youth on the road, his destination unknown, but his determination unquestioned. "Happy Traveler" carries, like "Merry Wanderer," an umbrella; but instead of thrust across his shoulder, the umbrella is held beneath his arm. He does not carry a satchel, such as "Merry Wanderer," which leads to the speculation that "Happy Traveler" is bound on a shorter journey. Rather than a full striding motion, "Happy Traveler" has one leg raised high and the other foot firmly planted on the ground.

There are three basic sizes, of which only two are still in production. Some confusion arises from the fact that the size indicator was dropped from the small version during the 1970s. The collector must keep reminding himself of the fact that 109 is merely a later production of 109/0 and that the two do not represent separate editions or sizes. This is further complicated by another circumstance, the existence of an old 109 designation while the 109/0 designation was in use. This designation appeared on the largest size, measuring 7¾″, but has been discontinued.

"Happy Traveler" was once known as "Wanderer," but this was too similar to "Merry Wanderer" and had to be changed. Otherwise this model has led a more or less unaltered existence in the more than 40 years of its production since its introduction in 1938. The boy wears a pastel or muted

**109** Happy Traveler

green jacket, very pale brown trousers which could almost be called white with brown highlighting, a white shirt, and gray shoes. He has a brown cap and carries a red umbrella. The figure stands on a small circular base. The 7½″ size, 109/11, was permanently retired in 1982.

| | Price Range | |
|---|---|---|
| ☐ 109/0, trademark CM, 4¾″–5″.................... | **170.00** | **255.00** |
| ☐ 109/0, trademark Full Bee, 4¾″–5″ .............. | **145.00** | **175.00** |
| ☐ 109/0, trademark Stylized Bee, 4¾″–5″.......... | **95.00** | **125.00** |
| ☐ 109/0, trademark 3-line mark, 4¾″–5″ .......... | **70.00** | **90.00** |
| ☐ 109, trademark Goebel/V, 5″ ..................... | **55.00** | **75.00** |
| ☐ 109, trademark Goebel, 5″ ....................... | **55.00** | **70.00** |
| ☐ 109/II, trademark CM, 7½″ ....................... | **495.00** | **555.00** |
| ☐ 109/II, trademark Full Bee, 7½″ ................. | **550.00** | **650.00** |
| ☐ 109/II, trademark Stylized Bee, 7½″.............. | **345.00** | **365.00** |
| ☐ 109/II, trademark 3-line mark, 7½″ .............. | **295.00** | **325.00** |
| ☐ 109/II, trademark Goebel/V, 7½″ ................ | **220.00** | **255.00** |
| ☐ 109/II, trademark Goebel, 7½″ ................... | **195.00** | **220.00** |
| ☐ 109, trademark CM, 7¾″ .......................... | **995.00** | **1105.00** |
| ☐ 109, trademark Full Bee, 7¾″ .................... | **745.00** | **830.00** |

## 110 LET'S SING

Figurine in current production. "Let's Sing" is a baseless model of a boy seated on the floor, playing a concertina on which a bird perches and joins him in song. The figure has been produced in three sizes of which there are a number of variations. Only two of these are still in production, the largest, 110 (4"), having been discontinued.

In addition to this figurine, the "Let's Sing" theme has been employed on a candy jar and bowl. The boy wears a green shirt or jacket, short maroon trousers, brown shoes highlighted with red, and white socks stroked with light touches of other colors. He wears a wide orange-red neckerchief tied in a bow at the side, decorated with yellow dots. The concertina has red sides and red hand straps. The bird is pale violet with a yellow beak. In some specimens the interior of the bird's mouth is red and in others yellow. This figure is sometimes found with a 1938 incised copyright date, but its presence or absence has no special bearing on value.

**110** Let's Sing

|  | Price Range | |
|---|---|---|
| ☐ 110/0, trademark CM, 3"–3¼".................... | 200.00 | 225.00 |
| ☐ 110/0, trademark Full Bee, 3"–3¼" ............. | 125.00 | 135.00 |
| ☐ 110/0, trademark Stylized Bee, 3"–3¼".......... | 90.00 | 100.00 |
| ☐ 110/0, trademark 3-line mark, 3"–3¼" .......... | 60.00 | 70.00 |
| ☐ 110/0 trademark Goebel/V, 3"–3¼" .............. | 55.00 | 65.00 |
| ☐ 110/0, trademark Goebel, 3"–3¼"................ | 50.00 | 60.00 |
| ☐ 110/I, trademark CM, 3½"–4" ................... | 200.00 | 220.00 |
| ☐ 110/I, trademark Full Bee, 3½"–4" ............. | 250.00 | 270.00 |

| | Price Range | |
|---|---|---|
| ☐ 110/I, trademark Stylized Bee, 3½"–4"........... | **125.00** | **135.00** |
| ☐ 110/I, trademark 3-line mark, 3½"–4"............ | **100.00** | **110.00** |
| ☐ 110/I, trademark goebel/V, 3½"–4"............... | **80.00** | **90.00** |
| ☐ 110/I, trademark Goebel, 3½"–4" ............... | **72.00** | **80.00** |
| ☐ 110, trademark CM, 4" .......................... | **350.00** | **385.00** |
| ☐ 110, trademark Full Bee, 4" ..................... | **250.00** | **275.00** |

## III/110 LET'S SING

Candy box in current production. The "Let's Sing" candy box was introduced to the line in 1938 and has the distinction of being the first Hummel candy box. There are two styles; the jar and the bowl. The jar has a flat lid and a rim on the lid overhanging the side of the base. The bowl has a sloping lid and a contoured bowl. The bowl style, produced for many years before introduction of the jar, is now a closed edition. So many were manufactured, however, that the edition is far from rare. The jar style was not introduced until 1964. There is a difference in size as the bowl style measures 6¼" and the jar 5¼".

**III/110** Let's Sing

| | Price Range | |
|---|---:|---:|
| ☐ III/110, trademark CM, 6¼"...................... | 495.00 | 555.00 |
| ☐ III/110, trademark Full Bee, 6¼" ................. | 445.00 | 498.00 |
| ☐ III/110, trademark Stylized Bee, 5¼" or 6¼" ...... | 345.00 | 390.00 |
| ☐ III/110, trademark 3-line mark, 5¼" .............. | 115.00 | 135.00 |
| ☐ III/110, trademark Goebel/V, 5¼"................. | 105.00 | 125.00 |
| ☐ III/110, trademark Goebel, 5¼".................. | 90.00 | 101.00 |

## 111 WAYSIDE HARMONY

Figurine in current production. "Wayside Harmony" was introduced in 1938 as part of a two-piece set. On the American market, it was called "Just Sittin'-Boy," while its companion piece, #112 "Just Resting" was "Just Sittin'-Girl." As has occurred with many Hummel figurines, the largest of the three sizes, III(5½"), of "Wayside Harmony" has been discontinued while sale of the two smaller editions continues.

The model depicts a Tyrolean-costumed boy seated on a low fence, alongside a chirping bird. The title suggests both are whistling in tune. The boy wears a green Robin Hood type shirt, richly enameled brown leder-

**111** Wayside Harmony

hosen with matching suspenders, light brown shoes, white socks with hints of green, and a conical green hat with red band and red feather. On the front crosspiece of the suspenders is an attractively colored floral motif. The bird is pale violet, with slightly stronger color on the wings and a yellow beak. On the ground are several red flowers with black centers.

The "Wayside Harmony" theme was used also for a lamp base and, in combination with "Just Resting," a set of bookends. See #II/111, #224, and #121. Size variations will be encountered in "Wayside Harmony." Some specimens bear a 1938 incised copyright date.

|  | Price Range | |
|---|---|---|
| ☐ 111/3/0, trademark CM, 3¾"–4" | 270.00 | 300.00 |
| ☐ 111/3/0, trademark Full Bee, 3¾"–4" | 170.00 | 200.00 |
| ☐ 111/3/0, trademark Stylized Bee, 3¾"–4" | 120.00 | 155.00 |
| ☐ 111/3/0, trademark 3-line mark, 3¾"–4" | 79.00 | 92.00 |
| ☐ 111/3/0, trademark Goebel/V, 3¾"–4" | 60.00 | 71.00 |
| ☐ 111/3/0, trademark Goebel, 3¾"–4" | 425.00 | 470.00 |
| ☐ 111/I, trademark CM, 5"–5½" | 270.00 | 300.00 |
| ☐ 111/I, trademark Full Bee, 5"–5½" | 170.00 | 200.00 |
| ☐ 111/I, trademark Stylized Bee, 5"–5½" | 120.00 | 150.00 |
| ☐ 111/I, trademark 3-line mark, 5"–5½" | 78.00 | 92.00 |
| ☐ 111/I, trademark Goebel/V, 5"–5½" | 68.00 | 82.00 |
| ☐ 111/I, trademark Goebel, 5"–5½" | 63.00 | 72.00 |
| ☐ 111, trademark CM, 5½" | 445.00 | 500.00 |
| ☐ 111, trademark Full Bee, 5½" | 295.00 | 335.00 |
| ☐ 111, trademark Stylized Bee, 5½" | 170.00 | 200.00 |
| ☐ 111, trademark 3-line mark, 5½" | 148.00 | 168.00 |

## II/111 WAYSIDE HARMONY

Lamp base, closed edition. The "Wayside Harmony" lamp base was introduced in the early 1950s and at first bore the number II/111. Shortly thereafter the model was renumbered 224 and the number II/111 retired as a "closed edition." Consequently this piece is not rare on the whole, since it is still in production, but specimens with the designator II/111 are scarce indeed. It is not known for certain whether any were made with the Crown trademark. The only examples of which there is record carry the Full Bee, but it is quite possible that some could have been stamped with the earlier mark. When the II/111 number was closed out a moderate restyling was done, its chief change being that the bird on the fence, shown in the "Wayside Harmony" figurine but omitted from the lamp base, was added. The boy's face is turned slightly more forward in the old version and the tree trunk is less textured.

| ☐ II/111, trademark Full Bee, 7½" | 2600.00 | 2860.00 |
|---|---|---|

## 112 JUST RESTING

Figurine in current production. "Just Resting", originally known as "Just Sittin'-Girl," was designed as a companion piece to "Wayside Harmony" and, like it, was subsequently incorporated into a lamp base and bookend set. Its first year of production was 1938. Some specimens bear an incised copyright date but the majority do not. The presence or absence of this feature has no influence on value. Some specimens carrying this date, however, do not have any trademark either incised or printed but do have the "M.I. Hummel" signature. As with "Wayside Harmony," there have been three basic sizes, of which the largest, 112 (5½"), has been discontinued.

"Just Resting" portrays a coquettish-looking girl seated on a fence with a basket on the ground. Her head is turned in a three-quarter profile toward her right, which appears no more than a random pose when the model is displayed by itself. The original intention was that "Wayside Harmony" and "Just Resting" be displayed together, with the girl on the boy's left. When this is done, a neat little scene is depicted in which the girl's glance is directed at her companion and his at her. The facial expression of "Just Resting" is one of those masterpieces that occur, even in Hummels, only occasionally. The figure is skillfully modeled, well colored, and, all things taken into account, ranks in the upper echelon of the factory's successes. Some observers see contentment in her face. Others find the expression

**112** Just Reading

one of curiosity, or intense interest. The subdued Mona Lisa smile is intentional on the girl's part and is directed across the fence to "Wayside Harmony," who seems so preoccupied with whistling that some means of distraction are needed. "Just Resting" wears a dark yellow short-sleeved blouse, a maroon vest, a skirt of sea green striped with blue, brown shoes, and white socks. On her head is a red kerchief tied in a bow at the chin. Both her hands are placed on the fence rail in a very natural attitude. A few red flowers plus the basket complete this composition. There is a rare type with no baskets, found in 112/I, but there is not sufficient information to offer a suggestion of prices.

|  | Price Range | |
|---|---|---|
| ☐ 112 3/0, trademark CM, 3¾"–4" ................ | 275.00 | 300.00 |
| ☐ 112 3/0, trademark Full Bee, 3¾"–4" ........... | 175.00 | 195.00 |
| ☐ 112 3/0, trademark Stylized Bee, 3¾"–4" ....... | 125.00 | 145.00 |
| ☐ 112 3/0, trademark 3-line mark, 3¾"–4" ........ | 80.00 | 90.00 |
| ☐ 112 3/0, trademark Goebel/V, 3¾"–4" .......... | 70.00 | 80.00 |
| ☐ 112 3/0, trademark Goebel, 3¾"–4" ............ | 63.00 | 73.00 |
| ☐ 112/I, trademark CM, 4¾"–5½" ................. | 425.00 | 450.00 |
| ☐ 112/I, trademark Full Bee, 4¾"–5½" ............ | 275.00 | 300.00 |
| ☐ 112/I, trademark Stylized Bee, 4¾"–5½" ........ | 175.00 | 195.00 |
| ☐ 112/I, trademark 3-line mark, 4¾"–5½" ......... | 125.00 | 137.50 |
| ☐ 112/I, trademark Goebel/V, 4¾"–5½" ........... | 110.00 | 120.00 |
| ☐ 112/I, trademark Goebel, 4¾"–5½" ............. | 94.50 | 105.00 |
| ☐ 112, trademark CM, 5½" .................... | 500.00 | 550.00 |
| ☐ 112, trademark Full Bee, 5½" .................. | 400.00 | 440.00 |
| ☐ 112, trademark Stylized Bee, 5½"............... | 250.00 | 275.00 |
| ☐ 112, trademark 3-line mark, 5½" ............... | 150.00 | 165.00 |

## II/112 JUST RESTING

Lamp base, closed edition. II/112 is the old Hummel number from the early 1950s, for the lamp base currently known as #225 "Just Resting". As the old number was removed from use after a brief period of production, specimens carrying this designation are quite scarce. There is not a great deal of stylistic difference between the two. The old version shows the girl and her basket to be somewhat larger than the present version and the tree trunk is not so extensively textured. For a description of this refer to #112 above. It has not yet been established whether or not II/112 exists with Crown trademark.

☐ II/112, trademark Full Bee, 7½" .................    2500.00   3500.00

## 113 HEAVENLY SONG

Candleholder, closed edition. This design was originally produced as a candleholder, but was also sold as a figurine without candle receptacle. It has long been a controversy whether or not the piece has been taken out of production. "Heavenly Song" was discontinued for a time during the

3-line trademark era. It was then reissued in limited quantities in 1978 with the Goebel/V trademark. It has now been officially classified as a closed edition by the factory. No specimens have been found bearing the plain Goebel trademark, but that is not to say one does not exist. Older examples are quite rare, especially in the US, probably because the Crown Mark pieces were not imported here at the time of their manufacture, but came over in very limited numbers after the first wave of popularity for Hummel collecting in the 1950s.

The composition is similar to #54 "Silent Night." The Christ Child lies on a bed of rushes, surrounded by an angel and two young children. From the left, the first figure wears a blue gown and a yellow overgarment with incised designing, and red shoes. The second figure wears a drab green gown, and the angel wears a reddish robe and has white, yellow, and blue wings. A few flowers appear on the base which is textured to represent rocks.

The prices given for specimens bearing obsolete trademarks are rough guides only, as sales have not occurred with sufficient frequency to establish dependable values.

|  | Price Range | |
|---|---|---|
| ☐ 113, trademark CM, 3½″ × 4¾″ ................. | 4000.00 | 4400.00 |
| ☐ 113, trademark Full Bee, 3½″ × 4¾″ ............ | 3000.00 | 3300.00 |
| ☐ 113, trademark Stylized Bee .................... | 2500.00 | 2750.00 |
| ☐ 113, trademark Goebel/V, 3½″ × 4¾″............. | 2300.00 | 2530.00 |

## 114 LET'S SING

Ashtray in current production. The motif of this ashtray is adapted from #110 "Let's Sing," to which the reader is referred for information on design and color. The original version, introduced during the Crown Mark period, has the figure on the right side of the dish. It was subsequently switched

**114** Let's Sing

to the left side and the bird slightly remodeled. Pieces with the Crown and Full Bee marks are considered moderately scarce.

| | Price Range | |
|---|---|---|
| ☐ 114, trademark CM, 3½″ × 6¼″ ................. | 995.00 | 1105.00 |
| ☐ 114, trademark Full Bee, 3½″ × 6¼″ ............. | 895.00 | 995.00 |
| ☐ 114, trademark Stylized Bee, 3½″ × 6¼″ ........ | 145.00 | 170.00 |
| ☐ 114, trademark 3-line mark, 3½″ × 6¼″ ......... | 98.00 | 115.00 |
| ☐ 114, trademark Goebel/V, 3½″ × 6¼″ ............. | 73.00 | 87.00 |
| ☐ 114, trademark Goebel, 3½″ × 6¼″ ............... | 65.00 | 76.00 |

## 115  GIRL WITH NOSEGAY

Candleholder in current production. "Girl with Nosegay" belongs to a trio of three figures, normally sold as a set, called in old catalogues "Advent Group", and currently "Christmas Angels." The latter designation may prove confusing as the figures are not only wingless, but are not dressed in anything even approaching angelic garb: Their costuming is that of earthly children. If they are angels, it is in a symbolic sense only. Each holds a candle receptacle. This figure holds a small bunch of flowers. She wears a blue dress with red polka dots, and wine-colored shoes. Her hair is sandy blonde and the flowers are mostly red. All of these figures stand on circular bases.

**115** Girl with Nosegay

**Price Range**

☐ 115, trademark CM, 3½″ ........................    150.00     165.00
☐ 115, trademark Full Bee, 3½″ ..................     80.00      90.00
☐ 115, trademark Stylized Bee, 3½″...............     60.00      70.00
☐ 115, trademark 3-line mark, 3½″ ................     40.00      45.00
☐ 115, trademark Goebel/V, 3½″ ..................     30.00      35.00
☐ 115, trademark Goebel, 3½″ ....................     26.50      32.50

## 116 GIRL WITH FIR TREE

Candleholder in current production. The second in the "Advent Group" or "Christmas Angels" (See #115 above and #117 below). She wears a white short-sleeved blouse, a black vest, an orange skirt, and has a red kerchief pulled over her head. In her left arm she carries a small Christmas tree.

☐ 116, trademark CM, 3½″ ........................    145.00     170.00
☐ 116, trademark Full Bee, 3½″ ..................     75.00      95.00
☐ 116, trademark Stylized Bee, 3½″...............     55.00      75.00

**116** Girl with Fir Tree

| | Price Range | |
|---|---|---|
| ☐ 116, trademark 3-line mark, 3½" ............... | 39.00 | 46.00 |
| ☐ 116, trademark Goebel/V, 3½" ................. | 29.00 | 36.00 |
| ☐ 116, trademark Goebel, 3½" .................... | 26.50 | 31.00 |

## 117  BOY WITH HORSE

Candleholder in current production. Last in the "Advent Group" or "Christmas Angels" set, and the only male figure in the lot. The horse is a wooden toy mounted on wheels, very handsomely modeled. Its owner wears a green jacket, a white shirt, short brown pants, and red shoes, which are very uncommon on Hummel figures.

| | | |
|---|---|---|
| ☐ 117, trademark CM, 3½" ........................ | 125.00 | 135.00 |
| ☐ 117, trademark Full Bee, 3½" ................... | 70.00 | 76.00 |
| ☐ 117, trademark Stylized Bee, 3½"............... | 45.00 | 52.00 |
| ☐ 117, trademark 3-line mark, 3½" ................ | 30.00 | 35.00 |
| ☐ 117, trademark Goebel/V, 3½" .................. | 28.00 | 32.00 |
| ☐ 117, trademark Goebel, 3½" .................... | 26.50 | 30.00 |

**117** Boy with Horse

## 118 LITTLE THRIFTY

Figurine (bank) in current production. This is the only bank ever manufactured by Hummel. It is not, however, classified as a bank but as a figurine. It is doubtful whether any specimens are ever used as banks: the thought of risking damage to an object worth $50 or more in the process of saving a few pennies is hardly pleasant. The receptacle portion of this composition is sometimes referred to by those unacquainted with its nature as merely a tall square box. It is in fact designed to represent an offerings box of the sort found in churches, commonly referred to at one time as "poor boxes."

A small girl is shown reaching high to deposit a coin in the box's slot. She wears a pale green dress, an orange apron with white polka dots, and black shoes. The original version is somewhat taller and less sharply colored than specimens bearing current or recent trademarks. This model is provided with a metal locking disc at the base and a key.

|  | Price Range | |
|---|---|---|
| ☐ 118, trademark CM, 5″–5½″..................... | 495.00 | 555.00 |
| ☐ 118, trademark Full Bee, 5″–5½″ ............... | 345.00 | 390.00 |
| ☐ 118, trademark Stylized Bee, 5″–5½″............ | 175.00 | 205.00 |

**118** Little Thrifty

**Price Range**

☐ 118, trademark 3-line mark, 5″–5½″ ............. **105.00**     **125.00**
☐ 118, trademark Goebel/V, 5″–5½″................ **83.00**     **96.00**
☐ 118, trademark Goebel, 5″–5½″................. **66.00**     **75.00**

## 119 POSTMAN

   Figurine in current production. "Postman" is a very accurate, attractive rendering of a Bavarian letter carrier of the early to mid 19th century. For those who collect Hummels with period themes, this is unquestionably the star item in the entire line. The boy representing the postman is attired and equipped in strictly authentic fashion. He carries, as was the custom in Europe in those days, the mail bag at his chest. Closer observation will reveal that the bag is not really a bag, but a box, in which the letters are arranged in a neat fashion in sequence. Decorating the box front is a symbol of the "posthorn," the horn traditionally sounded by mail carriers to announce their presence in the days preceding the time represented by this figure.

   This "Postman" can be dated historically to the 1850s, as his letters carry both postage stamps and wax seals. Postage stamps were introduced in

**119** Postman

Germany late in the 1840s and the use of wax seals for letters died out by the 1860s, so there is little guesswork involved in arriving at the date. "Postman" wears a long blue overcoat, a white shirt, brown shoes, and a blue official cap with brown brim. A red bow tie completes the visible portions of his outfit. The pose shows him holding aloft a letter and calling out; he is undoubtedly meant to be standing beneath a window.

This model was introduced in 1939 and has since been in continuous production. There is only one official size but numerous size variants, ranging from 5″ to 5½″. Minor differences will be noted in modeling in the earlier versions. The current edition of "Postman" has the textured finish.

|  | Price Range | |
|---|---|---|
| ☐ 119, trademark CM, 5″–5½″..................... | 375.00 | 400.00 |
| ☐ 119, trademark Full Bee, 5″–5½″ ................ | 225.00 | 265.00 |
| ☐ 119, trademark Stylized Bee, 5″–5½″ ........... | 150.00 | 170.00 |
| ☐ 119, trademark 3-line mark, 5″–5½″ ............ | 125.00 | 135.00 |
| ☐ 119, trademark Goebel/V, 5″–5½″................ | 95.00 | 110.00 |
| ☐ 119, trademark Goebel, 5″–5½″................. | 83.00 | 95.00 |

# 120  JOYFUL AND LET'S SING

Set of bookends, closed edition. This set of bookends was introduced in 1939, at the same time that Hummel placed two other bookend sets in production, #121 "Wayside" and "Just Resting" and #122 "Puppy Love" and "Serenade." All of these sets carried wooden bases and employed previously released themes. Unfortunately, they had a very brief lifespan. Whether any specimens of #120, #121, or #122 ever actually reached store shelves is doubtful, as they are just as rare as closed number designations. Their classification as closed editions means the designs were approved for production, but there is no way of determining what stage production reached. All were entered in the factory's books as closed editions on June 16, 1939. Perhaps the war clouds then hanging over Europe had something to do with closing the edition. It is all speculative.

Virtually nothing is available about these bookends as far as published information is concerned. There are no known examples, not even a factory sample. The designing approach was to take already marketed figures, remove their bases, and place the components on shallow blocks of wood, each set comprising two different themes. For a description of "Joyful" and "Let's Sing," the reader is referred to the comments made of #53 and #110. It is not known in what respects, if any, the bookend models differ from the separately produced figurines. It is pointless to attempt stating a price. If any of these sets came up for sale, it is certain it would be in a manner involving bids, either through auction or one of those familiar advertisements in which the owner asks bids, and in these situations the outcome is quite impossible to forecast.

## 121  WAYSIDE HARMONY AND JUST RESTING

Set of bookends, closed edition. See #120 (above). A description of these figures will be found by referring to #111 and #112.

## 122  PUPPY LOVE AND SERENADE

Set of bookends, closed edition. See #120 (above). The figures used in this set are Hummel #1 and #85, to which the reader should refer for information on their design. There is one recorded example, said to be a factory sample.

## 123  MAX AND MORITZ

Figurine in current production. "Max and Moritz," a model showing two boys standing side by side, was formerly known as "Good Friends." It was originally introduced in 1939. There is no special theme here other than the companionship of youth. There has been only one basic size, but many size variations are found. The majority of specimens carry an incised copyright date.

**123** Max and Moritz

The taller boy is wearing a plum jacket with muted striping, a white shirt, short gray pants with plaid stripes in black, dark brown or black high boots, and white socks. His companion is wearing a grayish jacket, a white shirt, long salmon-red trousers, and brown shoes. Both wear red bow ties. The facial expressions are quite different; the smaller youth reflects an appearance of smug satisfaction, which the other stands open-mouthed in an attitude of speaking. Just what the conversation may involve, and to whom it is addressed, are open to interpretation.

|  | **Price Range** | |
|---|---|---|
| ☐ 123, trademark CM, 5″–5½″..................... | 370.00 | 405.00 |
| ☐ 123, trademark Full Bee, 5″–5½″ ............... | 245.00 | 280.00 |
| ☐ 123, trademark Stylized Bee, 5″–5½″ ........... | 145.00 | 175.00 |
| ☐ 123, trademark 3-line mark, 5″–5½″ ............ | 95.00 | 125.00 |
| ☐ 123, trademark Goebel/V, 5″–5½″............... | 85.00 | 105.00 |
| ☐ 123, trademark Goebel, 5″–5½″................. | 77.50 | 89.00 |

## 124 HELLO

Figurine in current production. "Hello" is a figure of a boy in formal attire holding a telephone to his ear. There have been three different sizes, one of which, 124 (6¾″) is now a closed edition. Specimens of the larger versions with early trademarks are genuinely scarce. A number of color changes

**124** Hello

have been made at various times, but the model itself is basically the same today as when first introduced. In 1982, the 124/1 model was temporarily discontinued.

"Hello" has a tuxedo jacket, vest, striped pants, and black polished shoes. In the earliest specimens, with Crown trademarks, the jacket and pants are gray and the vest is primarily white with pale pink stripes. In the early 1950s they were recolored to brown jacket, green pants with dark green stripes, and a more intense pink vest. The current version, whose coloring was of 1960s origin, has a brown jacket, light brown trousers and a white shirt with hints of blue.

The facial expression of "Hello" does not seem to convey the message of the model's title, but is rather one of irritation, perhaps at a phone that never ceases ringing. "Hello" was once known as "The Boss," which might explain the irritability, and at other times, "The Chief." He might just as readily be taken for a hotel manager or other businessman. Despite his boyish face, he is undeniably intended as an adult in caricature. The phone he holds is black and cordless.

| | Price Range | |
|---|---|---|
| ☐ 124/0, trademark CM, 5¾″–6¼″ ................. | 200.00 | 300.00 |
| ☐ 124/0, trademark Full Bee, 5¾″–6¼″ ............ | 250.00 | 270.00 |
| ☐ 124/0, trademark Stylized Bee, 5¾″–6¼″........ | 150.00 | 170.00 |
| ☐ 124/0, trademark 3-line mark, 5¾″–6¼″ ......... | 100.00 | 120.00 |
| ☐ 124/0, trademark Goebel/V, 5¾″–6¼″ ........... | 85.00 | 95.00 |
| ☐ 124/0, trademark Goebel, 5¾″–6¼″ ............. | 77.50 | 90.00 |
| ☐ 124/I, trademark CM, 6¾″–7″ ................... | 1000.00 | 1200.00 |
| ☐ 124/I, trademark Full Bee, 6¾″–7″ .............. | 500.00 | 575.00 |
| ☐ 124/I, trademark Stylized Bee, 6¾″–7″.......... | 350.00 | 375.00 |
| ☐ 124/I, trademark Goebel/V, 6¾″–7″ ............. | 110.00 | 120.00 |
| ☐ 124/I, trademark Goebel, 6¾″–7″ ............... | 80.00 | 90.00 |

## 125 VACATION TIME

Wall plaque in current production. This attractive composition was originally known as "On Holiday" and is occasionally referred to as "Happy Holidays." It shows a boy and a girl in Bavarian native dress at a cottage window from which they salute and call to persons below. Apparently the vacation, or holiday, is summer recess from school.

Plaques are always a bit unpredictable. Even at best they are not the ideal vehicle for the Hummel type of art, which depends so much on three-dimensional modeling for its effect. So often a fine design, which seems perfect for a plaque, results in a disappointment. "Vacation Time" is agreed to be one of the factory's finest efforts in the medium. The modeling is lifelike and in high relief, the colors rich and well coordinated. The composition is handsomely balanced to create just the feeling Sister Hummel must have intended when sketching this subject.

The cottage window has no glass, but wooden Dutch doors that open outward, a type still to be seen in the Bavarian countryside. Hanging outside is a windowbox filled with red flowers. This windowbox, though not a central component of the design, provides the chief distinguishing feature between old and new specimens of "Vacation Time." In the old version, there are six wooden slats running vertically across the front of the box. There are only five in the current edition. Aside from this, the changes are very minor. It will be noted that the boy's left hand, which is raised and holding several flowers, is positioned slightly differently and that the contour of his mouth has changed.

The coloring in this model is exceptional; one can almost see the sunlight falling upon the figures. The girl wears a white short-sleeved dress, a black vest, and blue skirt. The boy has a white shirt, medium brown jacket with plaid striping, and a blue mountaineer type hat with brown band and feather. Behind them at the window is a set of cream-colored curtains, ornamented with arrangements of small red dots. The doors are reinforced with horizontal wooden slats and bear peepholes in the form of hearts, which are carved out of the wood.

The old version was furnished with a string hanger at the back. On new specimens there is merely a hole for hanging, designed to be slipped over a nail. It is important to take notice of the size difference. The old version is somewhat larger, measuring 4⅜″ × 5¼″, while the new style is 4″ × 4¾″. This variation is entirely in the frame as the subject is no larger or smaller.

**125** Vacation Time

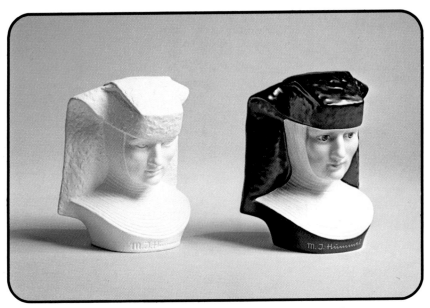

**HU-2, Portrait Bust of Sister Hummel**

(left to right) **205, German Store Plaque**
**187, Current Store Plaques in English**

**10, Flower Madonna, various sizes**

**214, Nativity Set**

(left to right) **25, Silent Night Candleholder**
**54, Angelic Sleep Candleholder**

(left to right) **251/A, Good Friends Bookend**
**251/B, She Loves Me Bookend**

**392, Little Band Music Box**

(left to right) **360/B, Boy Wall Vase**
**360/A, Boy and Girl Wall Vase**
**360/C, Girl Wall Vase**

(left to right) **44/A, Culprits Lamp Base**
**44/B, Out of Danger Lamp Base**

(left to right) **280, 1975 Anniversary Plate**
**281, 1980 Anniversary Plate**

(left to right) **222, Madonna Wall Plaque**
**273, 1980 Annual Plate**

(left to right) **701, 1979 Annual Bell**
**702, 1980 Annual Bell**
**700, 1978 Annual Bell**

(left to right) **III / 53, Joyful Candy Bowl and Candy Jar**

(left to right) **34, Singing Lesson Ashtray**
**166, Boy With Bird Ashtray**

| | **Price Range** | |
|---|---|---|
| ☐ 125, trademark CM, 4⅜″ × 5¼″ .................. | 515.00 | 580.00 |
| ☐ 125, trademark Full Bee, 4⅜″ × 5¼″ ............. | 355.00 | 400.00 |
| ☐ 125, trademark Stylized Bee, 4⅜″ × 5¼″ ......... | 215.00 | 245.00 |
| ☐ 125, trademark Stylized Bee, 4″ × 4¾″ ........... | 215.00 | 245.00 |
| ☐ 125, trademark 3-line mark, 4″ × 4¾″............. | 155.00 | 185.00 |
| ☐ 125, trademark Goebel/V, 4″ × 4¾″............... | 115.00 | 135.00 |
| ☐ 125, trademark Goebel, 4″ × 4¾″................. | 100.00 | 112.00 |

## 126 RETREAT TO SAFETY

Wall plaque in current production. "Retreat to Safety" was placed on the market at the same time as "Vacation Time" (See #125 above), early in World War II. If it is not quite equal to "Vacation Time" in composition, it is surely among the better Hummel plaques. The theme is at once charming and humorous: A boy leaping upon a fence to escape the advances of a not very menacing frog.

**126** Retreat to Safety

The primary color in "Retreat to Safety" is brown, with light beige background and a speckled frame edge. The boy wears a plaid striped jacket, short lederhosen, slippers, and Tyrolean hat with feather, all in rich wine brown. He also wears a white shirt and white socks. The fence, composed of twin horizontal slats on vertical posts, is grayish brown. On the ground in the background there are several flowers and reeds. All in all, the frog seems to steal the show as a plump, green splendid model. He has bulging eyes, a red mouth, and brown stripes at his back. Both frog and youth stare at each other intently. Though no major change has been made on this model, it will be observed that older specimens are somewhat larger than the recent and current editions. There are insignificant color variations.

| | Price Range | |
|---|---|---|
| ☐ 126, trademark CM, 4¾" × 4¾" to 5" × 5" ........ | **500.00** | **550.00** |
| ☐ 126, trademark Full Bee, 4¾" × 4¾" to 5" × 5" ... | **280.00** | **300.00** |
| ☐ 126, trademark Stylized Bee, 4" × 4¾" to 5" × 5". | **220.00** | **240.00** |
| ☐ 126, trademark 3-lin mark, 4¾" × 4¾" to 5" × 5".. | **160.00** | **180.00** |
| ☐ 126, trademark Goebel/V, 4¾" × 4¾" to 5" × 5" .. | **120.00** | **130.00** |
| ☐ 126, trademark Goebel, 4¾" × 4¾" to 5" × 5" .... | **100.00** | **110.00** |

## 127 DOCTOR

Figurine in current production. "Doctor," one of the more popular occupational Hummels, is a little girl whose doll's leg is broken. The girl looks down contemplatively at the patient who lies on the circular base at the girl's feet. Is surgery in order? Or will doses of tender care and affection suffice? A trip to the toyshop for a new doll seems out of the question. "Doctor" wears a white gown, a long cream-colored hospital type jacket with deep pockets, reddish slippers, and white socks highlighted with touches of red and brown. A pair of eyeglasses is pushed up on her forehead. Her hair is henna-colored with streaks of reddish brown. The doll is modeled as a wooden "walking puppet" of the mid 1800s, in the form of a male with reddish hair and large dots representing coat buttons at his chest.

There are numerous size variations. In the original version, which was introduced around 1940, the doll's feet overhang the base slightly. This is not found in later specimens. The current edition has a textured finish.

| | Price Range | |
|---|---|---|
| ☐ 127, trademark CM, 4¾"–5¼" ................... | **295.00** | **315.00** |
| ☐ 127, trademark Full Bee, 4¾" × 5¼" ............. | **165.00** | **185.00** |
| ☐ 127, trademark Stylized Bee, 4¾"–5¼" .......... | **121.00** | **132.00** |
| ☐ 127, trademark 3-line mark, 4¾"–5¼" .......... | **93.00** | **110.00** |
| ☐ 127, trademark Goebel/V, 4¾–5¼" .............. | **68.00** | **82.00** |
| ☐ 127, trademark Goebel, 4¾"–5¼" .............. | **63.00** | **71.00** |

**127** Doctor

## 128 BAKER

Figurine in current production. Another popular occupational theme, "Baker" has been a consistently good seller. Specimens are frequently used as window or interior decoration in European bakery shops, and to a lesser degree, in the U.S. There are some color variations and considerable differences in size, from 4¾" to 5¼" tall. A premium is generally given for the larger, older specimens, though this is in no way a rare figure. The current edition of "Baker" has the textured finish. "Baker" is holding a freshly decorated cake on a serving platter. He points to himself, with the index finger of his left hand, as if to say, "Any compliments to the chef should be directed here." If his creation is as appealing to the taste as to the sight, he will likely receive some. As experienced collectors are aware, foodstuffs are seldom rendered very successfully in porcelain, except perhaps for fruits. In most specimens, "Baker" wears a blue sweater, gray or pale violet trousers, and dark gray shoes. He has a white apron and a tall white chef's hat.

**128** Baker

| | Price Range | |
|---|---|---|
| ☐ 128, trademark CM, 4¾"–5"..................... | **350.00** | **385.00** |
| ☐ 128, trademark Full Bee, 4¾"–5" ............... | **200.00** | **220.00** |
| ☐ 128, trademark Stylized Bee, 4¾"–5"........... | **110.00** | **120.00** |
| ☐ 128, trademark 3-line mark, 4¾"–5" ............ | **100.00** | **110.00** |
| ☐ 128, trademark Goebel/V, 4¾"–5"............... | **82.00** | **90.00** |
| ☐ 128, trademark Goebel, 4¾"–5"................. | **72.00** | **80.00** |

## 129  BAND LEADER

Figurine in current production. This is a serious little fellow who is obviously at the head of a symphony orchestra, leading it in a classical selection. He mounts a wooden platform before an open book of musical composition which rests on a stand. As in the old tradition, he uses no baton but only movements of his hands to direct the musicians. His facial expression is that of intense concentration.

"Band Leader" was originally known simply as "Leader." There are numerous size and color variations, especially among the older specimens.

**129** Band Leader

The standard outfit is a green jacket, a white shirt, a greenish vest, rust-colored trousers, highly polished black shoes, and an oversized red bow tie. The high jacket collar suggests a dating of 1840–1860. Musical notations are indicated on the pages from which he conducts.

| | | Price Range | |
|---|---|---|---|
| ☐ 129, trademark CM, 5″–5⅞″..................... | | 395.00 | 425.00 |
| ☐ 129, trademark Full Bee 5″–5⅞″................. | | 245.00 | 275.00 |
| ☐ 129, trademark Stylized Bee, 5″–5⅞″............ | | 145.00 | 165.00 |
| ☐ 129, trademark 3-line mark, 5″–5⅞″ ............. | | 120.00 | 140.00 |
| ☐ 129, trademark Goebel/V, 5″–5⅞″................ | | 95.00 | 115.00 |
| ☐ 129, trademark Goebel, 5″–5⅞″.................. | | 88.00 | 98.00 |

## 130 DUET

Figurine in current production. Among the burst of occupational Hummels, numbered in the 120's and 130's, are several figures relating to the music profession or music in general: #129 "Band Leader," #131 "Street Singer," #134 "Quartet," #135 "Soloist" and the present #130 "Duet." "Duet" is a figure of two male singers, one of whom holds a score from which they

**130** Duet

both read. It was formerly known as "The Songsters." They are undoubtedly street carolers. They are dressed in mid 19th century style and are very Dickensian in appearance. There are size variations in this piece and other differences, the most notable of which is that the musical notations are incised and also painted in the earliest examples. Later specimens, from the Full Bee mark onward, have painted notations only.

The costuming is typical mid-Victorian street dress. One youth wears a red jacket, a white vest, red trousers, black polished shoes, and a tall green wide-brimmed hat. A red bow tie completes his outfit. His companion has a gray jacket, a white vest, grayish-green trousers, and black polished shoes. The second figure is hatless. He holds the music and stands with his other hand thrust into a trouser pocket.

|  | Price Range | |
|---|---|---|
| ☐ 130, trademark CM, 5"–5½"..................... | 450.00 | 470.00 |
| ☐ 130, trademark Full Bee, 5"–5½" ................ | 300.00 | 320.00 |
| ☐ 130, trademark Stylized Bee, 5"–5½"............ | 175.00 | 185.00 |
| ☐ 130, trademark 3-line mark, 5"–5½" ............. | 130.00 | 140.00 |
| ☐ 130, trademark Goebel/V, 5"–5½"................ | 115.00 | 125.00 |
| ☐ 130, trademark Goebel, 5"–5½"................. | 105.00 | 115.00 |

## 131  STREET SINGER

Figurine in current production. "Street Singer" is a representation of an occupation not familiar to Americans: The vagabond vocalist who went about the streets of European towns offering ballads or Christmas carols beneath the windows of residences. It was risky work. If his talents were appreciated he might be rewarded with a few coins. But if he chose the wrong house or wrong moment for a performance, he was likely to be doused with a bucket of water. The profession lingered on into the present century, but was at its height in the era before recorded music.

There is not much confusion with this model. Early specimens are very similar to those in current production. Only minor color variations are encountered. It has not been restyled or retextured. The size varies from 5" to 5½", but the latter appear no less plentiful than the former and no special premium is given for it. "Street Singer" was originally known as "Soloist."

The figure wears a tall top hat and holds a music folio in his left hand. His outfit consists of a beige-gray jacket, a white vest, a red bow tie, salmon pink-colored trousers and dark brown or black polished shoes. His hat is mahogany, touched along the brim and crown with red. His eyes turn upward to the window to which he directs his serenade.

**131** Street Singer

| | Price Range | |
|---|---|---|
| ☐ 131, trademark CM, 5″–5½″...................... | **295.00** | **335.00** |
| ☐ 131, trademark Full Bee, 5″–5½″ ................ | **170.00** | **200.00** |
| ☐ 131, trademark Stylized Bee, 5″–5½″............ | **115.00** | **129.00** |
| ☐ 131, trademark 3-line mark, 5″–5½″ ............. | **80.00** | **100.00** |
| ☐ 131, trademark Goebel/V, 5″–5½″................ | **73.00** | **87.00** |
| ☐ 131, trademark Goebel, 5″–5½″.................. | **66.00** | **76.00** |

## 132 STAR GAZER

Figurine in current production. "Star Gazer" is a figure of a youth, seated upon a rectangular base, peering into a telescope aimed at the heavens. Rather a different kind of theme for Hummel, the work is now regarded

**132** Star Gazer

mainly as a collector piece, rather than an item for the general public. The early specimens with the Crown trademark are moderately scarce. In the original version, the amateur astronomer wears a dark blue or dark pink and violet shirt. Later this was changed to pastel blue or a light pink with a suggestion of violet.

There have likewise been certain variations in the telescope's color, without an affect on the value. There is no doubt that the instrument is the center of interest. It is represented to be an old-fashioned telescope of the early to middle 1800s with a wooden frame, mounted on a fixed wooden tripod. Generally the telescope frame is a rich maple color, the tripod grayish brown. "Star Gazer" has a long-sleeved shirt, violet lederhosen with matching suspenders, brown shoes, and cream-colored socks with hues of brown and red. His hair is reddish and worn in an upsweep or peak at the front, infant style.

| | Price Range | |
|---|---|---|
| ☐ 132, trademark CM, 4¾" ........................ | 350.00 | 380.00 |
| ☐ 132, trademark Full Bee, 4¾" .................... | 225.00 | 245.00 |
| ☐ 132, trademark Stylized Bee, 4¾" ............... | 150.00 | 170.00 |
| ☐ 132, trademark 3-line mark, 4¾" ................ | 125.00 | 145.00 |
| ☐ 132, trademark Goebel/V, 4¾" ................... | 105.00 | 120.00 |
| ☐ 132, trademark Goebel, 4¾" .................... | 88.00 | 100.00 |

## 133 MOTHER'S HELPER

Figurine in current production. "Mother's Helper" is a little girl seated on a stool darning a sock. There is a ball of wool at her feet and, in the newer version, a stylized black cat who fixes its gaze on the woolen ball. Originally there was no cat in this composition. Whether it appears in Sister Hummel's drawing is not known, but it seems a natural enough accessory to this scene. The earlier specimens are somewhat larger in overall size, which can hardly be ascribed to mold growth. More likely the mold was refashioned at some point along the way. It will be noted, if a study is made of Hummels in production at various stages (say 1940, 1950, 1960, etc.), that the factory has placed more emphasis on smaller models within recent years, discontinuing the larger versions of figurines manufactured in several sizes and reducing slightly, in some cases, those produced in a single size.

"Mother's Helper" wears a rust orange dress with dotted ornamentation, a white bib tied around her neck, brown shoes, and white socks highlighted with strokes of gray and brown. She has a red ribbon in her hair. The sock she repairs is more or less identical to those she wears. Her stool is a rich mahogany and her cat is midnight black and glossy, except for its white eyes and ears. The expression on "Mother's Helper's" face can only be described as angelic.

| | | |
|---|---|---|
| ☐ 133, trademark CM, 4¾"–5" ..................... | 385.00 | 425.00 |
| ☐ 133, trademark Full Bee, 4¾"–5" ............... | 245.00 | 280.00 |
| ☐ 133, trademark Stylized Bee, 4¾"–5" ........... | 95.00 | 165.00 |
| ☐ 133, trademark 3-line mark, 4¾"–5" ............ | 120.00 | 150.00 |

**133** Mother's Helper

| | Price Range | |
|---|---|---|
| ☐ 133, trademark Goebel/V, 4¾"–5"............... | **95.00** | **125.00** |
| ☐ 133, trademark Goebel, 4¾"–5"................. | **88.00** | **102.00** |

## 134  QUARTET

Wall plaque in current production. "Quartet" has the distinction of featuring more figures than any other Hummel plaque. There is, of course, a much stricter limitation to the quantity of figures that can be included in a plaque, as opposed to a figurine, as all must be depicted on a common surface without the potential variations offered by a traditional model. This is a group of street singers, presumably carolers. They stand on cobblestoned pavement against a background of town rooftops and a street lamp. As the lamp contains a candle, this subject can be safely dated to the era before gas lighting, probably about 1830. Their heavy dress leads one to conclude that the season is winter, and this leads further to the assumption that "Quartet" is performing Christmas carols.

The original version is signed "M.I. Hummel" on the back. On subsequent versions the signature was placed on the front instead. The older models have a pair of holes through which a cord could be threaded for hanging; currently this plaque is supplied with one central hanging hole, designed to be slipped over a nail.

The basic coloring is green. Looking at the figures from left to right, they are attired as follows:

**#1**—This figure wears a short pastel green jacket, white vest with black buttons, light green-gray trousers with lozengework pattern, black shoes, and a black or dark green low-crowned hat similar to a beret. He holds a music folio in his left hand, from which he and figure #2 read.

**#2**—A somewhat taller boy, hatless. He wears a long green overcoat, white or light gray trousers, and black shoes.

**#3**—This figure may be regarded as the lead singer as he holds his own music folio. He wears a short brown jacket with dark brown plaid striping, grayish green trousers, black shoes, a white shirt, and red bow tie. He is wearing a tall stovepipe hat of dark gray with narrow brim.

**#4**—This snappily dressed figure is hatless. He wears a pink vest, green jacket, green pinstriped trousers, and black shoes. All of the figures have sandy blonde hair with light streaks of red.

There are two cottage roofs with attic windows to be seen in the background. There are minor size variations.

**134** Quartet

| | Price Range | |
|---|---|---|
| ☐ 134, trademark CM, 5½" × 6¼" ................. | 720.00 | 795.00 |
| ☐ 134, trademark Full Bee, 5½" × 6¼" ............. | 450.00 | 495.00 |
| ☐ 134, trademark Stylized Bee, 5½" × 6¼" ......... | 250.00 | 275.00 |
| ☐ 134, trademark 3-line mark, 5½" × 6¼" ......... | 200.00 | 220.00 |
| ☐ 134, trademark Goebel/V, 5½" × 6¼" ............. | 170.00 | 190.00 |
| ☐ 134, trademark Goebel, 5½" × 6¼" ............... | 147.00 | 162.00 |

# 135 SOLOIST

Figurine in current production. "Soloist" inherited the name previously applied to #131 "Street Singer." He had originally been known as "High Tenor," which may have seemed too esoteric for the general market. In any event it is important to draw the proper distinction between these two models, which might appear to be duplications in subject matter. #131 "Street Singer" is just that; a vocalist who does his work out-of-doors along the roads of villages and towns.

"Soloist" is instead a concert hall performer who sings with the accompaniment of music. As with so many Hummels, the older pieces, Crown and Full Bee, tend to be larger than those with recent trademarks, the varying in reported sizes being as much as half an inch.

The composition of this model is simple; a youth with one hand thrust in his trouser pocket, the other hand holding a music folio while he tilts his head upward in song. His face has a determined, confident appearance. "Soloist's" dress comprises a high-collared greenish gray jacket, pastel green trousers, a white vest, and a large red bow tie. His shoes are black.

"Soloist" has been a popular number over the years. The figure was produced in such quantity, even in its earlier years, that the Crown and Full Bee specimens are still easy to get.

**135** Soloist

|  | Price Range | |
|---|---|---|
| ☐ 135, trademark CM, 4½″–5″..................... | **245.00** | **275.00** |
| ☐ 135, trademark Full Bee, 4½″–5″ ............... | **145.00** | **175.00** |
| ☐ 135, trademark Stylized Bee, 4½″–5″............ | **95.00** | **125.00** |
| ☐ 135, trademark 3-line mark, 4½″–5″ ............. | **70.00** | **87.00** |
| ☐ 135, trademark Goebel/V, 4½″–5″............... | **58.00** | **72.00** |
| ☐ 135, trademark Goebel, 4½″–5″................. | **55.00** | **67.00** |

## 136  FRIENDS

Figurine in current production. "Friends" is a collector's Hummel because of the many variations some are quite rare which can be found. There have been three edtions, one of which, 136 (10½″) in a brown terra cotta finish, is no longer in production. This model was strictly a trail issue during the Crown trademark era. It seems to have remained in production very briefly

**136** Friends

as specimens are now met infrequently. In fact, the scarcity of this edition is such that some Hummel books do not even mention it, their compilers apparently being unaware of its existence. The model in terra cotta is handsome enough; however, public reaction, when it was introduced in the 1940s, presumably did not justify keeping it in production. It was expensive, because of the large size, and was being outsold by the enameled version. Undoubtedly it would enjoy a far different fate if reinstated. A terra cotta Hummel on the present market would be such a novelty that its success would almost be assured. Of the remainder of the series, 136/5, the large-size figures with arabic size designators, are also far from common though not in the class of #136.

"Friends" is a figure of a girl and young deer who has just taken food from her hand. The basic pose is of the girl standing beside the animal with one hand placed on the back of its neck as a sign of reassurance, the other held to its mouth. There are very noticeable differences in modeling between the terra cotta and the ordinary versions. An attempt was made in the terra cotta edition at strict naturalistic sculpturing with rich textured surfaces. The deer is depicted in a natural rather than stylized manner, the effect achieved being of wet clay. It is pleasing to view the sculptor's work with all the marks and prints left by his fingertips. All this is lost in the standard "Friends," in which the animal is devoid of body texture and assumes the appearance of a toy or storybook sketch. The girl is not well modeled in the enameled version, either, though she is less disappointing than the deer. In the terra cotta specimens her head is turned downward while enameled examples show it tilted to the side. There are also other differences that will be readily apparent by comparison, such as the attitude of the deer's head and the replacement of the girl's hand at its neck, which scarcely touches in the terra cotta version but is securely positioned in the enameled. In the terra cotta version, the base is also terra cotta. This used to be termed "natural finish" and was at one time highly regarded, especially in Europe, as it gave the suggestion of a wood carving. In the enameled version, "Friends" wears a white short-sleeved blouse, a black vest, a red skirt, tan shoes, and white socks banded with green and brown. She has a red ribbon in her hair. The deer is fawn brown, darker at the upper part of its body than at the legs, with white spots on its sides.

| | Price Range | |
|---|---:|---:|
| ☐ 136/I, trademark CM, 5″ | 500.00 | 520.00 |
| ☐ 136/I, trademark Full Bee, 5″ | 300.00 | 320.00 |
| ☐ 136/I, trademark Stylized Bee, 5″ | 150.00 | 170.00 |
| ☐ 136/I, trademark 3-line mark, 5″ | 125.00 | 135.00 |
| ☐ 136/I, trademark Goebel/V, 5″ | 100.00 | 110.00 |
| ☐ 136/I, trademark Goebel, 5″ | 88.00 | 100.00 |
| ☐ 136/V, trademark CM, 10¾″–11″ | 2000.00 | 2400.00 |
| ☐ 136/V, trademark Full Bee, 10¾″–11″ | 1500.00 | 1750.00 |
| ☐ 136/V, trademark Stylized Bee, 10¾″–11″ | 750.00 | 850.00 |
| ☐ 136/V, trademark 3-line mark, 10¾″–11″ | 600.00 | 650.00 |
| ☐ 136/V, trademark Goebel/V, 10¾″–11″ | 525.00 | 550.00 |
| ☐ 136/V, trademark Goebel, 10¾″–11″ | 300.00 | 330.00 |
| ☐ 136, trademark CM, 10½″ | 2000.00 | 2200.00 |
| ☐ 136, trademark CM, terra cotta, 10½″ | 2500.00 | 2750.00 |

## 137 CHILD IN BED

Wall plaque in current production. The success of the factory's #30 "Ba-Bee Rings" (see above) encouraged the search for a subject that could be similarly represented. "Child in Bed," originally known as the "Ladybug" plaque, is nearly identical to "Ba-Bee Rings." Instead of representing only the face, however, it shows the infant's shoulders and upper portion of its body, over which a blanket is drawn. The baby's head rests upon a pillow. Instead of a bumblebee, the insect to which the child's gaze is fixed is a less menacing ladybug, but his surprise or apprehension is equal to that of the figure in "Ba-Bee Rings." In any event, this is an attractive composition that has proved a good steady seller for many years. Its use among the non-collecting public has been primarily as an adornment for infant's nurseries.

As originally produced, "Child in Bed" was a set of two plaques, one in which the face turned left and the other right. The left-looking version, designated as #137/A, was quickly taken out of production, possibly before reaching store sale. Today this is a rarity of which no known examples are in circulation. Of the right-looking type, still in production, there are two designators, 137 and 137/B, the latter of which is discontinued. The frame is circular, finished in a cream glaze. The child's blanket has pale blue or violet striping, the pillow is white with a crimson stripe along its edge, and the ladybug perched on the frame is black and red.

**137** Child in Bed

|  | Price Range | |
|---|---|---|
| ☐ 137, trademark CM, 2¾" ........................ | **495.00** | **560.00** |
| ☐ 137, trademark Full Bee, 2¾" ................... | **245.00** | **275.00** |
| ☐ 137, trademark Stylized Bee, 2¾"............... | **107.00** | **122.00** |
| ☐ 137, trademark 3-line mark, 2¾" ................ | **49.00** | **59.00** |
| ☐ 137, trademark Goebel/V, 2¾" .................. | **40.00** | **47.00** |
| ☐ 137, trademark Goebel, 2¾" .................... | **31.50** | **36.00** |
| ☐ 137B, trademark CM, 2¾"....................... | **545.00** | **605.00** |
| ☐ 137B, trademark Full Bee, 2¾" ................. | **295.00** | **335.00** |
| ☐ 137B, trademark Stylized Bee, 2¾".............. | **105.00** | **125.00** |
| ☐ 137B, trademark 3-line mark, 2¾" .............. | **53.00** | **63.00** |

## 138 INFANT IN CRIB

Wall plaque, closed number. "Infant in Crib" is a variation on the "Ba-Bee Rings" theme that never reached production. The frame is oval instead of circular. The complete infant is shown lying in a crib, and there is no insect on the frame. Instead a huge sunflower grows up from behind the crib.

It is not positively known why #138 received closed number designation. One can put forward the theory that it and #137 "Child in Bed" (see above) were fashioned as factory samples at the same time for the purpose of choosing one or the other for marketing, since the designs are very similar. If that was the case it is not surprising that #137 was selected, as it more closely paralleled the already widely sold "Ba-Bee Rings." The face on "Infant in Crib" is not so well modeled as those of "Ba-Bee Rings" or "Child in Bed," but the composition is overall more charming. The child is covered by a white blanket striped in pastel violet. A large red sculptured heart decorates the foot of the wooden crib. Several small yellow flowers are on the ground. The large sunflower has yellow petals with a violet brown center. As a closed number designation, no information can be provided on value. At least one specimen is known to be in private hands. It measures 2¼" × 3".

## 139 FLITTING BUTTERFLY

Wall plaque in current production. "Flitting Buterfly" was also inspired, as were #137 and #138 (see above), by the previously released "Ba-Bee Rings." Here the frame is square, the child is shown seated in the frame, and the insect is not a bumblebee but a butterfly. "Flitting Butterfly" has also been known as "Butterfly" plaque. There are, thanks to redesignings, three major variations, which for want of better terminology are referred to as Original, Intermediate, and Current. They may be distinguished as follows:

**ORIGINAL:**

The child wears a solid-colored orange-red dress without pattern or other markings. Her gaze is focused directly at the butterfly in the upper left corner of the frame. Behind her head and left shoulder is a cut out area.

**139** Flitting Butterfly

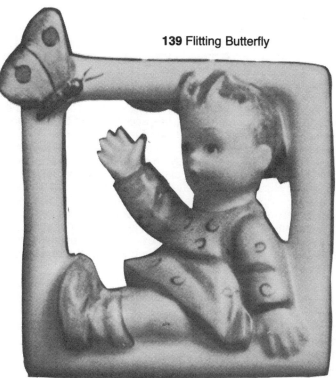

**Old Style**

**New Style**

## INTERMEDIATE:

The dress has gotten paler and blue dots have been added. Her shoes are a paler brown, tending toward gray. Her face no longer looks directly toward the insect, but is turned more in the viewer's direction. There are slight differences in the butterfly's coloration.

## CURRENT:

Similar to the intermediate version except the open portion behind the child's head and left shoulder is closed, this accomplished by positioning the figure further toward the right-hand side of the composition.

There are few observers who will not agree that the old version is the most visually effective of the three, mainly on strength of superior modeling of the face and stronger coloration. In a plaque with a white or cream frame such as this, pastel shades tend to be less appealing. The "M.I. Hummel" signature has always appeared on the reverse side of "Flitting Butterfly."

The model represents an infant girl reaching out to touch a butterfly. In this respect it presents a departure from the "Ba-Bee Rings" and "Child in Bed" (see above), in which the children show some anxiousness at the visitor's presence. The later versions have been equipped with a hanging cord.

|  | Price Range | |
|---|---|---|
| ☐ 139, trademark CM, 2½″ ......................... | 345.00 | 390.00 |
| ☐ 139, trademark Full Bee, 2½″ .................... | 275.00 | 315.00 |
| ☐ 139, trademark Stylized Bee, 2½″................ | 145.00 | 170.00 |
| ☐ 139, trademark 3-line mark, 2½″ ................ | 115.00 | 135.00 |
| ☐ 139, trademark Goebel/V, 2½″ ................... | 35.00 | 41.00 |
| ☐ 139, trademark Goebel, 2½″ ..................... | 31.50 | 38.00 |

# 140 MAIL IS HERE

Wall plaque in current production. "Mail is Here" is also known as "Mail Coach." A splendid piece of captured history, it shows a mail delivery wagon of the 1840s drawn by a pair of horses. The wagon is stopped while its driver, seated up front, raises the post horn to his lips and signals the arrival of mail. The horse-powered post wagon has disappeared even from remote European villages, but in its time it was a most familiar sight. It was employed in towns for the delivery of parcels too heavy to be borne by the foot carrier, and in rural areas for all mail delivery.

The wagon was small; there were no passengers in these vehicles. At the side is a door just large enough to permit the driver's entry. Piled on the roof are several bundles. The driver wears a blue striped jacket, a white shirt, salmon-colored trousers and high work boots. A tall black stovepipe hat is on his head. He holds the post horn firmly in both hands and gives it a mighty blast. His horses are grayish-white with black spots. They have cropped tails and wear eye blinders. The coach is a pale beige. Along the ground are a number of red flowers with dark centers.

During its early years of production, "Mail is Here" was sold in a cream overglaze version. Cream overglaze simply does not suit plaques, as the shallowness of the modeling does not afford sufficient play to light and shade. This is, nevertheless, a very scarce item highly prized by collectors.

**140** Mail is Here

|  | **Price Range** | |
|---|---|---|
| ☐ 140, trademark CM, cream overglaze, 4¼″ × 6¾″ | 1100.00 | 1400.00 |
| ☐ 140, trademark CM, 4¼″ × 6¾″ | 500.00 | 550.00 |
| ☐ 140, trademark Full Bee, 4¼″ × 6¾″ | 360.00 | 415.00 |
| ☐ 140, trademark Stylized Bee, 4¼″ × 6¾″ | 250.00 | 275.00 |
| ☐ 140, trademark 3-line mark, 4¼″ × 6¾″ | 180.00 | 200.00 |
| ☐ 140, trademark Goebel/V, 4¼″ × 6¾″ | 140.00 | 155.00 |
| ☐ 140, trademark Goebel, 4¼″ × 6¾″ | 126.00 | 137.50 |

## 141 APPLE TREE GIRL

Figurine in current production. Also known as "Spring" or "Springtime," "Apple Tree Girl" has a long and varied history. Within the past several years it has come to be regarded as one of the classic Hummels. It has the distinction of being the tallest model in the line, thanks to a giant 32″ version, #141/X, introduced in 1975. This super size model, one of three so far included in the "X" series (the other two being "Apple Tree Boy" and "Merry Wanderer") is frequently seen in the windows of shops selling Hummels. Invariably the proprietor has no additional specimens in stock. The impression is often felt that 141/X was intended mainly as a shop ornament. Whatever the intent, there has been sufficient collector and public interest in this oversized version to result in a fair number of sales. There are, of course, some persons to whom the unusual appeals merely on grounds of being unusual, and a nearly 3-foot-high Hummel is unusual indeed. But

**141** Apple Tree Girl

just consider the number of hobbyists working toward a complete collection of Hummels into which these oversized models must naturally be included.

There are four basic editions of the "Apple Tree Girl," all of which are still in current production, a situation that does not prevail with too many of the factory's works. There are numerous variations. This model was originally introduced in the two smaller sizes in the 1940s. When these proved popular the third largest size, 141/V, was put on the market, around 1971 or 1972. The gigantic version was first placed on sale in 1975. Opinions differ strongly on which of the four manufactured sizes shows this model to its best advantage.

The subject is a girl in Bavarian peasant costume seated on the branch of a tree, clasping another branch for balance and looking over her shoulder. The old versions of 141/3/0 and 141/I have highly textured brown bases intended to represent sod; in the current editions the bases are standard white. There are slight differences between versions in the position of the girl's head and her facial expression. The finest example of facial expression can be found in 141/V. The old types had a look of curiosity; this was subsequently altered to a sunny smile. One important distinction is that the smallest size, in both the original and current editions, is devoid of the small canary bird that perches atop the tree in 141/I, 141/V, and 141/X.

It is confusing to find 141/X listed sometimes as 29", or as 30" or 31", rather than its actual height of 32". This must result from measures failing to include the bird in their calculations, or attempting the job with a soft tapemeasure rather than the required carpenter's rule. The girl wears a white puffy-sleeved blouse, a black vest, a blue peasant skirt, wine red shoes, and white socks. She has a yellow apron and a red kerchief pulled down and tied round her chin. Along the tree's length there are a number of attractive pink flowers.

|  | **Price Range** | |
|---|---|---|
| □ 141/3/0, trademark CM, 4″–4¼″.................. | 260.00 | 285.00 |
| □ 141/3/0, trademark Full Bee, 4″–4¼″ ........... | 160.00 | 175.00 |
| □ 141/3/0, trademark Stylized Bee, 4″–4¼″........ | 100.00 | 110.00 |
| □ 141/3/0, trademark 3-line mark, 4″–4¼″ ........ | 80.00 | 90.00 |
| □ 141/3/0, trademark Goebel/V, 4″–4yy″ .......... | 65.00 | 71.50 |
| □ 141/3/0, trademark Goebel, 4″–4¼″.............. | 55.00 | 60.00 |
| □ 141/I, trademark CM, 6″–6¾″ .................... | 500.00 | 550.00 |
| □ 141/I, trademark Full Bee, 6″–6¾″ ............... | 280.00 | 310.00 |
| □ 141/I, trademark Stylized Bee, 6″–6¾″........... | 180.00 | 200.00 |
| □ 141/I, trademark 3-line mark, 6″–6¾″ ........... | 140.00 | 155.00 |
| □ 141/I, trademark Goebel/V, 6″–6¾″ .............. | 120.00 | 130.00 |
| □ 141/I, trademark Goebel, 6″–6¾″ ................ | 105.00 | 115.00 |
| □ 141/V, trademark 3-line mark, 10¼″.............. | 650.00 | 715.00 |
| □ 141/V, trademark Goebel/V, 10¼″................. | 560.00 | 615.00 |
| □ 141/V, trademark Goebel, 10¼″................... | 525.00 | 575.00 |
| □ 141/X, trademark Goebel/V, 32″.................. | 13000.00 | 14300.00 |
| □ 141/X, trademark Goebel, 32″.................... | 13100.00 | 14400.00 |

## 142  APPLE TREE BOY

Figurine in current production. The companion piece to "Apple Tree Girl" (see above), #142 has had a similar history, first introduced in two sizes only; a larger size was subsequently added at the same time as the second largest edition of "Apple Tree Girl" and finally a colossal #142/X. The jumbo size "Apple Tree Boy" is not quite as large as its feminine counterpart, measuring 30″ as compared to 32″. There are old and new versions of the two smaller sizes, their chief characteristic being that the old version has a brown textured base, while the later edition has a standard base. A bird perches in the tree in the three larger sizes; it is absent from the smallest size.

It may be observed that "Apple Tree Boy" is not quite the equal, compositionally, of its companion piece. The boy is not as appealing as the girl. She seems alive and playful, while his appearance is stiff and almost caricatured. The best version is unquestionably the new edition of 142/3/0 with a great improvement in facial expression and in naturalism over its predecessor.

"Apple Tree Boy" wears a blue short jacket with red plaid striping, a white shirt, maroon lederhosen held by matching suspenders, brown shoes, yellow socks, and a green Tyrolean style cap. Unlike the tree in which "Apple Tree Girl" sits, apples are growing from "Apple Tree Boy's" tree—extremely realistic ones.

**142** Apple Tree Boy

| | Price Range | |
|---|---:|---:|
| ☐ 142/3/0, trademark CM, 4″–4¼″ .................. | 195.00 | 215.00 |
| ☐ 142/3/0, trademark Full Bee, 4″–4¼″ ............ | 145.00 | 165.00 |
| ☐ 142/3/0, trademark Stylized Bee, 4″–4¼″ ........ | 95.00 | 115.00 |
| ☐ 142/3/0, trademark 3-line mark, 4″–4¼″ ........ | 70.00 | 90.00 |
| ☐ 142/3/0, trademark Goebel/V, 4″–4¼″ ........... | 35.00 | 50.00 |
| ☐ 142/3/0, trademark Goebel, 4″–4¼″ ............. | 65.00 | 72.00 |
| ☐ 142/I, trademark CM, 6″–6¾″ .................. | 50.00 | 70.00 |
| ☐ 142/I, trademark Full Bee, 6″–6¾″ .............. | 495.00 | 555.00 |
| ☐ 142/I, trademark Stylized Bee, 6″–6¾″ .......... | 395.00 | 445.00 |
| ☐ 142/I, trademark 3-line mark, 6″–6¾″ ........... | 295.00 | 335.00 |
| ☐ 142/I, trademark Goebel/V, 6″–6¾″ ............. | 75.00 | 86.00 |
| ☐ 142/I, trademark Goebel, 6″–6¾″ ............... | 105.00 | 116.00 |
| ☐ 142/V, trademark 3-line mark, 10¼″ ............. | 645.00 | 720.00 |
| ☐ 142/V, trademark Goebel/V, 10¼″ ............... | 555.00 | 620.00 |
| ☐ 142V, trademark Goebel, 10¼″ .................. | 525.00 | 578.00 |
| ☐ 142/X, trademark Goebel/V, 30″ ................. | 12995.00 | 14295.00 |
| ☐ 142/X, trademark Goebel, 30″ ................... | 13100.00 | 14395.00 |

**143** Boots

## 143 BOOTS

Figurine in current production. "Boots" is surely one of the more appealing occupational Hummels which the factory turned out in large numbers in the 1940s and 1950s. For some reason, the better occupationals are those with Old World flavor which "Boots" has in abundance. It depicts a shoemaker wearing his work apron, under one arm carrying a pair of heavy men's boots and delicately holding in the other hand stylish women's slippers. The shoes and the figure represent the mid 1800s. Originally "Boots" was known as "Shoemaker."

There are three editions of "Boots", of which 143 (6¾") has been discontinued. It should come as no surprise that the 6¾" size was closed out, as the factory has engaged over the past 20 or more years in a continuing practice of deleting from its line the largest versions of multiple size pieces. Within the two smaller sizes there are variations as indicated, but "Boots" has undergone no major restyling and exists today pretty much as he did three decades ago. The apron is blue, and "Boots" wears a white shirt with rolled up sleeves, brown trousers, and black shoes.

**Price Range**

☐ 143/0, trademark CM, 5″–5½″.................... **325.00** **357.00**
☐ 143/0, trademark Full Bee, 5″–5½″ .............. **220.00** **240.00**
☐ 143/0, trademark Stylized Bee, 5″–5½″ .......... **120.00** **130.00**
☐ 143/0, trademark 3-line mark, 5″–5½″ .......... **100.00** **110.00**
☐ 143/0, trademark Goebel/V, 5″–5½″............. **82.00** **90.00**
☐ 143/0, trademark Goebel, 5″–5½″................ **72.00** **80.00**
☐ 143/I, trademark CM, 6½″–6¾″ ................. **500.00** **550.00**
☐ 143/I, trademark Full Bee, 6½″–6¾″............. **350.00** **385.00**
☐ 143/I, trademark Stylized Bee, 6½″–6¾″ ........ **250.00** **275.00**
☐ 143/I, trademark 3-line mark, 6½″–6¾″ .......... **180.00** **200.00**
☐ 143/I, trademark Goebel/V, 6½″–6¾″ ............ **150.00** **165.00**
☐ 143/I, trademark Goebel, 6½″–6¾″ ............. **110.00** **120.00**
☐ 143, trademark CM, 6¾″ ......................... **750.00** **825.00**
☐ 143, trademark Full Bee, 6¾″.................... **500.00** **550.00**
☐ 143, trademark Stylized Bee, 6¾″................ **300.00** **330.00**
☐ 143, trademark 3-line mark, 6¾″ ................ **200.00** **220.00**

## 144  ANGELIC SONG

Figurine in current production. "Angelic Song" is a pair of figures who stand together as one model without a base. The angel song or angel music

**144** Angelic Song

theme has been used frequently by the factory. The angels in "Angelic Song" could be twins: They have a nearly identical facial appearance and are of equal height. Their dress is also similar. The left-hand angel is wearing a long flowing red gown with circular ornaments, while her companion wears the same style in an orange-red. The left-hand angel plays a lute; the other holds an open book from which she sings. Only one toe of one shoe is visible beneath the long gown of each figure, but even this small glimpse is sufficient to show that these musical angels have different tastes in footwear. The left-hand angel has red shoes, and her companion has bluish-green shoes.

This model was once known simply as "Angels" or as "Holy Communion," the latter being a reference that apparently proved unclear to many. It was undoubtedly meant to signify music being played in churches during communion service.

|  | Price Range | |
|---|---|---|
| ☐ 144, trademark CM, 4″–4½″...................... | 295.00 | 355.00 |
| ☐ 144, trademark Full Bee, 4″–4½″ ................ | 130.00 | 180.00 |
| ☐ 144, trademark Stylized Bee, 4″–4½″ ............ | 95.00 | 115.00 |
| ☐ 144, trademark 3-line mark, 4″–4½″ ............. | 80.00 | 98.00 |
| ☐ 144, trademark Goebel/V, 4″–4½″................ | 69.00 | 82.00 |
| ☐ 144, trademark Goebel, 4″–4½″.................. | 63.00 | 71.00 |

## 145 LITTLE GUARDIAN

Figurine in current production. "Little Guardian" belongs to the group that includes #144 "Angelic Song," #146 "Angel Duet," and #147 "Angel Shrine." It shows a young girl kneeling at prayer; alongside her stands her Guardian Angel, holding flowers in her arm and patting the girl's head. The girl wears flowers of a type similar to those held by the angel, made into

**145** Little Guardian

a band around her head. The normal color of these flowers is orange. There is a moderately scarce variety in which the kneeling figure is adorned with blue flowers (see below). The angel wears a long white grown decorated with colorless four-point stars and has gray-blue wings tipped in red. The kneeling figure wears a salmon pink gown and has a set of rosary beads dangling from her left wrist. The earlier specimens of "Little Guardian," especially those with Crown Mark, are generally somewhat larger than those of recent vintage.

| | Price Range | |
|---|---:|---:|
| ☐ 145, trademark CM, 3¾″–4″...................... | 200.00 | 220.00 |
| ☐ 145, trademark CM, blue flowers, 3¾″–4″ ....... | 300.00 | 330.00 |
| ☐ 145, trademark Full Bee, 3¾″–4″ ............... | 125.00 | 137.50 |
| ☐ 145, trademark Full Bee, blue floers, 3¾″–4″.... | 175.00 | 195.00 |
| ☐ 145, trademark Stylized Bee, 3¾″–4″ ........... | 85.00 | 95.00 |
| ☐ 145, trademark Stylized Bee, blue flowers, 3¾″–4″......................................... | 100.00 | 110.00 |
| ☐ 145, trademark 3-line mark, 3¾″–4″ ............. | 85.00 | 95.00 |
| ☐ 145, trademark Goebel/V, 3¾″–4″................ | 73.00 | 85.00 |
| ☐ 145, trademark Goebel, 3¾″–4″................. | 63.00 | 70.00 |

## 146 ANGEL DUET

Wall font in current production. "Angel Duet" is designed as a backless font, the figures themselves forming the back. The composition is similar

**146** Angel Duet

to #144 "Angelic Song." One angel plays a lute while the other, instead of holding a book and singing, has her hands clasped in prayer. The descriptions of the figures are as follows:

**#1 (left-hand angel)**—She wears a long blue gown fronted with pastel blue (white in some specimens). She has blonde hair, and the tip of a brown shoe can be observed peeking from beneath her gown.

**#2 (right-hand angel)**—She wears a green gown fronted with pastel green. She has reddish hair, green shoes, and she plays a maple-colored lute.

There is some variation in the wings. The facial expressions of the angels are almost identical.

|  | Price Range | |
|---|---|---|
| ☐ 146, trademark CM, 3¼″ × 4¾″ | 150.00 | 175.00 |
| ☐ 146, trademark Full Bee, 3¼″ × 4¾″ | 85.00 | 105.00 |
| ☐ 146, trademark Stylized Bee, 3¼″ × 4¾″ | 38.00 | 47.00 |
| ☐ 146, trademark 3-line mark, 3¼″ × 4¾″ | 34.00 | 41.00 |
| ☐ 146, trademark Goebel/V, 3¼″ × 4¾″ | 29.00 | 36.00 |
| ☐ 146, trademark Goebel, 3¼″ × 4¾″ | 23.00 | 29.00 |

## 147 DEVOTION

Wall font in current production. "Devotion" is also known as "Angel Shrine" and "Angelic Devotion." This well-balanced composition depicts a boy angel shown in profile, praying against a canopy surmounted wooden cross. The rear portion of the font is scalloped along the top and adorned with a number of orange flowers. The angel wears a greenish blue robe, brown shoes, and has red and brown wings. Variations will be noted in construction of the bowl but no major restyling of this model has been executed. The Crown Mark specimens are generally the largest, but so many size variations are reported that it is difficult to make any definite statement.

|  | Price Range | |
|---|---|---|
| ☐ 147, trademark CM, 3″ × 5″ to 3⅛″ × 5½″ | 95.00 | 115.00 |
| ☐ 147, trademark Full Bee, 3″ × 5″ to 3⅛″ × 5½″ | 30.00 | 47.00 |
| ☐ 147, trademark Stylized Bee, 3″ × 5″ to 3⅛″ × 5½″ | 28.00 | 41.00 |
| ☐ 147, trademark 3-line mark, 3″ × 5″ to 3⅛″ × 5½″ | 24.00 | 36.00 |
| ☐ 147, trademark Goebel/V, 3″ × 5″ to 3⅛″ × 5½″ | 22.00 | 29.00 |
| ☐ 147, trademark Goebel, 3″ × 5″ to 3⅛″ × 5½″ | 16.00 | 19.00 |

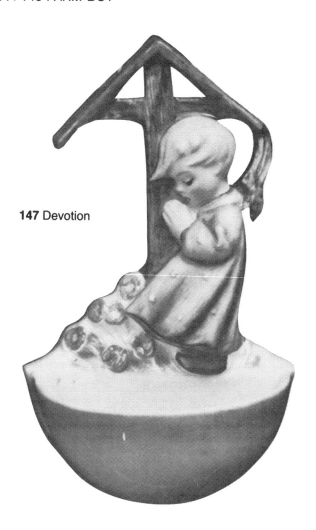

**147** Devotion

## 148 FARM BOY

Figurine closed number. "Farm Boy" was an effort to produce a figurine version of #60A, of the boy and two pigs who adorn a Hummel bookend, different from #66. It was never placed into production and was officially designated a closed number on February 28, 1941. Since no specimens or factory samples are available, no information can be given as to size or value. It would have probably carried the Crown trademark if put into production.

## 149 GOOSE GIRL

Figurine closed number. This is not the celebrated Hummel "Goose Girl," which is still in production, but a figurine version of the figure in #60B (one side of a bookend set). No information is available on this model, other than its listing as a closed number designation in the factory's records on February 28, 1941, the same date #148 was closed out (see above).

## 150 HAPPY DAYS

Figurine in current production. "Happy Days" has been previously known as "Happy Little Troubadors." Some may not agree with the opinion that Hummel frequently attains its best work when stepping out of character, but "Happy Days," a superb composition both in modeling and coloration, is not a typical Hummel. There is something definitely Latin about these two figures, one of which plays a guitar, and the other a lute or mandolin. One can well imagine them serenading in a Madrid or Barcelona square.

**150** Happy Days

There have been four editions of this model, one of which 150 (6¼″), is now closed. Two of the others, 150/0 and 150/I, were also closed but have been returned to production; thus there are three sizes currently being manufactured.

This motif was subsequently used for a lamp base (#232 and #235). The figures represent a boy and girl. The girl wears a long-sleeved white blouse adorned with black dots, a black vest, a long yellow skirt with wine red dots, brown shoes, and has her hair in pigtails tied with bright red ribbons. She plays a guitar. The boy has a dark gray jacket with black striping, a white shirt, pale blue trousers with blue pinstriping, brown shoes, and a yellow neckerchief dotted with red. He plays a lute or mandolin. The girl stands on a raised platform designed to represent sod. Both have their lips parted in song.

| | Price Range | |
|---|---:|---:|
| ☐ 150/2/0, trademark CM, 4¼″ | 255.00 | 295.00 |
| ☐ 150/2/0, trademark Full Bee, 4¼″ | 170.00 | 205.00 |
| ☐ 150/2/0, trademark Stylized Bee, 4¼″ | 120.00 | 150.00 |
| ☐ 150/2/0, trademark 3-line mark, 4¼″ | 98.00 | 122.00 |
| ☐ 150/2/0, trademark Goebel/V, 4¼″ | 95.00 | 117.00 |
| ☐ 150/2/0, trademark Goebel, 4¼″ | 83.00 | 99.00 |
| ☐ 150/0, trademark CM, 5″–5¼″ | 370.00 | 530.00 |
| ☐ 150/0, trademark Full Bee, 5″–5¼″ | 345.00 | 380.00 |
| ☐ 150/0, trademark Stylized Bee, 5″–5¼″ | 198.00 | 222.00 |
| ☐ 150/0, trademark Goebel/V, 5″–5¼″ | 145.00 | 168.00 |
| ☐ 150/0, trademark Goebel, 5″–5¼″ | 140.00 | 156.00 |
| ☐ 150/I, trademark CM, 6″–6½″ | 120.00 | 138.00 |
| ☐ 150/I, trademark Full Bee, 6″–6½″ | 1195.00 | 1325.00 |
| ☐ 150/I, trademark Stylized Bee, 6″–6½″ | 775.00 | 875.00 |
| ☐ 150/I, trademark Goebel/V, 6″–6½″ | 545.00 | 620.00 |
| ☐ 150/I, trademark Goebel, 6″–6½″ | 260.00 | 290.00 |
| ☐ 150, trademark CM, 6¼″ | 235.00 | 270.00 |
| ☐ 150, trademark Full Bee, 6¼″ | 1295.00 | 1425.00 |

## 151 MADONNA HOLDING CHILD

Figurine in current production. This is a tall stately model, the basic size in all editions being 12½″. References have been found in lists and elsewhere to specimens as tall as 14″. In the absence of substantiation, they must be classified as possibilities only, very likely victims of inaccurate measurements. There have been five varieties of "Madonna Holding Child," also known as "Blue Cloaked Madonna":

White or cream overglaze (uncolored).
Pastel blue cloak.
Dark blue cloak.
Brown cloak.
Ivory finish (uncolored).

It is important to note that, unlike the situation that generally prevails with color variations, these were issued as separate and distinct editions and are not the result of restyling or normal color variance. Currently only two of the five are in production, which the factory designates as #151/II

Color and #151/W White, the latter being the white or cream overglaze version, not the ivory finish. The present edition of the color version has a **pastel blue cloak**. Consequently, the editions no longer in production are: Dark blue cloak, brown cloak, and ivory finish. All of the closed editions are rare and costly. The most valuable, and indeed one of the most valuable of all Hummels, is the **brown cloak**. There are no common specimens of the brown cloak, regardless of trademark. It should, however, be pointed out that caution is the byword if one is encountered because of the danger of faking. As these models all carried the same trademark, a faker need only apply brown enamel to a blue-cloaked specimen to increase its value by thousands of dollars. There are no documented cases of such faking, but given the ease of the operation and the profits it offers, it would be most surprising if attempts have not been made.

The model depicts the seated Madonna holding the Christ Child on her lap. From whatever viewpoint one wishes to consider this work—modeling, naturalism, classicism, symmetry or on various other counts—it must unquestionably rank as one of the finest of the factory's products. The care and attention shown in its sculpturing is not exceeded by any other Hummel, nor is it likely to be. The old ivory finish edition has an appearance of real ivory so true that, when viewed from a distance, it cannot be distinguished from a hand carving. Even the colored editions are superb, thanks to perfect skin tone which fully equals the enameling on Italian terra cotta figures of the 16th and 17th centuries. Moreover, the details of this model, especially the folds in clothing, are so realistically presented that "Madonna Holding Child" is set well above other attempts, by various factories, to model this subject.

For a number of years this figurine was listed as a closed edition in all five varieties. The two currently produced are reinstatements made during use of the Goebel/V or Vee-Gee trademark, about 1977. Please understand that prices given for the rarer examples are approximations only, sales occurring too infrequently for firm levels to be established.

|  | Price Range | |
|---|---|---|
| ☐ 151/W, trademark CM, white or cream overglaze, 12½" | **2500.00** | **2750.00** |
| ☐ 151/W, trademark Full Bee, white or cream overglaze, 12½" | **2000.00** | **2200.00** |
| ☐ 151/W, trademark Stylized Bee, white or cream overglaze, 12½" | **2000.00 +** | **—** |
| ☐ 151/W, trademark Goebel/V, white or cream overglaze, 12½" | **200.00** | **220.00** |
| ☐ 151/W, trademark Goebel, white or cream overglaze, 12½" | **175.00** | **195.00** |
| ☐ 151, trademark CM, dark blue cloak, 12½" | **3000.00** | **3300.00** |
| ☐ 151, trademark Full Bee, dark blue cloak, 12½" | **2500.00** | **2750.00** |
| ☐ 151, trademark Stylized Bee, dark blue cloak, 12½" | **2000.00** | **2200.00** |
| ☐ 151/II, trademark Goebel/V, pastel blue cloak, 12½" | **525.00** | **575.00** |
| ☐ 151/II, trademark Goebel, pastel blue cloak, 12½" | **472.50** | **520.00** |

**Price Range**

☐ 151, trademark CM, brown cloak, 12½"......... **5000.00 +** —
☐ 151, trademark Full Bee, brown cloak, 12½" .... **200.00** **220.00**
☐ 151, trademark CM, ivory finish, 12½".......... **5000.00 +** —
☐ 151, trademark Full Bee, ivory finish, 12½"...... **2000.00 +** —
☐ 151, trademark Stylized Bee, ivory finish, 12½" **2000.00** **2200.00**

## 152A UMBRELLA BOY

Figurine in current production. "Umbrella Boy" was issued as a companion piece to #152B "Umbrella Girl" and they may originally have been marketed as a set. Both figures are of children seated on the ground holding an open umbrella. The models do not have bases. "Umbrella Boy" was issued in 1942, in two editions.

The smaller size, 152/A/0 (4¾") bears a copyright date of 1957, but was in fact on the market at least several years before then. As yet there is no definite information on whether #152/A/0 exists with the Crown trademark; it quite possibly does, and would be worth over $1,000 with such a mark. No precise values can be given since no sales records whatsoever are to be found. The same is true of "Umbrella Girl" (see #152/B below). Even with the later Stylized Bee mark this is by no means an easily obtainable figurine. The 8" size does exist with Crown Mark and is extremely rare. "Umbrella Boy" was called at various times "In Safety" or "Boy Under Umbrella." It has been incorrectly referred to as "Out of Danger," a title that may be appropriate enough, but is already in the Hummel series as #44 and #56.

**152/A**     **152A** Umbrella Boy     **152/B**

The figure is splendidly modeled and colored. There is no positive information, but one would certainly infer from the similarity in quality between the umbrella youths and #151 "Madonna Holding Child" released in the same year, that the same modeler was responsible for all three. The experienced connoisseur of Hummels will recognize the brilliance of these simple designs.

The larger size "Umbrella Boy" has undergone a restyling, resulting in his umbrella becoming thinner and the finish textured. He is sitting with his legs outstretched and his head is turned looking to his right. He wears a yellow jacket with plaid striping, blue lederhosen, grayish-blue shoes, and white bulky socks tinted with strokes of orange and blue. The umbrella handle is brown.

|  | **Price Range** | |
|---|---|---|
| ☐ 152/A/0, trademark Full Bee, 4¾"................ | 755.00 | 840.00 |
| ☐ 152/A/0, trademark Stylized Bee, 4¾" ........... | 395.00 | 445.00 |
| ☐ 152/A/0, trademark 3-line mark, 4¾"............. | 345.00 | 390.00 |
| ☐ 152/A/0, trademark Goebel/V, 4¾" .............. | 295.00 | 335.00 |
| ☐ 152/A/0, trademark Goebel, 4¾" ................. | 265.00 | 295.00 |
| ☐ 152/A/II, trademark Full Bee, 8" ................. | 1495.00 | 1648.00 |
| ☐ 152/A/II, trademark Stylized Bee, 8"............. | 995.00 | 1095.00 |
| ☐ 152/A/II, trademark 3-line mark, 8" ............. | 845.00 | 938.00 |
| ☐ 152/A/II, trademark Goebel/V, 8" ................ | 795.00 | 882.00 |
| ☐ 152/A/II, trademark Goebel, 8" .................. | 750.00 | 827.00 |

## 152B UMBRELLA GIRL

Figurine in current production. Most of the comments made about #152A "Umbrella Boy" (see above) are applicable to this model, both having a more or less common history. The basic difference is that "Umbrella Girl," though originally designed in 1942 at the same time as "Umbrella Boy," was withheld as an open number designation for seven years, not reaching production until 1949. Hummel has kept the retail prices on both sizes of #152B identical to those of #152A which have been manufactured and circulated in more or less equal quantities; their value on the secondhand or collector market is parallel.

"Umbrella Girl" wears a blue dress with decorations composed of triple raised dots, tan slippers or clogs, and white socks with thin strokes of various highlight colors. Her hair is braided in pigtails, in which she wears red ribbons.

| ☐ 152/B/0, trademark Full Bee, 4¾"................ | 760.00 | 835.00 |
|---|---|---|
| ☐ 152/B/0, trademark, Stylized Bee, 4¾"........... | 400.00 | 440.00 |
| ☐ 152/B/0, trademark 3-line mark, 4¾"............. | 350.00 | 385.00 |
| ☐ 152/B/0, trademark Goebel/V, 4¾" .............. | 300.00 | 330.00 |
| ☐ 152/B/0, trademark Goebel, 4¾" ................. | 265.00 | 290.00 |
| ☐ 152/B/II, trademark Full Bee, 8" ................. | 1500.00 | 1650.00 |
| ☐ 152/B/II, trademark Stylized Bee, 8"............. | 1000.00 | 1100.00 |
| ☐ 152/B/II, trademark 3-line mark, 8" ............. | 850.00 | 935.00 |
| ☐ 152/B/II, trademark Goebel/V, 8" ................ | 800.00 | 880.00 |
| ☐ 152/B/II, trademark Goebel, 8" .................. | 750.00 | 825.00 |

**153** Auf Wiedersehen

## 153  AUF WIEDERSEHEN

Figurine in current production. "Auf Wiedersehen," also known as "Good-bye," is a figure of two youths, a boy and a girl, waving a vigorous farewell to some person or persons unknown. The full history of this design is not yet known. It was introduced into the line during World War II, presumably in late 1942 or early 1943. There are two basic sizes currently in production and the largest, #153 (7"), has been discontinued.

In addition, a variant of #153/0 was marketed in the 1940s, in which the boy wears a Tyrolean style green hat. Normally the model is hatless. "Auf Wiedersehen" with hat is not in the rarity class of the Brown Cloaked Madonna (see #151 above), but does carry a considerable cash value. The 7" closed edition is also quite rare. A large size "Auf Wiedersehen" with hat has never been produced; the variation exists only in the 5½"–6" version.

Both the large and small editions have been restyled. The girl and boy are standing together, each with right hand raised. In all instances the girl waves a handkerchief or similar object. In "Auf Wiedersehen" with the hat the boy waves with his empty hand. In specimens in which the boy is hatless he waves a handkerchief. Her costume is made up of an orange long-sleeved dress, a pale yellow smock decorated with circular ornaments, brown shoes, and socks that range from white to a pale beige. Her hair is short and combed forward. The boy wears a blue (various shades de-pending on age) jacket with dark blue plaid striping, a white shirt, brown lederhosen with matching suspenders, black shoes, white, or yellow or pale brown socks, and a red bow tie. In the case of the version with hat, the boy wears a green conical hat with a white feather.

**Price Range**

| | | |
|---|---:|---:|
| ☐ 153/0, trademark Full Bee, green hat, 5¼" ...... | 2495.00 | 2745.00 |
| ☐ 153/0, trademark Full Bee, 5½"–6" .............. | 270.00 | 305.00 |
| ☐ 153/0, trademark Stylized Bee, 5½"–6" .......... | 195.00 | 225.00 |
| ☐ 153/0, trademark 3-line mark, 5½"–6" ........... | 135.00 | 157.00 |
| ☐ 153/0, trademark Goebel/V, 5½"–6"............... | 103.00 | 118.00 |
| ☐ 153/0, trademark Goebel, 5½"–6"................ | 94.50 | 107.00 |
| ☐ 153/I, trademark CM, 6¾"–7" .................... | 995.00 | 1105.00 |
| ☐ 153/I, trademark Full Bee, 6¾"–7" .............. | 545.00 | 598.00 |
| ☐ 153/I, trademark Stylized Bee, 6¾"–7"........... | 445.00 | 498.00 |
| ☐ 153/I, trademark 3-line mark, 6¾"–7" ........... | 348.00 | 389.00 |
| ☐ 153/I, trademark Goebel/V, 6¾"–7" .............. | 137.00 | 158.00 |
| ☐ 153/I, trademark Goebel 6¾"–7" ................ | 125.00 | 140.00 |
| ☐ 153, trademark CM, 7" .......................... | 995.00 | 1095.00 |
| ☐ 153, trademark Full Bee, 7" ..................... | 545.00 | 605.00 |
| ☐ 153, trademark Stylized Bee, 7"................. | 445.00 | 498.00 |

## 154  WAITER

Figurine in current production. "Waiter" is a figure of a boy holding a salver or serving tray on which is a bottle marked "Rhein Wine" and a

**154** Waiter

drinking glass. "Waiter" was originally known as "Chef of Service." There have been three editions, of which the largest, #154 (6½"), has been discontinued.

In the earlier stages of production, and especially in the closed edition #154, the costume includes gray pinstriped trousers and a gray jacket. This was later changed to pale blue jacket and rust-colored pinstriped trousers. There is also a change of color to be noted in the bow tie, so small as to easily escape observation. In models with gray jacket and trousers, the bow tie is black; in others bright blue. The salver changes from light tan in the old version to red in the new. Shoes are charcoal gray in the former, dark brown or black in the latter. "Waiter" holds a towel over his left arm and appears to be crouching just slightly, as if about to place his salver on a table. His face has been remodeled at least three times with three very distinct expressions ranging from ready alertness to an almost sleepy-eyed look, the last to be found in the gray outfit specimens. It should also be noted that the bottle, pale green or blue in color, does not invariably state "Rhein Wine" on its label. This is the most frequently encountered wording but numerous others have been recorded, including simply "Whisky" (obviously for specimens directed to the U.S. and British market), leading to the presumption that enamelers were free to fill in the label with whatever legend they deemed appropriate. Hummel collecting has not yet reached the point where premiums are given depending on the label wording.

|  | Price Range | |
| --- | --- | --- |
| ☐ 154/0, trademark CM, 6"–6¼" .................. | 400.00 | 440.00 |
| ☐ 154/0, trademark Full Bee, 6"–6¼" ............. | 280.00 | 310.00 |
| ☐ 154/0, trademark Stylized Bee, 6"–6¼" ......... | 180.00 | 198.00 |
| ☐ 154/0, trademark 3-line mark, 6"–6¼" ......... | 125.00 | 137.50 |
| ☐ 154/0, trademark Goebel/V, 6"–6¼" ............. | 100.00 | 110.00 |
| ☐ 154/0, trademark, 6"–6¼" ...................... | 88.00 | 98.00 |
| ☐ 154/I, trademark CM, 6½"–7" .................. | 750.00 | 825.00 |
| ☐ 154/I, trademark Full Bee, 6½"–7" ............. | 400.00 | 440.00 |
| ☐ 154/I, trademark Stylized Bee, 6½"–7" ......... | 210.00 | 230.00 |
| ☐ 154/I, trademark 3-line mark, 6½"–7" ......... | 130.00 | 145.00 |
| ☐ 154/I, trademark Goebel/V, 6½"–7" ............. | 125.00 | 135.00 |
| ☐ 154/I, trademark Goebel, 6½"–7" ............... | 110.00 | 120.00 |
| ☐ 154, trademark CM, 6½" ....................... | 1000.00 | 1100.00 |

## 155 MADONNA WITH CLOAK

Figurine closed number. Not much information is available on this work. Factory records list it as "Madonna with Cloak, Sitting with Child on Her Lap." This would lead strongly to a suspicion that the design is related to #151 "Madonna Holding Child," a Hummel that successfully reached production and has been on the market nearly 40 years. It was perhaps a smaller version of #151 with enough alteration in design to warrant a separate number. Lacking even a factory sample for observation, however, it is unlikely that this theory can be substantiated.

## 156 SITTING WOMAN

Wall plaque, closed number. It is apparent that if this work had reached production its title probably would have been something more elegant than "Sitting Woman." For the sake of identification, we give the name, as taken from factory records, which state, "Wall picture with sitting woman and child." Very likely the sitting woman was a Madonna and the child a Christ Child, although the possibility of a portrait of an adult woman and a child is not entirely out of the question. It was listed as a closed number on May 18, 1943, the same day on which #155 "Madonna with Cloak" was closed out (see above). There appears to be no existing sample.

## 157 BOY WITH FLOWER BASKET

Figurine, closed number. Factory records list this as "Boy standing with flower basket." This work was entered as a closed number in the factory's books on September 17, 1943. A factory sample was made, but was never placed into production for reasons unknown.

## 158 GIRL WITH DOG

Figurine, closed number. Factory records list this as "Girl standing with dog in her arms." The number was closed on September 17, 1943, along with four other designs (#157, #159, #160, and #161). A factory sample was made, but was never placed into production for reasons unknown.

## 159 GIRL WITH FLOWERS

Figurine, closed number. Listed in factory records as "Girl standing with flowers in her arms," it was given a closed number designation on September 17, 1943. Apparently, the uncertain market conditions brought about by World War II resulted in this group of models (#155–162) being closed out before reaching production. Export to the U.S. was impossible and, even in Europe, many shops that had sold Hummels were shut down. A factory sample was made, but was never placed into production for reasons unknown.

## 160 GIRL IN TIERED DRESS

Figurine, closed number. Mistakenly referred to sometimes as "Girl in Tiered Dress." Factory records list it as "Girl standing in tiered dress and bouquet of flowers." A factory sample was made, but was never placed into production for reasons unknown.

## 161 GIRL WITH HANDS IN POCKETS

Figurine, closed number. Factory description reads, "Girl standing with hands in her pockets." This sounds as though it would have yielded an appealing model, but unfortunately it was never produced. A factory sample was made, but was never placed into production for reasons unknown.

## 162 GIRL WITH POCKETBOOK

Figurine, closed number. Closed out on October 11, 1943, giving the year 1943 a total of eight closed numbers (obviously because of the war). There are no factory samples or photographs of this piece.

## 163 WHITSUNTIDE

Figurine in current production. "Whitsuntide" ("White Sunday," a term more familiar to British ears than American) was introduced to the line in

**163** Whitsuntide

the mid 1930s. After about 25 years of manufacturing, it was temporarily discontinued, then reinstated with the Goebel/V trademark and is now being produced with the current mark. It is not yet positively established whether any received the 3-line trademark. A price of $800 is given for such a specimen in a reference book currently on the market; this however, most likely results from the author merely giving a price for the 3-line mark based on values for other markings, and was entered without any research. If such a specimen did exist, it would surely be valued well in excess of $800, probably as high (or higher than) the Crown trademark.

"Whitsuntide" was previously known as "Christmas" or "Happy New Year." The model is unusual in being chiefly architectural, the human figures playing only a subordinate role. A cathedral belltower is pictured surmounted by a mosque style canopy, giving this design a distinctly Turkish or Persian flavor. A pair of trumpeters lean over the belltower facade, while an angel stands at the base, sometimes holding a candle and in other specimens bearing empty hands with a hole where the candle should be attached. On the tower is a clock indicating several minutes before midnight. Shrubbery and flowers adorn the base, while inside the belltower a large western style bell can be seen. The trumpeters wear green and orange; the angel has a yellow gown and brown wings tipped in red; the tower's canopy is bright crimson, with a textured effect suggesting shingling. Generally the candle is present in older models and may be red or yellow. Yellow is somewhat less common. Older specimens tend to be somewhat larger by as much as half an inch.

|  | Price Range | |
|---|---|---|
| ☐ 163, trademark CM, 6½"–7".................... | 1195.00 | 1398.00 |
| ☐ 163, trademark Full Bee, 6½"–7" ............... | 995.00 | 1198.00 |
| ☐ 163, trademark Stylized Bee, 6½"–7"........... | 748.00 | 825.00 |
| ☐ 163, trademark Goebel/V, 6½"–7"............... | 148.00 | 173.00 |
| ☐ 163, trademark Goebel, 6½"–7"................. | 125.00 | 146.00 |

## 164 WORSHIP

Wall font in current production. "Worship" depicts a primly attired young girl seated at the edge of the holy water bowl, her legs over the side, with hands clasped in prayer. At her back (the upright portion of the model) is an indistinct figure of the Madonna and Child, set into a shrine topped by a sloping canopy. At the base are a number of red flowers with black centers, and there is an extension of red coloring from the flowers downward into the bowl. The girl wears a white short-sleeved blouse, a red skirt, brown shoes, and white socks. There is some color variation to be encountered on the lip of the bowl. The original version has no projection on the rear side of the bowl.

| | | |
|---|---|---|
| ☐ 164, trademark CM, 3¼" × 5"..................... | 250.00 | 275.00 |
| ☐ 164, trademark Full Bee, 3¼" × 5"................ | 160.00 | 180.00 |
| ☐ 164, trademark Stylized Bee, 3¼" × 5" ........... | 60.00 | 65.00 |

**164** Worship

|  | **Price Range** | |
|---|---|---|
| ☐ 164, trademark 3-line mark, 3¼″ × 5″. . . . . . . . . . . . | **50.00** | **55.00** |
| ☐ 164, trademark Goebel/V, 3¼″ × 5″. . . . . . . . . . . . . . | **40.00** | **45.00** |
| ☐ 164, trademark Goebel, 3¼″ × 5″. . . . . . . . . . . . . . . . | **26.50** | **30.00** |

## 165 SWAYING LULLABY

Wall plaque in current production. "Swaying Lullaby" was introduced in the 1940s and manufactured with the Crown, Full Bee, and Stylized Bee marks. It was then taken out of production and listed as a closed edition. In 1978 it was reinstated in time to receive the Goebel/V mark and is currently being produced with the Goebel mark. It is not known whether any specimens exist with the 3-line mark used during the years this number was discontinued. If so they would be quite rare and command a premium price. All the old specimens, prior to discontinuation and reinstatement, are scarce. It was never apparently in full production. The old version has the Hummel signature on the back, while on the reinstated edition the signature appears in the lower right front corner. There is only one size with no reported size fluctuations, another indication of limited production.

The old name for "Swaying Lullaby" was "Child in a Hammock." It shows an infant lying in a hammock with eyes tightly shut, the hammock ends

**165** Swaying Lullaby

strung to the upper left and upper right corners of the frame. A canary bird perches on the child's left knee. The background is composed of vine leaves, floral stems, and a number of varieties of flowers, including tulips and both yellow and red roses. The child wears a white gown and white bib decorated with red dots. He has rosy cheeks, red lips, and auburn hair. At the lower portion of the design, beneath the hammock, is a banner carrying the inscription "Ertraumt von besseren Zeiten" or "Dreaming of better Times." The frame itself is finished in shades of brown, primarily mocha.

| | Price Range | |
|---|---|---|
| ☐ 165, trademark CM, 4½″ × 5¼″ ................. | 1095.00 | 1215.00 |
| ☐ 165, trademark Full Bee, 4½″ × 5¼″ ............ | 795.00 | 885.00 |
| ☐ 165, trademark Stylized Bee, 4½″ × 5¼″ ......... | 555.00 | 605.00 |
| ☐ 165, trademark Goebel/V, 4½″ × 5¼″............. | 88.00 | 101.00 |
| ☐ 165, trademark Goebel, 4½″ × 5¼″............... | 80.00 | 91.00 |

## 166 BOY WITH BIRD

Ashtray in current production. This appealing, brightly colored design shows a boy in Alpine costume reclining on his stomach and elbows on the ashtray rim, alongside a canary bird resting on a bush. The detail on these tiny figures is well presented. There have been no major variations of this model. The boy wears a dark blue jacket with black plaid striping, salmon-colored long trousers, brown shoes, yellow socks, and a cone-shaped Tyrolean cap in green with red band. He also wears a red bow tie. The bird is yellow with touches of brown and violet.

**166** Boy with Bird

|  | **Price Range** | |
|---|---|---|
| ☐ 166, trademark CM, 3¼″ × 6″ ..................... | **380.00** | **420.00** |
| ☐ 166, trademark Full Bee, 3¼″ × 6″ ................ | **250.00** | **275.00** |
| ☐ 166, trademark Stylized Bee, 3¼″ × 6″ ........... | **150.00** | **165.00** |
| ☐ 166, trademark 3-line mark, 3¼″ × 6″ ............. | **125.00** | **135.00** |
| ☐ 166, trademark Goebel/V, 3¼″ × 6″ ............... | **100.00** | **110.00** |
| ☐ 166, trademark Goebel, 3¼″ × 6″ ................. | **80.00** | **90.00** |

## 167 ANGEL BIRD

Wall font in current production. It has been known as "Seated Angel," "Angel-Bird," and "Angel with Bird." "Angel Sitting" is the title given in the latest Hummel catalogue. There are not many variations except for one major difference. Older models have the hanging hole in back, while the current edition is holed near the top directly beneath the frame.

The subject is an angel in a red dress with tiny beige wings, tipped in red, seated alongside a singing yellow canary bird that looks up to her

**167** Angel Bird

while she down at him. Her hair is brown and curly. Perhaps the most intriguing component in this composition is the frame, composed of a design suggesting thin branches woven together to form an arcade, entwined with pale blue flowers.

| | Price Range | |
|---|---|---|
| ☐ 167, trademark CM, 3¼"x4⅛".................... | **245.00** | **265.00** |
| ☐ 167, trademark Full Bee, 3¼"x4⅛"............... | **145.00** | **165.00** |
| ☐ 167, trademark Stylized Bee, 3¼"x4⅛".......... | **45.00** | **65.00** |
| ☐ 167, trademark 3-line mark, 3¼"x4⅛"............ | **35.00** | **55.00** |
| ☐ 167, trademark Goebel/V, 3¼"x4⅛".............. | **25.00** | **34.00** |
| ☐ 167, trademark Goebel, 3¼"x4⅛"................ | **23.00** | **29.00** |

## 168 STANDING BOY

Wall plaque in current production. "Standing Boy," introduced in the 1940s, was discontinued around 1960 and reinstated in 1978. While out of production it became quite a collector's item, with high price levels achieved. Resumption of manufacturing the figurine so far has not dampened interest in pieces with the obsolete trademarks. Most valuable are those with Crown Marks, but any old Standing Boy is scarce and desirable. There are no special points to notice, except that the "M.I. Hummel" signature appears on the front in CM/Full Bee/Stylized Bee examples, while on the back of current production pieces. The existence of "Standing Boy" with the 3-line trademark has been conjectured, but so far neither proven nor disproven. If such a specimen is brought to light it would undoubtedly be worth over $1,000 and possibly a good deal more.

The design shows a raucous-looking boy dressed in a white rolled-sleeve shirt, short brown lederhosen with matching suspenders, brown shoes, white socks, and a slightly askew red bow tie. Under one arm he holds a heart-shaped box (Valentine candy) and in the other a bottle closed with a cork whose contents are unidentified (wine or mineral water). This design is enhanced a great deal by the accessory work surrounding it, comprising a network of delicately colored vine leaves. There are two large flowers, one blue and the other yellow with a brown center. A tiny canary bird is also included. It is not known why this composition is called "Standing Boy" when it might more profitably have been titled "Valentine's Day" or something similar, but there are few endeavors in which time can be so successfully wasted as trying to fathom the motivation behind Hummel titles.

|  | Price Range | |
| --- | --- | --- |
| ☐ 168, trademark CM, 4⅛″ × 5½″ .................. | 1100.00 | 1210.00 |
| ☐ 168, trademark Full Bee, 4⅛″ × 5½″ ............. | 850.00 | 935.00 |
| ☐ 168, trademark Stylized Bee, 4⅛″ × 5½″ ......... | 600.00 | 660.00 |
| ☐ 168, trademark Goebel/V, 4⅛″ × 5½″............. | 100.00 | 110.00 |
| ☐ 168, trademark Goebel, 4⅛″ × 5½″............... | 80.00 | 90.00 |

## 169  BIRD DUET

Figurine in current production. "Bird Duet" was introduced in the late 1940s. During the period of the Stylized Bee trademark in the 1960s, it was restyled with so many alterations that even the following enumeration may not be totally complete. Basically the scene is an angel in orange gown, whose color has remained constant, standing before a wooden music rack on which an open music folio is placed. "A pair of birds are perched atop the music rack." The angel looks toward her feathered pupils and instructs them with a baton. That is the original composition. Here are the variations:

**Original Version**—The angel has brown hair, an infantish face, a chubby body, and blue touches on her wings. The music stand is yellow. One canary is yellow, and the other pale orange with brown wings. The black baton the angel holds is raised and appears to be pointing to the musical notations as the birds sing along.

**Current Version**—The angel has blonde hair, an older face, no blue on wings, and a more svelte body. Both canaries are grayish-brown, and the music stand is maple brown; angel's baton is orange, and the musical notations are different. The baton appears to be resting in a position at the bottom of the music stand.

There is a distinct flaw in this model which, unfortunately, was not corrected in the restyling: The baton is held in a most unnatural attitude too close to the music to provide for free movement.

**169** Bird Duet

|  | Price Range | |
|---|---|---|
| ☐ 169, trademark CM, 3¾″–4″..................... | **295.00** | **315.00** |
| ☐ 169, trademark Full Bee, 3¾″–4″ ................ | **170.00** | **190.00** |
| ☐ 169, trademark Stylized Bee, 3¾″–4″............ | **123.00** | **138.00** |
| ☐ 169, trademark 3-line mark, 3¾″–4″ ............. | **89.00** | **99.00** |
| ☐ 169, trademark Goebel/V, 3¾″–4″................ | **84.00** | **97.00** |
| ☐ 169, trademark Goebel, 3¾″–4″.................. | **66.00** | **73.00** |

## 170 SCHOOL BOYS

Figurine in current production. This attractive composition was the factory's first really successful attempt at a figurine comprised of three components. Originally known as "Difficult Problems," it shows a group of three boys pondering over a mathematical problem on a slate. The subject of their concern is $7 \div 7 =$, which may seem less frightening when compared to New Math, but is surely difficult enough to tax the abilities of these young boys. There have been three editions of "School Boys" the largest of which, #170 (10″), has been discontinued. Model #170/III was permanently discontinued in 1982.

The larger size was introduced some years prior to the small size. It seems to have been in circulation since the late 1940s, while 170/I was not manufactured until 1961 and bears a 1961 copyright date. The currently

**170** School Boys

marketed large version, 170/III, bears a 1972 copyright date, but it should not be inferred that this was the year of introduction. The 1972 copyright date refers only to the restyling, carried out after "School Boys" had been in production about 25 years. At that time it received the new textured finish, which suits this composition a bit better than some others. Since many color variations will be encountered, the following description should not be taken too seriously; it merely indicates the colors most frequently found.

**Boy #1** (going from left to right)—Carries a dark brown school satchel over his shoulder from which the top of a measuring stick protrudes. He wears a dark pink jacket with red plaid striping, red lederhosen, brown clogs, and pinkish socks.

**Boy #2**—Holds slate on which the mathematical problem is written in chalk. He wears a pink jacket highlighted violet and black plaid striping, similar lederhosen, a white shirt, tall brown boots with brownish-green pastel socks, a red bow tie, and a Tyrolean style red hat with a broad floppy brim, crimson banding, and a black and white feather.

**Boy #3**—Holds one finger to his chin in an attitude of contemplation. He is wearing a tomato red jacket with black plaid striping, a white striped shirt, green lederhosen, tall brown boots, and stockings similar to those worn by **#2**.

All of the youths have blonde hair and all are of comparable height.

**Price Range**

| | | |
|---|---|---|
| ☐ 170/I, trademark Stylized Bee, 7¼"–7½" ........ | 750.00 | 825.00 |
| ☐ 170/I, trademark 3-line mark, 7¼"–7½" .......... | 600.00 | 660.00 |
| ☐ 170/I, trademark Goebel/V, 7¼"–7½" ............ | 550.00 | 600.00 |
| ☐ 170/I, trademark Goebel, 7¼"–7½" ............. | 500.00 | 550.00 |
| ☐ 170,/III, trademark CM, 10"–10¼"................ | 2500.00 | 2800.00 |
| ☐ 170/III, trademark Full Bee, 10"–10¼" ........... | 2000.00 | 2200.00 |
| ☐ 170/III, trademark Stylized Bee, 10"–10¼"....... | 1500.00 | 1700.00 |
| ☐ 170/III, trademark 3-line mark, 10"–10¼" ........ | 1400.00 | 1600.00 |
| ☐ 170/III, trademark Goebel/V, 10"–10¼" .......... | 1350.00 | 1550.00 |
| ☐ 170/III, trademark Goebel, 10"–10¼" ............ | 1310.00 | 1500.00 |
| ☐ 170, trademark CM, 10" ......................... | **RARE** | |
| ☐ 170, trademark Full Bee, 10" .................... | **RARE** | |
| ☐ 170, trademark Stylized Bee, 10" ............... | **RARE** | |

## 171  LITTLE SWEEPER

Figurine in current production. "Little Sweeper," formerly known as "Mother's Helper" (a title which would, if retained, conflict with #133), is a girl in mid 19th century Bavarian peasant dress wielding a broom along the floor. There has not been much alteration in this long-produced model; nor has there been any significant variation in size. The girl wears a white rolled-sleeved dress, black vest, green apron decorated with floral motifs, brown shoes, and has a red kerchief tied around her head in typical domestic service fashion. The broom is naturally colored.

**171** Little Sweeper

**Price Range**

□ 171, trademark CM, 4¼"–4½" .................. **245.00    272.00**
□ 171, trademark Full Bee, 4¼"–4½" ............. **145.00    172.00**
□ 171, trademark Stylized Bee, 4¼"–4½" ......... **95.00    122.00**
□ 171, trademark 3-line mark, 4¼"–4½" .......... **73.00     87.00**
□ 171, trademark Goebel/V, 4¼"–4½" ............. **64.00     76.00**
□ 171, trademark Goebel, 4¼"–4½" ............... **55.00     66.00**

## 172 FESTIVAL HARMONY WITH MANDOLIN

Figurine in current production. "Festival Harmony with Mandolin" is a figure of a standing angel playing that instrument. The official title is merely "Festival Harmony." It is called "Festival Harmony with Mandolin" to distinguish it from #173 "Festival Harmony with Flute" (see below). Currently two sizes are in production. A third edition #172 (10¾"), made with the Crown trademark and possibly others, has been closed out.

The larger size, #172/II, is the older, having been introduced in the 1940s, and has undergone two restylings in its approximately 35 year history. In the original or Crown version, a tall growth of stems surmounted

**172** Festival Harmony with Mandolin

by flowers and leaves decorate the base at the angel's feet, and a yellow and brown canary bird perches on one stem. In the first restyling in the 1950s, the height of the flowers was sharply reduced and the bird dispossessed from them; he now alights on the mandolin's neck, and his color has changed to brown. The second restyling has a textured finish, flowers on the base (not growing up from it), and the bird has now become blue and has moved slightly more toward the mandolin head. There are no such variations with #172/0, which was not introduced until the middle 1960s and has undergone no change. In all models the angel's gown is pastel yellow, her hair blonde with touches of red and her wings reddish-brown. She stands on a circular base.

**Price Range**

| | | |
|---|---|---|
| ☐ 172/0, trademark 3-line mark, 8″ ............. | 150.00 | 170.00 |
| ☐ 172/0, trademark Goebel/V, 8″ ............... | 130.00 | 150.00 |
| ☐ 172/0, trademark Goebel, 8″ ................. | 115.00 | 125.00 |
| ☐ 172/II, trademark Full Bee, 10¼″–10¾″......... | 1000.00 | 1200.00 |
| ☐ 172/II, trademark Stylized Bee, 10¼″–10¾″ .... | 400.00 | 425.00 |
| ☐ 172/II, trademark 3-line mark, 10¼″–10¾″...... | 300.00 | 320.00 |
| ☐ 172/II, trademark Goebel/V, 10¼″–10¾″........ | 250.00 | 270.00 |
| ☐ 172/II, trademark Goebel, 10¼″–10¾″.......... | 220.00 | 240.00 |
| ☐ 172, trademark CM, 10¾″...................... | 2500.00 | 2800.00 |
| ☐ 172, trademark Full Bee, 10¾″................. | 2000.00 + | — |

## 173 FESTIVAL HARMONY WITH FLUTE

Figurine in current production. Companion piece to #172 "Festival Harmony with Mandolin" (see above). The history of its production closely parallels that of #172, and most of the comments made above can be applied to it. The chief exception is that the canary bird in "Festival Harmony with Flute" has never perched upon the flowers at the angel's feet, but has always been stationed on her left arm. As with #172 there have been two style changes in the larger version, involving the shortening of flowers and some alterations in the bird. The original or Crown Mark specimens have a large bird, who shrinks down to about one-half the size in the first restyling and remains more or less the same dimensions in the third or current edition. There are color variations in the bird and the present version has a textured finish. The larger specimens are a bit taller than #172.

It should of course be borne in mind that measurement includes the wings, not merely the top of the angel's head, and these account for an additional inch or more in height. The old discontinued 11-inch version is very scarce and should not be confused with 173/II. "Festival Harmony with Flute" is occasionally referred to as "Festival Harmony with Horn."

| | | |
|---|---|---|
| ☐ 173/0, trademark 3-line mark, 8″ ............. | 145.00 | 169.00 |
| ☐ 173/0, trademark Goebel/V, 8″ ............... | 127.00 | 141.00 |
| ☐ 173/0, trademark Goebel, 8″ ................. | 115.00 | 127.00 |
| ☐ 173/II, trademark CM, 10¼″–11″ .............. | 775.00 | 805.00 |
| ☐ 173/II, trademark Full Bee, 10¼″–11″.......... | 995.00 | 1195.00 |
| ☐ 173/II, trademark Stylized Bee, 10¼″–11″ ...... | 395.00 | 427.00 |

**173** Festival Harmony with Flute

| | | |
|---|---|---|
| ☐ 173/II, trademark 3-line mark, 10¼″–11″......... | **295.00** | **327.00** |
| ☐ 173/II, trademark Goebel/V, 10¼″–11″........... | **225.00** | **235.00** |
| ☐ 173/II, trademark Goebel, 10¼″–11″............. | **220.00** | **231.00** |
| ☐ 173, trademark CM, 11″......................... | **2500.00 +** | — |
| ☐ 173, trademark Full Bee, 11″.................... | **2000.00 +** | — |

## 174 SHE LOVES ME, SHE LOVES ME NOT

Figurine in current production. "She Loves Me, She Loves Me Not" is another Hummel variation on the daisy-plucking theme. Here the lovestruck child is a boy. This is a small model standing only 4¼″. Size variations have not been reported. There have, however, been several restylings which totally altered the boy's facial attitude and expression. In the original version,

**174** She Loves Me, She Loves Me Not

bearing the Crown trademark, he wears a pensive, soulful look. The current edition has a more offhandish expression; instead of staring off blankly into space, he concentrates methodically on the task at hand, removing each petal from the flower to discover if the final petal is a "She Loves Me" or a "She Loves Me Not."

The boy wears a violet short jacket with plaid striping, brown trousers, black clogs, and a brown Tyrolean hat with feather whose color varies. Two small flowers are on the ground and a canary bird in bright yellow perches on the post of a fence against which the boy's figure reclines. Specimens with the Full Bee, Stylized Bee, and 3-line marks have a flower on the left fencepost, opposite the bird. This is not present in the Crown version nor in those currently being marketed in the Goebel/V and plain Goebel marks. The current edition is sometimes described as having his eyes closed; but while they indeed appear closed, the intention is to show that the boy is gazing downward. These variations should correctly be termed "eyes open" and "eyes downcast."

|  | **Price Range** | |
|---|---|---|
| ☐ 174, trademark CM, 4¼" .......................... | 370.00 | 420.00 |
| ☐ 174, trademark Full Bee, 4¼" .................... | 245.00 | 275.00 |
| ☐ 174, trademark Stylized Bee, 4¼". ............... | 145.00 | 175.00 |
| ☐ 174, trademark 3-line mark, 4¼" ................. | 95.00 | 125.00 |
| ☐ 174, trademark Goebel/V, 4¼" ................... | 75.00 | 92.00 |
| ☐ 174, trademark Goebel, 4¼" ..................... | 72.00 | 81.00 |

## 175 MOTHER'S DARLING

Figurine in current production. "Mother's Darling," formerly known as "Happy Harriet," is a figure of a girl in peasant dress carrying a pair of empty laundry bags. At one time there was a tendency toward this type of model, who might carry an empty basket, bag or the like, as it was presumed buyers might wish to place candies, artificial flowers or other articles in them. Having discovered this not to be a prime selling point, no new figures of this sort have been introduced in recent yers.

"Mother's Darling" is apparently a helpful little tyke who cannot wait to get washday started. Washday in the mid 1800s era represented by this composition was not a 45 minute visit to the automatic laundry but truly an all-day affair. Resigned to her fate, "Mother's Darling" wears a cheery smile and a "let's get going" expression on her face. Her outfit comprises a white long-sleeved blouse, green dress, a white apron with wine red circular ornaments, brown shoes, and a red kerchief tied beneath her chin. Both laundry sacks are pale blue. One sack has blue dots, and the other sack has red dots. A few small reddish flowers appear at her feet on the model's

**175** Mother's Darling

circular base. Older specimens have no polka dots on the head kerchief, but a few white dots appear on the current editions. Also her laundry sacks were different colors in these earlier models. The sack in her right hand had blue polka dots on a pink background, and the one in her left was blue-green with red dots. These older specimens in the Crown, Full Bee, and Stylized Bee trademarks carry a premium evaluation.

|  | Price Range | |
|---|---|---|
| □ 175 trademark CM, one laundry bag pastel blue-green and one pastel pink, 5½″............. | 390.00 | 440.00 |
| □ 175, trademark CM, 5½″ ...................... | 300.00 | 330.00 |
| □ 175, trademark Full Bee, one laundry bag pastel blue-green, one pink, 5½″...................... | 250.00 | 275.00 |
| □ 175, trademark Full Bee, 5½″ ................... | 200.00 | 220.00 |
| □ 175, trademark Stylized Bee, one laundry bag pastel blue-green and one pink, 5½″............. | 150.00 | 165.00 |
| □ 175, trademark Stylized Bee, 5½″............... | 175.00 | 195.00 |
| □ 175, trademark 3-line mark, 5½″ ................ | 125.00 | 137.50 |
| □ 175, trademark Goebel/V, 5½″ .................. | 100.00 | 110.00 |
| □ 175, trademark Goebel, 5½″ .................... | 88.00 | 98.00 |

## 176 HAPPY BIRTHDAY

Figurine in current production. "Happy Birthday" is a figure of two girls standing alongside each other. One holds a cake at which the other looks admiringly. The second girl clutches a nosegay in her left hand. This simple composition is well modeled and effective. It has been produced in three editions, one of which, #176 (5½″) has been closed out.

The small size has an oval base while the larger edition is supplied with a circular base. Girl #1 (left) wears a white puffy-sleeved blouse with red polka dots, a black vest, a blue skirt with red polka dots, brown shoes, and white socks with red and brown brushstrokes. Girl #2 has a salmon-colored dress with red polka dots, brown shoes, socks identical to her companion's, and wears a red ribbon in her hair. The first girl has red hair while the second girl's hair is fawn-colored. The nosegay is yellow and green with reddish tips on the flowers. There has been speculation concerning a possible reinstatement of the discontinued #176 (5½″), but after more than two years of such rumors it is still not in production.

| □ 176/0, trademark CM, 5″–5¼″.................... | 245.00 | 328.00 |
|---|---|---|
| □ 176/0, trademark Full Bee, 5″–5¼″ ............. | 295.00 | 325.00 |
| □ 176/0, trademark Stylized Bee, 5″–5¼″ ......... | 170.00 | 198.00 |
| □ 176/0, trademark 3-line mark, 5″–5¼″ .......... | 118.00 | 141.00 |
| □ 176/0, trademark Goebel/V, 5″–5¼″............. | 100.00 | 120.00 |
| □ 176/0, trademark Goebel, 5″–5¼″................ | 94.00 | 112.00 |
| □ 176/I, trademark CM, 5¾″–6″ ................... | 645.00 | 705.00 |
| □ 176/I, trademark Full Bee, 5¾″–6″ .............. | 495.00 | 580.00 |
| □ 176/I, trademark Stylized Bee, 5¾″–6″.......... | 345.00 | 380.00 |
| □ 176/I, trademark 3-line mark, 5¾″–6″ ........... | 295.00 | 335.00 |

**176** Happy Birthday

| | Price Range | |
|---|---|---|
| ☐ 176/I, trademark Goebel/V, 5¾″–6″ .............. | 150.00 | 168.00 |
| ☐ 176/I, trademark Goebel, 5¾″–6″ ............... | 136.50 | 149.00 |
| ☐ 176, trademark CM, 5½″ ...................... | 745.00 | 830.00 |
| ☐ 176, trademark Full Bee, 5½″ ................... | 495.00 | 555.00 |

## 177  SCHOOL GIRLS

Figurine in current production. "School Girls," originally known as "Master Piece," is a feminine version of #170 "School Boys," whose production history closely parallels that work. Three girls of equal age and size are shown standing together. Instead of working out a mathematical problem as in "School Boys," the subject of attention is a piece of crocheting being performed by one of the group. One familiar component from "School Boys" will be readily recognized: The brown schoolbag with measuring rule protruding, which in this composition is carried by the girl on the right. There are three versions of "School Girls", and as in most cases of Hummel models, the original edition #177 was discontinued. In 1982, #177/III, the 9½″ model, was permanently retired. They are:

    #177/I, 7½″
    #177/III, 9½″, discontinued
    #177, 9½″, discontinued

When originally introduced only the larger size, #177/III, was sold and this remained the case until 1961, when 177/I was placed into production

**177** School Girls

carrying an incised 1961 copyright date. The larger size was restyled with the modern textured finish around 1972 and has a 1972 incised copyright date. It should not be presumed that the model was introduced in that year. The copyright date refers only to the restyling.

The knitting girl reappears later as an individual statuette in #255 "Stitch in Time" and again in #256 "Knitting Lessons," this time in combination with a figure who closely resembles the middle girl in "School Girls." As some color variations exist, the following descriptions should not be relied upon to apply in all cases.

**Girl #1** (left to right)—She wears a red dress, a black vest, a pale blue apron, gray shoes, and pink socks. She holds a pair of crocheting needles and a partially completed work of unidentifiable nature (possibly the sleeve of a sweater) whose color is primarily yellow.

**Girl #2**—She is dressed in a pastel brown short-sleeved blouse, a black vest, a light blue skirt with red circular ornaments, brown shoes, and white socks with touches of tan, and a blue hair ribbon.

**Girl #3**—She wears a red-orange dress or jacket with black plaid striping, brown slippers, white socks with strokes of blue, red hair ribbon, and carries a brown school satchel.

On the base is a ball of wool from which Girl #1 works and an indistinct reddish flower. The high values of this composition, similar to the prices of "School Boys," should require no explanation. Because of its size and the fact that three figures are involved, the work has always carried a much stiffer retail price than small single figurines. Thus the progression of older specimens into the four-digit category does not represent nearly so sharp a proportional advance as small figurines that began at prices of $8 or $10 and now sell for $400 or $500.

|  | Price Range | |
|---|---:|---:|
| □ 177/I, trademark Stylized Bee, 7½″ .............. | 750.00 | 825.00 |
| □ 177/I, trademark 3-line mark, 7½″............... | 650.00 | 715.00 |
| □ 177/I, trademark Goebel/V, 7½″ ................. | 550.00 | 605.00 |
| □ 177/I, trademark Goebel, 7½″ .................... | 525.00 | 580.00 |
| □ 177/III, trademark CM, 9½″........................ | 2500.00 | 2750.00 |
| □ 177/III, trademark Full Bee, 9½″ ................. | 2000.00 | 2200.00 |
| □ 177/III, trademark Stylized Bee, 9½″ ............. | 1500.00 | 1650.00 |
| □ 177/III, trademark 3-line mark, 9½″ .............. | 1400.00 | 1550.00 |
| □ 177/III, trademark Goebel/V, 9½″................. | 1350.00 | 1485.00 |
| □ 177/III, trademark Goebel, 9½″................... | 1310.00 | 1440.00 |
| □ 177, trademark CM, 9½″ .......................... | 2500.00 | 2750.00 |
| □ 177, trademark Full Bee, 9½″ .................... | 2000.00 | 2200.00 |
| □ 177, trademark Stylized, 9½″.................... | 1500.00 | 1650.00 |

## 178  THE PHOTOGRAPHER

Figurine in current production. Photography might appear an offbeat subject for representation by a Hummel, insofar as the themes are largely all set in the period 1830–1860. Photography was not, however, unknown

**178** The Photographer

during the latter part of that era. The camera used by "The Photographer" seems a fair likeness of an 1850s design, lacking only the light shield curtain which the picture taker in those days placed around his head and shoulders. This model was introduced in 1948, but originally did not carry a copyright date. The 1948 copyright date was added later in conjunction with a re-styling. The Crown Mark pieces are generally at least 5″ high, up to as much as 5¼″, while the current edition is more often 4¾″ to 5″. There are some color alterations to be noticed especially on the camera.

Basically the subject is a young boy who crouches down to peer through the viewfinder of a box style camera mounted on wooden tripod. The camera has black accordion sides and a tubular black lens covering at the front. On the base sits a dachshund type dog, maroon-colored, who looks up towards the camera. The boy is dressed in a pale green shirt with circular decorations, black lederhosen, brown shoes, and white or pale brown low socks. He wears a red neckerchief with yellow polka dots and has sandy-brown rumpled hair.

|  | Price Range | |
|---|---|---|
| ☐ 178, trademark CM, 4¾″–5¼″ ................. | 495.00 | 545.00 |
| ☐ 178, trademark Full Bee, 4¾″–5¼″ ............ | 295.00 | 334.00 |
| ☐ 178, trademark Stylized Bee, 4¾″–5¼″......... | 195.00 | 227.00 |
| ☐ 178, trademark 3-line mark, 4¾″–5¼″ .......... | 123.00 | 147.00 |
| ☐ 178, trademark Goebel/V, 4¾″–5¼″ ............ | 112.00 | 127.00 |
| ☐ 178, trademark Goebel, 4¾″–5¼″ ............. | 105.00 | 124.00 |

## 179 COQUETTES

Figurine in current production. The dictionary defines coquette as "a woman who endeavors, without sincere affection, to gain the attention and admiration of men." That there are child coquettes no one can doubt, and very likely the proportion of them is higher than among adults. Here we have two of their species, resplendent in their best attire, perched fetchingly on a fence. One holds a nosegay of red flowers. Their expressions, especially of the girl on the right, are what used to be called prissy. One need only call into play a bit of imagination to picture a young boy strolling by and the scene is completed.

This is a most handsomely designed and executed composition. Not only are the figures well modeled and enameled, but the fence, whose uprights consists of sturdy tree trunks, must be ranked among the finest representation of its type by the factory. So well modeled and colored are these components that they have the appearance of real wood, a condition rare in a porcelain model. Both the wood grain and texture are lifelike. At either side of the girls there is a canary bird colored green with a yellow underside and brownish wings. The first girl wears a red-orange dress, a black cape, black clog shoes, and blue peaked kerchief tied around her head. Her companion has a salmon-colored puffy-sleeved blouse, white dress with floral ornamentation, black clogs and a red kerchief. Several red flowers adorn the fenceposts. Minor color variations occur. The current edition of "Coquettes" has been restyled. Generally the Crown Mark examples are somewhat larger in size but the variation as reported is slight.

**179** Coquettes

| | Price Range | |
|---|---|---|
| ☐ 179, trademark CM, 5″–5¼″..................... | 290.00 | 490.00 |
| ☐ 179, trademark Full Bee, 5″–5¼″ ............... | 200.00 | 305.00 |
| ☐ 179, trademark Stylized Bee, 5″–5¼″ ........... | 120.00 | 175.00 |
| ☐ 179, trademark 3-line mark, 5″–5¼″ ............ | 100.00 | 125.00 |
| ☐ 179, trademark Goebel/V, 5″–5¼″................ | 110.00 | 120.00 |
| ☐ 179, trademark Goebel, 5″–5¼″................. | 80.00 | 100.00 |

## 180 TUNEFUL GOODNIGHT

Wall plaque in current production. "Tuneful Goodnight" is also referred to as "Happy Bugler." It shows a very young boy blowing into a bugle which he holds with one hand. The other hand clutches a flower, stem, and several leaves. Perched on the child's left knee is a bird, whistling in tune with the music. The design is rather unusual in that the figure, shown against a red heart-shaped frame, is modeled almost entirely in three dimension in the manner of a figurine, not the bas-relief common to Hummel plaques. In fact, his legs and feet hang over the base. This could well be termed a wall figurine.

"Tuneful Goodnight" has been redesigned. Introduced during the Crown Mark period, it was taken out of production in the 3-line mark era and reinstated in the late 1970s. However, the work does exist with all six marks.

**180** Tuneful Goodnight

It is quite scarce with the first four, apparently having never been in extensive production. Some color variations will be noted. The general format is for the child to wear a blue nightgown with dark blue hearts across it, brown slippers, and pale brown or white socks. The bird is generally blue, pale green, and red, with a salmon-colored beak.

|  | **Price Range** | |
|---|---|---|
| ☐ 180, trademark CM, 5″ × 4¾″ .................... | 745.00 | 830.00 |
| ☐ 180, trademark Full Bee, 5″ × 4¾″ ............... | 545.00 | 595.00 |
| ☐ 180, trademark Stylized Bee, 5″ × 4¾″ .......... | 395.00 | 445.00 |
| ☐ 180, trademark 3-line mark, 5″ × 4¾″ ............ | 298.00 | 331.00 |
| ☐ 180, trademark Goebel/V, 5″ × 4¾″ ............... | 148.00 | 167.00 |
| ☐ 180, trademark Goebel, 5″ × 4¾″ ................ | 94.50 | 104.00 |

## 181 OLD MAN READING NEWSPAPER

Figurine, closed number. This is one of the four figures (#181, 189, 190, 191) commonly referred to as "The Mommas and the Poppas." All are representations of adults engaged in various activities, #181 being a figure of a grandfather-type seated on a stool reading a newspaper. None of the four ever reached production. When submitted to the Seissen Convent for approval they were rejected as not being representative of Sister Hummel's work. As the objection was founded upon the fact that adults rather than children were depicted, no effort was made at restyling. "Old Man Reading Newspaper" was listed in the factory's books as a closed number on February 18, 1948. Why there should have been such negative feeling about adult figures, when such figures were often sketched by Berta Hummel, is difficult to understand. In any event these are extremely rare pieces. A specimen of "Old Man Reading Newspaper" is in the collection of Mr. Robert L. Miller of Eaton, Ohio, the nation's foremost Hummel enthusiast. There appear to be no others in private hands and it is quite likely only this one factory sample exists.

The figure measures 6¾". The old man sits in a hunched posture, and the close proximity of his face to the newspaper suggests a need for spectacles. He wears a yellow and blue jacket with black plaid striping, yellow trousers brushed with muddy blue, beige slippers, and white socks with blue and yellow vertical striping. A salmon-colored stocking cap is pulled over his head. The stool is a pale yellowish-brown, suggesting raw oak. The figure is contained on a rectangular base.

Speculation on the value would be pointless; it is obviously an extremely valuable item whose price, if it reached sale, would depend on the level reached in competitive bidding. There has never been any speculation on the possibility of Hummel bringing these four models into production, but the intense interest shown in them in recent years could well lead to such a move. The kindly facial expression of #181 is worth noticing. One can only wonder about the model for this composition; very likely it was a member of Sister Hummel's family (see #202).

## 182 GOOD FRIENDS

Figurine in current production. "Good Friends" is a bright, appealing study of a young girl and her lamb done in strong sharp colors. This model was introduced about 1948, and after nearly 30 years of production was restyled in 1976 by Goebel's chief sculptor, Gerhard Strobek.

The current version retains the basic coloration of the old version, but it is somewhat larger and the girl's face is turned slightly upward rather than looking straight forward. She is seated, wearing a white long-sleeved blouse with blue polka dots, a maroon vest, a white skirt with blue plaid striping, brown shoes, and a reddish kerchief tied around her head. In her hands she holds several yellow and orange flowers. The lamb, naturalistically modeled, stands behind her. The expression in the new edition seems to be saying, "Buy my flowers." "Good Friends" was originally called simply "Friends."

**182** Good Friends

| | Price Range | |
|---|---|---|
| ☐ 182, trademark CM, 4″–4¼″...................... | 450.00 | 475.00 |
| ☐ 182, trademark Full Bee, 4″–4¼″ ................ | 250.00 | 275.00 |
| ☐ 182, trademark Stylized Bee, 4″–4¼″............ | 150.00 | 160.00 |
| ☐ 182, trademark 3-line mark, 4″–4¼″ ............. | 120.00 | 125.00 |
| ☐ 182, trademark Goebel/V, 4″–4¼″................ | 95.00 | 105.00 |
| ☐ 182, trademark Goebel, 4″–4¼″.................. | 83.00 | 90.00 |

## 183 FOREST SHRINE

Figurine in current production. A rare example of a Hummel which has no human figure in its motif. The theme of children stopping by or worshiping at wayside shrines was earlier used by the factory. In "Forest Shrine" they have been replaced by a pair of young deer. "Forest Shrine" was originally known as "Doe at Shrine." Introduced about 1948, the first postwar "shrine" design for the factory, it had been closed out during use of the 3-line trademark, but was again reinstated several years ago. This is, however, a rare item when it bears any of the three earlier marks. Prior to its listing as a closed edition, it was not likely to be discovered selling under $1,000.

**183** Forest Shrine

It was at first probably made in limited quantity to monitor public reaction to an animal–only composition.

In the currently manufactured edition the deer have a naturalistic matte finish, while in the pre-discontinued examples their bodies are almost plastic-looking. One deer reclines on the ground while her companion stands viewing an enamel plaque of the Madonna and Child. The plaque is affixed to a wooden stand and protected by a sloping wood canopy set into the side of a tree. At the tree's base and the plaque's base are a number of red and yellow flowers with leaves growing out of branches. The tree trunk is naturalistically textured. Both of the does are a light fawn color.

|  | Price Range | |
|---|---|---|
| ☐ 183, trademark CM, 9″ ......................... | 1498.00 | 1698.00 |
| ☐ 183, trademark Full Bee, 9″ ..................... | 998.00 | 1198.00 |
| ☐ 183, trademark Stylized Bee, 9″................. | 498.00 | 698.00 |
| ☐ 183, trademark Goebel/V, 9″ .................... | 298.00 | 318.00 |
| ☐ 183, trademark Goebel, 9″ ...................... | 273.00 | 305.00 |

## 184 LATEST NEWS

Figurine in current production. "Latest News," introduced in 1948, is a figure of a boy seated on a wooden stool reading a newspaper. There is an old and new version. In the original edition, this model has a square base and the boy's head is positioned so that his gaze falls more or less upon the central portion of the open double page paper. In the restyling, which occurred in the middle 1960s, the base is oval and his head is turned to one side in an attitude of reading the left-hand page. There are few size variations to be encountered. The restyling did not attempt to change the size.

Some square base specimens have been discovered carrying both the Crown Mark and Full Bee trademarks. They also have a raised vertical and horizontal bar on the underside of the base, which divides it into four equal squares. One trademark appears in one square; the other trademark in another. The chief matter of interest in this composition is the newspaper, which sometimes is blank and sometimes carries a masthead. The paper can be found with numerous different titles, mostly in the German language, but also including N.Y. Times, St. Louis Post, and the names of other American dailies. The obvious assumption is that the latter were intended for the U.S. market, but there is more to the story. It is reliably reported that for a long while, plain specimens were kept at the factory to be painted with any lettering desired by those who visited the Goebel gift shop on the premises. It is hardly surprising then that such a variety of titles should exist. Things have not yet reached the point where premiums are given for certain titles, but there is always the possibility that this might occur at some future time. "Latest News" is occasionally listed in old Hummel literature as #184/O.S. O.S. stands for "Ohne Schrift" which means no lettering.

**New Style**　　**184** Latest News　　**Old Style**

|  | **Price Range** | |
|---|---|---|
| ☐ 184, trademark CM, no title on paper, 5″–5¼″ ... | 350.00 | 385.00 |
| ☐ 184, trademark CM, title on paper............... | 500.00 | 550.00 |
| ☐ 184, trademark Full Bee, no title on paper, 5″–5¼″......................................... | 300.00 | 330.00 |
| ☐ 184, trademark Full Bee, title on paper, 5″–5¼″ | 350.00 | 385.00 |
| ☐ 184, trademark Stylized Bee, 5″–5¼″............ | 225.00 | 245.00 |
| ☐ 184, trademark 3-line mark, 5″–5¼″ ............. | 155.00 | 170.00 |
| ☐ 184, trademark Goebel/V, 5″–5¼″................ | 130.00 | 145.00 |
| ☐ 184, trademark Goebel, 5″–5¼″.................. | 115.50 | 125.00 |

## 185 ACCORDION BOY

Figurine in current production. There has been only one basic edition of this model of boy playing what appears to be a concertina rather than an accordion, but sizes vary considerably. The Crown Mark specimens are

**185** Accordion Boy

generally around 5¼". During the 1950s they grew a bit larger, occasionally reaching 6". They have since come down a bit. "Accordion Boy" is one of the works advanced as evidence by supporters of the "mold growth" theory (see Glossary), but the variations in size of this figure hardly provide proof, as far more Hummels have decreased than increased in size.

Originally this model was known as "On the Alpine Pasture," suggesting that the youth is a wandering troubador who plays his music for the entertainment of any who may be within hearing range including sheep and other livestock. He wears a pale green jacket, maroon lederhosen, black shoes, and yellow socks. The only difference in color between old specimens and new specimens is that the bellows of the concertina are darker, with yellow and red mixed in the old specimens. The youth has his lips parted in song.

| | Price Range | |
|---|---|---|
| ☐ 185, trademark CM, 5"–6"...................... | 698.00 | 748.00 |
| ☐ 185, trademark Full Bee, 5"–6".................. | 224.00 | 234.00 |
| ☐ 185, trademark Stylized Bee, 5"–6" ............. | 148.00 | 158.00 |
| ☐ 185, trademark 3-line mark, 5"–6"............... | 98.00 | 111.00 |
| ☐ 185, trademark Goebel/V, 5"–6"................. | 89.00 | 99.00 |
| ☐ 185, trademark Goebel, 5"–6"................... | 83.00 | 91.00 |

## 186 SWEET MUSIC

Figurine in current production. "Sweet Music," a figure of a boy playing a cello, was released at the same time as #185 "Accordion Boy" (see above) and may be considered a companion to it. There have not been such extensive size variations with this model. It was restyled with alterations limited mainly to enameling. In the original edition the boy has a gray railroad conductor's cap, a green medium length jacket, pale yellow shirt, brown baggy trousers, white slippers with black striping, and a red neckerchief. The version currently produced has a charcoal gray hat of the same type, with pale gray band, brown slippers without striping, and a lighter red neckerchief. The hair has also undergone some minor change in color, from sandy to a lighter brown. This is considered one of the more successful of the factory's efforts to model musicians. Its original name was "Playing to the Dance," undoubtedly referring to Bavarian folk dance. If this figure were in motion, the bow would be seen drawing back and forth vigorously.

| ☐ 186, trademark CM, 5"–5½"...................... | 750.00 | 825.00 |
|---|---|---|
| ☐ 186, trademark Full Bee, 5"–5½" ................ | 250.00 | 270.00 |
| ☐ 186, trademark Stylized Bee, 5"–5½"............ | 150.00 | 170.00 |
| ☐ 186, trademark 3-line mark, 5"–5½" ............. | 100.00 | 120.00 |
| ☐ 186, trademark Goebel/V, 5"–5½"................ | 90.00 | 100.00 |
| ☐ 186, trademark Goebel, 5"–5¼"................... | 83.00 | 90.00 |

**186** Sweet Music

## 187 STORE PLAQUE IN ENGLISH

Store plaque in current production. The factory began issuing store display plaques in 1947. Currently, they are listed by Hummel as "Display Plaques" and carry the mold number 187/C. Two varieties are now marketed: The traditional shop plaque, intended as an attention-getter and an assurance that the shop deals in genuine Hummels, and another for collectors. There are, of course, many variations, both in design and wording, but so far all have conformed in two essential regards: They are oval-shaped, measuring 4″ × 5½″ (the oval laid upon its side horizontally), and feature a likeness of the "Merry Wanderer" on the left-hand side.

The original version, in the Crown Mark and Full Bee editions, had a prominent bumblebee placed at the top of the oval. This was subsequently replaced in the Stylized Bee era by a badge carrying a stamped impression of that symbol in blue, and was later altered in the Goebel/V period to a simple printing of the symbol in the upper portion of the plaque. The badge in the Stylized Bee specimens extends upward beyond the plaque. It is also noteworthy that the original edition had a sculptured effect rather than being a perfectly symmetrical oval, which was adopted for the Stylized Bee plaques and has been retained since. There is also an effort at shading in

**187** Store Plaque in English

the early plaques to give a relief appearance while those in current production are smooth and flat.

Generally, in the Crown and Full Bee specimens the wording "Hummel Figures" appears in pale red with other lettering in black, but some examples have all of the wording in black. The Stylized Bee plaques normally have the factory name in red with accessory text in blue, and this practice carried over into the present design. There are, however, variations and exceptions, so no hard-and-fast rules can be laid down. The most common basic wording found on the original edition is "The Original Hummel Figures," followed by the "M.I. Hummel" signature as it appears on models. Sometimes the word "Hummel" is enclosed within inverted commas, sometimes not. The Stylized Bee plaques often carry this wording also, but will occasionally be found reading "Authorized Dealer" or something of that nature. The word "Figures" is replaced by "Figurines" in the new version, obviously for the American consumer's benefit. (In Britain the word "figure" is automatically taken to signify "statuette," but in this country one cannot be so certain.) Inclusion of the company's address was begun in the Stylized Bee era, though is not to be found on the majority of Stylized Bee plaques. It is now standard, along with a copyright cypher and the words "By W. Goebel Porzellenfabrik, Rodental, W. Germany." A registry cypher, the letter "r" within a circle, appears alongside the trademark, signifying registration in all countries protected by international patent laws. There have been two copyright dates, 1947 and 1976. Plaques are sometimes found with the names of dealers printed on them.

Because of the many variations that exist, the following prices should be taken as rough guidelines only. The latest design plaque is marked 187/A and is available to collectors in the last two trademarks. The words "Authorized Dealer" have been omitted on these editions.

| | Price Range | |
|---|---|---|
| ☐ 187, trademark CM, 4″×5½″ | 1498.00 | 1648.00 |
| ☐ 187, trademark Full Bee, 4″×5½″ | 798.00 | 878.00 |
| ☐ 187, trademark Stylized Bee, 4″×5½″ | 498.00 | 548.00 |
| ☐ 187, trademark 3-line mark, 4″×5½″ | 398.00 | 438.00 |
| ☐ 187/A, trademark Goebel/V, 4″×5½″, retailer plaque | 49.00 | 54.00 |
| ☐ 187/A, trademark Goebel/V, 4″×5½″, collector plaque | 41.00 | 51.00 |
| ☐ 187/A, trademark Goebel, 4″×5½″, retailer plaque | 42.00 | 51.00 |
| ☐ 187/A, trademark Goebel, 4″×5½″, collector plaque | 42.00 | 51.00 |

# 188 CELESTIAL MUSICIAN

Figurine in current production. "Celestial Musician" is a very occidental-looking angel playing a violin. Some specimens carry a 1948 copyright date, which, according to the best available information, is the year this figure was first placed on the market. "Celestial Musician" has not been restyled and there are no reported size variations. Some compilers of Hum-

**188** Celestial Musician

mel books are apparently unaware that this model exists with the Crown trademark as it is omitted in their listings. 1948 was definitely not too late to receive the Crown Mark. Some figures released even in 1949 are known with such markings. There is a rare version of "Celestial Musician" in cream overglaze, marketed at the outset of production, on which no reliable pricing information can be obtained. This variety is probably not found with any mark besides the Crown.

The figure stands and is dressed in a long sweeping green gown decorated with golden five-pointed stars and has grayish-white wings. There is some speculation about the leather bag carried by the angel at his right side. Though suggested at one time to be a case for the violin, it is too small for that purpose, unless carried with the neck protruding. It more than likely bears no connection to the instrument, but is a receptacle for hymnals or other music books.

|  | Price Range | |
|---|---|---|
| ☐ 188, trademark CM, 7″ ......................... | 750.00 | 800.00 |
| ☐ 188, trademark Full Bee, 7″ ..................... | 350.00 | 370.00 |
| ☐ 188, trademark Stylized Bee, 7″................. | 200.00 | 220.00 |
| ☐ 188, trademark 3-line mark, 7″ .................. | 150.00 | 170.00 |

|  | Price Range | |
|---|---|---|
| □ 188, trademark Goebel/V, 7″ ..................... | 130.00 | 140.00 |
| □ 188, trademark Goebel, 7″ ....................... | 115.00 | 125.00 |
| □ 188, trademark Goebel, 5½″ ..................... | 80.00 | 90.00 |

## 189 OLD WOMAN KNITTING

Figurine, closed number. This model and the two following (#190 and 191), as well as #181 "Old Man Reading Newspaper," comprise the celebrated group known as "The Mommas and the Poppas," a series of adult figurines never placed into production because the Seissen Convent regarded them as too drastic a departure from the norm. They exist today as factory samples only. "Old Woman Knitting" was listed as a closed number on May 14, 1948. The only complete set of factory samples of this group known to be in private hands is owned by Mr. Robert L. Miller of Eaton, Ohio. Whether or not the factory possesses any examples is not known. The knitter in "Old Woman Knitting" wears a light violet blouse with red polka dots, a long green dress, a pale pink apron, and violet colored slippers with red plaid striping. She sits on a wooden stool on a rectangular base. The model is 6¾″ high.

## 190 OLD WOMAN WALKING TO MARKET

Figurine, closed number. This is another in "The Mommas and Poppas" series. It shows a grandmotherly type strolling along with an umbrella in one hand and a basket over her arm. In the basket is a bottle. She wears a light beige long-sleeved blouse, a charcoal gray skirt, a blue apron with dark blue plaid striping, brown boots, and a blue kerchief on her head tied in the back. Listed as a closed number on May 14, 1948.

## 191 OLD MAN WALKING TO MARKET

Figurine, closed number. Perhaps the most intriguing of "The Mommas and Poppas" series, this figure is modeled with strong classical lines and reflects keen observation. It is also a charming vignette of German rural life in the 19th century. The marketer carries a basket containing a pig on his back. He is apparently planning a visit to the butcher. He wears a bluish-gray cutaway jacket, an orange vest, a gold watchchain, brown trousers, and tall brown hiking boots. A green porkpie style hat and bright crimson umbrella complete the composition. Growing up from the base are a few flowers. One may feel sad for the pig, but sadder yet are collectors deprived of owning this excellent design, which was listed as closed on May 14, 1948.

## 192 CANDLELIGHT

Candleholder in current production. "Candlelight," formerly known as the "Carrier of Light," is a likeness of an angel carrying a ceramic candle. There is sound historical basis for this figure. The light bearer is of ancient origin and is known in all cultures and societies. During the Greek and Roman periods, torches made of bundles of reeds were used in processions and to light the path of dignitaries or wealthy citizens at night. Common folk had no choice but to grope in the darkness. In the Middle Ages, when candles became more plentiful, they were generally used in place of torches. They were made bigger and bigger in order to obtain greater light. Some candles used in medieval churches attained heights of ten feet and diameters of more than two feet at the base.

"Candlelight" has been made in two distinct versions. The original edition comes with a long red ceramic candle that extends from the figurine's base to above the angel's head. This type was produced during the periods of the Crown, Full Bee, and Stylized Bee trademarks. While the Stylized Bee was being used, the design was revised. The candle was removed and in its place a candle receptacle, into which a real candle may be inserted was substituted. This second version, usually referred to as the no candle type, is found with Stylized Bee, 3-line, Goebel/V, and the current mark. The variety with candle is more valuable, not because of the candle, but because of its age and relative scarcity compared to specimens with the more recent marks. Generally the Crown Mark specimens are a bit taller, measuring to

**192** Candlelight

the top of the angel's head. There has not been any significant change in modeling or coloration.

The angel wears a dark grayish brown robe with white ornaments, brown shoes, long white stockings, wings colored identically to the robe but with reddish marking, and has sandy-blonde hair. The figure stands on a circular base.

| | Price Range | |
|---|---|---|
| ☐ 192, trademark CM, 6¾"–7"...................... | 798.00 | 878.00 |
| ☐ 192, trademark Full Bee, 6¾"–7" ............... | 648.00 | 710.00 |
| ☐ 192, trademark Stylized Bee, 6¾"–7", long candle............................................ | 370.00 | 410.00 |
| ☐ 192, trademark Stylized Bee, 6¾"–7", new version............................................ | 298.00 | 328.00 |
| ☐ 192, trademark 3-line mark, 6¾"–7" ............. | 109.00 | 122.00 |
| ☐ 192, trademark Goebel/V, 6¾"–7"................ | 91.00 | 100.00 |
| ☐ 192, trademark Goebel, 6¾"–7".................. | 70.00 | 79.00 |

## 193  ANGEL DUET

Candleholder in current production. "Angel Duet" shows a pair of angels singing hymns from an open book. One of them holds the book while the other holds the candle receptacle. This design was subsequently marketed without the candleholder as #261 "Angel Duet." "Angel Duet" was introduced in 1948; some specimens bear this copyright date, while others carry no copyright date. Its presence or absence has no bearing on value. It is mistakenly presumed by some that this figure does not exist with the Crown Mark but such specimens, while not plentiful, are found. It has been reported as having been at one time discontinued, but is known with all six marks. There is a rare version with cream overglaze finish; no reliable information is available to offer a suggestion of value.

The left-hand angel wears a long green gown studded with red polka dots and holds a red-covered book. His companion is clad in a pale violet robe in which hints of pink are usually noticeable. Both have brown shoes, brown wings, and sandy hair.

| | Price Range | |
|---|---|---|
| ☐ 193, trademark CM, 5" ......................... | 450.00 | 490.00 |
| ☐ 193, trademark Full Bee, 5" ..................... | 245.00 | 265.00 |
| ☐ 193, trademark Stylized Bee, 5"................. | 145.00 | 155.00 |
| ☐ 193, trademark 3-line mark, 5" .................. | 120.00 | 130.00 |

**193** Angel Duet

|  | | Price Range | |
|---|---|---|---|
| ☐ 193, trademark Goebel/V, 5″ .................... | | **100.00** | **110.00** |
| ☐ 193, trademark Goebel, 5″ ...................... | | **84.00** | **90.00** |

## 194 WATCHFUL ANGEL

Figurine in current production. "Watchful Angel" holds a candle, but the model is not classified as a candleholder as the candle is ceramic and is an integral part of the composition. "Watchful Angel" was introduced in 1948 and sometimes carries a 1948 copyright date; its presence has no influence on the price or desirability. Contrary to the opinion advanced by some commentators, the figure **is** found with the old Crown Mark, as well as with the other five marks. There has been speculation that the figure was discontinued temporarily during the Stylized Bee era on the grounds that it was absent from a 1966 catalogue. This omission was probably the result of error or some other cause, such as an intention to discontinue it which

**194** Watchful Angel

was never carried out since it is not scarce with the Stylized Bee mark. "Watchful Angel" is also known as "Angelic Care." The Crown Mark pieces are customarily a bit taller than those with later markings.

The composition shows an angel holding a tall candle, standing beside a wooden crib in which a child slumbers. It is a matter of debate whether this is intended as the Christ Child; most observers assume it to be, but there is no evidence to support this contention. As with a number of Hummels, one may use whatever interpretation he wishes. The angel wears a long red robe and holds a green candle with a yellow and red flame. She has dark brown, highly textured wings and sandy hair. The child is swaddled in a white garment and rests on a blue blanket, which in turn is supported by straw. The crib, built on four legs, is a light beige intended to suggest freshly hewn raw wood. This model stands on an oval base. There has not been any restyling or major alterations in its 32 years of manufacture.

|  | Price Range | |
|---|---|---|
| ☐ 194, trademark CM, 6¼"–6¾" .................. | 648.00 | 712.00 |
| ☐ 194, trademark Full Bee, 6¼"–6¾" ............. | 348.00 | 378.00 |
| ☐ 194, trademark Stylized Bee, 6¼"–6¾" ......... | 248.00 | 268.00 |
| ☐ 194, trademark 3-line mark, 6¼"–6¾" .......... | 174.00 | 196.00 |
| ☐ 194, trademark Goebel/V, 6¼"–6¾" ............. | 148.00 | 168.00 |
| ☐ 194, trademark Goebel, 6¼"–6¾" .............. | 136.50 | 154.00 |

## 195 BARNYARD HERO

Figurine in current production. A rare example of a satirical title, this "hero" is a youth straddling a fence to escape the advances of a goose. There have been three editions, one of which, 195 (5¾"–6"), has been discontinued. Both the large and small versions have been restyled. This model was introduced in 1948 and sometimes carries a 1948 copyright date, which plays no role in the value.

This is not, of course, the only Hummel composition in which a youth encounters an animal whose acquaintance he does not wish to make (see #126 "Retreat to Safety," in which the cause of alarm is a bullfrog). But Mr. Goose, intent on striking a friendship, does not give up easily; he follows "Barnyard Hero" to the fence and nips at the elbow of his jacket, while the youth wears an expression of impending disaster. In the small edition, 195/2/0, it will be noted that the boy's hands are placed differently on the fence in the old version than in the new. This characteristic is not present in the large edition.

The boy wears a blue sport type jacket with dark blue plaid striping, brown lederhosen, pinkish-brown slippers, and white socks with pink tonal highlights. He has a green Tyrolean hat with a red flower and a red neckerchief knotted at the side. The goose is shown in naturalistic colors with a feathered texture. At the fence base are a few red flowers. The fence is composed of two horizontal wooden poles attached to posts.

**195** Barnyard Hero

|  | Price Range | |
|---|---|---|
| ☐ 195/2/0, trademark CM, 3¾″–4″.................. | **200.00** | **220.00** |
| ☐ 195/2/0, trademark Full Bee, 3¾″–4″ ............ | **195.00** | **215.00** |
| ☐ 195/2/0, trademark Stylized Bee, 3¾″–4″ ........ | **130.00** | **145.00** |
| ☐ 195/2/0, trademark 3-line mark, 3¾″–4″ ........ | **110.00** | **120.00** |
| ☐ 195/2/0, trademark Goebel/V, 3¾″–4″........... | **90.00** | **100.00** |
| ☐ 195/2/0, trademark Goebel, 3¾″–4″.............. | **72.50** | **82.50** |
| ☐ 195/I, trademark CM, 5½″...................... | **350.00** | **385.00** |
| ☐ 195/I, trademark Full Bee, 5½″.................. | **300.00** | **330.00** |
| ☐ 195/I, trademark Stylized Bee, 5½″ .............. | **210.00** | **230.00** |
| ☐ 195/I, trademark 3-line mark, 5½″................ | **155.00** | **170.00** |
| ☐ 195/I, trademark Goebel/V, 5½″ ................. | **145.00** | **160.00** |
| ☐ 195/I, trademark Goebel, 5½″ ................... | **125.00** | **137.50** |
| ☐ 195, trademark CM, 5¾″–6″..................... | **650.00** | **715.00** |
| ☐ 195, trademark Full Bee, 5¾″–6″ ............... | **550.00** | **605.00** |

## 196 TELLING HER SECRET

Figurine in current production. "Telling Her Secret" is one of a number of Hummel compositions that utilizes a component from another design. Two girls are shown, the one on the right being a duplication of the model #258 "Which Hand?" The motive is, of course, a savings on the design and construction of molds. Whether such consideration should be placed before artistic creativity is a matter for the buyer to decide. It was probably felt, 20 and 30 years ago, that the likelihood of any individual coming into possession of figurines with duplicating components was slim. Today, however, with so many persons collecting Hummels to acquire as many different issues as possible, in the fashion of postage stamps, this likelihood is considerably increased.

"Telling Her Secret" was originally titled "The Secret." It depicts one girl leaning close to another's ear and whispering. Just what the secret may be is privileged information, but to judge from the blushing expression of the second girl, it must be an item of no small interest. This model has been produced in three distinct editions, one of which, 196 (6¾″), has been discontinued.

It was introduced in 1948 and sold for many years without alteration but the recently produced specimens are slightly restyled. The left-hand girl, the one telling the secret, wears a short-sleeved white blouse, brown vest, green skirt with dotted ornaments, and a yellowish apron with brown plaid striping. She has brown slippers and white socks and a brown kerchief striped in dark brown tied around her head. Her confidante wears a similar blouse, a pink and violet skirt, a beige apron with maroon striping, brown shoes, and white socks. She wears a pink kerchief tied around her head and a pigtail with a red ribbon. Both stand on an oval base.

|  | Price Range | |
|---|---|---|
| ☐ 196/0, trademark CM, 5″–5½″.................... | **398.00** | **438.00** |
| ☐ 196/0, trademark Full Bee, 5″–5½″ .............. | **348.00** | **378.00** |
| ☐ 196/0, trademark Stylized Bee, 5″–5½″.......... | **198.00** | **218.00** |
| ☐ 196/0, trademark 3-line mark, 5″–5½″ ........... | **148.00** | **169.00** |

**196** Telling Her Secret

| | Price Range | |
|---|---|---|
| ☐ 196/0, trademark Goebel/V, 5″–5½″.............. | 134.00 | 156.00 |
| ☐ 196/0, trademark Goebel, 5″–5½″................ | 125.00 | 146.00 |
| ☐ 196/I, trademark CM, 6½″–6¾″ .................. | 798.00 | 998.00 |
| ☐ 196/I, trademark Full Bee, 6½″–6¾″............. | 748.00 | 828.00 |
| ☐ 196/I, trademark Stylized Bee, 6½″–6¾″ ........ | 448.00 | 488.00 |
| ☐ 196/I, trademark 3-line mark, 6½″–6¾″.......... | 298.00 | 328.00 |
| ☐ 196/I, trademark Goebel/V, 6½″–6¾″............. | 248.00 | 268.00 |
| ☐ 196/I, trademark Goebel, 6½″–6¾″ ............. | 240.00 | 264.00 |

## 197  BE PATIENT

Figurine in current production. "Be Patient," formerly known as "Mother of Ducks," shows a young girl holding a feed bowl and being accosted by two hungry ducks. Because the design is so different, it can scarcely be

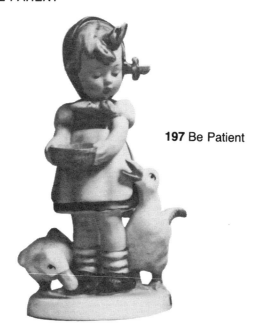

**197** Be Patient

regarded as a companion piece to #199 "Feeding Time." But both models were copyrighted 1948 and in both instances the birds are being fed, or are about to be fed. "Be Patient," is a less complex composition comprising fewer figures. There are three editions, one of which, 197 (6¼"), has been discontinued. Newer specimens bear a 1948 incised copyright date.

The girl wears a white short-sleeved blouse, a maroon vest, a green skirt, and a cream-colored apron. She has dark brown or black shoes, white socks with touches of dark brown, and wears a red kerchief tied around her head. She holds a small gray feed dish. "Be Patient's" facial expression perfectly conveys the message of this design, as the ducks attempt to leap for food in the dish rather than wait for its distribution on the ground.

|  | **Price Range** | |
|---|---|---|
| ☐ 197/2/0, trademark Full Bee, 4¼"–4½" .......... | 210.00 | 230.00 |
| ☐ 197/2/0, trademark Stylized Bee, 4¼"–4½" ...... | 130.00 | 145.00 |
| ☐ 197/2/0, trademark 3-line mark, 4¼"–4½" ....... | 110.00 | 120.00 |
| ☐ 197/2/0, trademark Goebel/V, 4¼"–4½" ......... | 95.00 | 105.00 |
| ☐ 197/2/0, trademark Goebel, 4¼"–4½" ........... | 77.00 | 87.50 |
| ☐ 197/I, trademark CM, 6"–6¼" ................... | 300.00 | 320.00 |
| ☐ 197/I, trademark Full Bee, 6"–6¼" .............. | 250.00 | 275.00 |
| ☐ 197/I, trademark Stylized Bee, 6"–6¼" .......... | 150.00 | 165.00 |
| ☐ 197/I, trademark 3-line mark, 6"–6¼" ........... | 125.00 | 137.50 |
| ☐ 197/I, trademark Goebel/V, 6"–6¼" .............. | 115.00 | 125.00 |
| ☐ 197/I, trademark Goebel, 6"–6¼" ................ | 105.00 | 115.00 |
| ☐ 197, trademark CM, 6¼" ........................ | 550.00 | 605.00 |
| ☐ 197, trademark Full Bee, 6¼" ................... | 450.00 | 495.00 |

## 198 HOME FROM MARKET

Figurine in current production. "Home From Market" is a figure of a boy holding an umbrella. Strapped to his shoulders is a wickerwork basket containing a live pig. It would seem more logical that the title be "Going to Market," or something similar, to explain the pig's presence. Generally, pigs were taken **to** the market, during the period represented by this composition (the mid 1800s), either for sale or for butchering (see #191 "Old Man Walking to Market.") The conclusion to be drawn is that either an unsuccessful effort was made to sell the pig, or the youth, instructed to carry the animal to a butcher, failed to complete his mission out of compassion. It is a cute pig indeed, and appears elated over its salvation.

There are three editions, one of which, 198 (5¾"–6"), has been discontinued. "Home From Market" was introduced in 1948, but only at a much later date was the practice of showing the 1948 copyright adopted. It appears on current examples. The older specimens are generally a bit larger,

**198** Home From Market

but this is not always the case. This model has been restyled, the major alteration is that the face of the boy looks directly forward in the revised version. It had previously been tilted somewhat skyward.

"Home From Market" wears a pastel violet jacket with violet-blue plaid striping, short brown pants, brown shoes, yellow socks, a red bow tie, and a grayish green conical cap with floppy brim. The umbrella is blue. Not much can be said of the pig. He stands upright in the basket in a human attitude with his front legs extended on the rim looking behind him. His color is cream with a light hint of pink. The figure is mounted on a circular base.

|  | Price Range | |
|---|---|---|
| ☐ 198/2/0, trademark CM, 4½"–4¾" .............. | 158.00 | 178.00 |
| ☐ 198/2/0, trademark Full Bee, 4½"–4¾" ......... | 148.00 | 168.00 |
| ☐ 198/2/0, trademark Stylized Bee, 4½"–4¾" ..... | 98.00 | 118.00 |
| ☐ 198/2/0, trademark 3-line mark, 4½"–4¾" ...... | 74.00 | 84.00 |
| ☐ 198/2/0, trademark Goebel/V, 4½"–4¾" ........ | 64.00 | 74.00 |
| ☐ 198/2/0, trademark Goebel, 4½"–4¾" .......... | 55.00 | 64.00 |
| ☐ 198/I, trademark CM, 5½" ...................... | 298.00 | 332.00 |
| ☐ 198/I, trademark Full Bee, 4½"–4¾" ............ | 248.00 | 268.00 |
| ☐ 198/I, trademark Stylized Bee, 4½"–4¾" ........ | 148.00 | 168.00 |
| ☐ 198/I, trademark 3-line mark, 4½"–4¾" ......... | 124.00 | 134.00 |
| ☐ 198/I, trademark Goebel/V, 4½"–4¾" ........... | 95.00 | 110.00 |
| ☐ 198/I, trademark Goebel, 4¼"–4¾" ............. | 88.00 | 114.00 |
| ☐ 198, trademark CM, 5¾"–6" .................... | 445.00 | 498.00 |
| ☐ 198, trademark Full Bee, 5¾"–6" .............. | 348.00 | 384.00 |

## 199 FEEDING TIME

Figurine in current production. It's morning in the barnyard and our little miss is tending to the feeding of her chickens; a rooster, a hen, and three chicks, one of which overzealously perches itself on the meal dish the girl carries. The bright cheeriness of this composition and the pleasing modeling of its livestock place it in the upper ranks of appealing Hummels. In the view of many authorities, this is one design which has profited immeasurably from restyling. The original version, sold for at least a dozen years in two sizes, in no way compares with the current "Feeding Time." In the old version the girl looked sad and confused, whereas in the new version she wears an expression appropriate to the occasion. The hen and rooster are more handsomely modeled. Of the three editions, 199 (5¾") has been discontinued. The current edition carries a 1948 copyright date.

The basic coloration has been maintained in both the original version and the restyling, the main difference being that the girl's hair, originally blonde, is now dark brown, with a reddish tint. She wears a white short-sleeved blouse, a red jumper, a blue apron with broad lozengework striping, fawn-colored shoes, and white socks. She has a blue kerchief tied around her head. The bowl she carries was grayish brown in the original version, and has now become a richer brown in the new version. The chicks are bright yellow with touches of red, while their parents are mainly brown with variegated highlighting. This model stands on an oval base. The current edition carries a 1948 copyright date.

**199** Feeding Time

|  | Price Range | |
|---|---|---|
| ☐ 199/0, trademark CM, 4¼″–4½″ ................. | **300.00** | **330.00** |
| ☐ 199/0, trademark Full Bee, 4¼″–4½″ ............ | **250.00** | **275.00** |
| ☐ 199/0, trademark Stylized Bee, 4¼″–4½″........ | **150.00** | **165.00** |
| ☐ 199/0, trademark 3-line mark, 4¼″–4½″ ....... | **130.00** | **145.00** |
| ☐ 199/0, trademark Goebel/V, 4¼″–4½″ .......... | **100.00** | **110.00** |
| ☐ 199/0, trademark Goebel, 4¼″–4½″ ............. | **88.00** | **98.00** |
| ☐ 199/I, trademark CM, 5½″–5¾″ ................. | **350.00** | **385.00** |
| ☐ 199/I, trademark Full Bee, 5½″–5¾″ ............ | **300.00** | **330.00** |
| ☐ 199/I, trademark Stylized Bee, 5½″–5¾″ ........ | **250.00** | **275.00** |
| ☐ 199/I, trademark 3-line mark, 5½″–5¾″.......... | **150.00** | **165.00** |
| ☐ 199/I, trademark Goebel/V, 5½″–5¾″ ........... | **105.00** | **115.00** |
| ☐ 199/I, trademark Goebel, 5½″–5¾″ ............. | **94.50** | **105.00** |
| ☐ 199, trademark CM, 5¾″ ........................ | **480.00** | **530.00** |
| ☐ 199, trademark Full Bee, 5¾″ ................... | **420.00** | **462.00** |

## 200 LITTLE GOAT HERDER

Figurine in current production. Formerly known as "Goat Boy," this model was designed in 1948 but the copyright date was not placed upon it until many years after its initial production. Current specimens carry the mark. "Little Goat Herder" has been restyled, with only minor variations. There are three editions:

200/0, 4½"–4¾"
200/I, 5"–5½"
200, 5½"–5¾", discontinued

A young boy stands with hands in pockets; his appearance is cavalier. With him are an adult goat and a kid. "Little Goat Herder" wears a white rolled-up sleeve shirt, maroon lederhosen with matching suspenders ornamented at the front with a red heart motif, brown shoes, and white socks with highlights of brown. He has an orange bow tie and a green conical Tyrolean-style hat. Contrary to the opinion advanced by some writers, "Little Goat Herder" **is** found bearing the crown mark.

|  | Price Range | |
|---|---|---|
| ☐ 200/0, trademark CM, 4½"–4¾" ................ | 250.00 | 275.00 |
| ☐ 200/0, trademark Full Bee, 4½"–4¾" ............ | 200.00 | 220.00 |
| ☐ 200/0, trademark Stylized Bee, 4½"–4¾"........ | 180.00 | 200.00 |
| ☐ 200/0, trademark 3-line mark, 4½"–4¾" ......... | 100.00 | 110.00 |
| ☐ 200/0, trademark Goebel/V, 4½"–4¾" .......... | 95.00 | 105.00 |
| ☐ 200/0, trademark Goebel, 4½"–4¾" ............. | 83.00 | 95.00 |

**200** Little Goat Herder

|  | **Price Range** | |
|---|---|---|
| ☐ 200/I, trademark CM, 5″–5½″ ................... | 275.00 | 300.00 |
| ☐ 200/I, trademark Full Bee, 5″–5½″ ............... | 225.00 | 250.00 |
| ☐ 200/I, trademark Stylized Bee, 5″–5½″........... | 175.00 | 195.00 |
| ☐ 200/I, trademark 3-line mark, 5″–5½″ ........... | 125.00 | 135.00 |
| ☐ 200/I, trademark Goebel/V, 5″–5½″ ............. | 105.00 | 115.00 |
| ☐ 200/I, trademark Goebel, 5″–5½″ ............... | 94.50 | 105.00 |
| ☐ 200, trademark CM, 5½″–5¾″ ................... | 450.00 | 495.00 |
| ☐ 200, trademark Full Bee, 5½″–5¾″ .............. | 350.00 | 385.00 |

## 201  RETREAT TO SAFETY

Figurine in current production. The design employed for this figurine has already been discussed under #126, the plaque version. The coloring here is somewhat different. Rather than attempting to achieve effect by the use of one basic shade, the figurine uses a number of colors. There are three

**201** Retreat to Safety

editions, as usual with 1948 models (but it should be noted that not all specimens bear the copyright date):

201/2/0, 3¾″–4″
201/I, 5½″–5¾″
201, 5¾″–6″, discontinued

As with #195 "Barnyard Hero," the restyled version of the smaller edition, #201/2/0, has the boy's hands placed differently on the fence than in the old version. There is no such variation between old and new specimens of #201/I. The motive for this change can only be speculated upon. "Retreat to Safety" was originally known as "Afraid." In the figurine the boy wears a blue cutaway jacket with dark blue plaid striping, charcoal gray lederhosen, brown slippers, pink stockings, a conical Tyrolean-style cap with red flower, and a red neckerchief tied into a bow at the side.

|  | Price Range | |
|---|---|---|
| ☐ 201/2/0, trademark CM, 3¾″–4″.................. | 168.00 | 188.00 |
| ☐ 201/2/0, trademark Full Bee, 3¾″–4″ ............ | 193.00 | 218.00 |
| ☐ 201/2/0, trademark Stylized Bee, 3¾″–4″ ........ | 124.00 | 144.00 |
| ☐ 201/2/0, trademark 3-line mark, 3¾″–4″ ......... | 98.00 | 118.00 |
| ☐ 201/2/0, trademark Goebel/V, 3¾″–4″............ | 78.00 | 88.00 |
| ☐ 201/2/0, trademark Goebel, 3¾″–4″.............. | 72.00 | 81.00 |
| ☐ 201/I, trademark CM, 5½″–5¾″.................. | 322.00 | 372.00 |
| ☐ 201/I, trademark Full Bee, 5½″–5¾″ ............. | 348.00 | 378.00 |
| ☐ 201/I, trademark Stylized Bee, 5½″–5¾″ ........ | 198.00 | 218.00 |
| ☐ 201/I, trademark 3-line mark, 5½″–5¾″.......... | 148.00 | 168.00 |
| ☐ 201/I, trademark Goebel/V, 5½″–5¾″ ............ | 103.00 | 114.00 |
| ☐ 201/I, trademark Goebel, 5½″–5¾″ .............. | 94.50 | 105.50 |
| ☐ 201, trademark CM, 5¾″–6″.................... | 505.00 | 595.00 |
| ☐ 201, trademark Full Bee, 5¾″–6″ ............... | 360.00 | 405.00 |

## 202 OLD MAN READING NEWSPAPER

Lamp base; closed number. The issuing of adult figures by the factory was approached with such ambition that both a figurine version (#181) and lamp base were prepared of "Old Man Reading Newspaper." When submitted for approval to the Seissen Convent, they were rejected on grounds of being untypical of Berta Hummel's work. Thus they were closed out before ever reaching production. The lamp version of "Old Man Reading Newspaper" stands 8½″ high. It was listed as a closed number on August 18, 1948. At least one factory sample is in private hands. The coloration is somewhat more intense than in the figurine.

## 203 SIGNS OF SPRING

Figurine in current production. "Signs of Spring" is another of the many models designed in 1948 (the first extensive series introduced after the war). As with most of the other models, a 1948 copyright date appears on

**203** Signs of Spring

recent specimens but is lacking on specimens with the old trademarks. There are three editions:

203/2/0, 4"
203/I, 5"–5½"
203, 5¼", discontinued

In the early stages of production 203/2/0 was designed with the central character, a girl standing at a fence, wearing both shoes. In the larger version she wore a shoe on the left foot only, and this is likewise true of current and recent examples of 203/2/0. The design is very simple. The girl points at a canary bird perched on the fencepost, who appears to be warbling a song. His presence provides the suggestion for the title. In the Bavarian Alps, where snow is common into April, the return of birds that had migrated south to the Mediterranean at the outset of winter is looked upon as an indication of spring's approach. The girl in "Signs of Spring" seems about to announce the bird's arrival to whomever might be in hearing distance. She wears a red long-sleeved dress, dark brown vest, blue polka-dotted apron, and—as we have mentioned—a brown shoe. Over her head is wrapped a red kerchief, tied beneath the chin. At the figure's base are a number of red flowers attractively modeled. The reason for "Signs of Spring" having one bare foot is not readily ascertained. Has she run so quickly through a meadow, following after this bird, that a shoe became lost? It may be observed that the old title was "Scandal," which hardly bears relation to "Signs of Spring" in its meaning. Taking that title, it may be suggested that the girl is admonishing her feathered friend not to reveal that he has seen her in this condition.

|  | Price Range | |
|---|---|---|
| ☐ 203/2/0, trademark CM, 4″, one shoe ............ | 350.00 | 385.00 |
| ☐ 203/2/0, trademark CM, 4″, two shoes ........... | 500.00 | 550.00 |
| ☐ 203/2/0, trademark Full Bee, 4″, one shoe ....... | 150.00 | 165.00 |
| ☐ 203/2/0, trademark Full Bee, 4″, two shoes ...... | 195.00 | 215.00 |
| ☐ 203/2/0, trademark Stylized Bee, 4″.............. | 125.00 | 140.00 |
| ☐ 203/2/0, trademark 3-line mark, 4″ ............... | 100.00 | 110.00 |
| ☐ 203/2/0, trademark Goebel/V, 4″ ................. | 85.00 | 95.00 |
| ☐ 203/2/0, trademark Goebel, 4″ ................... | 72.00 | 80.00 |
| ☐ 203/I, trademark CM, 5″–5½″ .................... | 275.00 | 300.00 |
| ☐ 203/I, trademark Full Bee, 5″–5½″ ............... | 225.00 | 275.00 |
| ☐ 203/I, trademark Stylized Bee, 5″–5½″........... | 175.00 | 195.00 |
| ☐ 203/I, trademark 3-line mark, 5″–5½″ ........... | 125.00 | 135.00 |
| ☐ 203/I, trademark Goebel/V, 5″–5½″ .............. | 110.00 | 120.00 |
| ☐ 203/I, trademark Goebel, 5″–5½″ ................ | 94.50 | 105.00 |
| ☐ 203, trademark CM, 5¼″ ......................... | 500.00 | 550.00 |
| ☐ 203, trademark Full Bee, 5¼″ .................... | 300.00 | 330.00 |

## 204  WEARY WANDERER

Figurine in current production. Previously known as "Tired Little Traveler," the "Weary Wanderer" is a forlorn-looking girl carrying a basket of flowers and a cloth bundle containing, perhaps, the remainder of her worldly goods. She has obviously come a long distance and along the way has lost her left shoe. It cannot be coincidence that this model and its numerical predecessor, #203 "Signs of Spring," both have one bare foot. The girl, though costumed differently, has the same hairstyle and appearance, leading one to conjecture that #203 and #204 are scenes of a continuing story (if so, it continues no further). It will be observed however that the right foot is bare in #203 and the left in #204. This composition was introduced in 1949 and has been manufactured only in a single size, of which there are some variations. The current version has a textured finish but is otherwise nearly identical. The majority of specimens bear an incised 1949 copyright date, but its absence should not be looked upon as indication of a scarce variety. It has been reported that only two specimens exist in which "Weary Wanderer" has blue eyes. If so, they are almost certainly color freaks resulting from one of the factory's enamelers misunderstanding his instructions. While such specimens may be of greater value than the normal, it is not often that extraordinarily high sums are associated with oddities of this nature. This is because of the ease with which such minute details can be counterfeited. We have declined to place a value guideline on this variety. To many collectors it would be worth no premium at all, while enthusiasts of "blunders" might pay thousands for it.

**204** Weary Wanderer

|  | Price Range | |
| --- | ---: | ---: |
| ☐ 204, trademark CM, 5½″–6″..................... | 498.00 | 548.00 |
| ☐ 204, trademark Full Bee, 5½″–6″ ................ | 298.00 | 348.00 |
| ☐ 204, trademark Stylized Bee, 5½″–6″ ........... | 198.00 | 218.00 |
| ☐ 204, trademark 3-line mark, 5½″–6″ ............. | 124.00 | 149.00 |
| ☐ 204, trademark Goebel/V, 5½″–6″................ | 98.00 | 108.00 |
| ☐ 204, trademark Goebel, 5½″–6″................. | 88.00 | 98.00 |

## 205 STORE PLAQUE IN GERMAN

Store plaque, closed edition. This is the German language version of
the Hummel dealer or retailer plaque, supplied to authorized dealers to
place in their shop windows or elsewhere on the premises. The German
plaque is stylistically similar to the English (see #187 above), with a large
bumblebee atop the oval and a striding "Merry Wanderer" at the righthand
side. The text reads "Verkaufsstelle Original Hummel-Figuren Hummel-
werk." There are three varieties of this early plaque, all quite scarce; one

**205** Store Plaque in German

with black lettering, one whose text is partly in red and partly in black, and one in all black letters with red capitals. It should be noted that the text is not printed, but hand painted with raised letters. The balance of this work is also hand painted. The existence of #205 with Stylized Bee trademark has been reported, but this is unlikely because it was listed as a closed edition on June 18, 1949, long before the Stylized Bee came into use.

|  | | Price Range | |
|---|---|---|---|
| ☐ 205, trademark CM, 5½" × 4¼" .................. | | **1100.00** | **1210.00** |
| ☐ 205, trademark Full Bee, 5½" × 4¼" ............. | | **900.00** | **990.00** |

## 206 ANGEL CLOUD

Wall font in current production. "Angel Cloud" could be more properly referred to as "Angel on Cloud," as the subject is a very content-looking angel seated upon a billowy white cloud, but nomenclature suffers sometimes at the mercy of saving space in lists. This composition was discontinued briefly during the period of the 3-line mark, but came back into production in the Goebel/V era and is currently being produced with the plain Goebel mark. The early, pre-discontinuation specimens are scarce but prices have not attained four-digit levels, probably because there is not quite such rabid collector interest in fonts as there is in figurines. A figure equally scarce in a figurine would undoubtedly bring a much higher sum.

This model was redesigned in 1949 but the copyright date was not applied to specimens immediately. There are several variations resulting from the restylings, the most notable being that early specimens do not have the rim on the rear side of the bowl. Despite the high number, this is

**206** Angel Cloud

a genuine old-time Hummel, released during the first year of Hummel manufacture. Although it has been so long in production, it has never been
extensively manufactured. Prior to the 1950s it seems to have been distributed primarily, or possibly exclusively, in Europe.

The angel wears a rust-red short gown and wine-colored shoes. In his
left hand he holds a nosegay of yellow flowers and is about to pick an
additional one which grows out of the cloud. Another flower, basically white
with light touches of violet, also grows out of the cloud. The cloud is attractively contoured, its puffs highlighted with brushstrokes of blue.

| | Price Range | |
|---|---|---|
| ☐ 206, trademark CM, 3¼″ × 4¾″ .................. | 548.00 | 598.00 |
| ☐ 206, trademark Full Bee, 3¼″ × 4¾″ ............. | 398.00 | 438.00 |
| ☐ 206, trademark Stylized Bee, 3¼″ × 4¾″ ......... | 298.00 | 328.00 |
| ☐ 206, trademark 3-line mark, 3¼″ × 4¾″ .......... | 78.00 | 88.00 |
| ☐ 206, trademark Goebel/V, 3¼″ × 4¾″............. | 28.00 | 36.00 |
| ☐ 206, trademark Goebel 3¼″ × 4¾″ .............. | 23.00 | 27.50 |

## 207 HEAVENLY ANGEL

Wall font in current production. The design is adapted from #21 "Heavenly Angel" (see above). The coloration, though perhaps somewhat paler, follows the same format as the figurine. Recent models bear a 1949 copyright date. This long manufactured font is readily obtainable with all trademarks, and would be suitable for a beginner who might want to form a complete set of the major trademarks. The older versions are holed at the back for hanging, while recent and current examples have this feature near the top background which provides somewhat greater security. It is a simple work without ornamentation of any kind. The background and bowl are entirely plain.

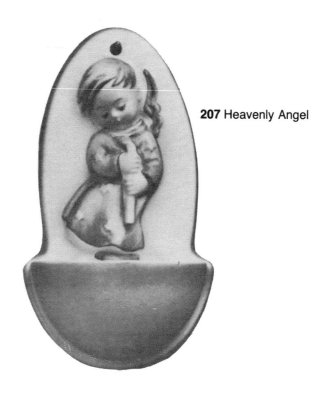

**207** Heavenly Angel

| | Price Range | |
|---|---|---|
| ☐ 207, trademark CM, 3″×5″ . . . . . . . . . . . . . . . . . . . . . . | 250.00 | 270.00 |
| ☐ 207, trademark Full Bee, 3″×5″ . . . . . . . . . . . . . . . . | 100.00 | 115.00 |
| ☐ 207, trademark Stylized Bee, 3″×5″ . . . . . . . . . . . . | 35.00 | 45.00 |
| ☐ 207, trademark 3-line mark, 3″×5″ . . . . . . . . . . . . . . | 30.00 | 40.00 |
| ☐ 207, trademark Goebel/V, 3″×5″ . . . . . . . . . . . . . . . . | 25.00 | 35.00 |
| ☐ 207, trademark Goebel, 3″×5″ . . . . . . . . . . . . . . . . . . | 23.00 | 35.00 |

## 208 STORE PLAQUE IN FRENCH

Store plaque, closed edition. This scarce plaque has the words "Figurines Originales Hummel" and is surmounted by the traditional bumblebee. There are two varieties, both of which are discontinued. In the early version the word "Hummel" is not enclosed by quotation marks. Later specimens have quote marks in addition to carrying the words "Reg. trademark." It may be of interest to the reader that France has long been one of the chief foreign (non-German) consumers of Hummels, though it does not buy as many as the U.S.

|  | **Price Range** |
|---|---|
| ☐ 208, trademark CM, 5½″ × 4″. . . . . . . . . . . . . . . . . . | **RARE** |
| ☐ 208, trademark Full Bee, 5½″ × 4″. . . . . . . . . . . . . . | **3000.00 +** |

## 209 STORE PLAQUE IN SWEDISH

Store plaque, closed edition. Reads "Akta Hummel figurer," accompanied by the Hummel signature. The word "Akta" means actual or authentic and is in black. "Hummel figurer" is in red, and the signature in black. This plaque is more scarce than most Hummel store plaques, presumably because the number of retail outlets for its products in Sweden could not have been as great as in more populated countries.

|  |  |
|---|---|
| ☐ 209, trademark CM, 5½″ × 4″. . . . . . . . . . . . . . . . . . | **RARE** |
| ☐ 209, trademark Full Bee, 5½″ × 4″. . . . . . . . . . . . . . | **5000.00 +** |

## 210 SCHMID BROTHERS STORE PLAQUE

Store plaque, closed edition. This is the only example of a Hummel store plaque bearing the name of an American dealer, Schmid Brothers, Inc. of Boston. The name does not appear on the plaque itself but on the satchel carried by "Merry Wanderer," and is raised in the mold rather than painted. Otherwise it is identical to other Hummel English text store plaques. For a more extensive description, the reader is referred to #187 (above). It is said that only one specimen of the Schmid Brothers plaque is known to exist. The price stated is a rough estimate only.

|  |  |
|---|---|
| ☐ 210, trademark CM, 5½″ × 4″. . . . . . . . . . . . . . . . . . | **RARE** |
| ☐ 210, trademark Full Bee, 5½″ × 4″. . . . . . . . . . . . . . | **5000.00 +** |

## 211 STORE PLAQUE IN ENGLISH

Store plaque, closed edition. This is a variation of #187 (see above) in which all lettering is in lower case and Oeslau is given as the place of manufacture. There is only one specimen reported to exist, in white overglaze. Apparently it was intended to be painted, as a colorless display sign would be ineffective. No information on its origins can be obtained and one can only speculate that it was produced as a factory sample.

|  | Price Range |
|---|---|
| ☐ 211, trademark CM, 5½″ × 4″..................... | RARE |
| ☐ 211, trademark Full Bee, 5½″ × 4″............... | 5000.00 + |

## 212 ORCHESTRA

Set of figures, closed number. No information is available on this work, which never reached production. It apparently belongs to the year 1951. The title "Orchestra" is obtained from a notation in an old factory list. There is some speculation that it was to have been a long set of figures playing various instruments, sold as a unit in the manner of the Nativity Set (#214). There are no known samples.

## 213 STORE PLAQUE IN SPANISH

Store plaque, closed edition. "Figures Legitimas 'Hummel'" and bears the Hummel signature and the words "Reg. trade mark." Capital and lower case letters were used, rather than all capitals. Only a few specimens are known to be in existence.

| | |
|---|---|
| ☐ 213, trademark CM, 5½″ × 4″..................... | RARE |
| ☐ 213, trademark Full Bee, 5½″ × 4″............... | 3000.00 + |

## 214 NATIVITY SET

Set of 14 or 15 figurines in current production. This was the first "Nativity Set" marketed by Hummel. It was placed on the market in 1952, and represented not only the most ambitious factory project up to that time, but also the most expensive Hummel product offered to the public. (Since then it has been exceeded in price by the jumbo "Nativity Set" and the oversized "Merry Wanderer," "Apple Tree Girl", and "Apple Tree Boy.")

As originally produced, it consisted of 14 figures. The present version, has 15, not because of the addition of a figure, but because the Virgin and Child, first designed as a single component with a common base, are now manufactured as separate pieces. This one-piece statue of the two figures is quite rare and commands a low to mid four-digit price, depending upon which trademark it bears and whether or not it is in color of white overglaze. Each piece is assigned a numerical designation based on the series number #214, followed by a slash and identifying letter. In the case of Virgin and Child, both pieces are known as 214/A, the number they were assigned when originally produced as a single construction. It should be noted that none of the figures are mounted on a base. The set consists of:

**214** Nativity Set     **White Version and Version with Color**

214/A Virgin Mary, 6¼″–6½″
214/A Infant Jesus, 1½″–3½″
214/B Saint Joseph, 7½″
214/C Angel Standing, 3½″
214/D Angel Kneeling, 3″
214/E We Congratulate, 3¾″
214/F Shepherd Standing, 7″
214/G Shepherd Kneeling, 5″
214/H Shepherd Boy with Flute, 3¾″–4″

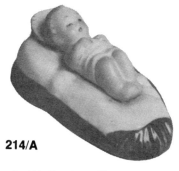 

**214/A**

214/J   Donkey, 5″
214/K   Ox or Cow, 3½″–6¼″
214/L   Moorish King, 8″–8¼″
214/M   King Kneeling on One Knee, 5½″
214/N   King Kneeling on Both Knees, 5½″
214/O   Lamb, 1¾″–2½″

The letter I is omitted from the the series as it would tend to cause confusion, this being the common designation for oversized Hummels. Each figure is produced in one size only, though it will be seen from this list that slight variations have occured in a few of the basic sizes. As presently offered in the 1981 catalogue, sets are packaged as follows:

Holy Family, three pieces (Virgin, Child, St. Joseph) in color.
Holy Family, three pieces as above, in white overglaze.
Nativity Set, 12 pieces, comprising the above figures but deleting 214/C, 214/D, 214/E and 214/H and including #366 Flying Angel (not designated as part of the original set).
Nativity Set, 16 pieces, which includes all the figures listed above plus #366 Flying Angel.

The barn or stable is not included, but one can be purchased for $50.

The figures chosen for inclusion have failed to meet with universal approval. Objection centers mainly upon "Congratulations," a figure of a young girl and boy in Bavarian costume that seems historically out of character in this setting. "Little Tooter," or "Shepherd Boy with Flute," is another figure incorrectly costumed for the time period represented. When viewed as a whole, it must be admitted that this set is both pleasing and appealing, and surely superior to the nativity sets of most other manufacturers. It may be said in the set's favor that the least significant components, such as the sheep, are modeled with equal care as the major figures, and that relative proportions are consistent. This set is frequently set up as a window display by dealers during Christmas season, and is used for such purposes by other retailers, restaurants, hotels, and various businesses, accounting in large measure of its extensive sale.

The complete set was once offered for sale in white overglaze but has since been discontinued. The only pieces available today in white are the three-piece set of Virgin Mary, Infant Jesus, and St. Joseph. A complete set in white is extremely scarce and commands a premium price.

It should be kept in mind that prices given here are for the complete sets and are calculated on the basis of all pieces bearing the same mark.

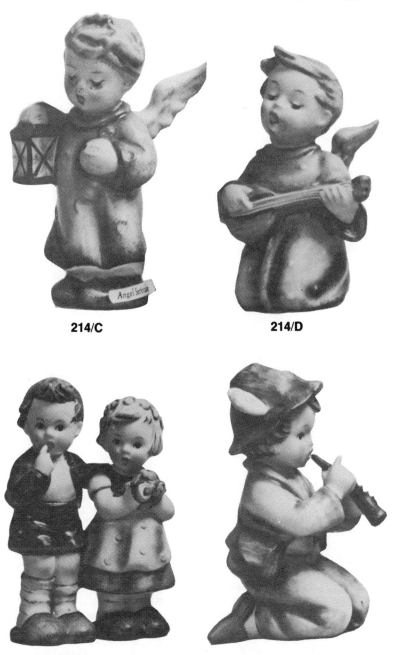

**214/C**

**214/D**

**214/E**

**214/H**

Mixed sets, in which two or more marks are included, are of less collector interest and generally bring lower prices. Prices are for sets without the stable. The set is reported to exist with the Crown Mark, but no reliable pricing information is available.

|  | Price Range | |
|---|---|---|
| ☐ 214, trademark Full Bee, ......................... | 2600.00 | 2860.00 |
| ☐ 214, trademark Stylized Bee,..................... | 1300.00 | 1430.00 |
| ☐ 214, trademark 3-line mark, ..................... | 1000.00 | 1100.00 |
| ☐ 214, trademark Goebel/V, ........................ | 950.00 | 1050.00 |
| ☐ 214, trademark Goebel, .......................... | 888.00 | 975.00 |

## 215  CHILD JESUS

Figurine, closed number. The only available information on this design is a notation in the factory's books describing it as a Child Jesus standing holding a lamb. It is not positively known whether this is a figurine or something else, but the former is more probable. It was listed as a closed number on August 16, 1951, and so far no samples have come to light.

## 216  JOYFUL

Astray, closed number. Listed as a closed number on September 10, 1951. It is described in factory records as an ashtray without cigarette rest. There are no known examples and no record of its dimensions.

## 217  BOY WITH TOOTHACHE

Figurine in current production. This figure, designed in 1951, was at first released without a copyright date, but recent specimens carry the copyright date incised. Its original name was "At the Dentist's" or simply "Toothache." There are no Crown Mark examples as "Boy with Toothache" was introduced during the Full Bee period. The older specimens are generally at least ⅛" taller than those presently manufactured.

The subject is one that could hardly fail to evoke compassion: A boy with a swollen jaw, who wears a cloth tied around his face and holds one hand to his cheek. This practice of bandaging the faces of toothache victims, not so widely known in America, was at one time common throughout the Old World. It is now obsolete and for good reason, as it had neither medical nor psychological effect. If anything, it increased the suffering as it reminded one of his misfortune. If "Boy With Toothache" appears unduly apprehensive, he must be excused. A dentist's office of the period represented by Hummel figureware (the mid 1800s) did not inspire confidence even in adults.

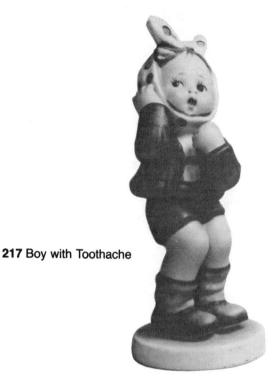

**217** Boy with Toothache

"Boy with Toothache" wears a light blue short jacket with darker blue plaid striping, brown lederhosen, brown shoes, and white socks. His facial bandage is white with red polka dotting. The figure stands on a circular base.

| | Price Range | |
|---|---|---|
| ☐ 217, trademark Full Bee, 5¼″–5½″ . . . . . . . . . . . . . | 180.00 | 197.00 |
| ☐ 217, trademark Stylized Bee, 5¼″–5½″ . . . . . . . . . | 122.00 | 137.00 |
| ☐ 217, trademark 3-line mark, 5½″–5½″ . . . . . . . . . . | 98.00 | 112.00 |
| ☐ 217, trademark Goebel/V, 5¼″–5½″ . . . . . . . . . . . | 84.00 | 94.00 |
| ☐ 217, trademark Goebel, 5¼″–5½″ . . . . . . . . . . . . . | 77.50 | 84.50 |

## 218 BIRTHDAY SERENADE

Figurine in current production. "Birthday Serenade" is one of the more discussed of the early 1950s Hummels due to its variations. It depicts a little girl and an even littler boy playing musical instruments, one a flute and the other a concertina. In some specimens the boy plays the flute and the girl plays the concertina; in others the instruments are switched around. In the original version the boy played the flute. When "Birthday Serenade" was restyled in 1965, the girl was given the flute while her companion inherited the concertina. The reason for this alteration, which was never officially explained, has been the subject of much conjecture. Of theories so far advanced, the most sensible seems to be that the flute was deemed a more feminine instrument, and the concertina a more masculine instrument. This revision, sometimes referred to as "mold reversal," creates a mistaken impression, because there is really no such procedure as mold reversal. A major change, such as the one presented in this model, requires the construction of entirely new molds. The use of a fresh mold can readily be distinguished in a number of other aspects of the design, notably the facial expressions on both figures and the attitudes of their heads. There are two sizes.

During the period of the 3-line trademark, 218/0 was discontinued but shortly thereafter reinstated during use of the Goebel/V. Early or prediscontinuation specimens of the larger size are moderately scarce and have been known to sell for high prices. The copyright date reads 1952. But since the model was redesigned in 1965, it should carry that date in keeping with factory tradition. As all specimens of the new version are identical, this can hardly be valued at a premium as an error.

The girl, who always stands on the right regardless of the instrument she plays, wears a pale blue (almost white) long-sleeved blouse, a blue vest, a long red skirt, and a yellow apron. She has brown shoes and white socks, and her pigtailed hair is tied with ribbons. The boy is outfitted in the old version in a pale blue jacket with blue plaid striping. In the revision the jacket becomes a darker blue. His trousers are gray in the old specimens, grayish-brown in the new. The most noticeable difference is that when playing the accordion or concertina in the new version, he wears a red neckerchief knotted into a bow tie. This is absent from the flute-playing boy. The figures stand on a textured and contoured base from which several reddish flowers grow.

**218** Birthday Serenade

**Old Style**

**New Style**

| | Price Range | |
|---|---:|---:|
| ☐ 218/2/0, trademark Full Bee, 4¼″–4½″ .......... | 500.00 | 550.00 |
| ☐ 218/2/0, trademark Stylized Bee, 4¼″–4½″ ...... | 450.00 | 495.00 |
| ☐ 218/2/0, trademark 3-line mark, 4¼″–4½″ ....... | 400.00 | 440.00 |
| ☐ 218/2/0, trademark Goebel/V, 4¼″–4½″ ......... | 90.00 | 100.00 |
| ☐ 218/2/0, trademark Goebel, 4¼″–4½″ ........... | 77.50 | 87.50 |
| ☐ 218/0, trademark Full Bee, 5¼″ .................. | 750.00 | 825.00 |
| ☐ 218/0, trademark Stylized Bee, 5¼″.............. | 650.00 | 715.00 |
| ☐ 218/0, trademark 3-line mark, 5¼″ .............. | 600.00 | 660.00 |
| ☐ 218/0, trademark Goebel/V, 5¼″ ................ | 140.00 | 155.00 |
| ☐ 218/0, trademark Goebel, 5¼″ .................. | 125.00 | 135.00 |
| ☐ 218, trademark Full Bee, 5¼″ ................... | 750.00 | 825.00 |
| ☐ 218, trademark Stylized Bee, 5¼″................ | 600.00 | 660.00 |

## 219 LITTLE VELMA

Figurine closed number. This is a coined name, one not applied by the factory, which was given to this figure by the renowned private collector, Robert L. Miller of Eaton, Ohio. A woman named Velma (surname not revealed) sold the specimen to Mr. Miller who titled it in her honor. Reference works have picked this title. The figure has come to be identified by this name since the factory's title for this composition is unknown.

The subject is a girl seated on a fence, looking with mild apprehension at a bullfrog poised on the ground as if about to leap. A similarity in concept, if not construction, will be noted between this figure and the more widely known "Retreat to Safety" (see #126 above). The reason for "Little Velma" never getting into production has been attributed to its lack of originality. The youth scared by a frog theme was in danger of overexposure. Only recently was it learned that a factory sample was not only preserved but in circulation. Factory records indicate that this figurine was produced in very limited numbers, but whether or not any other specimens are in circulation cannot be verified at this time.

The girl wears a white short-sleeved blouse, a brown vest, a sea blue skirt, brown shoes, and white socks. Her pigtailed hair is tied with red ribbons. Two reddish flowers decorate the fence. "Little Velma" is contained on an oval base and stands four inches tall. There is no information as to the date of listing as a closed edition, which undoubtedly occurred during 1952. Only an above estimate of a mid to high four-digit figure can be given for its value.

## 220 WE CONGRATULATE

Figurine in current production. "We Congratulate" is based upon, and in fact nearly identical to, the pair of figures known as "Congratulations" sold in the Hummel Nativity Set. Their presence in this set has been the subject of criticism, because their manner of dress does not agree with the historical

**220** We Congratulate

age represented by the nativity. However, as separate compositions they are typically and pleasingly Hummel. The chief differences between "We Congratulate" and its predecessor are that the former stands on a base, there are no floral ornaments in the girl's hair, and the boy now wears suspenders with his Alpine trousers. Why it was felt that suspenders would be out of place on a Nativity subject, when no article of the boy's attire was worn in the first century B.C., cannot be guessed at. The later pieces generally bear a 1952 incised copyright date but its presence or absence is not influential in the value. "We Congratulate" is found with 220 and 220/2/0 size markings. These are not two separate editions but merely represent a revision in numeration, adopted in 1965. Those marked 220/2/0 are earlier and worth a premium.

|  | Price Range | |
|---|---|---|
| ☐ 220, trademark Full Bee, 3¼"–4" ............... | **195.00** | **225.00** |
| ☐ 220, trademark Stylized Bee, 3¾"–4" ........... | **145.00** | **170.00** |
| ☐ 220, trademark 3-line mark, 3¾"–4" ........... | **98.00** | **112.00** |

## 221 HAPPY PASTIME

Candy box, closed number. The figure employed is the same as in #69, the figurine version of "Happy Pastime," with somewhat different coloring. The girl wears a whitish-gray long-sleeved blouse with red polka dots, a blue vest, and a pink skirt with red striping. She is wearing brown oxblood shoes and blue socks. Floral decorations circle the bowl. This piece, designed in 1952, was never placed into production. At least one factory sample is in private hands, possibly more. As with closed numbers in general, there is no record of sales to base prices upon.

## 222 MADONNA

Wall plaque, closed edition. This is the only example of a Hummel model employing metal in its construction. The subject is a handsomely rendered

**222** Madonna

Madonna and Child in classical style, fixed in a wooden frame and surrounded by wrought metal grillwork. Its appearance suggests a church window in Madrid or Barcelona. It is entirely un-German in nature. Whether or not the metal decoration was responsible, "Madonna" was not supported sufficiently enough to warrant remaining in production and was closed out during the Stylized Bee era after less than ten years of production. In consequence of its limited manufacture, the piece is now quite scarce and is almost a must for advanced Hummel collectors who wish to own examples of the full range of factory designs. Even if successfully marketed, it is unlikely that ornamental grillwork would have been applied to other plaques. It suited this design but was not apt to suit others unless very ingeniously constructed. There are some variations noted in the grillwork design. Specimens are occasionally found without grillwork. It is probable they were not sold in this fashion but that the grillwork was removed by the owners. If genuinely sold in that manner, it would be a rare version.

|  | Price Range | |
|---|---|---|
| ☐ 222, trademark Full Bee, 4″ × 5″................. | 1300.00 | 1430.00 |
| ☐ 222, trademark Stylized Bee, 4″ × 5″ ............. | 1000.00 | 1100.00 |

## 223  TO MARKET

Lamp base in current production. It is not often that a closed edition, especially one that had been closed for more than 20 years, makes such a successful comeback as the "To Market" lamp base. The design was originally introduced as #101 (see above), and closed out after a brief trial in 1937. Not until the 1960s was any effort made to revive it. The only real difference in the restyled version is that a flower grows from the tree trunk. "To Market" in this edition does not exist with the Crown Mark. It has been shown to be scarce even with the Full Bee mark.

| | | |
|---|---|---|
| ☐ 223, trademark Full Bee, 9½″ ................... | 548.00 | 610.00 |
| ☐ 223, trademark Stylized Bee, 9½″............... | 298.00 | 328.00 |
| ☐ 223, trademark 3-line mark, 9½″ ................ | 278.00 | 312.00 |
| ☐ 223, trademark Goebel/V, 9½″ ................... | 255.00 | 286.00 |
| ☐ 223, trademark Goebel, 9½″ .................... | 250.00 | 276.00 |

## 224  WAYSIDE HARMONY

Lamp base in current production. The motif of this lamp is adapted from #111. It is currently produced in two sizes but there have been a total of three editions; #224 (9½″) was discontinued in the 1950s.

224/II, though standing only two inches taller than 224/I, gives the ap-

**224** Wayside Harmony

**225** Just Resting

pearance of being considerably larger, because the base is also two inches wider (6¼″ as compared to 4¼″). The same is true of #225 "Just Resting" (see below). This work is not known to exist with the Crown Mark, though it is a possibility that such a specimen might be discovered.

| | Price Range | |
|---|---|---|
| ☐ 224/I, trademark Full Bee, 7½″.................. | 350.00 | 385.00 |
| ☐ 224/I, trademark Stylized Bee, 7½″ .............. | 250.00 | 275.00 |
| ☐ 224/I, trademark 3-line mark, 7½″................ | 210.00 | 230.00 |
| ☐ 224/I, trademark Goebel/V, 7½″.................. | 190.00 | 210.00 |
| ☐ 224/I, trademark Goebel, 7½″.................... | 180.00 | 200.00 |
| ☐ 224/II, trademark Full Bee, 9½″ .................. | 550.00 | 605.00 |
| ☐ 224/II, trademark Stylized Bee, 9½″.............. | 400.00 | 440.00 |
| ☐ 224/II, trademark 3-line mark, 9½″ .............. | 300.00 | 330.00 |
| ☐ 224/II, trademark Goebel/V, 9½″ ................. | 250.00 | 275.00 |
| ☐ 224/II, trademark Goebel, 9½″ ................... | 220.00 | 245.00 |
| ☐ 224, trademark Full Bee, 9½″ .................... | 550.00 | 605.00 |
| ☐ 224, trademark Stylized Bee, 9½″................ | 500.00 | 550.00 |

## 225 JUST RESTING

Lamp base in current production. Design taken from #112. The comments made about #224 (above) can be applied equally to this work.

| | Price Range | |
|---|---|---|
| ☐ 225/I, trademark Full Bee, 7½"................... | 345.00 | 388.00 |
| ☐ 225/I, trademark Stylized Bee, 7½" .............. | 247.00 | 277.00 |
| ☐ 225/I, trademark 3-line mark, 7½"................ | 208.00 | 228.00 |
| ☐ 225/I, trademark Goebel/V, 7½".................. | 188.00 | 212.00 |
| ☐ 225/I, trademark Goebel, 7½".................... | 180.00 | 202.00 |
| ☐ 225/II, trademark Full Bee, 9½".................. | 548.00 | 603.00 |
| ☐ 225/II, trademark Stylized Bee, 9½".............. | 395.00 | 438.00 |
| ☐ 225/II, trademark 3-line mark, 9½" .............. | 298.00 | 328.00 |
| ☐ 225/II, trademark Goebel/V, 9½" ................ | 248.00 | 278.00 |
| ☐ 225/II, trademark Goebel, 9½" .................. | 220.00 | 241.00 |

## 226 MAIL IS HERE

Figurine in current production. The design for "Mail is Here" has already been discussed under #140, the wall plaque version. Some inconsequential differences are to be noted in the figurine, including: the horses are a lighter shade of gray; the post horn is redesigned and held with the curved portion downward rather than upward; the carriage wheels are more richly colored; and bundles atop the carriage are bulkier.

**226** Mail is Here

Most of these specimens carry a 1952 incised copyright date. This has always been an expensive figure because of its size and complexity. it stands on a rectangular base on which several red flowers are painted.

|  | Price Range | |
|---|---|---|
| ☐ 226, trademark Full Bee, 4¼″ × 6″.............. | 800.00 | 880.00 |
| ☐ 226, trademark Stylized Bee, 4¼″ × 6″ .......... | 550.00 | 605.00 |
| ☐ 226, trademark 3-line mark, 4¼″ × 6″............ | 400.00 | 440.00 |
| ☐ 226, trademark Goebel/V, 4¼″ × 6″.............. | 300.00 | 330.00 |
| ☐ 226, trademark Goebel, 4¼″ × 6″................ | 265.00 | 295.00 |

## 227 SHE LOVES ME, SHE LOVES ME NOT

Lamp base in current production. The subject is adapted from #174, also titled "She Loves Me, She Loves Me Not," with minor alterations. It is noted that the boy's face does not match either the old or restyled version of its predecessor. He now wears a surprised expression, as if suddenly observed by the girl whose affections he wishes to determine.

**227** She Loves Me, She Loves Me Not

| | Price Range | |
|---|---|---|
| ☐ 227, trademark Full Bee, 7½″ .................... | 550.00 | 605.00 |
| ☐ 227, trademark Stylized Bee, 7½″................ | 300.00 | 330.00 |
| ☐ 227, trademark 3-line mark, 7½″ ................. | 210.00 | 230.00 |
| ☐ 227, trademark Goebel/V, 7½″ ................... | 187.00 | 205.00 |
| ☐ 227, trademark Goebel, 7½″ ..................... | 168.00 | 185.00 |

## 228 GOOD FRIENDS

Lamp base in current production. "Good Friends" table lamp takes its design from #182 (old style).

| | | |
|---|---|---|
| ☐ 228, trademark Full Bee, 7½″ .................... | 500.00 | 550.00 |
| ☐ 228, trademark Stylized Bee, 7½″................ | 300.00 | 330.00 |
| ☐ 228, trademark 3-line mark, 7½″ ................. | 210.00 | 230.00 |
| ☐ 228, trademark Goebel/V, 7½″ ................... | 187.00 | 205.00 |
| ☐ 228, trademark Goebel, 7½″ ..................... | 168.00 | 185.00 |

## 229 APPLE TREE GIRL

Lamp base in current production. "Apple Tree Girl" is one of a nonrelated group of six lamp bases designed in 1953 or 1954, all of which are still being produced. Its motif is too familiar to require any further comment here (see #141). The lamp is made, like the larger versions of the figurine, with a canary bird in the tree.

| | | |
|---|---|---|
| ☐ 229, trademark, Full Bee, 7½″ .................... | 750.00 | 825.00 |
| ☐ 229, trademark Stylized Bee, 7½″................ | 280.00 | 305.00 |
| ☐ 229, trademark 3-line mark, 7½″ ................. | 220.00 | 240.00 |
| ☐ 229, trademark Goebel/V, 7½″ ................... | 195.00 | 215.00 |
| ☐ 229, trademark Goebel, 7½″ ..................... | 168.00 | 185.00 |

## 230 APPLE TREE BOY

Lamp base in current production. (See #142). The lamp version of this popular Hummel design is the "bird in tree." It was formerly known as "Autumn" or "Fall."

| | | |
|---|---|---|
| ☐ 230, trademark Full Bee, 7½″ .................... | 700.00 | 770.00 |
| ☐ 230, trademark Stylized Bee, 7½″................ | 260.00 | 280.00 |
| ☐ 230, trademark 3-line mark, 7½″ ................. | 210.00 | 230.00 |
| ☐ 230, trademark Goebel/V, 7½″ ................... | 190.00 | 210.00 |
| ☐ 230, trademark Goebel, 7½″ ..................... | 168.00 | 178.00 |

**230** Apple Tree Boy

## 231 BIRTHDAY SERENADE

Lamp base in current production. "Birthday Serenade," utilizing #218 as its design (see above), was introduced into the line in 1954 along with a number of other lamp bases. It was taken out of production not long thereafter and reintroduced during use of the Goebel/V mark. Authorities are not in agreement on the matter of whether #231 exists with the Stylized Bee and 3-line mark. Since there is no information to confirm their existence, an attempt to suggest a price range cannot be made. If "Birthday Serenade" is found with either of these marks, it would be a highly desirable item. The Full Bee version, quite rare, conforms to the old style of #218, with the girl playing a concertina and the boy playing a horn. The current specimens, like those of the figurine, have the musical instruments reversed. The "Birthday Serenade" lamp base was manufactured in a large and a small size which, contrary to the usual Hummel practice in such situations, were assigned different numbers. #231 is the large version. See #234 for the smaller version.

|  | **Price Range** | |
| --- | --- | --- |
| ☐ 231, trademark Full Bee, 9¾" .................... | 2000.00 + | — |
| ☐ 231, trademark Goebel/V, 9¾" ................... | 270.00 | 297.00 |
| ☐ 231, trademark Goebel, 9¾" ..................... | 240.00 | 265.00 |

## 232 HAPPY DAYS

Lamp base in current production. Most of the comments made about #231 (see above) apply to "Happy Days." The design, a girl playing a guitar and a boy playing a mandolin or lute, is taken from the figurine issued as #150. Like "Birthday Serenade," it was discontinued during use of the Full Bee mark and not placed back into production until after adoption of the Goebel/V mark, thereby making it doubtful, though not impossible, that specimens exist with the two interim marks, Stylized Bee and 3-line. Any attempt to price such specimens would only be in the nature of a guess. As with "Birthday Serenade," there is a large and small version, #232 being the large. See #235 for the smaller version. Early specimens prior to discontinuation have a 1954 copyright date.

| ☐ 232, trademark Full Bee, 9¾" .................... | 1500.00 + | — |
| --- | --- | --- |
| ☐ 232, trademark Goebel/V, 9¾" ................... | 280.00 | 310.00 |
| ☐ 232, trademark Goebel, 9¾" ..................... | 240.00 | 265.00 |

## 233 BOY FEEDING BIRDS

Figurine, closed number. This is said to be the first figure sculptured by Gerhard Skrobek, currently the Master Modeler of Goebel, after joining the factory's staff. It was listed as a closed number on September 7, 1954. No samples are known to be in circulation. The design was, however, revised and issued as #300 Bird Watcher (see below). To what extent the revision differs from the original cannot be determined.

## 234 BIRTHDAY SERENADE

Lamp base in current production. This is the smaller version of #231, employing the motif of #218. As with #231, the early specimens show the girl playing the concertina and the boy playing the horn. The instruments in this version were subsequently switched. The only noticeable variation between this and the tall version is that #234 has no flower on the tree trunk. The trunk forms the lamp column and supports the socket. Although this smaller version was, like its prototype, discontinued for a time, it has been established to exist with all markings used since its introduction with the Full Bee trademark. It is scarce and seldom encountered with all markings except the last two.

|  | **Price Range** | |
|---|---|---|
| ☐ 234, trademark Full Bee, 7¾" .................... | 2000.00 + | — |
| ☐ 234, trademark Stylized Bee, 7¾" ............... | 1500.00 | 1650.00 |
| ☐ 234, trademark 3-line mark, 7¾" ................ | 1000.00 | 1100.00 |
| ☐ 234, trademark Goebel/V, 7¾" ................... | 240.00 | 265.00 |
| ☐ 234, trademark Goebel, 7¾" .................... | 210.00 | 230.00 |

## 235  HAPPY DAYS

Lamp base in current production. This is the smaller version of #232, differing both in size and the fact that no flower is shown on the tree trunk. It is a scarce item, but not quite in the class of #232. It bears a 1954 incised copyright date.

| ☐ 235, trademark Full Bee, 7¾" .................... | 1100.00 | 1210.00 |
|---|---|---|
| ☐ 235, trademark Stylized Bee, 7¾" ............... | 800.00 | 880.00 |
| ☐ 235, trademark 3-line mark, 7¾" ................ | 600.00 | 660.00 |
| ☐ 235, trademark Goebel/V, 7¾" ................... | 240.00 | 265.00 |
| ☐ 235, trademark Goebel, 7¾" .................... | 210.00 | 230.00 |

## 236  ?

Open number. Information regarding this design is not available, because the factory has made no announcement whatsoever.

## 237  STAR GAZER

Wall plaque, closed number. This was apparently an effort to fashion #132, also known as "Star Gazer" (see above), into a wall plaque. It was never placed on the market and the date of its termination has not been established. The only sample observed was in white overglaze and it is not known whether this still exists. No further efforts were made to produce this design as a wall plaque. The sample measured 4¾" × 5".

## 238/A  ANGEL WITH LUTE

Figurine in current production. This figure, part of the set known as "Angel Trio" comprising #238/A, 238/B, and 238/C, is a reissue of #38 without candleholder (see above). Normally the three pieces are retailed as a set, but as they frequently become separated after reaching private hands, it is not unusual to find them selling individually, especially the older examples. The nature of these pieces is such that they are occasionally used in conjunction with Nativity Sets. It is erroneously supposed by some commentators that the set can be found with marks as old as the Full Bee. Having been copyrighted and placed on sale in 1967, the existence of such specimens is doubtful.

**238/A** Angel with Lute

|  | **Price Range** | |
|---|---|---|
| ☐ 238/A, trademark 3-line mark, 2″–2½″ .......... | **55.00** | **60.00** |
| ☐ 238/A, trademark Goebel/V, 2″–2½″ ............. | **33.00** | **38.00** |
| ☐ 238/A, trademark Goebel, 2″–2½″ .............. | **23.00** | **28.00** |

## 238/B  ANGEL WITH ACCORDION

Figurine in current production. The second figure in the "Angel Trio" without a candleholder. This is an adaptation of #39 (see above).

| | | |
|---|---|---|
| ☐ 238/B, trademark 3-line mark, 2″–2½″ .......... | **55.00** | **60.00** |
| ☐ 238/B, trademark Goebel/V, 2″–2½″ ............. | **33.00** | **38.00** |
| ☐ 238/B, trademark Goebel, 2″–2½″ .............. | **23.00** | **28.00** |

## 238/C  ANGEL WITH TRUMPET

Figurine in current production. The third figure of the "Angel Trio" without a candleholder. Its design is a modification of #40. It carries an incised 1967 copyright date, the same as the other two components.

| | | |
|---|---|---|
| ☐ 238/C, trademark 3-line mark, 2″–2½″ .......... | **55.00** | **60.00** |
| ☐ 238/C, trademark Goebel/V, 2″–2½″ ............. | **33.00** | **38.00** |
| ☐ 238/C, trademark Goebel, 2″–2½″ .............. | **23.00** | **28.00** |

**238/B** Angel with Accordion

**238/C** Angel with Trumpet

**239/A** Girl with Nosegay

## 239/A  GIRL WITH NOSEGAY

Figurine in current production. In 1967 Hummel redesigned two earlier sets of candleholders as regular figurines: #238 "Angel Trio" and the set from which #239/A is derived, which is often called "Standing Children," "Children Standing," or "Children Trio." "Girl with Nosegay" is based upon #115 (see above) and carries a 1967 copyright date. It is normal at present for these figures (239/A, 239/B, and 239/C) to be distributed by the factory as a set, but they are frequently made available individually by retail dealers to suit the desires or requirements of customers. Extensive investigation on this set has not revaled any basis for the belief that it exists with either the Full Bee or Stylized Bee marks, in spite of information to the contrary supplied in certain works of reference.

|  | Price Range | |
|---|---|---|
| ☐ 239/A, trademark 3-line mark, 3½"............... | 55.00 | 61.00 |
| ☐ 239/A, trademark Goebel/V, 3½" ................. | 35.00 | 40.00 |
| ☐ 239/A, trademark Goebel, 3½" ................... | 25.00 | 29.00 |

**239/B** Girl with Doll

**239/C** Boy with Horse

### 239/B  GIRL WITH DOLL

Figurine in current production. Adapted from #116. See #239/A above for comments on the set of which this model is a component.

|  | Price Range | |
|---|---|---|
| ☐ 239/B, trademark 3-line mark, 3½"............... | **55.00** | **60.00** |
| ☐ 239/B, trademark Goebel/V, 3½"................. | **35.00** | **40.00** |
| ☐ 239/B, trademark Goebel, 3½"................... | **25.00** | **30.00** |

### 239/C  BOY WITH HORSE

Figurine in current production. Adapted from #117. See #239/A above for comments on the set of which this model is a component.

| | | |
|---|---|---|
| ☐ 239/C, trademark 3-line mark, 3½"............... | **55.00** | **62.00** |
| ☐ 239/C, trademark Goebel/V, 3½"................. | **35.00** | **40.00** |
| ☐ 239/C, trademark Goebel, 3½"................... | **25.00** | **30.00** |

**240** Little Drummer

## 240 LITTLE DRUMMER

Figurine in current production. "Little Drummer," a 1955 design, depicts a boy in a marching pose, clad in civilian dress, wearing a drum on a shoulder sling. In his hands he holds a pair of drumsticks. The boy's facial expression, one of extreme concentration, and the quality of motion captured by the modeling, has earned a deserved popularity for this model. It is probably one of the best Hummels of a child playing a musical instrument.

"Little Drummer" wears a white long-sleeved shirt highlighted by several red polka dots at the front, black or dark brown short trousers held with conventional suspenders, brown shoes, and white socks. His sandy hair is swept forward as if it were windblown. The drum is red and white, designed in a series of interlocking triangles. The figure stands on a small square base, on which the "M.I. Hummel" signature is incised. "Little Drummer," sometimes referred to merely as "Drummer," bears a 1955 incised copyright date. There is slight size variation.

|  | Price Range | |
|---|---|---|
| ☐ 240, trademark Full Bee, 4"–4¼" ............... | 150.00 | 170.00 |
| ☐ 240, trademark Stylized Bee, 4"–4¼" ........... | 100.00 | 110.00 |
| ☐ 240, trademark 3-line mark, 4"–4¼" ........... | 75.00 | 85.00 |
| ☐ 240, trademark Goebel/V, 4"–4¼" ............... | 60.00 | 70.00 |
| ☐ 240, trademark Goebel, 4"–4¼" ................ | 55.00 | 65.00 |

## 241 JOYOUS NEWS WITH LUTE

Wall font, closed number. The design for this font was adapted from #37 "Herald Angels," a triple-figure candleholder in which one of the components is a lute or mandolin-playing angel (see above). In the font she has an attractive blue gown touched with pink, green shoes, and wings of golden brown highlighted with red tips. The lute is red with white strings. Several red flowers are along the rear upper rim. This model was never officially produced. It was closed out on April 6, 1955, leaving only factory samples. The quantity in existence is not known.

## 241/B ANGEL LIGHTS

Candleholder in current production. This most unusual composition was introduced in the late 1970s. As the result of an error it was assigned the number 241, which already had been closed out on another design (see above.) To rectify this mistake the work is now known as #241/B. It would have normally been expected that a #241/A should exist, in keeping with the usual Hummel approach of numeration; but because of an oversight, there is no #241/A.

"Angel Lights" is made in two separate pieces: An arch supporting four candleholders plus a "Heavenly Angel" based upon #21, and a saucer on which this component rests. The novelty of this design has been the occasion of much comment, mostly favorable, as it presents an old traditional factory theme in an entirely fresh manner. The arch is of cream overglaze, decorated with fluting along its entire length, and surmounted by the "Heavenly Angel" figure at the center on a circular platform. Prices indicated are for specimens consisting of both components. When only the arch is present, the value is somewhat lower, while the saucer by itself would carry only a modest price. This work exists with the Goebel/V and Goebel marks only.

**241/B** Angel Lights

| | Price Range | |
|---|---|---|
| ☐ 241/B, trademark Goebel/V, 10½" × 8½" ......... | **150.00** | **165.00** |
| ☐ 241/B, trademark Goebel, 10½" × 8½" ........... | **142.00** | **157.00** |

## 242 JOYOUS NEWS WITH TRUMPET

Wall font, closed number. The design for this model was an adaptation of #27, with coloration and modeling somewhat changed. The angel's hair in #242 is more elaborately textured, for example. She wears a reddish gown, has a green shoulder satchel, brown shoes, and golden brown wings with reddish tips. Several violet flowers complete the composition. "Joyous News with Trumpet" was listed as a closed number designation on the same day as #241 "Joyous News with Lute" (see above), April 6, 1955. It is known to exist as a sample only.

## 243 MADONNA AND CHILD

Wall font in current production. During the mid 1950s, Hummel designed and placed on the market a number of wall fonts with mixed themes. These, taken as a whole are of great interest for the enthusiast of Hummel art, as they reflect major variations in style.

The Madonna is robed in red and the child in violet; the former has brunette hair and the latter sandy blonde. There are many small aspects of this design. The more they are studied, the greater they may be appreciated. A series of flowers is placed along the upper part of the font, where the figure meets the bowl. It is reported that this model was for a time discontinued, but there is no evidence in support of this belief. It bears a 1955 incised copyright date.

|  | Price Range | |
|---|---|---|
| ❏ 243, trademark Full Bee, 3⅛″ × 4″............... | 160.00 | 175.00 |
| ❏ 243, trademark Stylized Bee, 3⅛″ × 4″........... | 60.00 | 65.00 |
| ❏ 243, trademark 3-line mark, 3⅛″ × 4″............ | 40.00 | 45.00 |
| ❏ 243, trademark Goebel/V, 3⅛″ × 4″.............. | 33.00 | 38.00 |
| ❏ 243, trademark Goebel, 3⅛″ × 4″................ | 23.00 | 28.00 |

**243** Madonna and Child

## 244 ?

Open Number. No model has ever been produced with the number 244 and it has not been closed out. It is available for use when, and if, the factory elects. Why this number should have been skipped, that is, not officially listed as either open or closed, is a matter of speculation. It is possible that plans had been made to produce a sample which was never constructed. Or, the number could have been left open for possible application to a companion piece for an earlier Closed Number sample, for which plans were scrapped.

## 245 ?

Comments made regarding #244 above apply equally to this number.

## 246 HOLY FAMILY

Wall font in current production. During the mid 1950s, Hummel designed and placed on the market a number of wall fonts with mixed themes. These taken as a whole, are of great interest for the enthusiast of Hummel art as they reflect major variations in style. #246 is a grouping of the Virgin Mary, St. Joseph, and the Christ Child, the only instance in which these three figures appear in conjunction on one of the factory's wall fonts. The style may be regarded by some as casual in its modeling and coloration

**246** Holy Family

ut those familiar with art history will notice undeniable traces of Byzantine
nfluence in the pose and in the facial expressions. There is no doubting
hat the inspiration for it arose from Berta Hummel's observation of Byzan-
ne mosaics and fresco work in her native Germany.

St. Joseph and the Virgin are depicted half-length, their heads inclining
oward each other and touching. The child is seated before them on the
ont. St. Joseph wears a blue cloak and red cape. In his right hand, he
radles a white dove which the child touches. The Virgin is clad in a red
own and blue cape, while the child wears a green garment studded with
ur-pointed stars. He has yellow shoes. The hanger is ingeniously com-
osed of a short length of curved fabrique extending from the halo of St.
oseph to that of the Virgin. "Holy Family" bears an incised 1955 copyright
ate.

|  | | Price Range | |
|---|---|---|---|
| ] 246, trademark Full Bee, 3⅛″ × 4½″ | | 155.00 | 165.00 |
| ] 246, trademark Stylized Bee, 3⅛″ × 4½″ | | 100.00 | 110.00 |
| ] 246, trademark 3-line mark, 3⅛″ × 4½″ | | 60.00 | 65.00 |
| ] 246, trademark Goebel/V, 3⅛″ × 4½″ | | 36.50 | 40.00 |
| ] 246, trademark Goebel, 3⅛″ × 4½″ | | 26.50 | 30.00 |

## 247 STANDING MADONNA

Figurine, closed number. It is a great pity that this handsome model, a
ll, colored figure of the Virgin and Child, was never publicly marketed.
he piece stands 13″ high and shows the Virgin in a long blue robe, wearing
regal crown, and holding the Christ Child in her arms. The reason for its
ate has not been explained, nor has the date of its termination been re-
ealed. It is surely one of the most striking Madonnas in the Hummel line
modeling and composition.

In addition to the robe, the Virgin wears a yellow or pastel orange gown,
hile the Christ Child is clothed in white. Both carry sets of rosary beads.
he crown worn by the Virgin is especially worthy of note. Its fashion is of
e 15th or 16th century, in goldwork comprising arched components ter-
inating in triangular designs, and surmounted by a golden star. At the
ont is a large green jewel. Her robe is ornamented with a number of small
old crosses. "Standing Madonna" is known to exist in factory samples only.

## 248 GUARDIAN ANGEL

Wall font in current production. "Guardian Angel" was originally produced
large and small versions, of which only the small continues to be mar-
ted. Both 248/0 and 248/I were discontinued.

The model is a restyling of #29, which was removed from production
cause of the frailty of its wings. "Guardian Angel" is also known by the
ame "Kneeling Angel," which is the name used in the current Hummel
atalogue. The angel wears a dark red outer robe studded with white Greek
osses over a brownish-red gown. She kneels with hands clasped in prayer.

**248** Guardian Angel

Her wings are large and sturdily constructed. Not only are they fairly thi
but, for additional durability, are supported by a background piece design
to represent the angel's halo. The symmetry of this design, with the ange
wings curving downward toward the font or bowl, is particularly appealin
"Guardian Angel" carries a 1959 incised copyright date.

No evidence could be discovered to support the speculation that th
figure exists with the Full Bee mark and it is not possible to venture a gue
as to its value if such specimens do exist. One reference book gives t
value at $60, but this appears so unreasonable that one is led to belie
the compiler of this book priced the item without awareness of its rarity,
possible nonexistence, with the Full Bee mark. If such a price was inde
advertised by a dealer, it could only have resulted from being uninform
and does not represent a fair value for this item.

|  | Price Range | |
|---|---|---|
| ☐ 248, trademark Stylized Bee, 2¼″ × 5½″ ......... | **150.00** | **165.** |
| ☐ 248, trademark 3-line mark, 2¼″ × 5½″ .......... | **60.00** | **65.** |
| ☐ 248, trademark Goebel/V, 2¼″ × 5½″ ............. | **40.00** | **45.** |
| ☐ 248, trademark Goebel, 2¼″ × 5½″ ............... | **23.00** | **28.** |

## 249 MADONNA AND CHILD

Wall plaque, closed number. It is often stated that #249 is similar to an earlier plaque #48, but lacking the background and frame. This does the work an extreme injustice. While the subject and pose are the same, a half-length Virgin holding the Christ Child, the quality of modeling in #249 so far exceeds its predecessor that any comparison is impossible. Here, in fact, is one of the true gems of the Hummel line: A work so sensitively and carefully modeled, following strict Renaissance formula, that if hung amidst Italian enamels of the 16th and 17th centuries, it would scarcely be distinguishable. It would not be overzealous to state that the factory has never before, nor since, attained such perfection in any of its work, whether in figurine or other form. That it should be hidden away as a closed number designation, depriving the public of owning what can only be termed a masterpiece of its species, borders on the criminal. The reason for its failure to be marketed is not known; motive strong enough to prevent so fine a model from getting into production is inconceivable. That it could have been rejected by the convent (a common cause for closed number designations) seems less than possible. The Virgin wears a pale reddish cloak with billowing sleeves, and the Christ Child wears a white garment. Anyone having the opportunity to examine one of the samples or a photograph, should notice the contour and modeling of the child's legs, feet, and toes, all of which reflect an advanced understanding of classical sculpture. There is no information on the date this model was listed as a closed edition. The samples are rare. The factory would do collectors a service by resurrecting this design.

## 250/A AND B, LITTLE GOAT HERDER/FEEDING TIME

Set of bookends in current production. This set of bookends features #200 "Little Goat Herder" on one piece and #199 "Feeding Time" on the other. As these designs have already been discussed in some detail, the reader is referred to the earlier comments. The bases consist of wooden blocks cut square, on the side of which is constructed a fence, also of wood. As with Hummel bookends in general, their light weight renders them unsuitable for use with folio size volumes or any books that habitually refuse to stand upright, such as a shelf of unbound periodicals.

|  | Price Range | |
| --- | --- | --- |
| ☐ 250/A and 250B, trademark Full Bee, 5½"....... | 260.00 | 285.00 |
| ☐ 250/A and 250/B, trademark Stylized Bee, 5½" | 200.00 | 220.00 |
| ☐ 250/A and 250/B, trademark 3-line mark, 5½" ... | 170.00 | 190.00 |
| ☐ 250/A and 250/B, trademark Goebel/V, 5½" ..... | 180.00 | 200.00 |
| ☐ 250/A and 250/B, trademark Goebel, 5½" ....... | 170.00 | 190.00 |

## 251/A AND B, GOOD FRIENDS, SHE LOVES ME

Set of bookends in current production. This set was designed similarly to the preceding (see #250 above). #251/A Good Friends is #182 in the figurine series; #251/B She Loves Me, She Loves Me Not is #174. The reader is referred to the articles on these numbers for details of design and coloration. This set, like the one above and below, was originally marketed in Europe and not released to American distributors until 1964. While far from rare with the Full Bee mark, it is often difficult to locate in America because of this situation of withheld distribution.

**251/A** Good Friends

**251/A**                                                **251/B**

|  | Price Range | |
|---|---|---|
| ☐ 251/A and 251/B, trademark Full Bee, 5″ ........ | 300.00 | 330.00 |
| ☐ 251/A and 251/B, trademark Stylized Bee, 5″.... | 250.00 | 275.00 |
| ☐ 251/A and 251/B, trademark 3-line mark, 5″ ..... | 190.00 | 210.00 |
| ☐ 251/A and 251/B, trademark Goebel/V, 5″ ....... | 180.00 | 200.00 |
| ☐ 251/A and 251/B, trademark Goebel, 5″ ......... | 170.00 | 190.00 |

## 252/A AND B, APPLE TREE GIRL AND BOY

Set of bookends in current production. The motifs for this set of bookends are #141 "Apple Tree Girl," and #142 "Apple Tree Boy." The reader may refer back to these two Hummels for complete descriptions of these figures.

| | Price Range | |
|---|---|---|
| ☐ 252/A and 252/B, trademark Full Bee, 5"–5¼" .. | 300.00 | 330.00 |
| ☐ 252/A and 252/B, trademark Stylized Bee, 5"– 5¼" ............................................. | 250.00 | 275.00 |
| ☐ 252/A and 252/B, trademark 3-line mark, 5"– 5¼" ............................................. | 190.00 | 210.00 |
| ☐ 252/A and 252/B, trademark Goebel/V, 5"–5¼" | 180.00 | 200.00 |
| ☐ 252/A and 252/B, trademark Goebel, 5"–5¼".... | 170.00 | 190.00 |

## 253 GIRL WITH BASKET

Figurine, closed number. It is believed that this model represents a girl with a basket based upon the figure in #52 "Going to Grandma's" (see above). There are no recorded samples.

## 254 GIRL PLAYING MANDOLIN

Figurine, closed number. Supposedly similar to the girl in #150 "Happy Days," there appear to be no known samples of this figure, which is listed as being 4¼" tall. The date of its termination is not recorded.

**255** Stitch in Time

## 255 STITCH IN TIME

Figurine in current production. A variation on a theme twice employed, "Stitch in Time" bears close similarity to one of the figures in #177 "School Girls" and #256 "Knitting Lesson." In both of these other compositions, an additional figure or figures are included, whereas "Stitch in Time" is an individual model. The subject is a girl knitting. She wears a short-sleeved reddish dress, a dark brown vest, a seagreen skirt with black striping, blue shoes, light tan socks, and a red ribbon in her hair. "Stitch in Time" carries a 1963 incised copyright date, but was not marketed in the U.S. until 1964.

|  | Price Range | |
|---|---|---|
| ☐ 255, trademark Stylized Bee, 6½"–6¾" .......... | 250.00 | 270.00 |
| ☐ 255, trademark 3-line mark, 6½"–6¾" ........... | 125.00 | 145.00 |
| ☐ 255, trademark Goebel/V, 6½"–6¾" ............. | 105.00 | 120.00 |
| ☐ 255, trademark Goebel, 6½"–6¾" .............. | 94.00 | 105.00 |

**256** Knitting Lesson

## 256  KNITTING LESSON

Figurine in current production. "Knitting Lesson" depicts a girl knitting while another girl of similar age stands alongside her watching the process. Both figures are adaptations from #177 "School Girls." The girl who is knitting is almost identical to the "School Girls" knitter, but the girl who is watching differs in facial expression; she has a more quizzical look. They stand on an oval base.

This model carries a 1963 copyright date and was first sold in America in 1964. There are no reported size variations. The relatively high price of this model would seem to suggest scarcity, but in fact it results from manufacturing cost. This is a rather tall work (7½") for a multiple figure design, about two inches above the average. The factory has, especially in recent years, charged stiff premium prices for large constructions.

|  | Price Range | |
|---|---|---|
| ☐ 256, trademark Stylized Bee, 7½".............. | 350.00 | 375.00 |
| ☐ 256, trademark 3-line mark, 7½" ................. | 275.00 | 295.00 |
| ☐ 256, trademark Goebel/V, 7½" ................... | 240.00 | 260.00 |
| ☐ 256, trademark Goebel, 7½" .................... | 220.00 | 240.00 |

**257** For Mother

## 257 FOR MOTHER

Figurine in current production. This figure, copyrighted in 1963 when Hummel was relying heavily on the use of previously employed designs, is more original than most. It shows a girl in Bavarian village dress of the mid 1800s, holding a bouquet of flowers. There is some slight size variation in this model. The girl is wearing a white puffy-sleeved blouse, a tan vest, a green skirt, a white apron with red polka dots, brown shoes, and green socks. Her hair is brown and she holds yellow flowers with black centers. The figure stands on a circular base.

| | Price Range | |
|---|---|---|
| ☐ 257, trademark Stylized Bee, 5″–5¾″ ........... | 250.00 | 270.00 |
| ☐ 257, trademark 3-line mark, 5″–5¼″ ............. | 90.00 | 100.00 |
| ☐ 257, trademark Goebel/V, 5″–5¼″................ | 75.00 | 85.00 |
| ☐ 257, trademark Goebel, 5″–5¼″................. | 63.00 | 70.00 |

**258** Which Hand?

## 258 WHICH HAND?

Figurine in current production. The figure employed in "Which Hand?" bears a marked similarity to one of the girls in #196 "Telling Her Secret."

She stands with hands clenched behind her back, playing the old "which hand?" guessing game with a partner who is not portrayed in the composition. For those unfamiliar with this game, a brief description may be welcome. One player takes a small object, such as a penny, in one hand and places both hands behind his back, in order to switch hands if he so wishes. When the hands are extended, with closed fists, the other player must guess which hand holds the object. This is repeated several times and the score is kept. The object is passed to the second player, who then attempts to outscore his opponent. While it appears as though nothing but guesswork is involved, a skilled player can generally record a good score, through keen observation, mental persuasion, and misdirection. For example, the knuckles on the hand holding the object are usually whiter than those on the empty hand, because the player unconsciously closes that fist tighter. "Which Hand?" wears a puffy-sleeved blouse, a tan jumper, a pink apron with orange and dark brown striping, brown shoes, and white socks. A red kerchief is tied around her head and an orange ribbon decorates her pigtail.

| | Price Range | |
|---|---|---|
| ☐ 258, trademark Stylized Bee, 5¼"–5½".......... | 220.00 | 250.00 |
| ☐ 258, trademark 3-line mark, 5¼"–5½" ........... | 90.00 | 100.00 |
| ☐ 258, trademark Goebel/V, 5¼"–5½" ............. | 73.00 | 80.00 |
| ☐ 258, trademark Goebel, 5¼"–5½" ............... | 63.00 | 70.00 |

## 259 GIRL WITH ACCORDION

Figurine, closed number. This was an attempt to produce the accordion or concertina-playing girl from the old version of #218 "Birthday Serenade" as a separate composition. It was listed as a closed number on November 8, 1962, with only factory samples known to exist. The girl is modeled and colored identically to #218.

## 260 NATIVITY SET

Set of 16 figurines in current production. Following the popularity of the standard size Hummel Nativity Set, (see #214 above), it was decided to manufacture a larger version, comprised of the same components, but increasing the size. The result is a set that cannot be surpassed for pure grandeur on the commercial market and indeed rivals, in scale at least, the memorable Nativity Sets modeled in Italy in the 18th and 19th centuries. There is no doubting the fact that #260 was designed chiefly for use in churches, offices, and places of public assembly, as the set is too large for the average home. Its figures stand as tall as 12¾", accompanied by a stable measuring 31½" × 12½" × 23⅛". It should be noted that the stable, for all its bulk, serves primarily as background for the figures.

**260** Nativity Set (16 pieces)

The set consists of the following, which may be compared against the descriptions of #214 so far as size is concerned:

260/A  Madonna, 9¾"
260/B  Saint Joseph, 11¾"
260/C  Infant Jesus, 5¾" (horizontal measure)
260/D  Good Night, 5¼"
260/E  Angel Serenade, 4¼"
260/F  We Congratulate, 6¼"
260/G  Standing Shepherd, 11¾"
260/H  Sheep and Lamb, 3¾"
260/J  Kneeling Shepherd Boy, 7"
260/K  Shepherd Boy with Flute ("Little Tooter"), 5⅛"
260/L  Donkey, 7½"
260/M  Cow, reclining, 6" × 11"
260/N  Moorish King, 12¾"
260/O  King, standing, 12"
260/P  King, kneeling, 9"
260/R  Sheep, reclining, 3¼" × 4"

This set shows the new textured finish to its best advantage, probably because it was used with restraint on selected areas only. As might have been imagined, production is extremely limited. Though forecasts are always dangerous, there seems a strong likelihood that in the future specimens with the 3-line mark will become valuable because of inevitable breakage and loss. For a relatively new release it has already gained substantially.

Prices are for sets without the stable. The stable alone 260/S, is presently listed at $275.00 suggested retail by Hummel.

| | Price Range | |
|---|---|---|
| □ 260, trademark 3-line mark, ..................... | **3500.00** | **3850.00** |
| □ 260, trademark Goebel/V, ....................... | **3200.00** | **3520.00** |
| □ 260, trademark Goebel, ........................ | **2930.00** | **3230.00** |

**Incomplete sets.** The value of incomplete sets varies depending upon the extent and significance of pieces lacking. It is always possible to replace missing components, as all the figures are sold individually.

The storage of this set, if it is displayed only at Christmas and kept away the remainder of the year, should be carefully attended to. Because of the size and weight of these figures, they can be broken easily at the slightest accident. The safest and most logical procedure is to box each separately, wrapping it first in tissue and then cotton batting.

## 261  ANGEL DUET

Figurine in current production. "Angel Dust" is a standard figurine version of the design produced earlier as a candleholder (see #193 above). It is almost identical, except that the girl's left hand, instead of holding the candle

**261** Angel Duet

receptacle, now holds one side of the open music book. Her right arm is no longer at the boy angel's shoulder, but is around his waist. "Angel Duet" carries a 1968 copyright date.

|  | Price Range | |
| --- | --- | --- |
| ☐ 261, trademark 3-line mark, 5″ ................... | **325.00** | **355.00** |
| ☐ 261, trademark Goebel/V, 5″ ...................... | **95.00** | **105.00** |
| ☐ 261, trademark Goebel, 5″ ....................... | **88.00** | **98.00** |

## 262 HEAVENLY LULLABY

Figurine in current production. "Heavenly Lullaby" is a figurine version of the design marketed as a candleholder (see #24 above). The swaddling clothes of the infant are frequently of a deeper violet in this work than in its predecessor. Otherwise there is no material difference.

| | Price Range | |
| --- | --- | --- |
| ☐ 262, trademark 3-line mark, 3½″ × 5″............. | **355.00** | **385.00** |
| ☐ 262, trademark Goebel/V, 3½″ × 5″............... | **100.00** | **110.00** |
| ☐ 262, trademark Goebel, 3½″ × 5″................ | **80.00** | **88.00** |

**262** Heavenly Lullaby

## 263 MERRY WANDERER

Wall plaque, closed number. This was a bas-relief version without frame or background of the "Merry Wanderer" designed to be hung on a wall. From preserved samples it appears to be an attractive and effective piece of work, but a decision was made not to place it into production. It was listed as a closed number in the early 1960s. The samples measure 4″ × 5¾″. A hole for hanging is provided on the reverse side. (See #92 above).

## 264  ANNUAL PLATE, 1971

Limited production; sold out. #264 is perhaps the most historic number in the Hummel series as it represents the first of the factory's annual plates. It may be wondered why Hummel did not get into the practice of issuing such plates prior to 1971. The most logical explanation is that neither the factory nor the public was oriented toward commemorative or limited edition plates before that time. This can easily be demonstrated by inspecting hobby, antique, and other collector magazines of the 1960s, in which very little will be found in the way of advertising for such items. Hummel was in fact a trendsetter in the matter of annual plates. Since it began their manufacture on a regular basis, numerous other pottery works have followed their lead, encouraged by the successful sale of Hummel plates.

The series began innocently enough, without immediate plans to continue it regularly. It happened that 1971 was the 100th anniversary of Goebel Porzellenfabrik, which had long been in operation prior to its association with Sister Hummel and the manufacture of Hummel figurines. It was decided to produce a special work for distribution to factory staff by way of a celebration. This is occasionally done in such situations. As the factory was by then noted chiefly for its making of Hummels, there is no surprise that a Hummel design was selected. The choice was "Heavenly Angel" (see #21 above), incorporated as a shallow bas-relief on a plate measuring a modest 7½" in diameter. If it is wondered why the sries of Hummel Annual Plates are not larger physically in keeping with the dimensions of commemorative plates in general, the cause can be traced to this first issue. It was intended as a token only and no effort was made to design or style it to attract public notice. The Hummel mark was placed on the back of each specimen (at that time the 3-line mark) along with a stamped message reading, in German, "100 Jahre W. Goebel. Gewidmet Allen Mitarbeitern im Jubilaumsjahr. Wir Danken Ihnen fur Ihre Mitarbeit," expressing thanks to the employees for making the occasion possible. No decision had at that time been made to commercially sell the plate, but not long thereafter, it was in regular production. Neither the privately nor publicly issued editions bears any limitation notice, as in the case with subsequent additions to the series. It may, of course, be supposed that quantities were produced to meet whatever demand arose, and that production could well have spilled over into 1972 or even later. Based on available evidence, the most convincing being that these plates are invariably closed out quickly in the factory's catalogues, there seems to be no desire on the factory's part to profit from the desire of collectors to buy obsolete editions.

The Hummel Annual Plates may be regarded as a world unto themselves, insofar as there are numerous collectors concentrating upon them who have no wish to collect the factory's figurines and other products. This creates an enormous market for the plates, well exceeding that for figurines. Their nature as limited edition pieces also brings investors and speculators into the picture. The first plate was marketed with a $25 price and now sells for four figures, an increase of better than $100 per year on a very minimal investment. It would of course be pointless to suppose that subsequent editions will perform this well in price gain as the factory, having witnessed the demand for its 1971 plate, issued later ones in larger quantities. That they will advance in value more rapidly than newly issued figurines is, however, beyond doubt, even though the issue price has now reached the $100 level.

This first edition carries a representation of the "Heavenly Angel" motif. It was known originally as a "Christmas Plate" (a term no longer employed by the factory so as to permit use of a greater variety of designs) and carried, in the flat ground beside the angel, designs of the Star of Bethlehem and a pair of Christmas trees growing in a field. Missing from the reverse side is the now familiar advice, "Not To Be Used For Food."

"Heavenly Angel" is robed in deep green, her brown wings highlighted with touches of yellow, against a ground of white with light washes of brown and pinkish brown. The inner portion of the rim is dark brown. Arranged around the rim, in a practice followed thereafter on all Hummel Annual Plates, is a circular frame of five-point stars. The date appears in red beneath the central figure, another practice carried on subsequently. The style of lettering used for the date has been called Gothic. It is not in fact Gothic, the handwriting of late medieval Germany, but rather a modified version embodying Saxon influence. The collector of old European coins will immediately see the truth of this observation. As with all Hummel Annual plates, the stand on the reverse is punctured with a pair of holes through which a string is threaded for hanging.

With this 1971 edition a situation exists somewhat different than that for the remainder of the series. The plate exists in two distinct states: With and without the inscription giving thanks to factory workers. The version without the inscription is more valuable.

**264** Annual Plate 1971

| | | Price Range | |
|---|---|---|---|
| ☐ 264, trademark 3-line mark, 7½″, trade edition .. | | **1000.00** | **1400.00** |
| ☐ 264, trademark 3-line mark, 7½″, gift edition..... | | **2000.00** | **2500.00** |

## 265  ANNUAL PLATE, 1972

Limited production; sold out. The night watchman of #15 "Hear Ye, Hear Ye" was chosen as the motif for the second Annual Christmas Plate, as they were then commonly termed. The background consists of a star and a stylized version of a village church with a tall steeple. There are two varieties, one with the 3-line mark and another with Goebel/V, as the trademark was changed during production. This would seem to have created an ideal situation for a rarity, but in fact both versions are valued equally, neither being scarce. Issue price was set at $30.00

| | | | |
|---|---|---|---|
| ☐ 265, trademark 3-line mark, 7½″ ................. | | **100.00** | **110.00** |
| ☐ 265, trademark Goebel/V, 7½″ ................... | | **100.00** | **110.00** |

**265** Annual Plate 1972

## 266  ANNUAL PLATE, 1973

Limited production; sold out. Utilizes the "Globe Trotter" motif (see #79 above). Here the basket borne on the boy's shoulders is not empty, as in the figurine, but filled with blue flowers. There is a landscape background to the figure's left and a few blue flowers to the right. Issue price was set at $32.50.

**266** Annual Plate 1973

|  | Price Range | |
|---|---|---|
| ☐ 266, trademark Goebel/V, 7½" ................... | **250.00** | **275.00** |

## 267 ANNUAL PLATE, 1974

Limited production; sold out. The "Goose Girl" design was the motif for this plate (see #47 above). This was the first Hummel Annual Plate without a Christmas theme of any kind, although it was still referred to as a Christmas Plate. Issue price was set at $40.00.

| ☐ 267, trademark Goebel/V, 7½" ................... | **130.00** | **140.00** |
|---|---|---|

## 268 ANNUAL PLATE, 1975

Limited production; sold out. The "Ride Into Christmas" motif (see #396 below) shows a boy on a sled with a small Christmas tree and an old-fashioned lantern containing a candle. The figurine version of this design was released at the same time as the plate; the first time this was done in the annual plate series. Issue price was set at $50.00

| ☐ 268, trademark Goebel/V, 7½" ................... | **125.00** | **137.50** |
|---|---|---|

**267** Annual Plate 1974

**268** Annual Plate 1975

**269** Annual Plate 1976

## 269  ANNUAL PLATE, 1976

Limited production; sold out. The "Apple Tree Girl" motif with bird in tree (see #141 above). Issue price was set at $50.00.

|  | **Price Range** | |
|---|---|---|
| ☐ 269, trademark Goebel/V, 7½" .................. | **100.00** | **110.00** |

## 270  ANNUAL PLATE, 1977

Limited production; sold out. The "Apple Tree Boy" motif with bird in tree (see #142 above). Issue price was set at $52.50

| ☐ 270, trademark Goebel/V, 7½" .................. | **150.00** | **105.00** |
|---|---|---|

## 271  ANNUAL PLATE, 1978

Limited production; sold out. The "Happy Pastime" motif (see #69 above) but instead of the bird being seated on the girl's lap it is shown here perched on a low tree. Issue price was set at $65.00

| ☐ 271, trademark Goebel/V, 7½" .................. | **125.00** | **137.50** |
|---|---|---|

**270** Annual Plate 1977

**271** Annual Plate 1978

**272** Annual Plate 1979

**273** Annual Plate 1980

## 272 ANNUAL PLATE, 1979

Limited production; sold out. The "Singing Lesson" motif (see #63 above) but the bird perches on a tree instead of on the boy's shoe. Issue price was set at $90.00.

|  | **Price Range** | |
|---|---|---|
| □ 272, trademark Goebel, 7½" .................... | **125.00** | **137.50** |

## 273 ANNUAL PLATE, 1980

Limited production; sold out. The "School Girl" motif (see #81 above). Contrary to usual practice, the figurine is shown in profile rather than front view. It may be argued that #272 with "Singing Lesson" motif is also in profile, but this was a figurine intended for profile display, while "School Girl" was not. A village schoolhouse appears in the distance, suggesting that the girl is on her way to school. Her pigtails, which hang down in the figurine, are shown windblown. Issue price was set at $90.00.

| □ 273, trademark Goebel, 7½" .................... | **90.00** | **110.00** |
|---|---|---|

**274** Annual Plate 1981

## 274 ANNUAL PLATE, 1981

Limited production; sold out. The motif used is "Umbrella Boy" (see #152/A above). The colors are nearly identical to thsoe in the figurine.

| □ 274, trademark Goebel, 7½" .................... | **100.00** | **110.00** |
|---|---|---|

**275** Annual Plate 1982

**280** Anniversary Plate, 1975

## 275 ANNUAL PLATE, 1982

Limited production; currently available. The motif used is "Umbrella Girl" (see #152). The colors are nearly identical to those in the figurine.

|  | Price Range | |
|---|---|---|
| □ 275, trademark Goebel, 7½" ..................... | 100.00 | 110.00 |

## 276 ANNUAL PLATE, 1983

Limited production; currently available. The "Postman" design (see #119).

| □ 276, trademark Goebel, 7½" ..................... | 108.00 |
|---|---|

## 277 ANNUAL PLATE, 1984

Limited production; currently available. The "Little Helper" design (see #73).

| □ 277, trademark Goebel, 7½" ..................... | 108.00 |
|---|---|

## 278 ANNUAL PLATE, 1985

Limited production; currently available.

| □ 278, trademark Goebel, 7½" ..................... | 110.00 |
|---|---|

## 279 ANNUAL PLATE, 1986

Projected for release in autumn, 1985. "Playmates" motif (see #58 above). No available information on trademark or price.

## 280 ANNIVERSARY PLATE, 1975

Limited production; sold out. Hummel Anniversary Plates differ from the annual plates (see #264–279) in that they are larger, carry no date of issue on the front, and retail for a higher price. The series was begun in 1975 with the intention of releasing a new edition every five years. Consequently, there are now two in circulation, for 1975 and 1980, with the next scheduled for 1985. Numbers 282 to 299 inclusive have been set aside for future anniversary plates, the designs for which have not been made public, if indeed they have yet been decided. This would carry the series up to the year 2070.

What was the motive for anniversary plates, when Hummel already had annual plates? The obvious answer might be to take full advantage of the current collector demand for plates of all types, but this does not tell the whole story. When the annual plate series began, it was not intended to market them commercially and the size agreed upon was rather small by comparison to most commemorative or limited edition plates. Having once established this size, it was not possible to alter it in future editions. For several years after the annual plates had been issued, comments were widespread, especially in the collector press, that the small size tended to make them appear insignificant against the plates of many other factories. It was therefore resolved by Goebel to issue, for the benefit of persons to whom large plates have a special appeal, these anniversary plates, whose size of ten inches in diameter is closer to the normal dimensions of those produced by competitors.

It is presumed that the designs will not conflict with those on the annual plates. The 1975 edition features "Stormy Weather," a boy and girl huddled together under an umbrella (see #71 above). In this version the facial expressions differ markedly from the figurine as the children here are smiling broadly, while in the figurine they seem far from amused. A small five-point star appears in the left background and the "M.I. Hummel" signature is incised along the right-hand side. The anniversary plates have a rim composed of repeated ridges.

It may be supposed that, because of the higher original retail price of anniversary plates, their production is more limited than that of annual plates. Given the five-year intervals between issues, it is not plausible to place great faith in such an assumption. Only enough annual plates are manufactured to sell for a year, until release of the next, but the anniversary plates have a much longer potential selling period. As the factory gives out no information on these matters, it must remain open to speculation. There is no question that the reason for secrecy is the belief that if the number of specimens in circulation were known, this would decrease their sales appeal. Obviously, Hummel plates are made in greater quantities than those of most other manufacturers, as the number of Hummel buyers far surpass those who collect plates of other manufacturers. This does not mean that Hummel plates are not as good an investment, since the large output is balanced by an equally large demand. The issue price was set at $100.00.

|  | Price Range | |
|---|---|---|
| ☐ 280, trademark Goebel/V, 10″ .................... | 350.00 | 385.00 |

## 281 ANNIVERSARY PLATE, 1980

Limited production; currently available. The 1980 Anniversary Plate, which is the second in the series, was originally entitled "Spring Dance" (see #353) by the Goebel factory. Just before release, however, Goebel realized that only one of the figures on the plate was identical to one of the figures in the figurine version. The name was then changed to "Ring Around the Rosie." The design was a modification of the figurine version (see #349 below) since it used only the small girl in the brown dress and the girl to

**281** Anniversary Plate, 1980

her left with pigtails and blue scarf. It bears the current plain Goebel trademark and is listed at a suggested retail price of $225. The first Hummel Anniversary Plate tripled in value in five years. Should #281 follow suit, its value in 1985 will be close to $700, but these things are devilishly hard to forecast.

|  | **Price Range** | |
|---|---|---|
| ☐ 281, trademark Goebel, 10″ ..................... | **225.00** | **245.00** |

## 282 ANNIVERSARY PLATE, 1985

Limited production; currently available. The 1985 Anniversary Plate entitled "Auf Wiedersehen" will be the last plate in this series. It features a bas-relief rendition of the "Auf Wiedersehen" figurine #153. A boy and girl stand side by side with their right arms raised, waving goodbye with their handkerchiefs.

☐ 282, trademark Goebel, 10″ ..................... **225.00**

## 283-299 ANNIVERSARY PLATES

These numbers have been set aside for future editions of the anniversary plate, which was closed in 1985.

**300** Bird Watcher

## 300  BIRD WATCHER

Figurine in current production. "Bird Watcher" is based on a model designed by Gerhard Skrobek, said to be his first upon joining the factory staff in 1954. It was designated number 233 (see above) and terminated as a closed number on September 7th of that year. "Bird Watcher" is believed to be a close approximation of that model, though no samples of the previous design exist for comparison. Although not marketed until late in the 1970s, this figure carries a 1956 copyright date.

This figure shows a boy holding a slice of bread as three birds gather around him on the ground. It might be logical to assume that the boy is breaking away sections of the bread and feeding the birds, especially as two of them are pecking the ground in an attitude of eating. The original title, "Tenderness," provided some support for the feeding theory; to merely observe the birds would not be considered an act of tenderness.

The boy wears a long-sleeved blue shirt with pinstriping, orange or reddish trousers without suspenders, black shoes, and an orange scarf thrown round his neck. The costuming would suggest that "Bird Watcher" has stepped out-of-doors briefly on a chilly day, perhaps into his own back-yard; this might explain the absence of a jacket or more substantial clothing. The birds, of undetermined species, are colored mainly blue, green, and yellow. It should be noted that the slice of bread is half missing, but whether it has gone to the boy or birds remains to be settled. The figure stands on a textured oval base which gives the suggestion of snow on the ground.

|  | **Price Range** | |
|---|---|---|
| ☐ 300, trademark Goebel/V, 5″ .................... | 130.00 | 145.00 |
| ☐ 300, trademark Goebel, 5″ ...................... | 100.00 | 110.00 |

## 301 CHRISTMAS ANGEL

Figurine, open number. "Christmas Angel" is a figure of an angel carrying two empty baskets and a small decorated Christmas tree. This model was designed by Theodore Menzenbach in 1957. When submitted to the Seissen Convent it was not awarded approval, nor was it listed as a closed number. There is yet a possibility that it could, even after 23 years, be manufactured for public sale. To date, only samples are known. There were rumors of it being released in 1980, but it does not appear in the current Hummel list. "Christmas Angel" stands 6¼″. She wears a white or bone-colored long gown and has white wings touched with traces of yellow. Her hair is blondish red. The empty baskets might have been intended as receptacles for candy.

## 302 CONCENTRATION

Figurine, open number. "Concentration" is a figure of a girl knitting, bearing close resemblance to #255 "Stitch in Time" and several other compositions. A quizzical-looking boy stands by with his index finger to his mouth as if mystified by the procedure. This model was originally called "Knit One, Purl Two." The girl wears an orange polka dot dress, a brown vest, a blue apron with darker blue plaid striping, brown shoes and white socks with additions of gray and yellow. The boy is dressed in a short blue jacket also plaid-striped, with dark brown lederhosen, matching suspenders, brown tall boots, and yellow-white socks. "Concentration" stands 5″ high.

## 303 ARITHMETIC LESSON

Figurine, open number. The children in "Arithmetic Lesson," a boy holding a slate and a girl standing alongside him, are refugees with slight remodeling from previous designs. The boy appeared in #170 "School Boys," where he also held a slate, and the girl appeared in #177 "School Girls." He wears a matching suit of a blue plaid striped jacket and short pants, gray shoes, white socks, and a conical Tyrolean hat with feather. Her attire is an orange and rush jacket, gray oversized slippers, white socks, red hair ribbon, and a gray schoolbag slung behind her back on shoulder straps. They stand on an oval base.

**304** The Artist

## 304 THE ARTIST

Figurine in current production. "The Artist" bears a 1951 copyright date, but was not released for sale until the 1970s. This is a figure of a boy holding in one hand a palette of paints and brushes and in the other a brush loaded with paint. At his feet is an earthenware pitcher holding additional brushes. There is no canvas in the composition nor any hint of the artist's subject. The boy wears attire not typical for an artist, a pastel blue jacket with dark blue plaid striping, white short brown pants, wine-colored shoes, and white socks. His failure to don a smock has not resulted in the least bit of difficulty, and his clothing bears no evidence of paint staining. The nicely modeled earthenware pitcher is dark green. Red is the dominant color among the paints on "The Artist's" palette.

| | Price Range | |
|---|---|---|
| ☐ 304, trademark 3-line mark, 5½" ................ | 325.00 | 355.00 |
| ☐ 304, trademark Goebel/V, 5½" .................. | 110.00 | 120.00 |
| ☐ 304, trademark Goebel, 5½" .................... | 94.50 | 104.00 |

## 305  THE BUILDER

Figurine in current production. "The Builder," which was first sold in the U.S. in 1963 during use of the Stylized Bee trademark, carries a 1955 incised copyright date. It shows a mason at work, lifting a pair of bricks, while in the foreground there are three bricks assembled into what appears to be the foundation of a wall or some other structure. At the rear of the figurine is a bucket containing mortar and a trowel. This is by far the heaviest labor performed by any of the occupational Hummels. The figure is sometimes mistakenly referred to as a girl, because the shirt he wears happens to have bulging sleeves unlike those of a man's shirt. The intention was not to portray the sleeves as puffy, but to suggest muscular shoulders and upper arms, such as would be expected of a laborer. The shirt is pale blue with violet plaid striping. In addition, "The Builder" wears brown trousers and a white apron with blue pinstriping and black shoes. He has a brown narrow-brimmed hat and wears a red neckerchief.

**305** The Builder

| | **Price Range** | |
|---|---:|---:|
| ☐ 305, trademark Stylized Bee, 5½".............. | **2500.00** | **2700.00** |
| ☐ 305, trademark 3-line mark, 5½" ............... | **125.00** | **135.00** |
| ☐ 305, trademark Goebel/V, 5½" ................. | **105.00** | **110.00** |
| ☐ 305, trademark Goebel, 5½" ................... | **94.50** | **105.00** |

## 306  LITTLE BOOKKEEPER

Figurine in current production. The value of "Little Bookkeeper" is higher than that of other figurines issued around the same time, due to the complexity of its design. In addition to the title figure, there are several accessories in this composition: The chair on which he sits, the table, and, at the base, a terrier-type dog who ponders over the quaint and curious activities of his master. This model has an incised 1955 copyright date, but was not

**306** Little Bookkeeper

introduced to the American market until 1962. "Little Bookkeeper" intently studies an open book on the table while another book lies on the floor.

"Little Bookkeeper" wears a wine-colored jacket with plaid striping, brown short trousers, and mahogany-colored shoes. The stool is a light reddish brown. The table is similarly colored, its top and most of its base covered by a white cloth. The inquisitive dog is charcoal gray with a red collar. The open pages of the books have writing indicated by means of slashes. "Little Bookkeeper" is contained on an oval base. The model is often criticized for dull coloration, but this seems unjustified.

|  | Price Range | |
|---|---|---|
| ☐ 306, trademark Stylized Bee, 4¾".............. | 250.00 | 275.00 |
| ☐ 306, trademark 3-line mark, 4¾"................ | 160.00 | 175.00 |
| ☐ 306, trademark Goebel/V, 4¾" .................. | 140.00 | 155.00 |
| ☐ 306, trademark Goebel, 4¾" .................... | 115.00 | 127.50 |

**307** Good Hunting

## 307  GOOD HUNTING

Figurine in current production. "Good Hunting" was designed in 1955 and bears that copyright date, but was not released until the early 1960s. The subject, a hunter with rifle or shotgun slung over his shoulder, has occasionally been objected to as being contrary to Sister Hummel's love of animals. However it will be realized when studied at length, that the composition is merely a parody on hunting and does not seek to endorse the sport. The hunter peers through binoculars while the object of his search, a rabbit, sits placidly at his feet, totally unnoticed by him. That the gun is indeed a rifle or shotgun is questionable; it may well be a toy.

In any event, this is an attractive piece of work, both in modeling and coloration. The hunter wears a pastel brown jacket with hints of pink, green cuffs and dark plaid striping, wine-colored lederhosen and matching suspenders, tall brown boots, light tan socks, and a khaki-colored Tyrolean style hat with red feather. The rabbit is brown. "Good Hunting" has been restyled with some minor alterations. As the figure is not rare under any circumstances, these will not require special attention.

|  | Price Range | |
|---|---|---|
| ☐ 307, trademark Stylized Bee, 5″ | 250.00 | 270.00 |
| ☐ 307, trademark 3-line mark, 5″ | 175.00 | 185.00 |
| ☐ 307, trademark Goebel/V, 5″ | 110.00 | 120.00 |
| ☐ 307, trademark Goebel, 5″ | 94.50 | 105.00 |

**308** Little Tailor

## 308  LITTLE TAILOR

Figurine in current production. "Little Tailor" is one of a very small group of Hummels designed in 1955, but not released until considerably later. They have an intriguing and curious feature in common: They portray children engaged in activities using giant size props, making the figures appear to be Tom Thumbs or other miniatures. There are really only three: #308 "Little Tailor," #309 "With Loving Greetings;" and #312 "Honey Lover." Of these, "Little Tailor" is probably the best known. It shows a boy seated on a stool, holding a gigantic pair of scissors, with an equally gigantic spool of thread at his feet. While the basic compositions may follow Sister Hummel's sketches, it would be intriguing to know if her drawings show the accessories in this enlarged way.

"Little Tailor" is wearing a violet-gray jacket with red plaid stripes, green pinstriped trousers with suspenders, brown shoes, and an orange neckerchief. His blonde hair is closely cropped. There are two versions, differing mostly in facial expression but in other details as well. The old style from the 3-line mark era wears an apprehensive look, while currently the "Little Tailor's" expression is one of skepticism. It is generally agreed that the restyled version is more effective. The current version is taller.

|  | Price Range | |
|---|---|---|
| ☐ 308, trademark 3-line mark, 5¼″ ................ | **500.00** | **550.00** |
| ☐ 308, trademark Goebel/V, 5¾″ .................. | **115.00** | **125.00** |
| ☐ 308, trademark Goebel, 5¾″ .................... | **105.00** | **125.00** |

## 309  WITH LOVING GREETINGS

Figurine in current production. This composition shows a kneeling boy beside an open bottle of ink. A brush is thrust into the bottle. Instead of writing with the brush, the boy uses his finger. "Loving Greetings" is apparently fashioning a homemade greeting card.

| ☐ 309, trademark Goebel, 3½″ ..................... | **80.00** |
|---|---|

## 310  SEARCHING ANGEL

Wall plaque in current production. "Searching Angel" is an imaginative composition showing an angel kneeling on a cloud and looking downward to earth. A lantern containing a candle, set on the cloud, throws a beam of light downward. "Searching Angel" was originally called "Angelic Concern," but the object of her concern has been left to the viewer's imagination. She wears a pastel orange long gown ornamented with darker orange dots and has greenish gray wings with red tips. The lantern is chiefly green. "Searching Angel" carries a 1955 incised copyright date.

| ☐ 310, trademark Goebel/V, 4¾″ × 3¼″............. | **75.00** | **85.00** |
|---|---|---|
| ☐ 310, trademark Goebel, 4¾″ × 3¼″.............. | **63.00** | **73.00** |

**309** With Loving Greetings

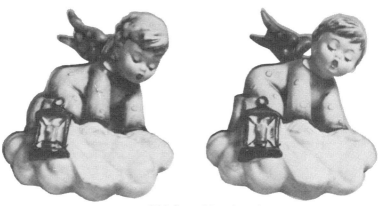

**310** Searching Angel

**311** Kiss Me

## 311  KISS ME

Figurine in current production. "Kiss Me," a figure of a girl holding and about to kiss a doll, was designed in 1955, but was not sold on the U.S. market until 1961. During the period of the 3-line trademark, it was redesigned at the request of the Seissen Convent, which had been disturbed over the fact that the doll was often being mistaken for a human baby. The convent stated that it was "too lifelike," so Goebel made the necessary alterations and the current version bearing the Goebel/V mark shows a more doll-like doll. As the change was made midway through use of the 3-line mark, this mark is found on both versions. The Stylized Bee mark appears only on the original version.

"Kiss Me" is slightly taller in the old version, though the difference is not great enough to be noticed without measuring. She is wearing a white puffy-sleeved blouse, an olive-brown skirt, a white apron with plaid striping, wine-colored shoes, white socks, and has red ribbons in her pigtailed hair. The doll has a reddish orange dress, a pastel yellow-green apron, and brown shoes. In the old version her socks are white with blue banding; in the new version they are all white. The doll has a blue ribbon in its hair. It is sometimes commented that the chief distinguishing characteristic is the presence of stockings on the doll in the original version, and that the new style is without socks. Both of these versions can be found bearing the 3-line mark. Consequently, there is a greater demand for the specimens with this trademark.

| | Price Range | |
|---|---|---|
| ☐ 311, trademark Stylized Bee, 6″–6¼″ ............ | 500.00 | 550.00 |
| ☐ 311, trademark 3-line mark, 6″–6¼″ ............. | 350.00 | 375.00 |
| ☐ 311, trademark Goebel/V, 6″–6¼″ ............... | 105.00 | 120.00 |
| ☐ 311, trademark Goebel, 6″–6¼″ ................. | 94.50 | 105.00 |

## 312 HONEY LOVER

Figurine, open number. "Honey Lover," called "In the Jam Pot" at the time of its designing in 1955, is a figure without a base of a boy seated on the floor, feeding himself jam or honey from a crockery vessel. Instead of a spoon, he uses his fingers. A bumblebee alights on the jar's side, busying itself with drippings, while another nibbles random drops on the boy's shoe. This design, although not yet placed into production, has occasionally been assailed for the messiness of its subject matter. It is doubtful, however, that this could explain its being held back as an open number, as a number of other 1955 designs have likewise not yet been manufactured. "Honey Lover" wears a long-sleeved beige shirt, blue trousers, and a long bib tied around his neck colored yellow with red polka dots. His shoes have textured soles; their basic color is brown. His socks are white with a mixture of pink and a few blue stripes. The honey pot is bright canary yellow. As for the expression on "Honey Lover's" face, it can only be described as that of one aware of wrongdoing. The model stands 3¾″.

## 313 SUNNY MORNING

Figurine, open number. This smaller yet complex model depicts an infant in a wooden crib beside a fence, over which grows a huge sunflower that inclines toward the infant. A bird perches on the fence. "Sunny Morning" was formerly called "Slumber Serenade," in reference to the bird's song. This handsome, chunky little figure has more than the usual decorating appeal, especially for its coloration. Both the modeling and enameling of the crib perfectly suggest roughly hewn wood, such as would be encountered in Bavarian village furniture of the period in question (the mid 1800s). The infant wears a white garment and rests on a white pillow ornamented with openwork violet polka dots. A beige blanket striped in white covers the crib, on which a heart-shaped motif is painted in folk style. The bird is blue and yellow with red at the throat. The sunflower, beautifully painted, is brown at the center with red crosshatch and has yellow petals. Its brawny stem and leaves are various shades of green, which show additions of yellow. Several small red flowers appear at the base. "Sunny Morning" measures 3¾″ to the top of the sunflower. It stands on an oval base.

**314** Confidentially

## 314 CONFIDENTIALLY

Figurine in current production. "Confidentially" is one of those love-hate Hummels that are considered adorable by some persons and less than delightful by others, chiefly because of its subject matter: A boy talking to a potted cactus plant. It should be observed that the figure was modeled in 1955, well before the theory was advanced that houseplants respond to the human voice. As originally designed, the plant stood upon a modern-looking stand. This was subsequently restyled to give the appearance of rough old wood. The boy, who holds his hands to his sides, wears a blue short jacket with dark blue pinstriping. In the revised version there are definite overtones of green in the jacket. He has brown lederhosen with suspenders, mahogany-colored slippers with crosshatch striping, and pale green socks. In the new version, he has a red neckerchief knotted into a bow tie, which was absent from the preceding type. The new version is also half an inch taller, 5¾" as opposed to 5¼", with some slight variations.

|  | Price Range | |
|---|---|---|
| ☐ 314, trademark 3-line mark, 5¼", no bow tie .... | 1350.00 | 1650.00 |
| ☐ 314, trademark 3-line mark, 5¾" ................. | 600.00 | 630.00 |
| ☐ 314, trademark Goebel/V, 5¾" ................... | 105.00 | 115.00 |
| ☐ 314, trademark Goebel, 5¾" .................... | 94.50 | 105.00 |

## 315 MOUNTAINEER

Figurine in current production. It seems only fitting, as so many of the youths in Hummel figures wear mountaineering outfits, that a model should be sold with the name of "Mountaineer." That it was designed in 1955 and carries that copyright date, but was not introduced to the U.S. market until 1964 when it was unveiled at the New York World's Fair, is little short of remarkable. This 5″ figurine shows a boy seated on a mountain top, pointing with one finger to a flower and feather in his Alpine style hat and holding in the other hand a stout walking stick. He wears a green jacket with maroon plaid striping, black lederhosen with matching suspenders, black shoes with textured soles, white socks touched here and there with red, and the aforementioned green hat, which has a narrow red band around its crown. His expression is one of supreme satisfaction. The lifelike posture of "Mountaineer's" body renders this a better-than-average composition, as does the strong coloring.

**315** Mountaineer

|  | **Price Range** | |
|---|---|---|
| ☐ 315, trademark Stylized Bee, 5¼″ ............... | **300.00** | **330.00** |
| ☐ 315, trademark 3-line mark, 5¼″ ................ | **125.00** | **145.00** |
| ☐ 315, trademark Goebel/V, 5¼″ .................. | **105.00** | **125.00** |
| ☐ 315, trademark Goebel, 5¼″ .................... | **94.50** | **115.00** |

## 316 RELAXATION

Figurine, open number. "Relaxation," originally termed "Nightly Ritual" and sometimes referred to as "Saturday Night," is a model of a boy in a wooden washtub. It has not yet been placed into production; therefore, no trademarks or prices can be listed. It cannot be assumed that the figure, when retailed, will agree wholly with its tentative designing and coloration. As it now stands, "Relaxation" is a basically brown and yellow composition. The youth is shown from shoulders upward; the remainder of his body, except for the tops of his knees, are hidden by the tub. He has reddish hair combed downward across his forehead, with one V-shaped shock falling between the eyebrows. He holds his left hand over the tub rim. The tub is constructed of roughly hewn wooden slats held in place by iron bands, and is a light tan shade mixed with yellow and strokes of dark brown to indicate graining. A green and yellow bird of unidentified species perches on the top, while over it hangs a large sunflower with brilliantly enameled yellow petals and reddish-brown center. A few stalks and other flowers (of much smaller size) plus a banner complete the composition. The boy's face wears an expression of delight. The work is contained on a scalloped green base designed to suggest a lawn.

## 317 NOT FOR YOU

Figurine in current production. "Not For You" is another Hummel variation of the child and dog theme, depicting a boy with hands held behind his back, hiding some treat or goodie from the anxious advances of his pet dog. There is certainly realism here. The youth in "Not For You" has obviously learned that, no matter how well a puppy is fed, nor how frequently, he will always want a sample of the thing the boy happens to be eating. He will want this sample even if the food does not appeal to him, just to make certain he is not missing something good. The type of dog is questionable. Perhaps it is merely a symbol of the universal hungry dog. The boy wears a smart, short-cut jacket of brown with green plaid striping, a red tie, a white shirt, brown lederhosen, tall tan-colored boots, and ribbed socks. The dog wears a red collar. It is a very simple construction, but with no lack of Hummel charm. "Not For You" was introduced into the line in 1955, but not sold in America until 1961; thus, it might be difficult locating a specimen in the States with a Stylized Bee mark. They are not, however, rare and the collector should not be tempted into paying a high price for one.

**317** Not For You

|                                                      | Price Range |        |
| ---------------------------------------------------- | ----------: | -----: |
| ☐ 317, trademark Stylized Bee, 5½″–6″ ............    | 300.00      | 330.00 |
| ☐ 317, trademark 3-line mark, 5½″–6″ .............    | 125.00      | 145.00 |
| ☐ 317, trademark Goebel/V, 5½″–6″................     | 105.00      | 125.00 |
| ☐ 317, trademark Goebel, 5½″–6″.................      | 94.50       | 115.00 |

## 318  ART CRITIC

Figurine, open number. "Art Critic" has been "on the shelf" roughly 25 years awaiting retail production. To date there has been no determination when, or if, the model will be released. No information can be provided on trademarks, sizes, or prices. The model represents a boy in a short pinkish brown smock jacket, holding a paintbrush and rolled paper or canvas in one hand and in the other hand, a framed picture which he studies. He wears oversized slippers of light and dark brown which are ornamented with lozengework designs. Beside him, on the figurine's base, rests a blue ink bottle without a cap.

**319** Doll Bath

## 319  DOLL BATH

Figurine in current production. "Doll Bath" was introduced into the line in 1956, but tested out on the European market for a number of years before U.S. distribution. There is an old "Doll Bath" and a new "Doll Bath," both bearing the number 319, the former having the traditional finish while new "Doll Bath" is textured. A little girl aged anywhere from five to eight is giving her doll a bath in a washbowl. She is standing and the washbowl is placed atop a wooden stool. The girl wears a black and white dress, a red apron highlighted with circular dots, grayish-green shoes, and a red ribbon in her hair, which is a short brown pageboy. The doll, depicted only from about shoulders upward, is shown as a very lifelike miniature person. The girl cradles the doll's head in one hand while scrubbing vigorously with the other. On the girl's face is an expression, not of determination, but of careful attention to the doll's welfare. The base is a nearly circular oval.

|  | **Price Range** | |
|---|---|---|
| ☐ 319, trademark Stylized Bee, 5″ ................. | 300.00 | 320.00 |
| ☐ 319, trademark 3-line mark, 5″ ................... | 150.00 | 160.00 |
| ☐ 319, trademark Goebel/V, 5″ ..................... | 105.00 | 115.00 |
| ☐ 319, trademark Goebel, 5″ ....................... | 94.50 | 105.00 |

## 320 THE PROFESSOR

Figurine, open number. Sometimes known as "Little Professor," this figure has not yet been released for public sale and there is no information on when, or if, it will be. "The Professor" is a boy wearing oversized adult slippers, pacing about the floor in deep thought, or so it may be presumed from the expression on his face. He wears a short plaid jacket whose primary colors are gray and pink, blue socks, and a red bow tie of exaggerated size. He carries an umbrella and, behind his back, a book plus a sheaf of folded papers bearing musical notations. His hair is shortly cropped and swept backward; its color varies from brown to strawberry blonde. "The Professor" was designed as a companion piece to #318 "Art Critic," also not yet released.

**321** Wash Day

## 321 WASH DAY

Figurine in current production. "Wash Day" is a model of a girl with a basket of laundry, about to hang an unidentified garment on a make believe clothesline. A simple composition, there is one brilliant little piece of artistry about this figure. The shape of the garment she holds, which is in the process of being shaken, appears to have a stop action quality about it, as if frozen by a camera in the midst of a good strong shake.

The girl is attired in typical washday fashion. A kerchief is pulled around her hair and tied at the back. She wears a short-sleeved dress with an apron, and a pair of house slippers. The colors are all basic white with pastel tintings, the kerchief having attractive additions of red and orange. Maybe the real scene stealer in "Wash Day" is the basket. It is a fine representation of wickerwork with ribbed banding and a pair of twisted-work handles. "Wash Day" was on the European market for about six years, 1957 to 1963, prior to U.S. distribution.

|  | Price Range | |
|---|---|---|
| ☐ 321, trademark Stylized Bee, 5½"–6" ............ | 300.00 | 330.00 |
| ☐ 321, trademark 3-line mark, 5½"–6" ............. | 125.00 | 145.00 |
| ☐ 321, trademark Goebel/V, 5½"–6" ................ | 105.00 | 125.00 |
| ☐ 321, trademark Goebel, 5½"–6½" ............... | 94.50 | 110.00 |

**322** Little Pharmacist

## 322  LITTLE PHARMACIST

Figurine in current production. "Little Pharmacist" is a figure of a boy in a white smock, with a pencil behind his ear and a pair of eyeglasses thrust upward on his forehead, holding a tub of medicine. Alongside him is a large bottle of "Vitamins," as the word reads in models designed for sale in English-speaking countries; and "Rizinusol," on German specimens. In his left hand, "Little Pharmacist" grasps a prescription booklet from which he appears to read aloud, perhaps advising a customer on dosage or other details.

He wears brown shoes and ribbed socks of a basically white color tinted with yellow and brown. The only bright color in this composition is his red tie, the red pencil behind his ear, and the liquid in his medicine tub is a reddish pink. "Little Pharmacist" has come to be a popular decoration for windows and interiors of drugstores, especially in Europe. The model was copyrighted in 1955, but not distributed for U.S. sale until 1962.

| | Price Range | |
|---|---|---|
| ☐ 322, trademark Stylized Bee, 5¾"–6" ............ | 300.00 | 330.00 |
| ☐ 322, trademark 3-line mark, 5¾"–6" ............. | 150.00 | 170.00 |
| ☐ 322, trademark Goebel/V, 5¾"–6"............... | 110.00 | 125.00 |
| ☐ 322, trademark Goebel, 5¾"–6".................. | 100.00 | 120.00 |

### 323  MERRY CHRISTMAS

Wall plaque in current production. "Merry Christmas" has a 1955 copyright date, but was not sold on the American market until 1979. It depicts an infant angel seated on a cloud holding a large lighted candle in both hands. An interesting variation in this design, from the usual Hummel treatment of angels, is that the halo is not on the angel, but surrounds the candle flame. The angel wears a long billowy blue-white gown highlighted with yellow four-point stars, brown shoes, and short blonde hair. His wings are chiefly a brownish gray with touches of yellow and some red at the tips. The candle is pastel violet, its flame a brilliant yellow and crimson, while

**323** Merry Christmas

the halo, an effective piece of work, is white with streaks of yellow and red. The dumpling-like cloud is white. As an experimental plaque without a frame or background, "Merry Christmas" is highly successful and is likely to become a standard item in the factory line for many years.

|  | Price Range | |
|---|---|---|
| ☐ 323, trademark Goebel/V, 5″ × 3½″ . . . . . . . . . . . . . . . | 70.00 | 77.00 |
| ☐ 323, trademark Goebel, 5″ × 3½″ . . . . . . . . . . . . . . . . | 63.00 | 70.00 |

## 324  AT THE FENCE

A figurine, open number. It depicts a very young boy and girl, standing at one side of a fence with a spaniel dog on the opposite side. The height is 4¾″.

## 325  HELPING MOTHER

Figurine, open number. "Helping Mother" is a little domestic scene of a girl seated on a stool, diligently sewing away at what appears to be a stocking. Beside her is a wooden table draped with a white cloth on which a candleholder rests. At her feet on the floor is a ball of sewing thread, or knitting yarn, and a cat. She is wearing an orange-rust dress, white socks banded with touches of ochre and maroon, shoes of orange-brown, and has an orange ribbon in her hair. The cat is black with gray and blue added for effect. A particularly intriguing aspect of this model is the folds of the tablecloth. As this model is not in distribution, no information on marks or prices can be provided. The height is 5″. "Helping Mother" was designed in 1955 and consequently has been an open number for 25 years.

## 326  BEING PUNISHED

Wall plaque, open number. "Being Punished" is one of a number of models designed and produced in the mid 1950s that have remained for many years in the open number classification not officially released for sale. It shows a youth seated in a corner, the corner being largely an imaginary one suggested by the presence of a few bricks on the right-hand side of the composition, next to a prison-type window covered with crosswork iron grating. A cat with a guilty look on its face peers at him intently. Exactly who is being punished may fairly be asked, as the cat appears far more disconsolate than the child. This composition is also known as "Naughty Boy." "Being Punished" is an engaging piece of craftsmanship, if only for the excellent modeling of the cat's face. The boy wears a pale shirt in which the predominant hues are green and yellow, speckled with orange dots, brown lederhosen held by suspenders, yellow socks, and brown shoes. He also sports a large red bow tie. The scene is set against the backdrop of a brick wall of cream color with a mixture of pink.

## 327 THE RUN-A-WAY

Figurine in current production. The "Run-A-Way" is a variation on the "Merry Wanderer" theme. Instead of a satchel, the boy now carries a basket on a wooden walking stick over his shoulder hobo fashion. Under his other arm is a mandolin. There are two versions of this model. Numerous alterations can be observed, though only one really major one. In the old or original type, introduced during the Stylized Bee era, the basket contains flowers, which are removed in the new version. It may be worthwhile to list some of the other differences:

**Old Version**—Boy's Tyrolean style hat is not sharply pointed; the crook or handle of the walking stick is turned outward; the basket is not strongly textured; his hair is combed to the side; his jacket is grayish-blue; the toe of his left shoe points upward.

**Restyled Version**—Boy's hat is more sharply pointed; the crook of the walking stick turns upward in a vertical plane with the figure; the basket is richly textured; the boy's hair is combed forward; his jacket is blue without any suggestion of gray; the toe of his left shoe does not point upward.

**327** The Run-a-way

In both versions he wears green lederhosen and dark brown, almost black, mountaineer boots. The restyled version has the new textured finish. The "Run-A-Way" bears a 1955 copyright date on the old version and 1972 on the new version. The restyling was done at the time of introduction of the Goebel/V trademark when many of the Hummel figures, including old ones, received the textured finish.

**Price Range**

☐ 327, trademark 3-line mark, 5¼".................. **750.00    825.00**
☐ 327, trademark Goebel/V, 5¼".................... **130.00    150.00**
☐ 327, trademark Goebel, 5¼"..................... **115.00    135.00**

### 328  CARNIVAL

Figurine in current production. "Carnival" is a sensitively modeled figure of a youth in clown costume. He stands with his hands at sides and his feet together, looking upward in wide-eyed and open-mouthed amazement, observing, it may be presumed, the wonders of a circus show. "Carnival's"

**328** Carnival

costume is pastel violet with oversized buttons or tassels of yellow and red, a white scalloped collar, green shoes, and a violet hood. The model carries a 1957 incised copyright date. An early specimen bearing the Full Bee trademark has been incised with a 1955 copyright date. This model is scarce and commands a premium.

|  | Price Range | |
|---|---|---|
| ☐ 328, trademark Full Bee, 6″ ...................... | 2100.00 | 3210.00 |
| ☐ 328, trademark Stylized Bee, 6″................... | 350.00 | 385.00 |
| ☐ 328, trademark 3-line mark, 6″ ................... | 150.00 | 165.00 |
| ☐ 328, trademark Goebel/V, 6″ ..................... | 100.00 | 110.00 |
| ☐ 328, trademark Goebel, 6″ ....................... | 77.50 | 85.00 |

## 329  OFF TO SCHOOL

Figurine, open number. "Off to School" has also been called "Kindergarten Romance." It shows a boy and girl strolling along, not exactly arm in arm, but so close that they can hardly be mistaken as close companions. The boy is the point of interest here. He walks in almost a marching gait, with chest thrust outward and thumbs tucked inside his suspender straps, as if he is proud to be in the girl's company. The girl, who carries a school satchel, gazes indifferently along the road in a state of perplexity at the attention she is receiving.

"Off to School" is novel and well executed, and it is a pity it is not on the market. The girl is attired in white, green, and yellow, with yellow socks and brownish-green shoes. Her hair is red. The boy wears a white shirt, brown lederhosen, a blue cap, and green shoes. He also has the traditionally red bow tie. His socks are white. "Off to School" stands 5″ tall. As an open number designation, there is no information on trademarks or prices.

## 330  BAKING DAY

Figurine, open number. Formerly called "Kneading Dough," "Baking Day" is a figure of a determined-looking little girl churning dough in a bucket. She wears a white dress highlighted with red dots, a green jumper, and a long white apron. Her hair is blonde, her cheeks rosy, and the look on her face is unmistakably one of firm resolve. Things are not progressing too well, however. The dough, although creamy and appetizing, is up to the bucket's rim and is beginning to spill over. Undaunted, the girl continues churning. The bucket is blue and rests on a low wooden stool. As an open number designation, there is no information to be given on trademarks or pricing. The height is 5¼″. This was released at $95.00

## 331 CROSSROADS

Figurine in current production. This large attractive model shows a pair of boys on a road standing before a waymarker pointing "East" in one direction and "West" in the other. They are apparently contemplating which to choose. One boy is carrying a trombone slung over his shoulder; the other is carrying a knapsack of possessions suspended from a rod. Whether they are intended as runaways or traveling musicians is not known. It is quite plausible that the title, "Crossroads," suggests they have reached not just a crossroad on the path, but a critical decision in life of whether to carry on the journey or return.

One boy is wearing a green and yellow jacket, a white shirt, and maple brown trousers. He has grayish shoes and a Sherlock Holmes sort of cap. His companion is wearing a brown jacket, green trousers, gray shoes, and a blue cap, and carries a walking stick. The signpost is intended to represent roughly assembled wood, of the type used to mark roadways in many areas of Europe at one time. Clusters of red flowers grow at the base. The original design for this model, made in 1955, is slightly different than the marketed version, and factory samples are desirable collectors items. These are quite rare. "Crossroads" bears a 1955 incised copyright date.

**331** Crossroads

**Price Range**

☐ 331, trademark Full Bee, 6¾" .................... 2500.00 +   —
☐ 331, trademark 3-line mark, 6¾" ................ 750.00   800.00
☐ 331, trademark Goebel/V, 6¾" .................. 195.00   215.00
☐ 331, trademark Goebel, 6¾" .................... 185.00   200.00

## 332  SOLDIER BOY

Figurine in current production. "Soldier Boy" wears a military-style jacket and cap and carries a rifle at his side. In the entire Hummel line, this figure represents one of the few departures from the tradition of providing subjects with 19th century costuming and accessories, as the cap is unquestionably modern. "Soldier Boy" bears a 1957 incised copyright date. He is wearing a pale orange jacket, grayish-green trousers, and black shoes with a high polish. His cap is greenish-brown. This work was restyled before reaching the American market, and older specimens with a 1955 incised copyright date are worth a premium.

**332** Soldier Boy

**Price Range**

| | | |
|---|---:|---:|
| ☐ 332, trademark Full Bee, 6¾" .................... | 2000.00 | 2200.00 |
| ☐ 332, trademark Stylized Bee, 5¾"–6" ............ | 250.00 | 270.00 |
| ☐ 332, trademark 3-line mark, 5¾"–6" ............. | 150.00 | 170.00 |
| ☐ 332, trademark Goebel/V, 5¾"–6"................ | 80.00 | 90.00 |
| ☐ 332, trademark Goebel, 5¾"–6".................. | 55.00 | 60.00 |

## 333  BLESSED EVENT

Figurine in current production. "Blessed Event" portrays a young boy and girl standing beside a crib in which a newborn infant reposes. The girl appears to be the older of the two children. She holds a harlequin-type doll of the 19th century and gestures, as if pointing out to her brother that the baby is a genuine version of the imitation she carries. "Blessed Event" was one of the Hummels introduced to America in the 1964 New York World's Fair. It has since then enjoyed considerable success. There are two versions: The original with 1955 copyright date and a later one bearing a 1957 date.

**333** Blessed Event

The infant is covered in a white blanket with red crosshatch designing and lays upon a white pillow. His crib is green, fashioned in a manner to suggest folk workmanship of olden time. The harlequin doll is very well modeled. "Blessed Event" stands on a circular base.

| | Price Range | |
|---|---|---|
| ☐ 333, trademark Stylized Bee, 5¼"–5½" ......... | **2000.00** | **2250.00** |
| ☐ 333, trademark 3-line mark, 5¼"–5½" .......... | **200.00** | **220.00** |
| ☐ 333, trademark Goebel/V, 5¼"–5½" ............. | **165.00** | **180.00** |
| ☐ 333, trademark Goebel, 5¼"–5½" .............. | **147.00** | **158.00** |

## 334  HOMEWARD BOUND

Figurine in current production. Modeled in 1955, "Homeward Bound" was not released for sale until the 3-line mark era. Shortly thereafter, in 1975, it was restyled with the new textured finish. The subject is a girl leading a goat along a road, accompanied by a much younger girl. This gives the impression at first of a hiking scene, especially as the first girl carries a walking stick. The more likely probability is that the trio is headed home from the market or a short journey.

**334** Homeward Bound

The older girl wears a white long-sleeved blouse, a black or deep green jumper, a tan apron with white polka dots, brown shoes, and blue socks. Her companion wears a red dress with darker red plaid striping, brown shoes, and dark pink socks. The goat wears a brass bell on a leather strap around its neck. In her left hand, the smaller girl carries a nosegay of flowers, chiefly orange and blue. The chief variation between the original and current versions is that, in the former, the goat is shown walking over a rock or tree stump of moderate size, which is removed in the restyled version, probably to permit better visibility of the lower part of this design. There is also a red circle running around the outer edge of the base in the old version, which is not on the current specimens.

|  | Price Range | |
|---|---|---|
| ☐ 334, trademark 3-line mark, 5¼" ................ | **500.00** | **550.00** |
| ☐ 334, trademark Goebel/V, 5¼" ................... | **350.00** | **375.00** |
| ☐ 334, trademark Goebel, 5¼" .................... | **157.00** | **175.00** |

## 335 LUCKY BOY

Figurine, open number. "Lucky Boy" is a youth returning from the fair with his prize: A pig that he carries beneath his right arm. In his left hand he holds an umbrella. Though never having actually been in production, the subject of "Lucky Boy," formerly known as "Fair Prizes," has aroused some debate. Is the pig intended as a real pig or merely an ornament or savings bank?

The boy gazes skyward. He wears a blue jacket highlighted with white, a white shirt, a large red bow tie, brown orange trousers flared at the cuffs, and a wide-brimmed conical hat. The umbrella is brown. As an open number designation there is no information on trademarks or pricing. "Lucky Boy" stands 5¾"–6" high.

## 336 CLOSE HARMONY

Figurine in current production. "Close Harmony" is a figure of two girls. One of the girls is playing a mandolin, while the other is holding a sheet of music. Both are singing. Introduced to the American market in 1963, "Close Harmony" may be found with either 1955, 1956, or 1957 incised copyright dates because the model was restyled a number of times. One significant restyling occurred after production began, affecting chiefly the sheet music holder. In the old version only one shock of hair is visible from beneath her kerchief, while in the restyling, considerably more hair is visible. Her stockings are higher in the restyled version and her facial expression somewhat altered.

The girl playing the mandolin is wearing a white long-sleeved blouse, a tannish-green skirt with lozengework striping (this striping is incised in the new version; it was previously indicated by painting), a blue vest, brown shoes, and white socks with additions of tan and ochre. Her companion is wearing a white short-sleeved blouse, a red jumper, black shoes, and a green kerchief tied around her head. They stand on an oval base.

**336** Close Harmony

| | Price Range | |
|---|---|---|
| ☐ 336, trademark Stylized Bee, 5¼″–5½″ ......... | **500.00** | **525.00** |
| ☐ 336, trademark 3-line mark, 5¼″–5½″ ........... | **350.00** | **370.00** |
| ☐ 336, trademark Goebel/V, 5¼″–5½″ ............. | **140.00** | **150.00** |
| ☐ 336, trademark Goebel, 5¼″–5½″ .............. | **125.00** | **135.00** |

## 337 CINDERELLA

Figurine in current production. How this model of a seated girl feeding doves from a saucer acquired the name "Cinderella" is not known, as there seems to be nothing in the composition relating to this well-known children's fable. Since the tale originated in Germany, popularized by the Brothers Grimm, it is fitting that it should be the subject of a Hummel. Undoubtedly, Sister Hummel read the story often. It was first published in 1821, roughly the time period most Hummel figures represent.

The girl is wearing a short-sleeved white blouse, a black jumper, a salmon pink apron with blue polka dots, fawn-colored shoes, and a red kerchief tied around her head. This model was restyled in 1972 and specimens produced after this date bear an incised 1972 copyright mark. The new version has a textured finish and only two birds; there are three in the original version. All the birds are pale blue. Differences will also be noted in the girl's hair and facial expression, particularly the eyes, which are opened wide and looking forward in the old examples, downcast and almost closed in the restyling.

**Old Style**  **337** Cinderella  **New Style**

|  | Price Range | |
|---|---|---|
| ☐ 337, trademark 3-line mark, 4½″ ................. | 700.00 | 770.00 |
| ☐ 337, trademark Goebel/V, 4½″ ................... | 120.00 | 130.00 |
| ☐ 337, trademark Goebel, 4½″ .................... | 115.00 | 120.00 |

## 338  BIRTHDAY CAKE

Candleholder, open number. "Birthday Cake" was modeled in 1956 and at that time was called "A Birthday Wish." The composition is simple. It shows a figure of a girl seated on an oval base holding a platter containing a cake, the central portion of which is hollowed out as a candle receptacle. The girl wears a long-sleeved white blouse, a green vest, a blue skirt, and wine-colored shoes. It would appear that the cake is intended as a rumcake or something similar judging by its design. The platter on which it rests has a scalloped base. "Birthday Cake" stands 3¾″.

## 339 BEHAVE

Figurine, open number. "Behave," also known as "Walking Her Dog," shows a girl with a dachshund dog. She holds one finger in the air as if to admonish the dog. In the other hand she cradles an antique type doll, representing a man with red hair. The doll's age suggests this as a period piece of 1840–1870. The girl wears a white dress decorated with red circular ornaments, green collar and a red ribbon in her hair. She is blonde and wears her hair combed forward. She has brown boots. The dog is shown in naturalistic shades of light and medium brown. As an open number designation not released for public sale, there is no information on trademarks or price. "Behave" stands 5¼"–5¾".

## 340 LETTER TO SANTA CLAUS

Figurine in current production. This model, first designed in 1956, was placed on the American market in 1971. The subject is a girl about five or six years old, who stands upon tiptoe to deposit a letter in a mailbox attached

**340** Letter to Santa Claus

to a wooden post. The base is textured to represent snow and both the mailbox and post are snowcapped. A wooden sled, which the girl had presumably been riding, is parked alongside her on the ground.

This appealing figure has been restyled with the new textured finish. A number of alterations have been made, including the following:

**Original Version**—The girl has white leggings; her stocking cap is pale gray and blue; the mailbox is decorated on its side with a V-shaped motif terminating in twin loops.

**Current Version**—The girl has red leggings; the letter she mails carries a stamp affixed to the side facing the mailbox; her cap is more darkly colored; the mailbox bears an image of the post horn.

In both versions she is wearing a heavy white jacket, apparently intended to represent animal fur.

| | Price Range | |
|---|---|---|
| ☐ 340, trademark Full Bee, 7″–7¼″ ................. | 2500.00 + | — |
| ☐ 340, trademark Stylized Bee, 7″–7¼″ ............ | 2000.00 | 2200.00 |
| ☐ 340, trademark 3-line mark, 7″–7¼″ ............. | 600.00 | 660.00 |
| ☐ 340, trademark Goebel/V, 7″–7¼″................ | 170.00 | 190.00 |
| ☐ 340, trademark Goebel, 7″–7¼″.................. | 137.00 | 150.00 |

## 341 BIRTHDAY PRESENT

Figurine, open number. This is a model of a girl holding a flowerpot from which violet flowers are growing. "Birthday Present" is colored attractively. She wears a pageboy hairstyle, a white blouse, a red and black vest, a long green-yellow skirt, and red-brown shoes. She is gazing at the flowerpot which, because of its large size, is in danger of slipping from her grasp. As an open number designation there is no information on trademarks or prices. "Birthday Present" stands 5″–5⅓″.

## 342 MISCHIEF MAKER

Figurine in current production. "Mischief Maker," introduced to the American market in 1972 when many of the older Hummels were restyled, is a figure of a boy seated on a fence, looking attentively at a crow perched on a nearby tree. The cause of mischief might not at first be ascertained, but it becomes clear enough when this composition is studied at length. It will be observed that the boy is holding a horn, which he was presumably attempting to play until interrupted by the crow's cackling.

The frustrated musician wears a deep violet jacket with plaid striping, white shirt, brown short trousers, brown boots, and a tall green Tyrolean hat with feather. The crow is dark blue, almost black. Several flowers adorn the base, which is colored and textured to represent sod. "Mischief Maker" may be found with 1958 or 1960 incised copyright date.

**342** Mischief Maker

|  | Price Range | |
|---|---|---|
| ☐ 342, trademark 3-line mark, 5″ ................... | **350.00** | **375.00** |
| ☐ 342, trademark Goebel/V, 5″ .................... | **120.00** | **140.00** |
| ☐ 342, trademark Goebel, 5″ ..................... | **110.00** | **130.00** |

## 343  CHRISTMAS SONG

Figurine in current production. "Christmas Song" is a figure of a standing angel with her mouth open in song. In one hand she is holding a lantern containing a candle, and in the other hand she is holding a long staff topped with a six-pointed star. She wears a long flowing red robe with white areas and five-pointed stars, brown shoes, and brown mittens streaked with red. Her wings are beige, tipped in red. "Christmas Song" was originally known as "Singing Angel." Until its release in 1982, this piece was an open number.

**343** Christmas Song

**Price Range**

☐ 343, trademark Goebel, 6¼" . . . . . . . . . . . . . . . . . . . .  **90.00      100.00**

## 344  FEATHERED FRIENDS

Figurine in current production. This popular design, copyrighted in 1956 but not introduced until considerably later during the 3-line trademark era, makes effective use of color contrast. It shows a girl leaning over a fence to observe a swan and its young swimming in a pool on the opposite side. Another bird is perched on one of the fenceposts, its head held high and its beak opened in song. In sharp departure from usual Hummel practice, the fence is colored a very dark brown, nearly black, and is not surrounded by flowers, as is generally done with works of this nature, but with shrubbery and leaves. The girl is attired chiefly in white and blue, her skirt having pale red openwork polka dots, and her blue kerchief tied around her head is ornamented with darker blue plaid striping. The bird atop the fencepost is chiefly violet. The model has an oval base.

**344** Feathered Friends

|  | Price Range | |
|---|---|---|
| ☐ 344, trademark Full Bee, 4¾" .................... | RARE | |
| ☐ 344, trademark Stylized Bee, 4¾"................ | RARE | |
| ☐ 344, trademark 3-line mark, 4¾" ................ | 250.00 | 260.00 |
| ☐ 344, trademark Goebel/V, 4¾" ................... | 120.00 | 130.00 |
| ☐ 344, trademark Goebel, 4¾" .................... | 110.00 | 125.00 |

## 345  A FAIR MEASURE

Figurine in current production. "A Fair Measure" shows a boy measuring some kind of liquid into a vessel which stands on one side of a pair of scales. On the other side are iron counterweights. This model was designed in 1956, but was not immediately released. Early specimens carry a 1956 copyright date. In 1972 "A Fair Measure" was, along with a number of other Hummels, redesigned with the new textured finish. The new version can be easily distinguished by the fact that the boy's eyes look downward at his task rather than ahead, as they did in the original version. The textured surface applied to this composition is not so extreme as that received by some models in the line. The work exists in one size only but there are, within this single edition, variations to be encountered.

**345** A Fair Measure

| | Price Range | |
|---|---|---|
| ☐ 345, trademark Full Bee, 5½″–5¾″ .............. | **RARE** | |
| ☐ 345, trademark Stylized Bee, 5½″–5¾″ ......... | **RARE** | |
| ☐ 345, trademark 3-line mark, 5½″–5¾″ ........... | **350.00** | **370.00** |
| ☐ 345, trademark Goebel/V, 5½″–5¾″ ............. | **125.00** | **135.00** |
| ☐ 345, trademark Goebel, 5½″–5¾″ .............. | **115.00** | **125.00** |

## 346  SMART LITTLE SISTER

Figurine in current production. "Smart Little Sister" is engaged in some kind of writing task. She sits outdoors with a tablet and pen, concentrating hard on her work, while her younger brother moves in for a close inspection of its progress. The girl is wearing a white long-sleeved blouse, a violet jumper, a yellow apron with floral motifs, and red shoes. She has sandy-colored hair. Her companion is dressed in a similar shirt, violet lederhosen, brownish shoes with suggestions of violet, beige socks, and likewise has sandy hair. The oval base is colored and textured to represent grass. "Smart Little Sister" has a 1956 incised copyright date.

**346** Smart Little Sister

| | Price Range | |
|---|---|---|
| ☐ 346, trademark Stylized Bee, 4¾"............... | **500.00** | **550.00** |
| ☐ 346, trademark 3-line mark, 4¾"................. | **125.00** | **145.00** |
| ☐ 346, trademark Goebel/V, 4¾".................. | **105.00** | **115.00** |
| ☐ 346, trademark Goebel, 4¾"................... | **94.00** | **110.00** |

## 347 ADVENTURE BOUND

Figurine in current production. No matter what the factory may choose to model in future years, it is difficult to comprehend any work surpassing "Adventure Bound" in ambition. No less than seven full sized figures are presented in the largest group composition ever attempted by Hummel. As far as price is concerned, it will probably be argued by some that other models in the line, such as the oversized editions of "Apple Tree Girl," "Apple Tree Boy," and "Merry Wanderer," are considerably more expensive to manufacture. It must be borne in mind, however, that these are merely large versions of figurines, whose basic size is small and whose price is moderate. There are no inexpensive versions of "Adventure Bound." It is produced in just one size, 7½" × 8¼", and while those measurements may not appear a sufficient excuse for its price, the labor it entails is far greater than any other single work. Although the number of molds for this figure is not known, figuring just five molds each for arms, legs, etc. would mean thirty-five molds yielding thirty-five components to be fitted together. The introduction of such a model called for great faith in the public's willingness to invest heavily in Hummels. It is not, of course, a limited edition, but quite obviously is not produced in numbers approaching those of lower-priced models. Except with the principal Hummel dealers, this is a special order item not kept in regular stock, but obtained from the distributor when required by a customer.

"Adventure Bound" is also known as "The Seven Swabians." Modeled by Theodore Menzenbach, it depicts a group of youths, intent apparently on storming a castle or other fortification, armed with a battering ram and hammer. One carries a lantern, suggesting the scene is taking place at night. The theme of "Seven Swabians" is perhaps borrowed from a German folk tale or ballad. The model bears a 1957 incised copyright date. It should be pointed out that, because of its heavy weight (much heavier than the size might suggest) and the complexity of its workmanship, "Adventure Bound" is likely to be damaged beyond reasonable repair by any accident. Those fortunate enough to own a specimen ought to take great pains in giving it special care.

**347** Adventure Bound

|  | Price Range | |
|---|---|---|
| ☐ 347, trademark 3-line mark, 7½" × 8¼" .......... | **2600.00** | **2860.00** |
| ☐ 347, trademark Goebel/V, 7½" × 8¼" ............. | **1850.00** | **2035.00** |
| ☐ 347, trademark Goebel, 7½" × 8¼" .............. | **1790.00** | **1970.00** |

## 348 RING AROUND THE ROSIE

Figurine in current production. "Ring Around the Rosie," modeled by Gerhard Skrobek in 1957 and carrying a 1957 copyright mark, is a figure of four girls with hands joined, dancing round in a circle to the familiar juvenile rhyme which provides the title. Had "Adventure Bound" (see #347 above) not been designed in the same year containing seven figures, this composition might have been considered crowded. Two of the girls were subsequently removed from it and released as a separate model, #353 "Spring Dance." "Ring Around the Rosie" captures a pleasing sense of motion and rhythm. A brief description of the costumes follows:

**Girl #1**—She wears a yellow short-sleeved blouse, a maroon vest, a green peasant skirt, a pink apron with yellow crosshatch pattern, a blue kerchief with dark blue striping, red hair ribbons, brown shoes, and reddish textured stockings.

**Girl #2**—She is clad in a white short-sleeved blouse, a green jumper, a yellow apron with brown polka dots, and a garland of flowers in her hair.

**Girl #3**—She is dressed in a white long-sleeved blouse with pin-striping, a maroon vest, a green peasant skirt, a yellow apron with red polka dots, a green kerchief, brown shoes, and reddish stockings.

**348** Ring Around the Rosie

**Girl #4**—She wears a white puffy-sleeved blouse with lozenge-work pattern, a mahogany jumper, a yellow apron, black shoes, and no head covering.

|  | **Price** | **Range** |
|---|---|---|
| ☐ 348, trademark Stylized Bee, 6¾" ............... | **2000.00** | **2200.00** |
| ☐ 348, trademark 3-line mark, 6¾" ................ | **1750.00** | **1950.00** |
| ☐ 348, trademark Goebel/V, 6¾" .................. | **1500.00** | **1700.00** |
| ☐ 348, trademark Goebel, 6¾" .................... | **1310.00** | **1500.00** |

## 349 THE FLORIST

Figurine, open number. "The Florist" presents a young tousle-haired boy wearing a long bib and holding a flower in one hand. Its original title, "The Flower Lover," was surely more descriptive, as "The Florist" could only suggest to most English-speaking persons a merchant who sells flowers. The boy is a ragamuffin; he appears to have wandered long through a field before coming upon these red and yellow flowers. He wears a white striped shirt with sleeves rolled up above the elbows. His short pants are brownish violet. As an open number designation there is no information on trademarks or prices. "The Florist" stands 7"–7½".

## 350 ON HOLIDAY

Figurine in current production. "On Holiday" is a figure of a girl holding an umbrella, empty basket, and bunch of flowers. She wears a grayish brown dress, a reddish apron, a red kerchief over her head, and brown shoes. The umbrella is black and the flowers are yellow with black centers. "On Holiday" was formerly called "Holiday Shopper." This model was an open number prior to its release in 1982.

☐ 351, trademark Goebel, 4" ......................     **90.00**     **100.00**

## 351 THE BOTANIST

Figurine in current production. "The Botanist" is a figure of an angelic-looking girl seated upon a rock, examining a blue flower which she holds in her hand. When first designed in 1963, "The Botanist" was called "Remembering," on the strength of her pensive expression. She has a white long-sleeved blouse, a black vest, a yellow skirt with raised dotted ornaments, brown shoes, and red ribbons in her pigtailed hair. A yellow and blue bird sits on a tree stump alongside her, and there are several more blue flowers on the ground. The base is colored and textured to represent grass. "The Botanist" had been an open number until its release in 1982.

☐ 351, trademark Goebel, 4" ......................     **88.00**     **110.00**

**350** On Holiday

**352** Sweet Greetings

## 352 SWEET GREETINGS

Figurine in current production. "Sweet Greetings" is a figure of a girl with a marvelously modeled, expressive face, who holds a heart-shaped box that presumably contains Valentine candy. The object could be a greeting card or homemade decoration. Its bearer wears a white long-sleeved blouse, a black jumper, canary yellow apron with red polka dots, and brown shoes. There is a violet and yellow bird. Three red flowers grow up at the base, which is partially textured and colored to represent grass. "Sweet Greetings" was originally known as "Musical Good Morning," a reference to the bird's chirping. This model had been on open number until its release in 1982.

|  | **Price Range** | |
|---|---|---|
| ☐ 352, trademark Goebel, 4″ ...................... | **85.00** | **90.00** |

## 353 SPRING DANCE

Figurine in current production. "Spring Dance" is an adaptation of two of the figures from #348 "Ring Around the Rosie" (see above). The girls join hands in a dance celebrating the arrival of spring to the Bavarian Alps and the thawing of the snow, an event eagerly awaited each year. This

**353** Spring Dance

model, unusual for a recent work, was produced in two sizes until 1982 when the larger size, 353/1 was temporarily discontinued.

The smaller size was closed out after very limited production with the Stylized Bee and 3-line trademark and not reinstated until late in the Goebel/V period. Consequently, specimens with the old marks are rare. All specimens carry an incised 1963 copyright date. The base is colored and textured to represent sod.

|  | Price Range | |
|---|---|---|
| ☐ 353/0, trademark Stylized Bee, 5¼" ............. | 1450.00 | 4500.00 |
| ☐ 353/0, trademark 3-line mark, 5¼" .............. | 1500.00 | 1750.00 |
| ☐ 353/0, trademark Goebel/V, 5¼" ................ | 150.00 | 170.00 |
| ☐ 353/0, trademark Goebel, 5¼" .................. | 115.00 | 125.00 |
| ☐ 353/1, trademark Stylized Bee, 6¾" ............. | 500.00 | 550.00 |
| ☐ 353/1, trademark 3-line mark, 6¾" .............. | 350.00 | 380.00 |
| ☐ 353/1, trademark Goebel/V, 6¾" ................ | 300.00 | 330.00 |
| ☐ 353/1, trademark Goebel, 6¾" .................. | 265.00 | 285.00 |

## 354/A ANGEL WITH LANTERN

Wall font, open number. "Angel with Lantern" was designed as a component in a three-piece set, the additional pieces being #354/B "Angel with Trumpet" and #354/C "Angel with Bird and Cross" (see below). To date none have been officially released. "Angel with Lantern" is a kneeling figure of an angel, robed in green, holding an iron lantern containing a candle. The lantern's design, composed of vertical and horizontal strips of iron, may be of interest to antique buffs. Beige and yellow are the chief colors of the angel's crimson tipped wings. A small red and white flower is on the ground. The bowls of these fonts are very small. The overall measurement is 3¼" × 5".

## 354/B ANGEL WITH TRUMPET

Wall font, open number. This model differs from its companion pieces #354/A and 354/C in that it has a pointed rather than a curved top. The angel faces left. She wears a reddish gown highlighted with yellow stars, black shoes, and has white wings touched with yellow and blue. There are several small red flowers on the ground.

## 354/C ANGEL WITH BIRD AND CROSS

Wall font, open number. The angel is posed in essentially the same manner as #354/A, except that her hands are clasped in prayer. She kneels alongside a wooden cross staked into the ground. A yellow canary bird is perched on the cross. Several red flowers complete the design. The angel wears a blue gown studded with groupings of circular ornaments. She has brown shoes and white and yellow wings tipped in red.

## 355 AUTUMN HARVEST

Figurine in current production. From the title one might expect a farm boy with a produce-filled wagon, but instead the figure in "Autumn Harvest" is a girl carrying, not vegetables, but a basketload of apples. This model has a 1964 copyright date. The girl is wearing a beige puffy-sleeved blouse, a wine-colored vest, a charcoal gray skirt, and a red apron with white polka dots. She has oxblood clogs, white socks, and a red ribbon on each of her braided pigtails. In her left hand she is clutching a bouquet of flowers. Her expression suggests that "Autumn Harvest" may be selling the apples in her basket to passersby. A more likely possibility, in view of the flowers that she carries, is that her mission is a visit to a friend or relative.

**355** Autumn Harvest

|  | **Price Range** | |
|---|---|---|
| □ 355, trademark 3-line mark, 4¾" . . . . . . . . . . . . . . . . | **375.00** | **410.00** |
| □ 355, trademark Goebel/V, 4¾" . . . . . . . . . . . . . . . . . | **110.00** | **120.00** |
| □ 355, trademark Goebel, 4¾" . . . . . . . . . . . . . . . . . . | **88.00** | **98.00** |

## 356 GAY ADVENTURE

Figurine in current production. "Gay Adventure" was originally called "Joyful Adventure." It carries a 1971 incised copyright date. The subject, a girl marching along with all her worldly possessions in a knapsack over her shoulder, is more or less a feminine version of #327 "The Run-A-Way." A 3-line mark specimen shows this model in the original version. It was later altered to the new textured finish. Other slight variations will be noticed between the old edition and the restyling. The adventurous girl wears a grayish-brown dress, tan shoes, and white socks with hints of brown and red. In her right hand she carries a small bunch of flowers of various colors, and in her left a walking stick, thrown over her shoulder, to which is tied a red bundle. On the end of the walking stick perches a brown and reddish canary bird. Flowers decorate the circular base.

**356** Gay Adventure

|  | **Price Range** | |
|---|---|---|
| ☐ 356, trademark 3-line mark, 4¾″ ................ | 325.00 | 355.00 |
| ☐ 356, trademark Goebel/V, 4¾″ .................. | 85.00 | 93.00 |
| ☐ 356, trademark Goebel, 4¾″ .................... | 75.00 | 82.00 |

## 357  GUIDING ANGEL

Figurine in current production. "Guiding Angel," sometimes referred to as "Angel with Lantern," is one of a trio of three small figurines often sold as a set, the other two being #358 "Shining Light" and #359 "Tuneful Angel" (see below). Each figure bears a 1960 incised copyright date. "Guiding Angel" kneels. In her right hand she holds a lantern from which a candle flame is visible. She wears a green gown and, like her companions, has sandy-brown hair. Specimens with the Stylized Bee trademark were not originally sold in the U.S., as this figure (and the two following) was released for American distribution only in 1972.

**357** Guiding Angel

|  | Price Range | |
|---|---|---|
| ☐ 357, trademark 3-line mark, 2¾" ................ | 70.00 | 77.00 |
| ☐ 357, trademark Goebel/V, 2¾" .................. | 52.00 | 58.00 |
| ☐ 357, trademark Goebel, 2¾" .................... | 42.00 | 47.00 |

**358** Shining Light

## 358 SHINING LIGHT

Figurine in current production. The second in a series of three small models of angels, each measuring 2¾". "Shining Light" kneels and holds in her left hand a candle. She attempts to prevent the flame from extinguishing in the wind by cupping her right hand over it. She wears a pale blue gown with openwork polka dots of dark blue. The candle is red and has a realistic appearance of wax.

|  | Price Range | |
|---|---|---|
| ☐ 358, trademark 3-line mark, 2¾" ................ | 80.00 | 90.00 |
| ☐ 358, trademark Goebel/V, 2¾" .................. | 60.00 | 68.00 |
| ☐ 358, trademark Goebel, 2¾" .................... | 42.00 | 48.00 |

## 359 TUNEFUL ANGEL

Figurine in current production. "Tuneful Angel" is seated, unlike the companion pieces in this trio, and plays a trumpet of the old Biblical type, fashioned from the horn of a ram or other animal. At her side, she has a lantern, somewhat different in design from the lantern held by #357 "Guiding Angel." She wears a red gown and has dark brown or black shoes.

**359** Tuneful Angel

|  | Price Range | |
|---|---|---|
| ☐ 359, trademark 3-line mark, 2¾" ................ | **50.00** | **65.00** |
| ☐ 359, trademark Goebel/V, 2¾" .................. | **31.00** | **39.00** |
| ☐ 359, trademark Goebel, 2¾" .................... | **31.00** | **39.00** |

## 360/A WALL VASE, BOY AND GIRL

Wall vase in current production. This model, plus the two following (#360/B and 360/C, see below), comprise the extent of Hummel's efforts at producing wall vases. Introduced during the Stylized Bee era, they were received with enthusiasm by collectors, but apparently not by the public at large, as they were soon discontinued. The fresh wave of Hummel popularity in the 1970s encouraged their reinstatement, with the Goebel/V mark. It is not positively known whether specimens were manufactured with the 3-line mark, but this is a distinct possibility. Their existence with Crown or Full Bee marks has never officially been observed, and is highly doubtful despite their occasionally being listed with such marks in reference works. These works are scarce with the Stylized Bee mark and would probably command even higher prices (based on rarity) if they were figurines, the collector demand for figurines being somewhat stronger.

Artistically, the Hummel wall vases are undeniable successes. Executed in the manner of plaques, they feature fully molded three-dimensional designs, not the low bas-relief designs of plaques, against backgrounds shaped and colored to give the appearance of vases. They are not, of course, real vases, the difficulty and awkwardness of hanging such articles upon a wall

**360/A** Wall Vase, Boy and Girl

being readily apparent. "The Boy and Girl" model is somewhat more costly in the Stylized Bee specimens than those depicting the boy alone and girl alone, not by reason of rarity as all three are about equally hard to get, but the fact that collectors have a habit of prizing multiple designs more highly than those representing single figures.

The motifs are similar to, though not borrowed directly from, "Apple Tree Boy" and "Apple Tree Girl." In #360/A the boy sits on the branch of a tree. The tree is used in all three wall vases, though designed slightly differently in 360/B and 360/C. He plays a horn, while the girl is seated on a lower branch holding in her lap a bunch of flowers. A brown and white bird also perches in the trees. The boy wears a grayish-blue jacket with blue plaid striping, salmon or pale orange trousers, brown shoes, and a grayish Tyrolean style hat with feather. His companion is attired in a white long-sleeved blouse, a brown vest, and a yellow skirt. She has a yellow kerchief tied around her head. The vase portion of this design is primarily white with strategic hints of blue to suggest contour. Stylistically, Hummel's wall vases are among the finest of its products.

|  | **Price Range** | |
|---|---|---|
| ☐ 360/A, trademark Stylized Bee, 4½″ × 6″ . . . . . . . . . | 520.00 | 570.00 |
| ☐ 360/A, trademark Goebel/V, 4½″ × 6″ . . . . . . . . . . . . | 80.00 | 90.00 |
| ☐ 360/A, trademark Goebel, 4½″ × 6″ . . . . . . . . . . . . . . | 63.00 | 68.00 |

## 360/B  WALL VASE, BOY

Wall vase in current production. Identical to the preceding #360/A except that the girl and the branch on which she sits are omitted.

**360/B** Wall Vase, Boy

|  | Price Range | |
|---|---|---|
| ☐ 360/B, trademark Stylized Bee, 4½″ × 6″ ......... | 520.00 | 570.00 |
| ☐ 360/B, trademark Goebel/V, 4½″ × 6″ ............. | 80.00 | 90.00 |
| ☐ 360/B, trademark Goebel, 4½″ × 6″ .............. | 63.00 | 68.00 |

## 360/C  WALL VASE, GIRL

Wall vase in current production. Identical to #360/A except lacking the boy and the branch on which he sits.

**360/C** Wall Vase, Girl

| | Price Range | |
|---|---|---|
| ☐ 360/C, trademark Stylized Bee, 4½″ × 6″ . . . . . . . . | **520.00** | **570.00** |
| ☐ 360/C, trademark Goebel/V, 4½″ × 6″ . . . . . . . . . . . | **80.00** | **90.00** |
| ☐ 360/C, trademark Goebel, 4½″ × 6″ . . . . . . . . . . . . . | **63.00** | **70.00** |

## 361 FAVORITE PET

Figurine in current production. "Favorite Pet" is a lamb and its mistress is a little girl who kneels down beside it, placing one hand on its back and holding a flower in the other. This model bears a 1960 incised copyright date, and was introduced to the American market at the 1964 New York World's Fair. The girl wears a white short-sleeved blouse, a black vest, and red skirt. She has red ribbons in her braided hair and wears a floral wreath. Over her right arm is an empty basket. The base of this work is colored to represent grass.

**361** Favorite Pet

| | Price Range | |
|---|---|---|
| ☐ 361, trademark Stylized Bee, 4½″ . . . . . . . . . . . . . . | **300.00** | **310.00** |
| ☐ 361, trademark 3-line mark, 4½″ . . . . . . . . . . . . . . . | **125.00** | **135.00** |
| ☐ 361, trademark Goebel/V, 4½″ . . . . . . . . . . . . . . . . | **110.00** | **120.00** |
| ☐ 361, trademark Goebel, 4½″ . . . . . . . . . . . . . . . . . | **100.00** | **110.00** |

## 362 I FORGOT

Figurine, open number. Originally called "Thoughtful," "I Forgot" is a figure of a girl in a state of bewilderment, holding one finger to her chin in an effort to remind herself of something. A simple composition, "I Forgot" derives its charm from the facial expression and a little accessory object: A doll clutched tightly by the girl, but in an offhand manner so that it almost drags on the floor. Over the girl's left arm is an empty wickerwork basket, suggesting that perhaps she has gone to market and forgotten what to buy. Little Miss "I Forgot" wears her sandy-blonde hair in braids. She has a long red dress highlighted with tones of pink and white, a pastel green vest, and a blue apron adorned with small yellow decorations. The doll, a clown type, has a striped shirt and red stocking cap. Its trousers are green. Because this is an open number model, no information can be given regarding prices. "I Forgot" stands 5½".

## 363 BIG HOUSECLEANING

Figurine in current production. "Big Housecleaning" portrays a girl with a huge scrub brush and bucket, busily cleaning a floor. She kneels and pushes the brush with both hands, a look of placid determination on her

**363** Big Housecleaning

face. The girl wears a white long-sleeved dress striped in blue, with the sleeves rolled up. Over this, she has a yellow apron with red openwork polka dots. On her head is a red kerchief with white polka dots. The bucket is brown. The base is incised to resemble the wooden slats of a floor. "Big Housecleaning" carries a 1960 incised copyright date.

|  | Price Range | |
| --- | --- | --- |
| ☐ 363, trademark 3-line mark, 4″ .................. | 360.00 | 400.00 |
| ☐ 363, trademark Goebel/V, 4″ ..................... | 140.00 | 155.00 |
| ☐ 363, trademark Goebel, 4″ ...................... | 115.00 | 125.00 |

## 364 SUPREME PROTECTION

Figurine in current production. "Supreme Protection" is a well-modeled standing version of the Madonna and Child in color. The Madonna is clothed attractively in a golden robe. On the robe appears an intricate network of raised ornaments. Over this she has a blue heavy robe, likewise decorated with raised ornaments but of a slightly different variety. She wears a large golden crown, sculptured and studded with gems. The Christ Child wears a violet and gold robe, the violet portion of which carries raised beaded ornaments. "Supreme Protection" was originally known as "Blessed Madonna and Child." This very special figurine was released by Goebel to commemorate the 75th Anniversary of the birth of Sister Berta Hummel. It was available only during 1984.

☐ 364, trademark Goebel, 9¼″ .................... **150.00**

## 365 LITTLEST ANGEL

Figurine, open number. "Littlest Angel," originally called "The Wee Angel," is a seated angel with bumblebee wings instead of the usual variety. She wears a charcoal gray gown with a yellow collar and yellow trimming, and touched with red. She gazes upward at a sight which the viewer's imagination must supply. Sizes have varied on the pre-production samples from 2½″–2¾″.

## 366 FLYING ANGEL

Figurine in current production. Though classed as a figurine, "Flying Angel" is designed for hanging and is often sold with the Hummel Nativity Set (see #214, above). The figure represents the angel Gabriel with his trumpet, announcing the birth of the Christ Child. "Flying Angel" is made in both a colored version and in white overglaze. There is some speculation, as yet unresolved, over whether this model exists with the Stylized Bee mark. If so, it would be quite rare; however, the assertion that specimens of the white overglaze version with 3-line mark are rare is certainly false.

**366** Flying Angel

**366/Color**　　　　　　　　　　　　　　**366/White**

They are, in fact, plentiful. Undoubtedly this mistaken belief, now spread far and wide throughout the world of Hummel collecting, arises from the rarity of a number of other white overglaze figures. But these were issued only in small quantities as an experiment, whereas from the outset the overglaze version of "Flying Angel" was a standard production item. It has never been discontinued or been in short supply on the American market. The version with color wears a grayish-violet robe, has gray wings tipped in orange and sandy hair. "Flying Angel" carries a 1964 copyright date.

|  | Price Range | |
|---|---|---|
| ☐ 366, trademark 3-line mark, 3½″ . . . . . . . . . . . . . . . | **52.00** | **68.00** |
| ☐ 366/W, trademark 3-line mark, 3½″ . . . . . . . . . . . . . | **26.00** | **34.00** |
| ☐ 366, trademark Goebel/V, 3½″ . . . . . . . . . . . . . . . . . | **65.00** | **70.00** |
| ☐ 366/W, trademark Goebel/V, 3½″. . . . . . . . . . . . . . . . | **15.00** | **18.00** |
| ☐ 366, trademark Goebel, 3½″ . . . . . . . . . . . . . . . . . . . | **55.00** | **60.00** |
| ☐ 366/W, trademark Goebel, 3½″. . . . . . . . . . . . . . . . . . | **15.00** | **18.00** |

## 367  BUSY STUDENT

Figurine in current production. "Busy Student," a girl writing on a slate, will be recognized as #346 "Smart Little Sister" (see above), shown here without her companion. Very little alteration was made in the figure. "Busy Student" bears a 1963 incised copyright date.

|  | Price Range | |
|---|---|---|
| ☐ 367, trademark Stylized Bee, 4¼"................ | 260.00 | 285.00 |
| ☐ 367, trademark 3-line mark, 4¼" ................. | 110.00 | 120.00 |
| ☐ 367, trademark Goebel/V, 4¼" ................... | 82.00 | 92.00 |
| ☐ 367, trademark Goebel, 4¼" ..................... | 72.00 | 80.00 |

## 368  LUTE SONG

Figurine, open number. "Lute Song" shows a girl playing a lute and singing. It was formerly called "Lute Player." She wears a white long-sleeved blouse, a blue vest, and attractive green skirt decorated with incised lozengework. Her shoes are beige with additions of mahogany, and her socks white with touches of brown and red. She has red and yellow ribbons in her hair, which is worn braided in Gretel fashion. She stands on a small plain circular base. As an open number designation not yet released for public sale, there is no information on trademarks or prices. "Lute Song" stands 5". The figure was adapted from the lute player in #336 "Close Harmony."

**368** Lute Song

## 369 FOLLOW THE LEADER

Figurine in current production. A large multiple figure grouping that represents the factory at its best in modeling and coloration but which is, even in current specimens, beyond the budget of many collectors. "Follow the Leader" is a trio of children, two girls and a boy, holding each other's shoulders and playing the game known by that title. All have bright smiles of radiate enjoyment. To describe them briefly, from the left:

**Figure #1 (girl)**—She wears a yellow long-sleeved blouse with openwork red polka dots, a dark green apron with polka dots, a blue skirt, brown shoes, and she carries an empty basket over her right arm.

**Figure #2 (boy)**—He wears a short blue jacket, a white shirt, black lederhosen, oxblood boots, a red bow tie, and he has red hair.

**Figure #3 (girl)**—She wears an off-white long-sleeved blouse, a red skirt, a violet apron with crosshatch striping, dark brown shoes, and ribbons in her braided hair. She holds three red flowers in her left hand.

A small grayish-brown, nondescript dog completes this scene. He stands behind the figures, as if confused by their actions. The base is textured and colored to represent sod.

**369** Follow the Leader

|  | Price Range | |
| --- | --- | --- |
| ☐ 369, trademark 3-line mark, 7″ ................. | **750.00** | **825.00** |
| ☐ 369, trademark Goebel/V, 7″ .................... | **550.00** | **605.00** |
| ☐ 369, trademark Goebel, 7″ ...................... | **450.00** | **495.00** |

## 370 COMPANIONS

Figurine, open number. Originally known as "Brotherly Love," "Companions" was modeled by Gerhard Skrobek, one of the factory's chief sculptors, in May of 1964. Since then, it has remained an open number designation, not released for public sale. There is no available information on trademarks or prices. The model portrays two boys, presumably brothers, standing side by side with arms around each other. One boy has an empty basket over an arm; the other boy has his free hand thrust into a trouser pocket. The first child wears a short brown jacket highlighted with soft tones of pink and maroon through which red plaid stripping runs. He has a white shirt, pastel green trousers, brown shoes, brown suspenders, and a prominent red bow tie. The second child is similarly attired except he wears short pants combining shades of brown, pink, and red, tall brown boots and white and brown socks. Their faces, with eyes raised and mouths opened wide, are nearly identical. They stand on a plain oval base. "Companions" measures 4¼″–4¾″ high.

## 371 DADDY'S GIRLS

Figurines, open number. "Daddy's Girls," formerly known as "Sisterly Love," is a companion piece to #370 "Companions," the two children being girls instead of boys. As in "Companions," the taller of the two holds an empty basket over one arm, but the girls do not have their arms around each other. The smaller girl has her arms behind her back, while her sister holds two small yellow flowers. Both girls wear short skirts and white aprons, the taller of the figures being attired mainly in brown, and the other in red. Both girls wear brown shoes with touches of gray and heavy wool socks that are primarily white highlighted with light brush strokes of yellow and brown. The smaller girl has a red ribbon in her hair; the other wears ribboned braids. Note should be taken of the smaller girl's facial modeling, which is extremely lifelike. As an open number designation, there is no available information on trademarks or prices. "Daddy's Girls" stands 4¾″.

## 372 BLESSED MOTHER

Figurine, open number. "Blessed Mother," formerly titled "Virgin Mother and Child," was modeled by Gerhard Skrobek of Goebel in May, 1964. It has not been distributed. The model is a standing figure of the Madonna holding the Christ Child, the Madonna being similar in design to #46 "Madonna Standing." The work could well be classified as modern, as it conforms to Sister Hummel's usual method of portraying the Madonna in svelte sweeping lines that place geometrical symmetry above strict adherence to natural body contour. She does not cradle the Child in her arms but holds him aloft, and he faces the viewer full front with his arms upraised in benediction.

The Child is not represented as an infant but as 1½–2 years of age, with curly, short-cropped hair and a sensitive facial expression. The Madonna's head tilts to one side as she gazes downward upon the Child. It is an effective presentation, complimented by its light pastel coloring. The Madonna wears a salmon-colored gown and a pale violet robe. The Child's gown is white. They stand on a small square plain base with corners cut away. As an open number designation, there is no information to be given regarding trademarks or prices. The height is 10¼".

## 373  JUST FISHING

Figurine, open number. "Just Fishing," which was previously known as "The Fisherman," is another in the factory's attempts to create figurines that portray full scenes, rather than merely individual figures. It shows a boy with a fishing line seated at the edge of a pond. He has just brought up his line and discovers that it is attached not to a fish, but a battered old boot. Not an entirely original theme perhaps, but very well handled and certainly one of the more successful scenic Hummels. The boy's expression is one of surprise mixed with mild dismay. The pond is the figurine's circular base, complete with water and ripples that appear quite realistic. The junior fisherman is wearing a cutaway green jacket, short maroon trousers, maple-colored boots, and high socks. He has a Tyrolean cap and a red bow tie. "Just Fishing" was modeled by Gerhard Skrobek in December, 1964, the same year in which many of the other Hummel open number designations were modeled. No information can be given on trademarks or prices. "Just Fishing" measures 4¼" × 4½".

## 374  LOST STOCKING

Figurine in current production. "Lost Stocking" is a variation on a theme repeated several times by the factory. This model was designed by Gerhard Skrobek in January, 1965, and carries a 1965 copyright date. It was not sold in the U.S. until 1972, but since then has become one of the more popular new Hummels on the American market. The subject is a boy who wears a brown shoe on his right foot and neither shoe nor stocking on his left. No hint is given for the loss. The boy appears in no way concerned over his plight. He wears long green trousers, a short jacket colored in shades of violet, a brown wide-brimmed cap, and a red bow tie. The expres-

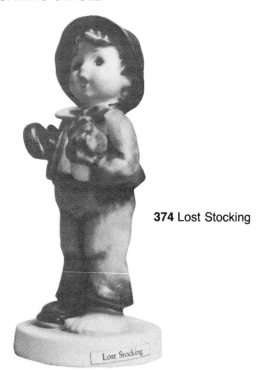

**374** Lost Stocking

sion on his face could only be described as passive. He carries an umbrella in one arm and an unidentified object in the other. His hair is brown. Careful observers of Hummel design will note that the "Lost Stocking" boy is a bit chubbier than usual for the factory's figures.

|  | Price Range | |
|---|---|---|
| ☐ 374, trademark Stylized Bee, 4½″............... | 175.00 | 195.00 |
| ☐ 374, trademark 3-line mark, 4½″ ................ | 350.00 | 370.00 |
| ☐ 374, trademark Goebel/V, 4½″ .................. | 70.00 | 80.00 |
| ☐ 374, trademark Goebel, 4½″ .................... | 63.00 | 73.00 |

## 375 MORNING STROLL

Figurine, open number. Originally titled "Walking the Baby," "Morning Stroll" was modeled by Gerhard Skrobek in November, 1964 and has remained an open number designation. It shows a young girl pushing her toy doll in a baby carriage, while her pet dog scampers alongside. Charm is lent to this composition by the carriage's design, which represents a wooden playtoy, complete with wooden wheels, of the mid 1800s. The girl wears a brown vest, a pale gray skirt highlighted with red dots, a white blouse, dark gray shoes, and socks of yellow and gray. She has a bow in her swept back hair. Anyone who collects or admires antique toys will find the carriage a delight. The basic color is light brown, but strokes of darker brown are cleverly added to give the appearance of rough wood graining. There are small decorations at the sides composed of circular blue dots. The carriage hood is gray with a white fringe. The dog is a dachshund type, colored a deep rust-brown. He is posed as if in motion, his face pointed upward with mouth partially open as if about to lick the hand of the doll, which rests on the carriage side. The immediate impression of this design is not typically Hummel, but a worthy composition nonetheless. It stands on a plain oval base. As an open number designation there is no available information on trademarks or values. "Morning Stroll" stands 4¼" high.

## 376 LITTLE NURSE

Figurine in current production. "Little Nurse" had remained an open number for years until its release in 1982. The subject is a girl playing nurse to a boy with an injured finger. The finger has been bandaged, but traces of blood are seen soaking through the bandage. Lying on the ground is a rather large knife which is also smeared with blood. This is clearly spelled out. The girl points toward the knife with one hand and shakes the other hand, as if admonishing the boy to be more careful in the future. It is the work of Gerhard Skrobek, Hummel's Master Sculptor. "Little Nurse" wears a long blue hospital gown with a front pocket from which the top of a thermometer protrudes. She has a white band around her head with a Red Cross symbol. The boy has an Alpine outfit of a white shirt, a reddish pink plaid jacket, short green trousers, gray-blue shoes, and a blue conical hat with feather. He wears a blue bow tie. The only other prop in this composition is the stool on which the patient sits and a yellow-orange flower growing in the ground.

|  | **Price Range** | |
|---|---|---|
| ☐ 376, trademark Goebel, 4" ..................... | **100.00** | **110.00** |

## 377 BASHFUL

Figurine in current production. Modeled by Gerhard Skrobek in 1966, "Bashful" carries a 1966 copyright date. It was not, however, released for American distribution until 1972. The subject is a girl, carrying a basket of flowers behind her back, who looks sideways to the viewer with a kind of timid but still charming smile on her rosy-cheeked face. She wears a white blouse, a reddish brown vest, a white apron highlighted with beige, and green skirt. She has brown slippers and white ribbed socks to which strokes of yellow, red, and deep brown are added. Her wicker basket contains several violet-colored flowers with white centers. There is a red ribbon in her brown hair. Apparently, the cause of her bashfulness is the fact that her skirt is being raised slightly by the wind.

**377** Bashful

|  | Price Range | |
|---|---|---|
| ☐ 377, trademark 3-line mark, 4¾" ................ | **300.00** | **330.00** |
| ☐ 377, trademark Goebel/V, 4¾" ................... | **100.00** | **110.00** |
| ☐ 377, trademark Goebel, 4¾" .................... | **77.50** | **85.00** |

## 378 EASTER GREETINGS

Figurine in current production. "Easter Greetings" carries a 1971 copyright date. It was first distributed on the American market in 1972. The subject is a boy in Tyrolean or Alpine costume, holding, on one arm, a basket of Easter treats, and, in the other hand, a bunch of flowers. He holds one finger to his chin in an attitude of self-consciousness, as if he were attempting to muster the confidence to present his gift to a female friend. He wears a white shirt, a pink plaid jacket, green trousers with black suspenders decorated with a tiny red heart, brown house slippers, and a blue conical hat with broad brim and feather. A red bow tie completes his outfit. The wickerwork basket is highlighted with touches of red.

**378** Easter Greetings

|  | Price Range | |
|---|---|---|
| ☐ 378, trademark 3-line mark, 5¼″–5½″ ........... | **325.00** | **355.00** |
| ☐ 378, trademark Goebel/V, 5¼″–5½″ ............. | **110.00** | **120.00** |
| ☐ 378, trademark Goebel, 5¼″–5½″ ............... | **88.00** | **94.00** |

## 379 DON'T BE SHY

Figurine, open number. Originally titled "One For You, One For Me," "Don't Be Shy" was modeled by Gerhard Skrobek in February 1966. It has not yet been released for distribution. The composition is extremely attractive, showing a girl in full Bavarian peasant costume offering a treat to a bird perched on a fence. It is often the case with Hummels that the simplest or least original designs result in the most pleasing compositions, and that seems definitely the case with "Don't Be Shy." Child and bird has been repeated many times in the series, but seldom with greater effect than here. The girl's face reflects tenderness and sensitivity not easily captured in a porcelain model. Skrobek is indeed a master. Occasionally, in transferring a sculpture to a finished piece, the subtle features on which the nuance of expression depend are lost. Here they have been retained successfully, and collectors can only lament the fact that "Don't Be Shy" is not at this time available for sale. The girl wears a white billowy-sleeved dress dotted with red open circles, a dark vest that is almost black, a green apron with crosswork designing, a long full maroon skirt, and a blue kerchief pulled down over her head and tied beneath the chin. Clutched in her left arm is a red flower with dark center. The bird perches on the post of a wooden fence. Its coloring is chiefly yellow with a reddish head and back. Two flowers, similar to those held by the girl, are growing up from the ground. The base is colored and textured to represent turf. As an open number designation, there is no available information on trademarks or prices. "Don't Be Shy" stands 4¼"–4½".

## 380 DAISIES DON'T TELL

Figurine, limited edition; sold out. The status of this figure changed in 1981 from an open number designation to actual production. It is the Goebel Collectors' Club exclusive design for their fifth special edition issue for members only. Purchase is limited to new or renewal memberships and must be accompanied by a redemption card. A representation of the "He

**380** Daisies Don't Tell

Loves Me, He Loves Me Not" theme, "Daisies Don't Tell" pictures a girl pulling petals from a daisy. Originally its title was "Does He?" This is another in the group of models designed by Gerhard Skrobek in the mid 1960s, dating to February, 1966.

The girl is wearing a white short-sleeved blouse, a maroon vest, a green skirt, and an attractive apron in pastel violet with touches of gray, ornamented with raised circular decorations in white with red outlines. Her shoes are brown and her socks yellow with brown banding. Her blonde hair is being blown about in the wind. A violet flower with a dark center grows up from the otherwise plain base.

|  | **Price Range** | |
|---|---|---|
| ☐ 380, trademark Goebel, 4½" ..................... | **80.00** | **90.00** |

## 381 FLOWER VENDOR

Figurine in current production. The appeal of "Flower Vendor" lies chiefly in its presentation of a theme from 19th century Bavarian country life: The street hawker who sold flowers from a basket on his back. Here the vendor is a small boy, which is not a historical inaccuracy as many street merchants of that time were indeed children. "Flower Vendor" bears a 1971 copyright

**381** Flower Vendor

date. It was distributed to the U.S. market beginning in 1972. The boy wears a Tyrolean hiking or mountaineering outfit of a blue jacket with plaid striping, brown lederhosen with suspenders, tall brown boots, red socks, a green wide-brimmed hat with a white and pink feather. He carries a walking stick fashioned from a tree branch. His basket is of wickerwork with dark and light bands interlaced, his flowers are red and orange. His suspenders are ornamented on the front horizontal strap with a red openwork heart. The boy looks down to check the footing as he walks, suggesting that he is perhaps on a hillside.

|  | Price Range | |
|---|---|---|
| ☐ 381, trademark 3-line mark, 5¼" ............... | 350.00 | 370.00 |
| ☐ 381, trademark Goebel/V, 5¼" .................. | 110.00 | 120.00 |
| ☐ 381, trademark Goebel, 5¼" .................... | 100.00 | 120.00 |

## 382  VISITING AN INVALID

Figurine in current production. "Visiting an Invalid" carries a 1971 copyright date. It was first introduced to the American market in 1972. The subject is a determined-looking girl, marching along with basket in one arm

**382** Visiting an Invalid

and umbrella under the other. Among the basket's contents is a bottle of wine. On the basket rim a canary bird is perched. The girl wears a long-sleeved white blouse, a maroon vest, a blue apron interlaced with dark blue strapwork designing, brown shoes, and a maroon kerchief tied around her head. The umbrella is red with grayish-brown handle.

| | Price Range | |
|---|---|---|
| ☐ 382, trademark 3-line mark, 5" .................. | 350.00 | 380.00 |
| ☐ 382, trademark Goebel/V, 5" ..................... | 105.00 | 125.00 |
| ☐ 382, trademark Goebel, 5" ...................... | 94.50 | 115.00 |

## 383 GOING HOME

Figurine, open number. Modeled by Gerhard Skrobek in 1966, "Going Home" was originally called "Fancy Free," but the faces of these figures, which appear to reflect fatigue, hardly agree with this title; the new one seems more appropriate. A boy and girl are represented hiking along a road. The boy holds a walking stick, while the girl carries bundles. The sombre coloration of this model adds to its effectiveness. The boy wears a white shirt with very pale lozengework striping, brown trousers with suspenders, black boots, a green Tyrolean style hat with a white and red feather, and a red bow tie. A knapsack is slung over his back. The girl has a white long-sleeved blouse and a gray jumper with polka dots, brown rugged boots and a red kerchief with polka dots around her head. The base is textured to represent sod. It measures 4¾" and was released at $125.00

## 384 EASTER TIME

Figurine in current production. "Easter Time" is a figure of two seated girls, one of whom holds a rabbit on her lap while the other girl pets it. Another rabbit is on the ground nearby. Originally known as "Easter Playmates," this model has a 1971 incised copyright date. The girl on the left wears a white short-sleeved blouse, a dark brown jumper, and a red apron with polka dots. She has a red polka dot kerchief tied around her head. Her companion is dressed primarily in blue, with blue kerchief and brown shoes. The base is colored and textured to represent sod.

**385** Chicken-Licken

| | Price Range | |
|---|---|---|
| ☐ 384, trademark 3-line mark, 4″ .................. | 350.00 | 370.00 |
| ☐ 384, trademark Goebel/V, 4″ ..................... | 140.00 | 150.00 |
| ☐ 384, trademark Goebel, 4″ ...................... | 125.00 | 135.00 |

## 385 CHICKEN-LICKEN

Figurine in current production. The subject is a proud-looking girl holding an open sack containing a number of baby chicks. She stands alongside a fence on which another chick perches. "Chicken-Licken" carries a 1971 incised copyright date. The girl has a white long-sleeved blouse, a maroon vest, and a dark green skirt. She wears brown shoes and has a red kerchief pulled around and tied under her head. Several flowers decorate the base. The sack is beige mixed with salmon, and decorated with red plaid striping.

**384** Easter Time

| | Price Range | |
|---|---|---|
| ☐ 385, trademark 3-line mark, 4¾" ................. | 350.00 | 370.00 |
| ☐ 385, trademark Goebel/V, 4¾" .................... | 140.00 | 150.00 |
| ☐ 385, trademark Goebel, 4¾" ..................... | 125.00 | 135.00 |

## 386  ON SECRET PATH

Figurine in current production. "On Secret Path" may be regarded as a young "Merry Wanderer." The subject is a boy of about five or six years of age, trudging along a road, carrying a candle in one hand, and a walking stick in the other. He is wearing a red jacket with black plaid striping, a white shirt, brown trousers, black mountaineer boots, and a pink long-shoreman's peaked cap on his head. "On Secret Path" carries a 1971 incised copyright date.

**386** On Secret Path

| | Price Range | |
|---|---|---|
| ☐ 386, trademark 3-line mark, 5¼" ................ | **325.00** | **355.00** |
| ☐ 386, trademark Goebel/V, 5¼" ................... | **125.00** | **135.00** |
| ☐ 386, trademark Goebel, 5¼" .................... | **115.00** | **119.00** |

## 387 VALENTINE GIFT

Figurine, limited edition, sold out. "Valentine Gift" was issued as the first special edition available only to members of the Goebel Collectors' Club, to be closed out after the supply on hand was sold. This has been done, and now the figure can only be obtained through collector channels. Its year of issue was 1977 and the original price was $45. The demand for these figures has been so great that many of the specimens have sold for $200 to $300. It may be presumed that the output was much smaller than that of the regularly produced models.

"Valentine Gift" exists with the Goebel/V mark, but specimens with the 3-line mark have sold for as much as $1000.00. It carries an inscription "Exclusive Special Edition No. 1 for Members of the Goebel Collectors' Club." The figure is of a girl holding a heart on which appears the message "i hab di gern," or "I love you very much." Undoubtedly, the heart is intended as a Valentine greeting. The girl also carries a basket with several flowers. She wears a white short-sleeved blouse, a green skirt, and a yellow apron

**387** Valentine Gift

with red crosshatch striping. Her shoes are brown and she has a garland of flowers in her hair.

|  | **Price Range** | |
|---|---|---|
| ☐ 387, trademark Goebel/V, 5¼″ .................. | **85.00** | **95.00** |

## 388 LITTLE BAND

Candleholder in current production. "Little Band" candleholder is comprised of three child musicians, two girls and a boy, seated around a circular base at the center of which is a candle receptacle. These figures of a girl playing a horn, a boy playing an accordion or concertina, and a girl holding a music sheet and singing, were also issued as individual figurines, as #389, #390, and #391, to which the reader should refer for descriptions.

**388** Little Band

|  | Price Range | |
|---|---|---|
| ☐ 388, trademark 3-line mark, 3″ × 4¾″............. | **180.00** | **200.00** |
| ☐ 388, trademark Goebel/V, 3″ × 4¾″............... | **150.00** | **165.00** |
| ☐ 388, trademark Goebel, 3″ × 4¾″................. | **132.00** | **145.00** |

## 388/M  LITTLE BAND

Music box in current production. Identical to #388 (see above), but with a wooden base containing a musical mechanism. As it plays, the platform holding the figures turns in a circular motion. The same music box is made without a candle receptacle as #392. The base is attractively contoured.

| | | |
|---|---|---|
| ☐ 388/M, trademark 3-line mark, 3″ × 4¾″.......... | **185.00** | **205.00** |
| ☐ 388/M, trademark Goebel/V, 3″ × 4¾″............ | **165.00** | **180.00** |
| ☐ 388/M, trademark Goebel, 3″ × 4¾″.............. | **165.00** | **180.00** |

## 389 GIRL WITH SHEET OF MUSIC

Figurine in current production. "Girl With Sheet of Music" is one of the "Little Band" figures employed on a candleholder, #388, and the non-candleholder version of the trio, #392. Normally these three figurines, #389, #390, #391 are sold as a set. All are seated without bases. The girl wears a white short-sleeved blouse, a maroon vest, and a yellow green polka dot skirt. She has brown shoes, white socks, and red ribbons in her braided hair. The set is often referred to as "Children Trio."

**389** Girl with Sheet Music

|  | Price Range | |
|---|---|---|
| ☐ 389, trademark 3-line mark, 2½" ................ | 55.00 | 61.00 |
| ☐ 389, trademark Goebel/V, 2½" ................... | 40.00 | 46.00 |
| ☐ 389, trademark Goebel, 2½" .................... | 31.50 | 36.00 |

## 390 BOY WITH ACCORDION

Figurine in current production. "Boy With Accordion" is the second of the three figures in the "Little Band" or "Children Trio" set. He has a grayish-blue rolled-sleeved shirt, dark brown short trousers, brown shoes, yellow socks, and a red neckerchief. The accordion or concertina is chiefly salmon colored.

**390** Boy with Accordion

| | Price Range | |
|---|---|---|
| ☐ 390, trademark 3-line mark, 2½" ................. | **55.00** | **62.00** |
| ☐ 390, trademark Goebel/V, 2½" ................... | **40.00** | **48.00** |
| ☐ 390, trademark Goebel, 2½" .................... | **31.50** | **36.00** |

## 391 GIRL WITH TRUMPET

Figurine in current production. The final figure in the "Little Band" or "Children Trio" set (see #389, and #390, above). "Girl With Trumpet" wears a red dress highlighted with yellow polka dots, greenish-gray slippers, and white socks. She has a red neckerchief tied around her neck.

| | | |
|---|---|---|
| ☐ 391, trademark 3-line mark, 2½" ................. | **55.00** | **61.00** |

**391** Girl with Trumpet

|  | Price Range | |
|---|---|---|
| ☐ 391, trademark Goebel/V, 2½" ................... | **40.00** | **46.00** |
| ☐ 391, trademark Goebel, 2½" ..................... | **31.50** | **36.00** |

## 392 LITTLE BAND

Figurine in current production. This is the figurine version of the candle holder issued as #388 (see above). For descriptions of the figures, refer to their listings as individual figurines, #389, #390, #391. "Little Band" has a 1968 incised copyright date. It is sometimes referred to as "Little Band on Base."

**392** Little Band

|  | Price Range | |
|---|---|---|
| ☐ 392, trademark 3-line mark, 3″ × 4¾″............. | **170.00** | **182.00** |
| ☐ 392, trademark Goebel/V, 3″ × 4¾″............... | **142.00** | **150.00** |
| ☐ 392, trademark Goebel, 3″ × 4¾″................. | **132.00** | **139.00** |

## 392/M  LITTLE BAND

Music box in current production. The same as #388/M but without a candle receptacle. There are some variations in the base style as well as in the music it plays.

| | | |
|---|---|---|
| ☐ 392/M, trademark 3-line mark, 3″ × 4¾″ .......... | **224.00** | **245.00** |

**392/M** Little Band

|  |  | Price Range |  |
|---|---|---|---|
| ☐ 392/M, trademark Goebel/V, 3″ × 4¾″ ............ | | **214.00** | **235.00** |
| ☐ 392/M, trademark Goebel, 3″ × 4¾″ .............. | | **214.00** | **235.00** |

## 393 DOVE

Wall font, open number. This font, designed by Gerhard Skrobek in 1968, has not yet been marketed for public sale. It shows a bluish-white dove in flight, viewed from the front, before a Greek cross and sunburst from which yellow beams radiate. An inscribed ribbon circles the top of the font. Its basic color is white. It measures 2¾″ × 4¼″.

## 394 TIMID LITTLE SISTER

Figurine in current production. Designed by Gerhard Skrobek in 1972, "Timid Little Sister" is a model of a boy and girl standing together, the girl

**394** Timid Little Sister

apprehensively viewing a bullfrog seated on the ground. This is a brightly colored work, the boy wearing a yellow shirt with green plaid striping, charcoal gray lederhosen and suspenders, brown shoes, and light tan socks in which can be noticed traces of other colors. He has a green Tyrolean style hat with narrow red band and a red and yellow feather, and a red neckerchief. The girl, not quite his equal in fashion, has a red short-sleeved dress, a gray vest, and a pale yellow apron with violet polka dots. She wears oxblood shoes and has red ribbons in her braided hair. The frog is green and yellow. This model remained an open number until its release in 1982.

**Price Range**

☐ 394, trademark Goebel, 6¾″ ..................... **200.00    220.00**

## 395  SHEPHERD BOY

Figurine, open number. Designed by Gerhard Skrobek, "Shepherd Boy" was originally called "Young Shepherd." The modeling was done in 1971, but to date this figure has not been released for sale. The subject is a boy and a sheep. He strokes the animal gently on its head and it responds with an almost human-like smile of satisfaction. "Shepherd Boy" is wearing a green short jacket with plaid striping, a white shirt, gray trousers, greenish-black shoes, and a pale red hat. The figures stand alongside a fence on which a violet and yellow bird perches. Several flowers are on the base. "Shepherd Boy" stands 6"–6½" tall.

## 396  RIDE INTO CHRISTMAS

Figurine in current production. "Ride into Christmas" was designed by Gerhard Skrobek in 1970 and bears a 1971 incised copyright date. Its design of a boy on a sled riding through the snow was used for the 1975 Annual Plate (see #268, above). The base of the figurine is attractively modeled to represent snow. There is somewhat more interest in this figure than might otherwise be the case because of the subject's use as a plate motif. Only one size of this model was produced until the release of 396/0, a 4½" model, in 1982.

**396** Ride into Christmas

|  | | Price Range | |
|---|---|---|---|
| ☐ 396/0, trademark Goebel, 4½" .................. | | 100.00 | 120.00 |
| ☐ 396, trademark 3-line mark, 5¾" ................ | | 750.00 | 800.00 |
| ☐ 396, trademark Goebel/V, 5¾" .................. | | 225.00 | 245.00 |
| ☐ 396, trademark Goebel, 5¾" .................... | | 185.00 | 205.00 |

### 397?

Comments made regarding #244 (above) apply equally to this number.

## 398?

Comments made regarding #244 (above) apply equally to this number.

## 399 VALENTINE JOY

Figurine, limited edition; sold out. This number had previously been listed as an open number designation. In 1980, it became the design for the fourth special edition issued for the Goebel Collectors' Club. Purchase is limited to fourth year members only with redemption cards. The figure is that of a boy who is very similar and could be a companion piece to the girl of #387 "Valentine Gift."

**399** Valentine Joy

|  | Price Range | |
|---|---|---|
| ☐ 399, trademark Goebel, 5¼" .................... | **100.00** | **110.00** |

## 405 SING WITH ME

This figurine was modeled by Gerhard Skrobek in 1973, and kept its original name to become one of 1985s new M.I. Hummel releases. It measures 5" and the release price is $125.00.

## 409 COFFEE BREAK

Figurine, limited edition, currently available to Goebel Collectors' Club members only. This is the 1985 special edition and can be purchased only by showing the redemption card issued to club members. This is the eighth in the series.

The figurine is of a little boy seated on the ground next to a handled jug. He is wearing a cap which has a bright yellow feather in the band, an orange jacket with a jaunty orange bow tie to the side and olive green plaid trousers and suspenders. His eyes are closed and he appears to be taking a nap.

                                                     **Price Range**

☐ 409, trademark Goebel, 4″ ...................... **90.00** —

## 414 IN TUNE

Figurine in current production. First introduced in 1981-82, this design was used on the #703 Annual Bell, 1981. The figurine is of a little girl sitting on an oblong base which is textured and painted to resemble grass. The

**414** In Tune

girl faces a songbird perched on a thin stump. The girl sits with her legs pulled up in front of her with her hands clasped about her knees. She wears a black jumper over a white long-sleeved blouse, a red kerchief and apron. The bird is yellow and purple.

**Price Range**

☐ 414, trademark, Goebel, 3¾"..................... **120.00    140.00**

## 415  THOUGHTFUL

Figurine in current production. Although first released in 1981-82, this figurine is the same as the design for #704 Annual Bell, 1980. This piece is almost a perfect match to #3 "Bookworm," except #415 is a boy instead of a girl.

This model has no base and shows a very young boy seated with a book open across his lap. The child leans over the book with one hand pointing down at the pages while the other hand points up in an absent-minded gesture while he concentrates intensely. He wears a long-sleeved red shirt with a blue and green bib over it, crumpled socks with touches of yellow, and brown shorts and shoes.

**415** Thoughtful

|  | Price Range | |
| --- | --- | --- |
| ☐ 415, trademark Goebel, 4¼" .................... | 115.00 | 125.00 |

## 416 COMMEMORATIVE FIGURINE "JUBILEE"

This has been released for $200.00. It measures 6¼".

**416** Commemorative Figurine Jubilee

## 421 IT'S COLD

Figurine, limited edition. This was the Goebel Collectors' Club design for their sixth special edition issue for members only. This could be purchased only by showing the redemption card issued to club members.

The figurine is of a boy wrapped up against the cold, his hands clasped together in front of him in mittens, and his muffler and cap windswept. His hat and jacket are a muted blue and green with brown shadings. His muffler and mittens are red, his shoes black.

|  | Price Range | |
| --- | --- | --- |
| ☐ 421, trademark Goebel, 5" ...................... | 80.00 | 90.00 |

## 422  WHAT NOW?

Figurine, limited edition. This was the 1984 Goebel Collectors' Club design for their seventh special edition for members only. This could be purchased only by showing the redemption card issued to club members.

The figurine is of a little girl with a blue bow in her hair holding a Pierrot doll in her left arm and a basket over her right arm. She wears a blue and lavender polka dot dress with a pinafore, slightly rumpled knee socks, and brown shoes which are outlined in black.

**Price Range**

☐ 422, trademark Goebel, 5¾" . . . . . . . . . . . . . . . . . . . .     **90.00**    —

## 432  KNIT ONE, PURL ONE

Figurine in current production. Newly released in 1983, this charming piece depicts a little girl seated on the floor with feet outstretched before her, working on her knitting. She wears an orange bow in her hair, has an

**432** Knit One, Purl One

orange kerchief around her neck and wears a blue apron with white polka dots over a burnt orange dress. A ball of orange yarn rests near her right knee.

**Price Range**

☐ 432, trademark Goebel, 3″ ...................... **52.00  —**

## 442  CHAPEL TIME

This is the very first M.I. Hummel clock, a new release.

## 466  MINIPLATE, "LITTLE MUSIC MAKERS" SERIES, 1984

Miniplate, limited edition, in current production. This 4″ plate titled "Little Fiddler" is the first issue in the series. A miniature 3″ companion figurine is also available. See "Little Fiddler" #2/4/0.

☐ 466, trademark Goebel, 4″ ...................... **30.00  —**

## 467  MINIPLATE, "LITTLE MUSIC MAKERS" SERIES, 1985

Miniplate, limited edition, in current production. This 4″ plate titled "Serenade" is the second issue in the series. A miniature 3″ companion figurine is also available. See "Serenade" #85/4/0.

☐ 467, trademark Goebel, 4″ ...................... **30.00  —**

## 468  MINIPLATE, "LITTLE MUSIC MAKERS" SERIES, 1986

This is the third edition of the "Little Music Makers" Series, "Soloist."

## 690  SMILING THROUGH

Wall plaque, limited edition; sold out. This plate-shaped plaque was the second edition in the series of limited production items sold only to members of the Goebel Collectors' Club, the first being #387 Valentine Gift (see above). It was first issued in 1978. It has not been as popular as the first edition for club members. "Smiling Through" features a seated girl holding a basket. Over her head is an open umbrella. She is apparently "smiling through" a rain shower. A small canary bird and red flower are at her feet. Unfortunately, there are no holes provided by which to hang the plaque. Lettering which reads "Collectors' Club Member" appears at the top in raised characters. On the back appears a decal reading: "Exclusive Special Edition No.2 Hum 690 for Members of the Goebel Collectors' Club."

**690** Smiling Through

| | Price Range | |
|---|---|---|
| ☐ 690, trademark Goebel/V, 5¾" .................. | **75.00** | **85.00** |

## 700 ANNUAL BELL, 1978

Limited production; sold out. This, the first in a series of Hummel Annual Bells, was a project which was greeted with some skepticism when announced, but it has now been firmly established as a commercial success. The annual bells are 6" high and carry a motif on one side and a date in red on the other. The 1978 edition has a "Let's Sing" design (see #110, above). The trademark is inside the bell. It was issued with a $50 suggested retail price.

**700** Annual Bell, 1978

**Price Range**

☐ 700, trademark Goebel/V, 6″ ..................... **195.00    215.00**

## 701 ANNUAL BELL, 1979

Limited production; sold out. The second Hummel Annual Bell, this 1979 edition carries a "Farewell" motif (#65, see above). It was issued with a suggested retail price of $70. It may still be found on the shelves of some dealers ("sold out" means it is no longer available from the factory).

**701** Annual Bell, 1979

| | Price Range | |
|---|---|---|
| □ 701, trademark Goebel/V, 6″ .................... | **85.00** | **95.00** |

## 702 ANNUAL BELL, 1980

Limited production; sold out. The 1980 Bell has a "Thoughtful" motif of a boy seated on the floor with a large open book on his lap. Issued with a suggested retail price of $85, it carries the current Goebel plain trademark. This design was made into a figurine, #415, in 1981.

**702** Annual Bell, 1980

|  | Price Range | |
|---|---|---|
| ☐ 702, trademark Goebel, 6″ ...................... | **85.00** | **95.00** |

## 703 ANNUAL BELL, 1981

Limited edition, currently available. The 1981 Annual Bell is titled "In Tune." The motif features a little girl seated on the ground facing a small bird which is perched on a branch. The two appear to be whistling with each other, as if sharing a common language. The design did not exist as a figurine until 1981 when #414 was released.

**703** Annual Bell, 1981

|  | Price Range | |
|---|---|---|
| ☐ 703, trademark Goebel, 6″ ...................... | **85.00** | **90.00** |

## 704 ANNUAL BELL, 1982

Limited edition, currently available. The 1982 Bell is titled "She Loves Me, She Loves Me Not." The motif for this bell is almost identical to the figurine, #174, of the same name. A little boy is sitting near a fencepost plucking petals from a daisy.

**704** Annual Bell, 1982

<table>
<tr><td></td><td style="text-align:right">**Price Range**</td></tr>
</table>

|  | Price Range | |
|---|---|---|
| □ 704, trademark Goebel, 6″ ...................... | **85.00** | **90.00** |

## 705  ANNUAL BELL, 1983

Limited edition, currently available. The 1983 Bell is titled "Knit One." The motif for this bell is a little girl sitting and studiously knitting.

**705** Annual Bell, 1983

| | Price Range |
|---|---|
| ☐ 705, trademark Goebel, 6″ ...................... | **90.00** — |

## 706  ANNUAL BELL, 1984

Limited edition, currently available. The 1984 bell is titled "Mountaineer" and depicts a little boy with a walking stick seated on a hilltop among the edelweiss.

☐ 706, trademark Goebel, 6½″ .................... **90.00** —

## 707  ANNUAL BELL, 1985

Limited edition, currently available. The 1985 Bell is titled "Girl With Sheet Music." It depicts a little girl with braids seated on the ground, holding her sheet music before her as she sings.

☐ 707, trademark Goebel, 6½″ .................... **90.00** —

## 708 ANNUAL BELL, 1986

This is entitled "Sing Along."

## HU-1, HU-2 BUST OF SISTER HUMMEL

Portrait bust, discontinued. The only portrait bust ever marketed by the factory, this model pictures the woman whose art work has served as the basis of its figurine designs, Sister M. I. Hummel. It is not numbered in the main sequential series.

This work was modeled by Gerhard Skrobeck in 1965. As originally issued, the work stood 15″ tall and was manufactured in a white bisque finish. It was discontinued shortly thereafter, during the 3-line mark era; the exact date is not a matter of public record. This model is scarce.

Reintroduction of the piece in 1967 was due to collector demand. Production was heavier of this smaller version which stands only 5¾″ tall. It appealed to enthusiasts who wished to include this work among their collection but found the large specimen's price beyond their means. At a suggested retail price of $15 to $17, it made a handsome addition to any collection. These specimens in white bisque also experienced a short life, on the market for only two years.

When it was discontinued in 1979, HU-2/W was followed by HU-2 in color. This was manufactured as a limited edition issued exclusively to third year members in the Goebel Collectors' Club. The original issue price was $75.00.

Pricing information on these busts is difficult to obtain due to their short life span. The item has not been listed in either the 1980 or 1981 Hummel catalogue, since all editions have been discontinued. Estimated current price levels are based on the best available data.

**HU-2/White**     **Hu-1 and Hu-2** Bust of Sister Hummel     **HU-2/Color**

|  | **Price Range** | |
| --- | --- | --- |
| ☐ HU-1, trademark 3-line, 15″, white ............... | 1000.00 + | — |
| ☐ HU-2/W, trademark 3-line mark, 5¾″............. | 110.00 | 120.00 |
| ☐ HU-2/W, trademark Goebel/V, 5¾″ ............... | 60.00 | 65.00 |
| ☐ HU-2, trademark Goebel/V, 5¾″.................. | 75.00 | 85.00 |

# HUMMEL NUMERICAL INDEX

To identify your Hummel, look at the number impressed on the base. Locate the number in the list below; the name of your piece follows. You can then go directly to the information given for that Hummel name by referring to the Table of Contents.

# How did your plates do?

Reco's "Little Boy Blue" by John McClelland

# UP 214% in 1 Year

Some limited edition plates gained more in the same year, some less, and some not at all...But *Plate Collector* readers were able to follow the price changes, step by step, in Plate Price Trends, a copyrighted feature appearing in each issue of the magazine.

Because *The Plate Collector* is your best source guide...has more on limited editions than all other publications combined...and gives you insight into every facet of your collecting...you too will rate it

### Your No. 1 Investment
### In Limited Editions

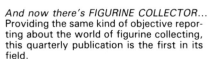

*Plate Collector*, established in 1972, was the first publication to feature limited editions only. Since then it's expanded, adding figurines, bells and prints, earning such reader raves as "Objective and impartial," "...has great research," "...a major guide to the plates I buy," and "It is the best collector magazine on the market."

To bring you the latest, most valuable information every month, our editors travel the world. Sometimes stories lead them to the smaller Hawaiian islands, or to the porcelain manufactories of Europe.

Their personal contact with artisans, hobby leaders, collectors, artists and dealers lets you share an intimate view of limited editions.

Each fat, colorful, monthly issue brings you new insight, helps you enjoy collecting more.

You'll find *Plate Collector* a complete source guide. Consider new issue information and new issue announcements. Use the ratings of new releases and wide array of dealer ads to help you pick and choose the best.

Read regular columns and check current market values in Plate Price Trends to add to your storehouse of knowledge.

Learn about clubs (perhaps there's one meeting near you) and the growing number of collector conventions and shows. Profit from tips on insurance, decorating with limited editions, safeguarding your collectables...just a sample of recurring feature subjects.

Read *Plate Collector* magazine to become a true limited edition art insider. Order now. See new and old plates in sparkling color.

*And now there's FIGURINE COLLECTOR...*
Providing the same kind of objective reporting about the world of figurine collecting, this quarterly publication is the first in its field.

*Figurine Collector* lets you in on what's new in this rapidly growing area. A veritable feast of information, it will instruct and entertain you with valuable information on a wide range of topics from how figurines are made to how they're doing on the secondary market.

To help you stay on top of what's happening in plate and figurine collecting, subscribe to both publications from Collector's Media, Inc., at the special combined rate.

16 issues (12 issues Plate Collector + 4 issues Figurine Collector) $30
Plate Collector only...12 issues (1 year) $24.95
Figurine Collector only...4 issues (1 year) $9.95

## Collector's Media, Inc.

**P.O. Box 1729-HS          San Marcos, TX 78667-1729**

To use VISA and MasterCard, include all raised information on your card.

# The HOUSE OF COLLECTIBLES Series

☐ Please send me the following price guides—
☐ I would like the most current edition of the books listed below.

## THE OFFICIAL PRICE GUIDES TO:

| | | |
|---|---|---|
| ☐ 753-3 | **American Folk Art** (ID) 1st Ed. | |
| | | $14.95 |
| ☐ 199-3 | **American Silver & Silver Plate** 5th Ed. | 11.95 |
| ☐ 513-1 | **Antique Clocks** 3rd Ed. | 10.95 |
| ☐ 283-3 | **Antique & Modern Dolls** 3rd Ed. | 10.95 |
| ☐ 287-6 | **Antique & Modern Firearms** 6th Ed. | 11.95 |
| ☐ 755-X | **Antiques & Collectibles** 9th Ed. | 11.95 |
| ☐ 289-2 | **Antique Jewelry** 5th Ed. | 11.95 |
| ☐ 362-7 | **Art Deco** (ID) 1st Ed. | 14.95 |
| ☐ 447-X | **Arts and Crafts: American Decorative Arts, 1894–1923** (ID) 1st Ed. | 12.95 |
| ☐ 539-5 | **Beer Cans & Collectibles** 4th Ed. | 7.95 |
| ☐ 521-2 | **Bottles Old & New** 10th Ed. | 10.95 |
| ☐ 532-8 | **Carnival Glass** 2nd Ed. | 10.95 |
| ☐ 295-7 | **Collectible Cameras** 2nd Ed. | 10.95 |
| ☐ 548-4 | **Collectibles of the '50s & '60s** 1st Ed. | 9.95 |
| ☐ 740-1 | **Collectible Toys** 4th Ed. | 10.95 |
| ☐ 531-X | **Collector Cars** 7th Ed. | 12.95 |
| ☐ 538-7 | **Collector Handguns** 4th Ed. | 14.95 |
| ☐ 748-7 | **Collector Knives** 9th Ed. | 12.95 |
| ☐ 361-9 | **Collector Plates** 5th Ed. | 11.95 |
| ☐ 296-5 | **Collector Prints** 7th Ed. | 12.95 |
| ☐ 001-6 | **Depression Glass** 2nd Ed. | 9.95 |
| ☐ 589-1 | **Fine Art** 1st Ed. | 19.95 |
| ☐ 311-2 | **Glassware** 3rd Ed. | 10.95 |
| ☐ 243-4 | **Hummel Figurines & Plates** 6th Ed. | 10.95 |
| ☐ 523-9 | **Kitchen Collectibles** 2nd Ed. | 10.95 |
| ☐ 080-6 | **Memorabilia of Elvis Presley and The Beatles** 1st Ed. | 10.95 |
| ☐ 291-4 | **Military Collectibles** 5th Ed. | 11.95 |
| ☐ 525-5 | **Music Collectibles** 6th Ed. | 11.95 |
| ☐ 313-9 | **Old Books & Autographs** 7th Ed. | 11.95 |
| ☐ 298-1 | **Oriental Collectibles** 3rd Ed. | 11.95 |
| ☐ 761-4 | **Overstreet Comic Book** 18th Ed. | 12.95 |
| ☐ 522-0 | **Paperbacks & Magazines** 1st Ed. | 10.95 |
| ☐ 297-3 | **Paper Collectibles** 5th Ed. | 10.95 |
| ☐ 744-4 | **Political Memorabilia** 1st Ed. | 10.95 |
| ☐ 529-8 | **Pottery & Porcelain** 6th Ed. | 11.95 |
| ☐ 524-7 | **Radio, TV & Movie Memorabilia** 3rd Ed. | 11.95 |
| ☐ 081-4 | **Records** 8th Ed. | 16.95 |
| ☐ 763-0 | **Royal Doulton** 6th Ed. | 12.95 |
| ☐ 280-9 | **Science Fiction & Fantasy Collectibles** 2nd Ed. | 10.95 |
| ☐ 747-9 | **Sewing Collectibles** 1st Ed. | 8.95 |
| ☐ 358-9 | **Star Trek/Star Wars Collectibles** 2nd Ed. | 8.95 |
| ☐ 086-5 | **Watches** 8th Ed. | 12.95 |
| ☐ 248-5 | **Wicker** 3rd Ed. | 10.95 |

## THE OFFICIAL:

| | | |
|---|---|---|
| ☐ 760-6 | **Directory to U.S. Flea Markets** 2nd Ed. | 5.95 |
| ☐ 365-1 | **Encyclopedia of Antiques** 1st Ed. | 9.95 |
| ☐ 369-4 | **Guide to Buying and Selling Antiques** 1st Ed. | 9.95 |
| ☐ 414-3 | **Identification Guide to Early American Furniture** 1st Ed. | 9.95 |
| ☐ 413-5 | **Identification Guide to Glassware** 1st Ed. | 9.95 |
| ☐ 412-7 | **Identification Guide to Pottery & Porcelain** 1st Ed. | $9.95 |
| ☐ 415-1 | **Identification Guide to Victorian Furniture** 1st Ed. | 9.95 |

## THE OFFICIAL (SMALL SIZE) PRICE GUIDES TO:

| | | |
|---|---|---|
| ☐ 309-0 | **Antiques & Flea Markets** 4th Ed. | 4.95 |
| ☐ 269-8 | **Antique Jewelry** 3rd Ed. | 4.95 |
| ☐ 085-7 | **Baseball Cards** 8th Ed. | 4.95 |
| ☐ 647-2 | **Bottles** 3rd Ed. | 4.95 |
| ☐ 544-1 | **Cars & Trucks** 3rd Ed. | 5.95 |
| ☐ 519-0 | **Collectible Americana** 2nd Ed. | 4.95 |
| ☐ 294-9 | **Collectible Records** 3rd Ed. | 4.95 |
| ☐ 306-6 | **Dolls** 4th Ed. | 4.95 |
| ☐ 762-2 | **Football Cards** 8th Ed. | 4.95 |
| ☐ 540-9 | **Glassware** 3rd Ed. | 4.95 |
| ☐ 526-3 | **Hummels** 4th Ed. | 4.95 |
| ☐ 279-5 | **Military Collectibles** 3rd Ed. | 4.95 |
| ☐ 764-9 | **Overstreet Comic Book Companion** 2nd Ed. | 4.95 |
| ☐ 278-7 | **Pocket Knives** 3rd Ed. | 4.95 |
| ☐ 527-1 | **Scouting Collectibles** 4th Ed. | 4.95 |
| ☐ 494-1 | **Star Trek/Star Wars Collectibles** 3rd Ed. | 3.95 |
| ☐ 088-1 | **Toys** 5th Ed. | 4.95 |

## THE OFFICIAL BLACKBOOK PRICE GUIDES OF:

| | | |
|---|---|---|
| ☐ 092-X | **U.S. Coins** 27th Ed. | 4.95 |
| ☐ 095-4 | **U.S. Paper Money** 21st Ed. | 4.95 |
| ☐ 098-9 | **U.S. Postage Stamps** 11th Ed. | 4.95 |

## THE OFFICIAL INVESTORS GUIDE TO BUYING & SELLING:

| | | |
|---|---|---|
| ☐ 534-4 | **Gold, Silver & Diamonds** 2nd Ed. | 12.95 |
| ☐ 535-2 | **Gold Coins** 2nd Ed. | 12.95 |
| ☐ 536-0 | **Silver Coins** 2nd Ed. | 12.95 |
| ☐ 537-9 | **Silver Dollars** 2nd Ed. | 12.95 |

## THE OFFICIAL NUMISMATIC GUIDE SERIES:

| | | |
|---|---|---|
| ☐ 254-X | **The Official Guide to Detecting Counterfeit Money** 2nd Ed. | 7.95 |
| ☐ 257-4 | **The Official Guide to Mint Errors** 4th Ed. | 7.95 |

## SPECIAL INTEREST SERIES:

| | | |
|---|---|---|
| ☐ 506-9 | **From Hearth to Cookstove** 3rd Ed. | 17.95 |
| ☐ 504-2 | **On Method Acting** 8th Printing | 6.95 |

| TOTAL | |
|---|---|
| | |

**SEE REVERSE SIDE FOR ORDERING INSTRUCTIONS**

## FOR IMMEDIATE DELIVERY

*VISA & MASTER CARD CUSTOMERS*

# ORDER TOLL FREE!
# 1-800-638-6460

This number is for orders only; it is not tied into the customer service or business office. Customers not using charge cards must use mail for ordering since payment is required with the order—sorry, no C.O.D's.

## OR SEND ORDERS TO

**THE HOUSE OF COLLECTIBLES**
*201 East 50th Street*
*New York, New York 10022*

### POSTAGE & HANDLING RATES
First Book . . . . . . . . . . . . . . . . . . . . . . . . . . . . . . . . $1.00
Each Additional Copy or Title . . . . . . . . . . . . . . . . . $0.50

Total from columns on order form. Quantity_____$_____

☐ Check or money order enclosed $_____ (include postage and handling)

☐ Please charge $_____to my: ☐ MASTERCARD ☐ VISA

Charge Card Customers Not Using Our Toll Free Number Please Fill Out The Information Below

Account No. _____Expiration Date_____
(all digits)
Signature_____

NAME (please print)_____PHONE_____

ADDRESS_____APT. #_____

CITY_____STATE_____ZIP_____

| DESCRIPTION | DATE PURCHASED | COST | DATE SOLD | PRICE | CONDITION |
|---|---|---|---|---|---|
| | | | | | |
| | | | | | |
| | | | | | |
| | | | | | |
| | | | | | |
| | | | | | |
| | | | | | |
| | | | | | |
| | | | | | |
| | | | | | |
| | | | | | |
| | | | | | |
| | | | | | |
| | | | | | |
| | | | | | |
| | | | | | |
| | | | | | |
| | | | | | |
| | | | | | |
| | | | | | |
| | | | | | |
| | | | | | |

| DESCRIPTION | DATE PURCHASED | COST | DATE SOLD | PRICE | CONDITION |
|---|---|---|---|---|---|
| | | | | | |
| | | | | | |
| | | | | | |
| | | | | | |
| | | | | | |
| | | | | | |
| | | | | | |
| | | | | | |
| | | | | | |
| | | | | | |
| | | | | | |
| | | | | | |
| | | | | | |
| | | | | | |
| | | | | | |
| | | | | | |
| | | | | | |
| | | | | | |
| | | | | | |
| | | | | | |
| | | | | | |
| | | | | | |
| | | | | | |

| DESCRIPTION | DATE PURCHASED | COST | DATE SOLD | PRICE | CONDITION |
|---|---|---|---|---|---|
| | | | | | |
| | | | | | |
| | | | | | |
| | | | | | |
| | | | | | |
| | | | | | |
| | | | | | |
| | | | | | |
| | | | | | |
| | | | | | |
| | | | | | |
| | | | | | |
| | | | | | |
| | | | | | |
| | | | | | |
| | | | | | |
| | | | | | |
| | | | | | |
| | | | | | |
| | | | | | |
| | | | | | |
| | | | | | |
| | | | | | |

| DESCRIPTION | DATE PURCHASED | COST | DATE SOLD | PRICE | CONDITION |
|---|---|---|---|---|---|
| | | | | | |
| | | | | | |
| | | | | | |
| | | | | | |
| | | | | | |
| | | | | | |
| | | | | | |
| | | | | | |
| | | | | | |
| | | | | | |
| | | | | | |
| | | | | | |
| | | | | | |
| | | | | | |
| | | | | | |
| | | | | | |
| | | | | | |
| | | | | | |
| | | | | | |
| | | | | | |
| | | | | | |
| | | | | | |
| | | | | | |
| | | | | | |
| | | | | | |